HMS HERMES
and the Virgin Sailor

Christopher P Clark

ISBN-10 1516917790
ISBN-13 978-1516917792

CONTENTS

The deceitful liar said the files did not exist. Fate gave me the laptop and, of course, the files were there - that's why I was able to complete this work. Like the Sun and the Moon the Truth cannot stay hidden for long.

ACKNOWLEDGMENT

The greatest of thanks go to my beautiful wife who encouraged me to complete this work. She gave me time, support and peace.

Listen to Sambo Song here:-
http://www.horntip.com/mp3/fieldwork/horntip_collection/p/micca_patterson/sambo_was_a_lazy_coon__asshole_rules_the_navy.htm

Listen to Dinah song here:-
http://www.horntip.com/mp3/1990s/1994_rugby_songs_sing-a-long__chubby_chalfont_and_the_chafers_(CD)/03_dinah_dinah.htm

Listen to the Zulu Warrior song here (unfortunately not a shanty version)
https://www.youtube.com/watch?v=RfwdNpx10dQ

1: THE DRAFT

HMS Hermes is what it said on the draft chit. It stood out on the paper as bold as brass. HMS Hermes is not a small ship! It's a big ship! In fact, it's a bloody great aircraft carrier! Everyone said small ships are best—best for everything!

'What have you got, Budgie?' I asked, dreading a reply to say he had one of the small Leander Class Frigates or even a County Class Destroyer.

'Fucking Hermes.'

I felt somehow relieved. At least he had no better than I, and I could go to my first ship with someone I knew.

I was sixteen years old and I had just completed my secondary training at HMS Collingwood. I had been in the Navy for just 10 months, but I was eager to get to sea. I was a Junior Ordinance Electrical Mechanic, second class, newly qualified. Budgie had been in my class and we had qualified together. He was my mate. The same age as me and we did most things together.

'Come on! Move along!' said the stern-faced RPO (Regulating Petty Officer) at the 'Draft Out' window of the RCO (Rating Control Office).

We shuffled out of the wooden framed building and down the steps to the road.

The sun was still shining brightly on this October afternoon, but we knew it would not last long; it was already 3:30 and soon it would be setting.

'Let's go to the automat,' I said, and we walked some way in silence. 'What do you reckon to Hermes then, Budge?'

'Not much,' he mumbled, clearly unimpressed.

'At least it's only another week of this place.'

'Yeah, then we'll be over the Pompey side and have some good runs ashore.'

When we got to the automat it was empty except for the NAAFI cleaning girl, who was busy sweeping the floors and cleaning tables. Normally the place was packed, but we had momentarily forgotten we had finished our training and it was still tuition time, meaning the myriad of people who would normally be here were still at their desks being lectured by toffee nosed pillocks, such as our Lieutenant Schreiber. It somehow felt good—but also a bit naughty!—that we were here at this time.

The front wall of the automat was covered in vending machines (hence its name), dispensing drinks, chocolate bars, packets of crisps and traditional NAAFI pies. We got ourselves a carton of milk each and found a newly cleaned table at which to sit. We each took a position where we could keep an eye on the cleaning girl. She must have been about 20 years old and not bad looking. But we weren't interested in her face; she had a gorgeous body. Her ample breasts were constrained under a tight jumper, and long slender legs disappeared up into a very short mini skirt. Everyone fantasised about her. We all dreamed of shagging her to death. We sat in silence watching her out of the corner of our eyes as she floated around, sweeping and stretching over tables, wiping them over. We knew she soon would have to bend down to brush the rubbish into her dustpan, and we waited in eager anticipation to see if we could catch a flash of the colour of her knickers or even a cheeky glimpse of stocking tops.

The door burst open and in came a panting Maxmore, having run all the way from the RCO. 'I've got the fucking Hermes,' he said, panting more. 'What have you got?'

'Fucking Hermes,' we said in unison.

His face lit up. 'That's brilliant! At least we'll still be together!' He sat down next to us and snatched Budgie's milk carton and took a swig.

'You bastard,' Budgie said, and thumped him hard on his shoulder muscle whilst trying to retrieve his milk.

Max spilt milk down his shirt and stood up quick with a look of indignation on his face. 'Now look what you've done! Moron!'

'Serves you right.'

The door slammed again as the cleaning girl walked out, having finished her chores. Budgie and I looked at each other, knowing we'd missed a golden opportunity. 'Bastard,' we said in unison.

It seemed the majority of our class had got the Hermes for our first sea-going ship.

The next few days were spent traipsing around Collingwood doing our drafting routine. We had to take round a chit of paper to the sickbay, dentist, pay office, armoury (to return our gaiters and have our gas masks checked), stores office, laundry, training office, accommodation office (to return bedding) and several other places some we had only visited once before when we had done our joining routines six months earlier. At each place we received a stamp and signature in the box provided. When all boxes were decorated with a signature and stamp, we returned them to the RCO 'Draft Out' window and presented them to the same miserable-faced RPO, who snatched them from us, and turned his back and sauntered down a row of files to process the paperwork. His big boots made loud clapping sounds on the wooden floor of the building, and we could feel the structure shake with each step. The tinny old filing cabinets clattered as he opened and slammed drawers. *What an existence*, I thought as I watched him carry out his mindless tasks. He had probably been in the Navy for more than twenty years, and this was the culmination of his experience and training. At least I had a trade. I was in the electrical branch, though I hadn't a clue what I would have to do once I got to sea. I just knew I wouldn't end up like *this* guy.

'Clark!' he barked.

'Yes, PO,' I replied, stepping forward.

'Here's ya leave pass, but you can't go till 16:30. And here's your travel warrant—don't fucking lose it! Give this envelope to the reg. office on your new ship when you get there. Where ya going?' he asked, knowing full well. 'Ah! Hermes. Never mind.'

I picked up the paperwork without saying another word and turned to the door. Budgie was next, and he received the same treatment and dialogue.

Behind Budgie came Fingers Toes (his real name was Patrick but everyone called him Fingers) and Mick Briggs. These two were older than Budgie and me, and we were jealous of the freedom their age afforded them. Fingers was already eighteen but looked older. He shaved—and when I say that, I mean he shaved properly! He had a black shadow across his cheeks and under his chin. He was never called 'skin'. I hated being called 'skin'. I wish I had proper whiskers so when some Junior came up to me I could call *him* 'skin'. If I shaved, I only did so as I had heard once you start then you don't stop, but it didn't seem to make much difference. Budgie was the same except he had gingerish hair and his complexion was pinkish. I was quite swarthy looking with dark hair and deep brown eyes. I suntanned easily. It was easy for me to look sullen. In fact, it was quite difficult for me to look anything but! Many people thought I was miserable or sulking all the time. My saviour was I was quick-witted with a good sense of humour.

When you're eighteen and in the Navy, you get about three times the pay you get when you're only sixteen. I was on £6 a fortnight, but we made do.

Fingers came bundling out of the RCO door grinning from ear to ear as he always does. He was a big lad—bordering on fat—and his face seemed to be bloated with joviality. His eyes were always bright and beady, but betrayed his thoughts. You knew he was always thinking of how he could take the piss out of you for the benefit of his and others' selfish humour. Occasionally, I could get Fingers on my side because I was far more intelligent and manipulative. Mostly, though, I'd be on the receiving end.

I got in first this time. 'You having a beer at the station, Fingers?' I asked, knowing his answer would be only if I was buying. Fingers was my best chance of getting a beer before I got on the train. There is no way I could get served—or even Budgie, for that matter: we were just too young.

'I will if you're buying,' he replied as per my prediction.

'I'll get the first.'

'And Budgie'll get the next fucker if he knows what's good for him,' replied Fingers with the usual menace in his voice.

Fingers was a powerful young man and, even though I was undefeated in the boxing ring, I knew I would stand no chance with him. I knew how to play this game.

Mick Briggs was the next to come out of the RCO door. Fingers shouted to him, 'Mick, Clarkie's getting the beers in at the station.'

'Well done, Clarkie! 'bout fucking time!'

'It's about time you two prats got the first beers in for a change,' I challenged but, not wanting to blow my chances, quickly added, 'but I'll let you off this time.'

Mick was even older than Fingers, but funnily enough didn't shave. His face was as smooth as mine save for a few whiskers on his upper lip and at the point of his chin. Because he was older, he was never called 'skin', though. When Mick got a round in, sometimes he was asked for his ID card to prove his age. Mick had a funny way of looking at things: his head would be slightly cocked to one side and always pointing to the left of the direct line of vision. His eyes always pointed the right way, though. He had small chubby ears, one of which was slightly bent over at the top. He walked with slightly hunched shoulders and had distinct bow legs.

Mick reached inside his tunic and pulled out a packet of Blue Liners. 'Who wants a fag?' he asked, throwing one to me and deliberately throwing one over Budgie's head knowing he couldn't catch for toffee. He offered the packet to Fingers for him to take one.

Fingers giggled at Budgie's poor attempt to catch his cigarette. 'Useless prick.'

All our kit was packed and lay cluttered in the road outside the RCO. We each had a large kit bag, a pusser's (Navy issue) grip and tool box. We all had the weekend off before we joined our new ships the following Monday. This meant we had to take this lot home with us and bring it back next week. We were all dressed in our uniforms; Number 1 suits with gold badges. None of us could wait to rip off the HMS Collingwood cap tallies and replace them with our new ones—even if it *was* HMS Hermes. However, we would have to wait till Monday for that.

We smoked our cigarettes and sky-larked around whilst Max, Mortiman, Ward and the rest of the class joined us.

At 16:00, the transport arrived; an old ten-tonne lorry with a canvas-covered back. It was chaos for a while as we threw our gear in and clambered up the tailgate to find a seat. The rear seat on either side was the favourite place; these, of course, were won by Fingers Toes and Mick Briggs. I made do standing at the front, leaning with my back to the driver's cab.

The lorry got under way, and I looked intently at the receding sites of Collingwood. We pulled out of the side road of the RCO and skirted around the parade ground. The lorry took us behind the drill shed, an enormous building with an open side facing the parade ground. It then turned down the main drag towards the main gate. I could see the parade ground falling further behind us, and beyond that the new accommodation buildings under construction. I visualised Howe section to the left of the furthest left-hand corner of the parade ground. Howe section had its own small parade ground where we would muster twice daily before marching off to our lessons way off to the far right of the establishment from where I now viewed it. Beyond Howe section parade ground and Howe section office was our old accommodation. Wooden huts dating from the war. Each hut housed about twenty people and had two rows of cast iron beds lining either side of each dormitory. At each end of every hut was a door. One end led out to the roadway whilst the other led into a common corridor with a concrete floor that ran at right angles to each hut and so connecting them all. Midway down this corridor was the heads (toilets) and bathrooms. There was no central heating in these huts and very seldom hot water in the bathrooms. Once out of the warm bed, it was sheer murder. The duty killick (leading hand) would walk through each hut tipping people out of their beds if they were not already up. If you had to be tipped out too often, you were charged with 'slack hammocks', which usually was followed by Number 9's or Number 14's punishment—otherwise translated to loads of extra work. Number 14's was mustering at ridiculous times of the day whereas 9's was extra work in the morning, before normal call; the hands, as well as mustering at ridiculous hours during the day and night, and an extended stint of extra work during early evening.

I always managed to avoid the slack hammocks charge, but I will never forget the coldness of running down the concreted corridor to take a cold shower and the even colder return to the mess. You could not take your clothes into the bathroom but had to go and return with only a towel wrapped around you. To not take a shower would be considered crabby. Being crabby was a great sin in the Navy. If you did not wash your knicks (underpants) and socks every day and shower in the mornings, you would be out-casted and victimised beyond tolerance.

I knew the last six months I had lived in the Howe section had been an endurance, but I also knew I would reflect upon it with fondness.

As we proceeded down the main drag, we passed the NAAFI Shop on our left, with the canteen next door. I was told the bar in the canteen was in the Guinness Book of Records for having the longest bar in the country, which was a fact that always made me feel a bit important because *I* had seen it. The next building was the automat where we spent many leisure hours. This was like the bar for the Juniors, where we would spend our time drinking cartons of milk and eating chocolate bars, whilst dreaming we were old enough to go into the main bar and drink beer and get pissed like *real* sailors do.

We slowed as we approached the reg. office and guard room. I knew the front of the lorry was adjacent to the Officer of the Watch's (OOW) caboose, and somehow I drew back further into the gloom of the canvas -covered lorry; I didn't want to be singled out for anything if a beady eyed RPO or Leading Regulator came peering into the back of the vehicle. This was an insecurity in myself, but I didn't recognise that at the time. We had no worries as we kept on moving, and I caught a glimpse of the OOW as he bent forward over some paperwork—not even acknowledging the fact we were leaving. I thought this was rather bazaar: today was a monumental day in our careers; we had finished our training and were about to go to sea and serve our country, and the OOW had no clue of this major event. It seemed to trivialise things a little.

Finally, we swept through the main gate and out onto the main road. We all cheered and celebrated the fact we would not have to return for a long time. We knew we would have to come back for advancement training, but that was so far in the future it felt almost like never.

The sun was lowering now, and I knew by the time we got to the Gosport ferry the air would be cool. This meant it would be bloody freezing on the ferry as it chugged across the harbour.

I was not looking forward to the next few hours. We all had this kit to haul around, and I know every single one of us was as nervous as the next with regard to its safety and security, particularly when considering the tool box. We would all pile into the train station bar, and me and Budgie would have to keep a low profile and sup our beer in a corner whilst relying on Fingers and Mick to fetch it from the bar. I didn't really like drinking; I couldn't handle it. After just a couple, I could feel I wasn't in control—and it made me feel funny. I had to do it, though: everyone drank beer and you had to drink several pints to gain the right status. It was all bravado.

Fingers lived on the South Coast, so would be catching a different train to the rest of us. Budgie, me and Mick would travel together to London, where we then would go our separate ways. Mick would travel east to Ramsgate, and Budgie to the north, from Euston to Northwich.

Budgie was very proud of Northwich, but whenever he told anyone where he came from, they always misunderstood him and thought he meant Norwich. I always smiled at this, but I know it infuriated him. When asked where Northwich was, he would say in the middle of a triangle made between Liverpool, Manchester and Chester. I, meanwhile, would journey north from Kingscross to Peterborough.

The bar at the station would be packed—it always was on a Friday, with all the Matelots going up the line. It would be full of smoke, and there would always be some menacing characters pissed out of their minds, begging money and looking for trouble. These people frightened me, and I would try to keep out of their line of vision. I knew Mick would be half-pissed by the time we got on the train—and no doubt before we even hit London! He would be stormy and would be seeking out a fight with someone; it was my aim to make sure that person wasn't me. Anyhow, I'd have to sneak off to the heads to be sick. I always was after two or more pints. I could hide the fact well, though. No one ever knew. If they had known, I would never have been able to live the piss-taking down. My life would have been a misery.

Eventually, the train pulled into Peterborough at eight-thirty, and I struggled to get my gear off. People were looking at me—a sailor in uniform was a rare sight to be seen here. I had to compose myself and sling the kit bag over my shoulder, hold it with my left arm, and pick up my grip and tool box with the other hand, then march off as if it was no weight at all. I had to give the impression I had done this millions of times, that I was a real experienced sailor. In reality, however, I struggled: I was clumsy and I was feeling far from well, and like the icing on the cake, now I was getting embarrassed and with that came annoyance. But nonetheless, eventually I arrived at the ticket gate and handed over my ticket.

My father was waiting with my little sister Lesley. She beamed when she saw me, and rushed over to meet me. She was only nine, and I was surprised at myself with how much I had missed her. A genuine lump made itself known in my throat as she hugged me. I was still struggling with all my kit and felt a right fool. My father didn't move towards me; in fact, he turned to the door, all ready to return to the car.

The ticket collector called me as I had forgotten to take the return half of my ticket. I threw the kit bag to the floor and collected it. I pulled up my uniform tunic to put the ticket into my money belt.

'What's that?' Lesley asked in her squeaky voice, taking hold of the flap of the money belt.

'Don't you worry about that, Besley,' I said, pulling her hands free and readjusting my uniform (me and my brother always called her Besley—she hated it!). She tried to help me with my gear and succeeded in dragging my grip across the hard ticket office floor. I picked up my kit bag and tool box, and followed Lesley, helping her with my grip by shoving it along with my foot. My dad was in the car by now, which was parked right outside the station door. My emotions were in turmoil: I was mad with myself and knew I was not giving Lesley the reception she deserved.

I got in the car next to Dad, at which point he spoke for the first time. 'Now then. When you going back?'

I didn't much like my dad: I'd never felt comfortable in his company, and we never made eye contact. He wasn't really interested in me, only in what I achieved. I know he used to brag about me to his friends—the fact I was in the Navy and excelled in my studies, and now that I was going to sea on an aircraft carrier. I also knew he was proud of me.

Lesley sat in the back of the car and reached forward to stroke my collar and began asking me stupid questions about the Navy and Portsmouth. This, at least, gave me the excuse not to speak with my father. I managed to avoid conversation with him for the full duration of the thirteen-mile trip to our home village of Forty Foot.

At home, my grandmother was waiting, and she was almost in tears when she first saw me in my uniform. She kissed me and said I reminded her of the boys she had known during the war—whatever that meant. My brother, eighteen months my senior, looked up from the television but said nothing. I didn't have much in common with my brother, either:

he was always my father's favourite, and I disliked the way he always satisfied my father's wishes. He wasn't rebellious like me.

I felt uncomfortable. I dumped my gear in the bedroom and waltzed out. 'I'm going up the bridge.'

'What time you coming back?' my dad asked. 'Don't be late.'

I ignored him and shut the door behind me.

The bridge was exactly that: a bridge over the river that ran past our house. It was a local meeting place for the village people. We used to just hang around there and swap stories and chatter about nothing. As I walked up the road I smoked a fag and made sure I looked good. I would show off when I got there, and I knew all my old school mates and play friends would be envious of me. But first, my priority was to call Kay.

There was a red phone box outside the village shop, next to the bridge. Kay was my girlfriend, and I had shagged her for the first time when I last came home. I knew I was going to shag her again tomorrow when I would stay at her house. The thought of it aroused me, and I felt like going over there straight away, but it just wasn't possible: she lived twenty-odd miles away, I had no means of transport, and it was too late for the buses.

2: HMS ST.VINCENT

I woke Saturday morning with the sun streaming through our bedroom window. I knew it was early, and I could sense Nicky was still asleep. I lay motionless, planning the day: I would catch the 11:30 bus to Peterborough and visit my grandparents from my mother's side; I would also meet my mother there, and we would spend a couple of hours together; later in the afternoon, I'd get the bus from Peterborough to Spalding, where Kay would meet me; we would probably hang around Spalding for a few hours before going back to her place; and in the evening, her parents would go out and we could get down to some serious stuff. Sex was still quite new to me, and I wanted to have it all the time. I wanted to explore her body with my hands and eyes. I was greedy for sex.

Suddenly, Nick's alarm clock sounded, filling the room with its clanging ring. Nicky cancelled it almost immediately. He must have been awake also. I heard him get up and get dressed. I pretended to be asleep as I didn't want to talk to him. I waited till he had left the room, and then I rolled onto my back and stared up at the ceiling. He would leave for work soon, and then I would get up.

My mind drifted back to Kay. She was six months younger than me and the daughter of my dad's friends Rox and Sylvey. They went to the clubs, where my old man played music in the evenings, because they liked to dance the old fashioned way. Kay used to go along, and Dad decided to match-make us. We swapped letters for a while. We met and things went from there. I took her virginity one evening when her parents were dancing to the music played by my dad. I was vastly more experienced than she was: I had fucked some girl at the bottom of our playing fields before I joined the Navy; really, it was a none-event as I was too eager and she, the poor girl, hadn't a clue what was happening; I don't think there was any penetration. Unfortunately, she didn't have much of an experience to look back on. With Kay, though, I had more time. I was in better control and Kay loved me to death—meaning there was nothing she wouldn't let me do!

Tonight, I was going to have her with the light on. I was going to see every part of her. She was a very attractive girl, with blonde hair like her mother. She had a beautiful face with statuesque facial bone structure; a square-ish jaw and straight nose. Unfortunately, however, she did have a little too much facial hair. Not much—only at the corners of her upper lip—but enough for me to know she was not perfect. She had a wonderfully hairy fanny, though! I remember the first time I slithered my hand down her knickers and my fingers sank deep into the thick bush of hair. I cupped her womanhood, and my whole hand held hair. It was truly wonderful. I hadn't seen it yet, though; I had only peered down and glimpsed it in the gloom of a darkened room with only the TV to cast its light. Tonight, though, I was going to get her starkers and openly look at her. The thought of this aroused me and I held my stiffening cock underneath the bed clothes and considered masturbating.

I heard the door slam as Nicky went outside and, shortly afterwards, his motorbike started. I listened to the noise abate as he rode down the road, and all was quiet again. I played with myself a little longer, then decided I'd wait. I jumped out of bed and dressed. Dad didn't have a shower; no-one here could call me crabby.

I went into the kitchen where Fay, Dad's fourth wife, was making him tea. 'Oh, hello, Christopher,' she said, cheerfully. 'Did you sleep alright?'

'Yeah, great. You off shopping today then?' I asked, knowing full well she was. She always went shopping on a Saturday morning and Dad always whinged about it.

'Yeah, we're going to Peterborough today for a change.'

Wowee! I thought.

'Do you want a cup of tea, Christopher?'

'Yes, please. I don't take sugar now, though.'

'I don't know how you can drink the bloody stuff without sugar. Your dad has four spoons in his, and if I don't stir it enough he goes potty!'

'How's Gran these days then?'

'Not too bad. She's always complaining about things, as she always does, but everyone just ignores her.'

My gran was still in bed. She was probably awake but remained in bed because she didn't want to disturb Lesley, who shared a room with her.

I took my tea outside and sat on the top of the steps leading down to the lake. The sun was beautiful, although not very warm. Wisps of mist rose from the water, and the surface was disturbed in places by flying insects and fish swimming beneath it. The tree opposite still had the rope dangling from it from where we had swung just a few years earlier. It still had the diving board that had been erected, but it had not been used for some years now, since Mr Edwards next door had forbidden us from swimming in his water. I always thought it strange that someone could own the water in a lake.

The fish pond still leaked—it was only half-full of manky water. I wondered if there were any fish in there, but decided not to get up to look. I was enjoying the rare quiet moment to myself.

I could see Cherry in her kennel. This aging Alsatian looked at me with sad, drooping eyes. It was a shame how Dad kept her cooped up all the time. I was going to take her for a walk later, and then the two of us could dissolve into our special world out in the fields. We had often gone off together in the past, roaming the fields and droves and the derelict farm sheds and buildings that were dotted about the landscape. I had many secret hideaways where I could go and dream of how I would one day be a millionaire. I would visit some of these places today with Cherry. I thought about waiting for Lesley to get up and taking her with me, but then again, no. I felt like I needed to be alone.

I finished my tea and left the cup by the back door. I ran down to Cherry's cage, and her eyes began to sparkle. 'Come on, girl, we're going for a walk.'

She began to get excited, and jumped up the side of the bars, her tail wagging furiously. Squeaky, whimpering sounds came from her, and her breath came in short pants. She yelped with sheer delight as I opened her cage, and she shot out and darted this way and that. 'Come on,' I said again, waving my arm in big circles towards the roadway. She ran off ahead of me.

We went down the Hollow, which meant we turned right at our gate. The road on which we lived was called Hollow Road, but everyone knew it as The Hollow. It ran parallel to the river, and all the houses were on the opposite side of the road to the river. We lived in a bungalow, and our neighbours were some way away in both directions.

I walked after Cherry, past our orchard and some waste ground before I came to the next batch of houses, where just a few sat huddled together. Once past these, I was standing at the top of Hollow Hill. This must have been the only hill for miles around. Forty Foot was in the middle of the fens. We were below sea level and, from this position, you could see for absolute miles. I loved this land. I only ever remember corn being grown in the fields, though I knew other crops had been grown in alternate years. In fact, sugar beet was a regular, as was potatoes, but these were dirty crops, and that's probably why I deleted them from my mind: you couldn't play in sugar beet fields like you could in corn fields; you could hide amongst the wheat and no-one could see you. Once the corn had been harvested, the bales of straw made wonderful building blocks; we would spend many hours making igloos, just like the Eskimos, but with straw bales instead of ice. We would make long entrance tunnels that wound around like a maze. I remember beautiful, long, Summer days when the sun shone all day in an enormous sky. It was like living in a giant upturned mixing bowl.

Hollow Hill was hardly a hill by most people's standards. To freewheel down by bike would only take a few seconds, and soon you would have to peddle again; you didn't need to get off the bike to push it back up again either. The descent was only about ten feet, maximum, but in the fens, it was a hill. From the top of Hollow Hill, the road swung slightly to the right, and then back to the left and went straight for about a mile, again parallel to the river but a little further away. It was possible to continue walking straight, by the river, on a disused footpath. This used to have a tarmac surface many years ago, and remnants of the tarmac could still be seen.

About 300 yards along the footpath was a derelict house standing by the river. I remember playing in this house as a kid and being frightened whenever we went inside. Of course, we thought it was haunted. We never ventured upstairs—that was far too scary. As we got older, we became bolder, but by then it was too late to show our bravery and mountains of courage: the stairs had rotted away, meaning we couldn't get up there.

I remember marigolds grew in the garden during the spring and what a stark contrast the bright orange colour made in amongst the weeds that had overgrown the garden. Another 300 yards farther up, there was a large farmhouse where an elderly farmer and his wife lived. In all the years I had lived in the area, I do not recall ever speaking to them. There were several farm tracks that turned off the main road, connecting these houses to the road and also to many farm buildings scattered about the countryside.

As I stood at the top of Hollow Hill, there was another farm track to my immediate right, which led behind the lake. I used to like walking down there. I would hide up in the trees at the opposite side of the lake from our house and spy on the people at home. The house looked strange from across the lake, and I always experienced a warm feeling of guilt and cheekiness as I hid in the bushes and observed what was going on. I had walked these roads and tracks on every possible permutation and repeated each hundreds of times throughout the course of my childhood. I knew where I was going today, but still I just wanted to linger a little longer.

There were no crops in the fields now. The corn had been cut, the straw bales had been removed, and some of the fields had been ploughed up, waiting for the frost to break up the big clods of earth.

I strolled down the road to the bottom of the hill, remembering the occasions gypsies had camped on the verge on the right-hand side of the road opposite to the track that led to the derelict house. I was always fascinated by gypsies, but my father warned me not to go near them and never to talk to them. I used to spy on their camp from the track by the river, but nothing very much ever happened. Occasionally, the man of the family would raise his voice to the children in a language where every other word sounded like a profanity. But there was a young girl that really interested me; she must have been around my age. Her hair was fabulous. I remember it being jet black and wavy. It would stream behind her as she ran and played, and it would bounce around her head, the sheen as deep as any ocean. She was only small but not skinny, and certainly not fat! I always looked out for her. One day, she caught me spying on the caravans. I was laid in the grass, and she must have been down by the river. She looked at me and then ran off.

I stopped where the road straightened again and turned down the track to my right, threading my way through the puddles. Cherry ran ahead of me and dived from one ditch, on one side of the track, to the other ditch on the other side. She kept popping her head up every now and then to see if I was still following. Half way down the track, I reached my destination. Off to the left was a make-shift dam, which held up the water in the ditch. The farmers could control the level of water in the dam dependent on the amount of irrigation required downstream.

The dam was constructed from vertical planks of wood, all driven into the ditch. Another plank of wood was imbedded in either side of the ditch, and ran behind the vertical ones, thereby supporting them against the pressure of water. The supporting plank then acted as a bridge. I used to sit on this bridge and contemplate the world. In the reservoir behind the dam, the water was deep and clear, and was alive with sticklebacks, water beetles, and a million other insects and reptiles. Occasionally, newts and frogs could be seen.

I laid down on the bridge and considered my future. I could hear Cherry rummaging through the reeds and bulrushes downstream, snorting and panting. I could also hear crickets rasping and bees and flies buzzing this way and that. I looked up to the sky, which was mainly clear but not blue. Although the sun was shining, it was low in the sky, which appeared a blue-grey colour. I had often laid here in the sun during the long, hot Summer days when I could sneak away from home during the school holidays. I used to roam these fields from one secret place to another. This was always my favourite when the sun shone. Had it been raining I would have carried on to the hut at the bottom of the track where, inside, there was always something to lie on and listen to the rain as it pounded the corrugated steel of the roof and walls.

I knew this would be the last time I would ever lay in this position. I knew I could never come home again; I had changed too much. In only 10 months, I had been exposed to too many changes and experiences.

I remember leaving on the train on January 23, 1967, to join the Navy. I was still 15 years old (I would be sixteen the following week, though). I travelled across London to Waterloo, and then found the train that would take me to Portsmouth Harbour Station. I was informed by my instructions I would be met at the station. When I arrived at Portsmouth Harbour Station, I looked for someone in Naval uniform, but I could see nobody. Soon, the station became almost deserted, all the passengers having left. I saw a ticket collector and approached him. He was elderly with a hunched-up back and a bloated face full of pock marks. His fingers and thumbs were like sausages, although he was quite dextrous. I observed him rolling a cigarette. He looked up at me as I approached, his eyes pale blue and fixed on me. I detected he was a kindly man and would not take the piss out of me for what I was about to ask him.

'I've come to join the Navy, Mister. Do you know where I should go?'

'Oh, you have, have you? How old are you then?' he asked, after a pause.

I thought maybe he didn't believe me. I wondered if he thought I'd bunked off school or something. 'Sixteen,' I lied.

'You don't look old enough to join the Navy.'

'Do you know where I should go, Mister?' I asked again, fearing I sounded a little pathetic.

'Yes,' he said quite jovially, and I detected he now believed me. 'Just sit down there and a Petty Officer will be with you soon. I think most of the other lot will be on the next train from London.'

'Thanks a lot,' I said, and wandered over to the wooden bench he indicated.

I sat in silence. I didn't read papers in those days, so I took stock of my surroundings. Portsmouth Harbour Station had only two platforms, and the trains went back out the same way they came in. I didn't know it, but we were right on the harbour edge. There were clear signs of how to get to the Isle-of-Wight ferry, and I wondered how many people made that trip.

I didn't know how long I would have to wait there. I didn't want to bother the old ticket collector again, and so resigned myself to do nothing but wait.

Suddenly, there was a man in front of me. 'Hello, lad,' he said. He was Scottish; his accent thick and easily identifiable. 'What's your name? Have you got your letter?'

I was panicking now: it was the Petty Officer the ticket collector had spoken of, and his uniform and crisp accent exuded authority. I fumbled for my letter and said, 'Yes,' followed by, 'Christopher Paul Clark,' then, while he looked at my letter, I added, 'Sir!' I felt it was necessary.

He gave me the letter back. 'You're early. You should have been on the next train.'

'Oh, I'm sorry. I didn't know.'

'Never mind,' he said in a voice that reassured me that I didn't have to worry. 'Now look,' he said, holding out a ticket, 'this is a ticket for the Gosport ferry. Go across the harbour on the ferry, and when you get to the other side, follow the path to the left-hand side to the bus station.' He held out his left arm as he said this and waved it round to the left. 'Take a number fifty-nine bus and get a seven-penny ticket. Ask the driver to let you know when you get to St Vincent. The bus stop is right outside the main gate. Watch how you cross the road, and report to Officer of the Watch.' He looked at me for some response. I nodded. 'You got your expenses with the letter did you? Five and threepence,' he added, nodding as he did so.

'Yes, Sir,' I said, reaching in my pocket to show him.

'It's okay. As long as you have money for the bus.' He then walked down the station and entered the bar.

I walked out of the station and past the old ticket collector. 'Good luck, Skin,' he said jovially. I couldn't help but wonder why he'd chosen to call me Skin.

Although it was the middle of Winter, it was bright outside after becoming accustomed to the gloom of the station. It was raining a drizzly rain that was more annoying than wetting. The harbour was on my left. A roadway led off to the right, at the end of which were tall Victorian buildings—mainly pubs, by the look of things. I could see the Dockyard gate; I recognised it from a previous trip I had made with my mother. From above the buildings in the dockyard, I could see the top of the mast of HMS Victory—Nelson's flagship. I felt wonderfully independent and proud to see the Victory and the dockyard. In some way, I felt that part of this belonged to me.

I walked down the steps and sudden panic set in: what on earth had the Petty Officer said? I wished I had listened more closely. I had to get a ferry then a bus. Oh my god, what was the number of the bus I should get and from where? *Bollocks!* I thought. Then again, first things first. Get the ferry. *Where is the ferry?* I had seen the signs in the station but that was the Isle-of Wight ferry. There must be two. *Don't get the wrong one!* I told myself.

I looked around but there were no clues. A lady was walking towards the station steps. 'Excuse me?' I blurted out, alarming her. She stopped abruptly and took a pace backwards. 'Where's the ferry?' I asked, not realising how rude I sounded. She looked indignant but just raised her arm and pointed off to my right. 'Cheers,' I said, turning before she could see me blush. The feeling of independence had given way to insecurity and embarrassment in only a few short seconds. In reality, I was so bloody vulnerable.

After a few steps, the concrete roadway began to slope downwards like a boat slip way. Groups of people were walking towards me with their heads down, straining under the pressure of the incline. They had obviously come off the ferry. I reached a barrier at the bottom of the slope that guarded the jetty of the ferry. A heavily tattooed greaser, in a sleeveless leather jacket, slammed the barrier shut as the last passenger passed through. This coincided with my arrival, and he looked down at me and sneered. He frightened me.

'I want to go to Gosport,' I said. 'I've come to join the Navy,' I added but wished I hadn't. I wished the earth would open and swallow me up. I was embarrassed once more.

'Poor bastard. This is the getting off end—you get on at that fucking end,' he sneered, raising a tattooed arm pointing to the bow. He turned his head in the direction of his pointing finger, and I saw tattoos on his neck. I looked in the direction he was pointing and saw other people getting on the ferry through a similar barrier. Another yobbo stood sentry, taking tickets from the boarding passengers as they passed him. There was no way I could get to the other end of the ferry as another barrier ran the length of the sloping roadway. 'You stupid bastard,' the greaser drawled as I turned my back on him and ran up the slope.

I ran round the barrier and down the other side. This walkway was narrow because there was a small ticket office selling ferry tickets. I ran past this and down to the ferry, only to have the barrier slam shut in front of me again.

It was the yobbo at the front end's turn to sneer at me now. 'Have to wait for the next fucker, sonny boy.'

I said nothing. The greaser at the back end was laughing. I quickly averted my eyes as I felt the sting of tears welling up. *Don't cry! Don't cry! Don't cry!* I commanded myself in my mind. I took a deep breath as the ferry pulled away. After some minutes, I was relieved to see another ferry ready to take its place at the now-vacant jetty. Other people were joining me as I stood waiting for the barrier to open. A similar character opened the barrier and held out a hand for my ticket. I passed it over, avoiding speaking or even looking at him. I took a seat in the semi-open bow section. I made sure I was out of the wind and rain, but I could feel the fresh air and see what was going on.

The ride across the harbour took only about 10 minutes, which allowed me to compose myself. I came to the conclusion that harbours were dirty places—that's the first thing that struck me about it. The tide must have been going out as the harbour was fringed with mud. There were some ships at anchor further in the harbour, exhibiting large areas of rust on their hulls and superstructure, the paintwork discoloured with oil and oxidation. Lots of little work boats were weaving about from one side to the other. Predominantly, these were black-hulled with yellow-painted cabins. Funnily enough, most had dogs in their bows, leaning into the wind with their ears swept back and tails wagging. Seagulls swarmed around, squawking and diving at random. Whilst I scanned around, I racked my brain, trying to remember which number bus I had to take, but to no avail. However, it didn't worry me too much—I would ask when I got to the bus station. I knew I had to get to HMS St Vincent so it should be easy enough.

I remember standing by the side of the road as the bus pulled away, looking at the awe-inspiring gates of HMS St Vincent. The Petty Officer was right: I was directly opposite, and I could see through the gates to the ceremonial mast, which stretched above the tops of the buildings behind. I had seen pictures of sailors manning such masts in their bell-bottom trousers and white caps, shaped like milk churn lids. They stood side by side on each limb of the mast, their arms outstretched. One would stand on the button, the round bit right at the very top, and chin-up the final part of the mast without the aid of rigging or ropes. *Well,* I thought, *this is it*, and with that I strode across the road into the gateway where I was met by a sailor in uniform.

'Can I help you?' he asked, politely.

'Yes,' I said. 'I've come to join the Navy.'

'Hang on there a minute,' he said, pointing to a chair.

I sat down whilst he wandered off to a corner to inform other people I was here. I was amazed by all the brass and gold surrounding me. The sailor who greeted me had three gold sergeant stripes on one arm. I later learned these stripes don't represent the position of sergeant as they do in the Army or Air Force. On the other arm, he had a very impressive badge, again in gold, depicting what looked like a torpedo and ropes and things. Another man had two gold rings around his cuff with a circle on the upper ring. He wore a more conventional cap with a peak, a big gold badge gleaming in the middle. Either side of the entrance to the Officer of the Watches' office, there were old cannon balls piled into pyramids and white painted ropes coiled into circles. The windows and doors were adorned with highly polished brass door knobs and window catches. I wondered if I would have to clean these at some stage.

The sailor came back to me and commanded that I follow. I followed him in silence as he led me across the parade ground and right under the mast, which appeared even more fearsome, and through an old door into one of the buildings. Inside the door, the floor was of reddened flagstone with such a deep shine I was amazed you were allowed to walk on it. I had never seen such a surface, and knew it was not gloss paint. I was led up stone stairs with black painted wrought iron work supporting a broadly rounded banister rail, which was polished by many hands sliding up and down it. On the second landing, the sailor led me through a door facing the landing and into a lobby area, where a door directly in front opened up into an enormous bathroom and toilet. Either side of us, there was a door leading into dormitories. We turned to the right; he opened the door and invited me in. The dormitory was huge. It stretched away in front of me for what seemed miles. It was bigger than any room I had ever been in. I could see through the windows at the end, and looked onto the ceremonial mast at the first gantry staging. The dormitory was lined with steel framed beds, one standing above the other. There were seven tiers on the left-hand side and seven on the right, with one single bed on its own opposite the door.

As we entered a boy jumped off this single bed and stood to attention at its foot and shouted, 'Sir!'

The sailor just looked at him and told me to wait. 'Saunders will show you the ropes,' he said. With that, he turned and left.

'You've come to join the Navy as well, have you?' Saunders asked in a very posh accent.

'Yes,' I said. 'My name's Chris Clark. What's yours?'

'Colin Saunders,' he informed me. Colin was taller than me; mind you, at this stage, I was only five-foot two-inches! His complexion was very clear and tanned to a light golden colour. When I tan, I go dark.

Colin was already sixteen, and his parents were living in Cyprus. He had arrived the week before, and had been living there on his own since then. He was wearing dark blue trousers and a lighter coloured blue shirt. This 'uniform' was referred to as Number 8s. I looked back down the dormitory and saw each bunk had a blue-and-white patterned counterpane with an anchor embroidered on it, covering the bed. All the anchors were facing the foot of the bed. At the head of each bed was a pile of blankets, although it was not clear how many. Atop the pile of blankets was a pillow. Adjacent to each bed was a silver coloured locker with two doors. Each was the height of a normal kitchen table. The lockers were made of aluminium, and some shone more than others. At the foot of each bed, facing the locker, was a single straight-backed chair made from a tubular steel frame with a light-coloured plywood seat and back. Along the centre of the room, equally spaced down the gap between the rows of beds, were six odd-looking bins. They were circular in shape and made of aluminium like the lockers. These were actually called spitkids and were used for spitting chewed tobacco in, although now used for collecting litter and bits of rubbish. The floor was the same red colour as the flagstones downstairs, but this red was a lino covering. It also shone, although a thin layer of dust had accumulated on it.

From outside, I could hear a rhythmic crunch, crunch, crunch sound getting progressively louder. Colin bolted down the dormitory to the windows at the end. 'Come and see,' he said, and I followed him. We peered out of the windows, both left and right, and off to our right we saw a group of trainee sailors marching under the instruction of a sailor in proper uniform. The crunching sound of their hobnailed boots on the roadway got louder still as they approached. They were marching in a line of three and about ten deep.

The sailor in charge shouted out, 'Squad, halt!' and with one last crunch, all fell silent. There was another command, and they all turned 90 degrees to face the real sailor with another enormous crunch. Again, momentary silence. Another command and another crunch, and the men were stood at ease. The sailor then spoke to the body of men in a normal voice; he was giving information, not commands. We could not hear what was said. Soon afterwards, the men were commanded to stand to attention. Another crunch sounded, followed by 'Dismiss!' Another crunch followed as they turned to the right then, after a moment's pause, all hell broke loose: they all ran off towards us, shouting and hollering. We heard them enter our building and run up the stairs. It was sheer bedlam! We heard them enter the dormitory beneath us and the noise abated a little. I was impressed with this display. I wanted to wear these Number 8 things, and the big boots and do what I had just seen them do! I knew Colin felt the same.

'Let's go for some dinner,' Colin said. I hadn't realised it was that late.

As we passed Colin's bunk, he took a plastic cup from his locker. 'You'll get one of these later,' he informed me, 'but in the meantime you can share mine.' He then led me down the stairs and out the door I had entered through previously. We turned right and he led me in front of the building and then down an alley way at the end 'This is a shortcut,' he said over his shoulder. At the end of the alleyway, we crossed the galley loading area and went out into the front of the galley.

The dining room was equally as enormous inside as our dormitory, with row upon row of dining tables and chairs. The galley serving counter was on our left-hand side, and I followed Colin as he collected a tray from a pile at the end. I could see men dressed in whites, all strategically placed behind the counter with serving spoons and other implements in their hands.

'We're lucky. If we had been a few minutes later, there would be a horrendous queue here.'

I took his word for it.

The first section of the serving counter we came to offered meat. There were three enormous roasting trays, each with the biggest joint of meat I had ever seen in my life. I couldn't believe it. One had beef, a second pork, and the last one lamb. I loved roast meat, but I never ever got my fill at home. I remember my dad carving on a Sunday and serving Sunday lunch. He would have loads of slices of meat whereas he would only give me a couple. Nicky was always given at least one more slice of meat than me, and his would always be thicker. Not only that, I'd always get the gristly bits. Dad wouldn't just carve and serve in turn; he'd be selective and dole the slices out dependent on their thickness, size and amount of fat and gristle. If I turned my nose up at it, he'd say it was good for me and to get on with it. He knew I liked roast meat, that's why he never allowed me to have a lot of it. If he thought for one minute I didn't like it, he would put more on my plate then take great joy in making me eat it. He would make me remain at the table and finish it all, regardless of how long it took. Maybe I should have done that.

Colin walked past the three carcasses to where a tray of roast chicken was on display. He helped himself to a juicy leg.

'What'll it be, Skin?' the man in white asked me, waving a carving knife.

That was the second time someone had called me that, and still I wondered what it meant. 'Some meat, please.'

'It's all fucking meat, sunshine!' he replied, casting his eyes to the heavens.

'This one,' I said, pointing to the beef. He carved two enormous slices, thicker than I'd ever seen before, and plonked them on my plate.

'More?' he asked.

'No, thanks,' I said, genuinely content with my lot. I could have taken another piece, but I didn't want to appear greedy. I had more roast beef on my plate than I had ever had in my life! More than Dad ever gave Nicky!

We moved along to the next section, and there was tray upon tray of potatoes; mashed potatoes, boiled potatoes, chipped potatoes and, best of all, roast potatoes. These roast potatoes were just like my granny cooked. Deep, golden brown, the corners darker still. You knew they'd be crisp and crunchy and wonderfully soft inside. Saliva gathered behind my back teeth, and I had to swallow before I could speak again. Another man in white stood behind the potatoes with a large spoon in each hand. I offered my plate toward the mashed potato tray, and he scooped up a large dollop and plopped it on it.

'Roasts?' he inquired, jutting his chin towards me.

'Yes, please.'

This was fantastic! I was going to have a feast!

The next section offered vegetables. Whole cauliflowers were placed regimentally on a tray forming geometric lines, which were covered in white sauce. Next was a mountain of carrots on a tray followed by a great aluminium vat of peas, looking firm and juicy. Finally, there was another vat containing sprouts. I chose carrots and peas. I had a wonderful plate of food on my tray. The colours were superb. Steam rose from the individual parts, carrying an aroma of mixed ecstasies that alerted my tummy that something really good was on its way! But then, just as I thought the dream was complete, I noticed large jugs of gravy. At least four stood in a row. This was help yourself. I recalled at home that I was never given enough gravy. I loved gravy, and my dad used to flood his plate with it and, when all the food was gone, he'd take a spoon and spoon up the gravy. The amount of gravy he allowed me to have never left enough to warrant a spoon. Now I could have as much as I wanted! I picked up a jug and slowly poured, making a circuit of the plate with the brown stream of steaming viscous liquid. I did it slowly so it filled all the crevices. Once it approached the rim, I stopped. Fantastic!

Colin had moved on to where the desserts were on offer. My eyes popped again. There was apple pie, a spongy thing with currents dotted throughout its mountainous mass. There was treacle tart and a vat of rice pudding at the end. Beyond the rice pudding, I saw large glass jugs of custard. It was almost too much for me to take in! I had a slice of the apple pie and flooded it with custard. I followed Colin to a table, trying to keep the gravy and custard on their respective plates. I also noticed Colin's plates were equally full.

'It's bloody good grub here,' Colin said. If ever I was in doubt as to what an understatement was, then there was no doubt now!

I tucked into my dinner with an enthusiasm I'd never experienced before. I kept thinking to myself over and over how fantastic it all was. It really was fantastic!

As I was attacking my apple pie and custard, the entrance door burst open and a herd of trainees stampeded through wearing their Number 8s and boots. They all clambered to put their hats on a row of hooks provided, and chased each other round to the start of the serving counter where the trays were stacked. The whole place was filled with noise; people talking, shouting, giggling and stamping feet. All this competed with the tinkling of cutlery and the banging and scraping of chairs. This was real chaos. Before long, the queue for dinner was out the door. Colin and I looked at each other, and he said, 'See what I mean?' referring to the queue.

We finished our food and took our dirty plates to the scullery, and handed them over to another heavily tattooed elderly man who was about the same height as me, although his waist measurement was probably five-foot-two as well!

'Cheers, Skin,' he said.

Again! I thought.

Colin went over to some brightly polished urns and filled his mug with steaming tea. He gingerly carried it back to our dormitory.

I sat with him as he explained a bit of what was to happen to us. As he had already been there a few days, he had spoken to the other recruits and had some idea of what was set to happen. It seemed the rest of our class would be arriving over the course of the afternoon and the next morning. Once we had all arrived, there would be a series of lectures about the Navy and what would be happening over the next few weeks. There would be a process of counselling and chats, some with the padre.

After a couple of days, we would be expected to sign on. Once this was done, we then would be inducted. Starting off with a haircut, the issuance of kit, the sewing on of badges, polishing boots, and learning drill and all other seamanship functions. Colin had already got some of his kit. He showed me his boots and explained how to polish them—the spit-and-polish method. *What a waste of time,* I thought. The toe caps shone with such a deep shine. It must have taken him ages, but there again he didn't have much time for anything else. He also explained we were not allowed out for the first week. The Navy probably thought we would all piss off at the first given opportunity!

During the afternoon and the following morning, the rest of our class arrived. Soon, our dormitory was full with young men and boys from all over the country. One even came from Rhodesia. There were a couple younger than I, which made me feel superior in some way.

For the first time, I was being exposed to different country accents and the richness of the diverse upbringing of the various recruits. I was amazed that people actually loved their parents! I had grown up without my mother, with only my sister's mother and, later, Fay as substitutes. My father was just that; he never became a friend or anyone I enjoyed being with, and I was never really comfortable in his company. I always felt better if someone else was in the room with us or in the car if we were going anywhere. I did not miss them. At night, some boys were heard crying in their bunks because they missed their mums.

My basic training at HMS St Vincent seemed to take ages, although it was only six weeks. Secondary training was at HMS Collingwood, where I learned all about electrics and was eager to put this newfound knowledge into practice. I wanted to go to all the wonderful places I had heard the older sailors speaking of: Honky Fid (Hong Kong), Singers(Singapore), Gib (Gibraltar) and Aussie(Australia), and many more. I wanted to do some of the many things I heard they had done; pissing-up and bagging off (drinking and shagging), mainly. Unfortunately, I was still only 16 years old (only looking 14!) so I still had some growing up to do.

I was aware of a large spider crawling over my chest. I lay still and allowed it to continue its journey. The sun was warmer now, having climbed higher in the sky. I could hear Cherry rooting around in the ditch on the other side of the track, and I called out to her. Soon her head appeared over the bank, and she came galloping up to me—she was filthy. I sat up and considered what I should do. Time was getting on, and I had much to do even though I didn't want to leave this place. All I really wanted to do was to be with Kay again and then get back to Portsmouth to join the Hermes. At long last, I would be going to sea.

I decided what I would do. I sprang to my feet and brushed myself down. Cherry was watching me in anticipation. 'Come on, girl,' I called, and jumped off the bridge and scrambled up the bank. I remembered Fay said she was going shopping in Peterborough, so I decided to go with them and save the money of a bus fare. I could also take my kit bag and tool kit, and leave these at 'Left Luggage' at the station, where I could retrieve them on Sunday when I returned from seeing Kay. This way I didn't have to return home. It all seemed so neat!

My dad pulled up outside the station and I got out of the car. He moaned all the way that I was not spending enough time with them at home before I went off to sea. But I just couldn't wait to be there. I pulled my kit bag and tool box out of the boot, and dumped them by the station door. Nicky had not returned from work before I left, which pleased me no end, and Lesley had left whilst I was walking Cherry, going off to spend the day with her mother, meaning I did not see her, which actually saddened me a little.

I turned to my dad and Fay, who were still in the car, and said, 'I'll see you then.'

Dad nodded. 'Yuh.' And then they pulled away.

''Bye, Christopher,' Fay shouted from the open window as they disappeared round the corner of The Station hotel. I stood there, looking after the car, and thought to myself, *Well, mate, that's it.* It was to be more than a year before I would see them again.

I visited my grandparents and was moaned at for not wearing my uniform. My mother turned up with her husband Tosh, and we played some cards for a while. I loved my mother, but not like some of the boys

I had joined the Navy with. I didn't miss her and I didn't cry at night for her, but I still loved her.

Saturday late-afternoon, I arrived at Spalding and was met by Kay. It was good to see her again, and instantly I felt a distinct stirring in my loins at just the sight of her. She was wearing a short mini skirt, which showed off her fantastically shaped legs, which were clad in knee-high boots. Her blouse was light and silky beneath a brown leather jacket. I couldn't wait for the evening when her parents would go out and leave us together for a few hours when she would once again get a thorough good seeing to.

That evening, I couldn't get enough of her. I fucked her on the settee, on the kitchen table, on the stairs, up the stairs, and finally on the carpet in front of the fire. I must have shot my duff at least half a dozen times, and I was always ready to go again. But it was all one-way traffic; I only fucked her—it was only for me. That's all I knew. I hadn't yet learned how to make love to a woman. I didn't know women needed pleasure and satisfaction also. I didn't know anything different, and to me it was only important to do it again and again. My whole time with her was only focused on the act of 'bagging off'. Really, it was sexual abuse with permission.

We had to stop and clear up a bit before her parents came home. After we had done this, Kay made a cup of tea and we sat in the kitchen chatting away, and she became tearful that I was going away for such a long time. I promised I would write and that I would not even look at another girl. She turned to the sink so I could not see her tears, and I embraced her from behind. In this position, my hands naturally fell to her breasts, which, again, aroused me. I had to have her one last time, and so I pulled her knickers down from behind and did it as we stood there, Kay just looking at our reflection in the kitchen window. It took all of two minutes, and she accused me of only wanting her for one thing. I tried to reassure her but I was only thinking I couldn't wait to tell Budgie how many times I had done it.

Rox took us to the station the next afternoon, and left Kay and I alone so we could say our goodbyes. I was in my uniform as I had to report to my new ship when I got to Portsmouth. We stood in a corner and held each other tight. She was crying again, and no matter what I said I couldn't console her. The reality of the situation was that I was dying for the train to come so I could get rid of her. She was ruffling up my collar, and her make-up was coming off and marking my tunic and white front.

Eventually, the train arrived, and I managed to prize myself away and get on-board. I waved her goodbye from on the train, and then felt guilty I could not return her obvious affection.

3: The Black Cat Cafe

At just after seven on Sunday evening, I stepped from the train onto the platform of Portsmouth Harbour Station once again. These surroundings were now familiar to me, and I hurried my way to the exit turnstiles, out of the station and down the steps to the pavement. I now had to find the Hermes within the dockyard—and I hadn't a clue where it would be! But nonetheless, I contented myself that the dockyard police would direct me.

From where I stood, the lights of the line of pubs outside the dockyard gate were a welcoming sight. You could anticipate the warmth of the pub interiors in contrast to the cold rain that had just started to fall and threatened to do so with increasing ferocity. I slung the kitbag over my shoulder and made my way towards the dockyard gate. Outside the gate was a large hotdog stall where some people were taking cover from the rain whist drinking hot Bovril or coffee and eating a chipolata sausage cradled in the slit of a finger roll, masquerading as a hot dog. There were a few sailors there in uniform also. I decided I'd go straight past and find my ship.

'Clark, ya prick!' I heard someone call out. 'Come 'ere!'

It was Budgie. 'What do you want, you toss pot?' I replied, but I was genuinely pleased to see him. I sidled up beside him and dumped my kitbag and tool box next to his. 'Fucking freezing, aint it, eh?' I said, then snatched the remaining morsel of his hot dog and put it in my mouth before he could protest.

'Seen any of the others?' he asked, and I shook my head as I munched his supper. 'Do you know where the ship is?'

'In there,' I motioned with my head.

'Fountain Lake Jetty. Seeing's how you've just had me hot dog, you can get the fags out.'

'I aint got any. In fact, I've had none all weekend. Have you?'

'Only blue liners. Here,' he said, offering me one.

The first drag sent my head in a spin and made me feel dizzy. This was quickly followed by a feeling of nausea, but I resisted it, pushing it away, until I recovered.

'Did you get your end away then?' he asked, smirking.

'All the time. More than ten times! I lost count in the end!'

'You lying bastard. I bet you got fuck all.'

'Just cos you've never had it, Budgie, doesn't mean it don't happen!'

'Piss off,' he said, trying to push me away.

We stood smoking whilst we observed what was happening around us. The pubs had just opened for the evening and were beginning to fill up. People were moving from one to the other, and every time a door opened the juke box could be heard along with the sound of bustle inside. We knew we couldn't go in on our own as we were too young and would never get served. Budgie must have been thinking the same thing as he turned to me and said, 'I wonder where Fingers or Briggsy is. Do you think they're maybe on-board already?'

'Maybe. Come on, let's go and see.'

We walked through the dockyard and found Fountain Lake Jetty. When we turned the corner HMS Hermes was there.

'It's fucking enormous!' Budgie said in wonderment.

We both stopped and stared at it. The ship was floodlit against the dark, and its grey sides rose out of the water and high above the surface of the jetty. The line of the Flight Deck was edged with guard rails where people leaned and looked out to the dockyard. The island towered even higher still, the mast holding navigation and safety lights. The big 984 radar antenna resembled a darkened search light. The flat surface of the ship's hull was broken with red square grills of fan intakes. Midway down from the Flight Deck were the Weather Decks; the forecastle at the front and the Quarterdeck nearest to us at the stern. A line of others interspersed between the whole length. There was a gang-plank going up to the Quarterdeck with a white canvas sheet tethered to the hand rail with HMS Hermes emblazoned upon it. This was for the exclusive use of the ships' officers and their guests. Towards the bow was another leading onto a Weather Deck, which obviously was intended for the lower-deck crew, i.e. us.

And then, aside from the enormity and magnificence of the sight, there was the noise. A pulsating hum throbbed away from within the vessel. The summation of a myriad of fans, pumps, motors, generators, compressors, steam and air bouncing through pipes and trunking, along with hammers hammering, spanners clanking, doors slamming, and the best part of two-thousand people going about their daily business.

'Fuck me,' I said in wonderment.

We walked along the jetty to our gang-plank and, as we approached the ship, we became aware of its smell. The smell got stronger the closer we got, yet it was a smell we would only experience a few times. Once you were on-board, the senses dulled to it and it only manifested itself when you had spent time away on leave and then returned. The smell is so unique; it's a culmination of all the smells—oil, grease, aviation fuel, steam, sewage, sweat, bilge water, food, paint; the combination of all the chemicals in the sickbay and dentist, all the chemicals in all the cleaning cupboards, and all the perfumes and deodorants in all the lockers, along with bacteria, beetles and backsides.

We walked up the gang plank and jumped off the end to the deck of the ship—no easy task when you are laden with a full kitbag and tool box, let me tell you!

We were expected. We were given a joining routine card to be completed the next day and were shown to our Mess Deck and bunk. All new recruits were to report to the Regulating Office at 8pm (in five minutes' time). As it transpired, Budgie and I were the last to arrive. Fingers, Briggsy and Maxmore were all on-board along with the others, their gear already stowed away.

Our Mess Deck was beneath the Junior Rates dining hall. The mess was large. It went from each side of the ship and spanned the entire area between two watertight bulkheads. 5E Mess, the fifth deck down from the Flight Deck, and Section E was the fifth watertight section from the bow, with A–D obviously in front of us. The access hatch was in the deck of the dining room at the centre line and adjacent to the forward bulkhead. Upon entering the mess, the centre line was the locker area, comprising two alleyways of lockers. The bunks were outboard of these. The Senior members were on the starboard side whilst the Juniors were on the port. I had a bottom bunk and Budgie was allocated the one above it. We just dumped our gear then went up to the Regulating Office. At exactly 8pm, the reg. office door swung open and out stepped a giant of a man dressed in a Petty Officer's uniform. He ducked under the top of the doorframe then turned to pull the door shut. As he bent to do so, his shoulders strained the seams of his jacket, such was his broadness. He swivelled around to face us as he placed his cap over a spiky crewcut hairstyle. He stood upright, his cap between pipes and trunking of the deck head (ceiling of the corridor). His complexion was craggy and rugged, and his jaw was square and strong. His nose was scarred, though straight. He had piercing pale blue eyes that could burn holes straight through you. I can appreciate that, to a woman, he was a handsome man.

'Right, men!' he barked, scaring the living daylights out of us all. 'Form a line two deep, stand to attention, and shit 'n it. Quickly now!' (I soon came to discover 'shit 'n it' meant to be quite).

We formed the two lines and stood in silence, not daring to look in his direction. Our eyes were staring directly in front of us—every single one of us did the same.

'My name's RPO McSnell!' he bellowed. 'That's spelt B, A, S, T, A, R, D.' He looked at us and slowly walked the length of the line, ducking his head under the obstacles on the deck head as he went. 'Don't fuck with me or your life will not be worth living! Do I make myself clear?'

'Yes, RPO!' we replied in unison.

I was standing to the right of the reg. office door, fixing my eyes on a bolt hole in the bulkhead. I sensed McSnell was staring at me. He moved towards me in silence, and a feeling of dread overwhelmed me. He stopped in my line of vision, but my eyes still focused beyond him on where the bolt hole would be.

'What's your name, boy?' he barked at me.

I almost wet myself—I could not speak such was my fright.

'Well?' he shrieked.

'Clark,' I said, rather lamely.

'Well, Clark. What the fuck is this on your white front?' He prodded his finger into my chest.

I looked down and he whipped his hand up with such speed his finger lashed the end of my nose like a whip lash.

'Stand still!' he commanded. 'You're stood to attention and when you are stood to attention you don't move!' His finger resumed its position on my chest. 'Do you?'

'No, RPO,' I replied, even more lamely.

'Well! What the fuck is it!'

'I don't know, RPO,' I managed to squeak out.

'You don't know, 'he said, mimicking my voice. 'I'll tell you what it is, lad! It's some brown hatter's make-up, that's what it is!' He turned away from me and walked down the line. 'Is that right, Clark?'

My fear meant I could only answer affirmatively, despite realising that a brown hatter was a colloquial term for a homosexual. 'Yes, RPO!'

'We don't have brown hatters on this ship, Clark! I'll be watching you.' RPO McSnell then produced a piece of paper and proceeded to lecture us on discipline, and about the various dos and don'ts, etc. I was relieved my ordeal was over—for now, at least. I knew Kay had left makeup on me but could do nothing about it.

We were informed we were going to sea the next day for our sea trials so we were to muster in one of the switchboards during harbour stations. Finally, we were informed we could go ashore if we wanted to as this would be the last opportunity for a couple of weeks. We were dismissed and proceeded to return to the mess.

As I was about to step through into the dining room, McSnell bellowed after me, 'Clark! Change that fucking white front!'

'Yes, RPO.' I answered in a voice more resembling that of a human being.

'He's got it in for you, Clarkie!' Fingers said as we went down the ladder to our mess.

'He don't bother me,' I lied. 'Are we off ashore then, Fingers?'

'Fucking right we are! Get that white front changed, PDQ!'

An RPO is a Regulating Petty Officer, and they are the policemen of the Navy. You cannot join the Navy in the regulating branch; you join the regulating branch because you cannot succeed in your own branch. Therefore, all regulators are failed seamen or stokers or even electrical mechanics like ourselves. Because of this, all regulators have big chips on their shoulders and despise anyone with intelligence. I didn't realise it at the time, but I was to have a long relationship with RPO McSnell throughout my time on Hermes.

At 9pm, Budgie, me, Max, Fingers and Mick Briggs went through the dockyard gate again, but this time in the opposite direction.

We were on the Hard—that's what the stretch of road was called from the main dockyard gate to the railway bridge, which crossed it some several hundred yards further onto the right was the harbour. To the left was pub after pub. The first was called The Apple Tree, and the last before the bridge was called The Victory. I was to become very familiar with The Victory—or rather a young girl that frequented it—as time went by.

Budgie and I were at the mercy of Fingers and Mick because they had to order our beer. They made the decision and we went into the first pub. On opening the door, we were greeted by the smell of tobacco, stale beer and cheap perfume. It was a smell I would become accustomed to in the future, and one I would welcome. The noise was also phenomenal. A deep rumble of shouting and the high-pitched screech of women's laughter mixed with the clatter of glasses and furniture moving on wooden floors. It was packed. Just the way I liked it. Fingers could get the beer, and me and Budgie could hide in a corner. Budgie had to pay for this one, and I knew it would be my turn next.

As I slumped in a corner, a drunken man next to me asked if I was in the Navy. I wondered what gave him that idea, particularly as I was in my uniform. He offered to buy me a beer, which I thought was very generous, but then Fingers and Mick arrived with our beer. 'Fuck off, knobber,' Fingers said to the man, which I thought was a bit rude till Max explained the man was a homosexual who had taken a fancy to me. Well, well! I'd met my first homosexual. Before I had time to taste my beer, Mick was halfway down his and suggesting we go to The Victory next and then work our way back to the dockyard gate. This was a good strategy, I supposed—at least *I* couldn't fault it.

Before I knew it, Mick said, 'Come-on then, let's go.' I was with the big boys and had to do my bit. I finished my beer and watched as Budgie finished his. We looked at each other with the recognition we could not keep this up all night.

We wandered past all the pubs to The Victory, which was, by comparison, a modern bar. Not from the Victorian age at all, but still decked out with the theme of the Navy. Inside was less crowded. John Lennon was professing from a juke box that all he wanted was money, which was rather too loud. Two drunken young girls were dancing on a beer-stained carpet, and all the eyes of the men present were upon them. Their mini skirts showed ample thighs and their tops advertised the non-use of bras. They turned me on. Flashes of the cheeks of their arses could be seen, and the bouncing of their breasts added to my excitement. I'd come a long way from Forty Foot!

Me and Budgie took a seat by the window, close to the dart board. There was a young girl playing darts who looked at me and whose eyes stayed on me longer than necessary. I looked away in embarrassment, hoping I would not blush. After a while, I chanced a look at her and saw long, slender, shapely legs, only disappearing at the last moment beneath a short skirt. She wore high heel shoes, which enhanced the shape of her legs. She had on a tight blouse, which covered more than ample breasts—fucking big tits, in other words! Much bigger than Kay's! Her shoulder-length hair was flaming red and shone in incandescent waves. Her face was narrow with a longish pointed nose, high cheek bones, and green all-knowing eyes. She was beautiful. I looked at her for far too long, and she caught my eye and, once again, I was embarrassed. I swore to myself I would not look at her again.

Once more, Mick was eager to move on. I still had best part of a pint and already was feeling heady.

'Do you two want a game of darts?' the redhead asked me and Budgie.

Confusion. Embarrassment. Shyness. All of these emotions came to the fore. Quickly, I could see a solution. I knew I could not keep up drinking with Fingers or Mick, and to linger with this girl and her partner would go down in some way as a bit of a victory. Budgie looked at me and we both knew it was on opportunity to bail out of a situation we couldn't handle.

'If you think you're good enough,' I said with bravado.

Budgie nodded and we stood and faced the board.

The redhead was called Dianne and she could throw well. Most people aim for the treble-twenty for a maximum score, but she chose treble-nineteen. Her darts took a looping trajectory, and it's a wonder they ever stuck the board. But stick they did, and Budgie and I took a bit of a beating.

Dianne had beautiful hands; long, slender fingers held together by such small palms. Everyone knew her, and more people offered to buy her Mackison (a dark bottled stout) than she could have ever wanted. I was so happy to be in her company, although I hadn't learned the social skills to be able to 'chat her up'. I knew she was interested in me, but she was also older and so much more assured. At least she was able to go to the bar and order beer for us, which we could drink at our own pace. Mick, Fingers and Max had moved on by this stage.

When the bell went for time, we all said our goodbyes. There was much more I wanted to say to her, and I knew she wanted to say much more to me, but I was too young to know what to do about these things.

Budgie and I ambled down the Hard back to the dockyard gate. This was an experience in itself: the pubs had kicked out, and drunken people flooded the street; some arguing, some telling jokes and laughing loudly, some fighting and some being sick. I was confused with too much alcohol. I wasn't old enough to be used to it—and I wasn't old enough to do the sensible thing, which was to circumnavigate myself around them to spend my first night on the ship, which was to become my home for the next three years.

As we passed the The Apple Tree, the knobber, as Fingers named him, tapped me on my shoulder and asked if I wanted a coffee and a hot dog. Budgie and I looked at each other, and I could tell he wanted to go back on-board. 'Just up here. The Black Cat café,' he said, pointing to his right.

It was only two doors away, and we could see people inside, and music was playing loudly and smoke was billowing out the door. To me, it looked inviting. It oozed danger and excitement, and I wanted to peek inside. 'Come on, Budge, let's go.'

'Chris! We have to be on-board by midnight and we're off to sea tomorrow!'

'I know, I know. We've got stacks of time and it'll be our last chance for days.'

'Okay. But I'm not going to be adrift.'

'Like I said, we have stacks of time and it's a free dog,' I said, referring to the hot dog on offer. I could tell Budgie wasn't happy, but I didn't want the evening to end.

'Come, my two sailor boys. Come and have a lovely hot dog with Frankie,' said the knobber, who now had a name. He put his arm around both of us and led us toward The Black Cat.

The Black Cat café looked its best at this time of night. The lights were low, it was full of smoke, and the crowd of people obscured the decrepit bar, the torn chairs, dirty tables and the overall filth of the place. Over-laced with the smell of tobacco was the smell of burnt lard from within the kitchen where our hot dogs would be cooked along with chips, ham burgers, sausages, bacon, and the myriad of dead flies and cockroaches that had accumulated during the day. Cat Stevens sang from the juke box about Matthew and his son.

I was excited by everything; I had never been in such a place. With so many 'grown up' people around, I somehow also felt grown up.

It seemed to me everyone I looked at was drunk. Sailors and dockyard workers were hanging on to their stools with tomato ketchup dripping from the ends of their hand-held supper, leaving red trails on their jackets and trousers. They didn't care. There were a few women also. Harlots of the night, mostly, although I wasn't to know this at the time. All I could take in were the short skirts, stocking tops, big breasts and abundance of make-up. Other people just jostling around.

As we entered, two of the aforementioned ladies alighted from the window seats, dragging two men with them. 'Quick! Sit!' said Frankie, pushing us into their vacant seats. 'Keep this seat for me,' he said, as he went off to place his order.

'I think we should piss off,' said Budgie. 'I don't like this and I don't like that bloke either.' He nodded towards Frankie.

'Come-on, Budge, let's have this free scoff then we'll make a dash for it,' I replied, trying to reassure him. 'The dockyard gate's only there.'

The next thing that happened was the door was blocked by the entrance of a giant of a man. He must have been six-foot-six if he was an inch, and although he had an enormous barrel chest, his belly led the way. He stopped just inside the door and peered into the gloom of the place—obviously looking for someone. He looked at me and I glanced away immediately. This man brought fear with him as most of the noise abated. People continued to talk but in hushed tones, with only the drunken ones continuing unaware of this man. He strutted in slowly, still scanning left and right. As he reached the serving counter, he turned, took one last look, and then headed back for the door. Obviously he didn't find who, or what, he was looking for. Relief descended as he left.

Budgie and I exchanged glances of relief, but before we could say anything we were interrupted by the serving lady from behind the bar. She was attired the same as all the ladies there. She was curvy; not fat but sensuous. Curvy breasts wobbled where they became exposed from her dress, causing the crevice of her cleavage to promise unthinkable delights. Her arms were also full but, again, not fat; just lightly toned. Her hips flared from a small waist, and the material of the dress wrinkled as it tightly pulled over her underwear. I could see lines of elastic and the various outlines of lace. This woman excited me. *Every* woman excited me, and I still had the residue of the excitement left me by Dianne earlier.

The lady wiped the table and the wobbly bits wobbled more. I knew she did not have to wipe the table with so much vigour, and I knew *she* knew what it was doing to her wobbly bits. Whilst she could have guessed the feelings it was stirring in me, she could never have guessed the severity of those feelings.

Hands still now, she continued to lean on the table and surveyed us knowingly. 'So, you're the two virgins eh? Frankie's virgins, eh?' She added, 'Maybe not just Frankie's virgins either, eh?' She looked intently at us both. She was looking at Budgie and I had lowered my gaze some.

She turned to me, and I looked up to see wide dark blue eyes staring into me. I could not look away from them. I was hypnotised by them. She was made up in such a way that every contour of her face was glamorised. Her cheek bones were higher, cheeks rosier, eyebrows more hooded. Her eyelashes were long and curved, and had globules of mascara across them. Her wrinkles had been filled, and I only saw a smooth youthful complexion free from spots and blemishes. She smiled at me and, when her luscious lips parted, they revealed beautiful white teeth—unusually white, which almost radiated light onto me in the gloom of this place.

'Don't worry, boys. Frankie's had to leave. The gorilla's after him.' She nodded to the door the gorilla had been blocking earlier. 'I let him out the back door. Frankie said if I give you two a hot dog, you're mine,' she said menacingly. 'So, standby.' And with that, she straightened up, pushed out her breasts, tossed her head back, and just shook her long wavy hair from her shoulders. She turned and walked back to the bar, lifting the serving hatch at the side as she headed towards the kitchen.

She left the serving hatch open, and my eyes followed the rotating motion of her hips and buttocks as she disappeared.

Budgie elbowed me in the ribs with severity, the surprise of which caused me instant annoyance. I had been well and truly awakened from my thoughts. 'Let's fuck off quick!' he said, and attempted to get up.

I grabbed him. 'Hang on! We'll get a free hot dog out of this and, you never know, something else as well!'

'Clark, you're barmy! She's a fucking pro! Go with her and you never know what you might get. Let's get back on-board before she comes back.'

'Hang on, for fuck sake! Let's just see what pans out. We've stacks of time to get back on-board.' Budgie relaxed a bit, resigned to wait for the hot dog to come.

She returned from the kitchen and perched on a stool behind the counter facing her customers on the other side. David Bowie turned into Major Tom and a Space Oddity was issued forth from the juke box. She lit a cigarette and turned her face towards us. She blew smoke in our direction as she simultaneously rotated her body on the stool. This motion was initiated by her swinging her right leg away from the counter; this pulled her hips around as the rotation started. However, the left leg did not follow immediately. Eventually, the rotation of her hips caused the left leg to follow the right. During the sequence, when she sat square on to us, her two legs were separated by about some 30 degrees. She was looking directly at me as a twinkle in her eye and a curl at the corner of her lips. I looked at the space between her knees. I could see the tightness of her stockings being stretched over her thighs. The colour of her legs had changed there; the tightness of the nylon had made them look lighter and also, because I was looking along the length of her inner thighs, the nylon took on a sheen that is not seen when viewed straight on. The sheen gave way to a darker band as the material was doubled up for reinforcement so the suspender clips wouldn't damage it. I often wonder what the stocking manufacturers had in their mind when they designed these things. Did they know? Beyond the dark band there immediately followed a white band of silky flesh.

My head was about to explode with the sheer excitement of it all.

Her customers could not see this; this was only for me and Budgie. Deeper into the junction of her legs, the whiteness gave way to a maelstrom of textures and shade of darkness. The flesh darkened with the shadow, then turned into furriness—or that could have been the underwear. The knickers, in other words, because that's how they must be described in this instance—and *sexy* knickers at that. It was not possible to determine what each texture was or where one started from the other. I knew this was what it was like being flashed. *I* was being flashed! I was being flashed by someone who was a professional at it. An artist deploying her trade. I had a stirring in my groin like never before. I could easily explode down there at any minute. Eventually, however, the left leg caught up with the right, and the flash was over.

My heart was beating so severely I was competing with Mr Bowie and wondered if anyone could hear me. 'Fucking hell, Budge. You see that?'

'What?' he said, looking up from the menu and surveying the room. 'What?' he said again.

'Nothing, Budge. Never mind.' I didn't know where to begin to tell him.

The lady came back to our table with our supper. When she placed mine in front of me, she said, 'You have come-to-bed eyes. They'll get you into trouble one day. I finish in half an hour. I'll meet you in the lobby next door and I'll really show you something.' I must have been bright red by this time. I knew I had to go. I knew I could never give up this opportunity. If I should die then, it would have to be after tonight. *God, please allow me this time*, I offered up in silent prayer.

'We have to be on-board at midnight, Miss,' Budgie said.

She just looked at him in unblinking silence for a second, then turned back to me. 'I'll see you later, Lover,' and with that she sauntered back to her stool.

'You're not going to meet her surely, Chris. She's a fucking prossy! She'll be riddled with VD! For fuck sake, come to your senses.'

'Budgie, I have to do this.'

'No you don't! Just forget it! You'll be in deep shit when you do come back.'

I took another bite from my hot dog roll and, after half a chew, said, 'I couldn't give a fuck! I'm going to shag that woman tonight if it's the last thing I do. If I miss the ship, I miss the ship.'

Budgie looked at me, shaking his head in resignation.

He left without saying any more to me. He was annoyed and dismayed. I knew he had some caring for me, but sometimes a young 16-year-old has to do what a young 16-year-old has to do! And that's what I was going to do!

I walked out and into the cold night air. Winter was on its way, so no surprise that the moisture in my breath condensed upon meeting the coldness. I felt it would rain soon. I don't know why I felt that as I could not see the night sky. I knew it had rained earlier, and I just had a feeling it would rain more.

I felt good. I knew I was being naughty; I still could feel the effects of the beer I had earlier, but I didn't feel sick. I was excited and also a little fearful of meeting this woman. It crossed my mind the big gorilla would be around and would only want me for my money. That would be a laugh considering two shillings and tuppence was all I had! No problem to lose that. I figured nothing more sinister would happen to me too near the dockyard gate. I'd just have to wait and see.

I entered the tenement block; the lobby was dark and cold. Somewhere up the five flights of stairs, there was a light that only showed me the stairs went up a long way. On each landing I could see two doors, one going off to the right, the other to the left. *Must be big rooms*, I thought to myself.

The building was old. The stairs had a wrought iron balustrade topped off with a wooden banister, highly polished by years of use. The stairs were of concrete, but the corners were edged with steel to prevent ware. The floor on which I stood was a mosaic of small tiles depicting a pattern of a sea battle. Tall-masted ships bounced around on ridiculous-looking waves. Randomly, some of the tiles were missing, leaving a square alien dot in the picture. The floor was uneven with wear. A furrow had developed from the door to the first step. There was the smell of urine.

I sensed she had entered the lobby before I saw her.

'Well, hello,' she said. 'Who's a little virgin looking for adventure then?'

It's a good job it was dark as I knew I was blushing again. I had the urge to run, but again there was such a stirring in my pants I knew I had to stay. I said nothing. I *couldn't* say anything. I didn't know *what* to say! What on earth do you say when you are of tender years and about to get fucked by a mass of wantonness?

She came up to me and stood with her nose almost touching mine. She took my hand and led it around her back, and pressed it against her buttock. My hard on got harder. She pushed herself against it and cooed. 'You had better come with me, my boy,' and with that she led me up the stairs.

I followed, my eyes level with her backside as we ascended, and I watched every bounce and rumble of flesh with each step we took. I was not disappointed to learn her room was at the very top.

At the top, she fished in her bag for her key and let us in. The room was the attic. The ceiling sloped from left and right to an apex in the centre. It was only one room with a toilet and small sink curtained off in the corner. A single light swung on a chord from the apex, which she illuminated from a switch by the door. All of a sudden, the room was bathed in light that revealed the shabbiness of it all. The carpet was stained and littered with ash and cigarette ends. Half-empty cups and glasses were strewn on almost every flat surface. One corner was full of crumpled paper that previously had held fish and chips, which seemed to be her staple diet. The bed was unmade and looked dirty and crumpled.

She lit a candle by the bed and then turned off the main light.

After entering the room, I had remained still and hadn't said a word. She began to get undressed in front of the candle. Slowly, she revealed herself to me. The dress was pulled over her head, and I could see all those secret and very exciting items of ladies' clothes that are often fantasised about. I did not see the over-flabby belly or the stretch marks.

She removed her bra and her breasts swung down and separated. They were fucking enormous. The nipples were dark and slightly oval in shape, with the largest diameter being vertical. I did not notice they were closer to the ground than they should have been. She then removed her knickers and stood there looking at me. She still wore the suspenders and stockings of such a wonderful dark shiny colour. Her pubic hair formed a perfect triangle although I did not see the grey flecks amongst the blackness.

'Well, darling, don't just stand there with your mouth open.'

Instinctively, I shut my mouth, not realising it had gaped open.

'You really are a virgin, aint you?' she said, her hands on her hips. 'Well, you aint got nothing to worry about. I've had stacks of virgins and no one's died yet.' She came around the bed to me and again stood close. Again, she took my hand and placed it on one of her pendulous breasts. How warm and soft she felt. 'Well, squeeze the fucker,' she said.

I did, and the texture I will never forget. Like a balloon full of warm water.

She took my other hand in both hers and placed it between her legs; pubic hair wiry and resilient. She pushed my fingers down deeper and I could feel the soft, warm flesh. Kay was different to this, which surprised me. I thought all women would be the same. I felt wet rubberiness with softness. I couldn't believe that, in a very few minutes, I would be putting my penis in there.

She began to undue my trousers and pushed them down. 'You'll have to do that fucking tunic thing. Never could I get used to those weird sailors' collars.' And then she turned away from me and climbed into bed. 'Cat got your fucking tongue, has it then?' she asked.

'No,' I said, using the business of getting undressed as a distraction from her. 'Don't really say much.'

'Ah, a doer are we. I like doers. You certainly look like you're a doer with that thing. How long you been hard?'

Little did she know I had been hard most of the night since playing darts with Dianne!

'Since I saw your knickers.'

'You liked that, then, did you?' she said. 'Most young uns do. Well, you better come here then and see what else I've got for you.'

I got into bed, and she steered me on top of her. Almost like magic, I was inside her. The heat, softness and passion of her made me shoot my first load almost before the first stroke ended. Premature ejaculation I was later to find it was called. Some say it's a problem, but I was still hard and I could ejaculate four or five times consecutively whilst keeping a hard-on for hours.

Lying on top of this woman, I could see the makeup beginning to slip. The lipstick smeared, and the blue-black eye makeup came together to form dark patches. I could see wrinkles that previously had been hidden; hidden behind the makeup and also behind my animal desire for her. No matter what she looked like, it could not detract from the feeling from being deep inside her.

After a while, she pushed me off saying, 'Sorry, Lover, I need a quick piss.' She disappeared behind the curtain, and I could hear the jet of urine as it bounced off the surface of the toilet pan or crashed directly into the water at the bottom. She emerged without flushing the pan or washing her hands. 'Okay, my lovely, I'm going to really crush you now.' She pushed me back and climbed on top of me.

Again, almost like magic, I was inside her. I could feel another wetness about her now which was cooler but no need to guess what it was. She then locked her mouth over mine. She had only kissed me delicately before so this was strange and different behaviour. There was a greater urgency about her and her hips were grinding into me. Her tongue probed into my mouth. Before it had played on my lips, but now inside my mouth. Between my cheeks and teeth, it went and then deep into my mouth. I could feel its roughness, like freshly plucked ostrich skin. I could taste tobacco and feel a coating of fur, which I knew would change its colour. I could soon see I would have had enough before long. I decided to get this tongue out of my mouth so thought that it would be a good idea to push it out with mine. She seemed to enjoy this battle of the tongues and writhed around on top of me with a new strength and vigour. I felt I was winning when I could get her tongue beyond her teeth but, to my horror, the teeth moved…

They tilted and fell on my tongue! They were false! No wonder they looked so white and perfect!

False teeth! I'm fucking a woman with false teeth!

With all my strength, I rolled her over. I put my face on the pillow by the side of her head. I wanted to clean my tongue on the pillow by licking it viciously, but noticed the dirt on the pillow. It shone. It must have been Brylcream from the blokes before. This was turning into a nightmare, and I was beginning to think I'd had enough of her. I rolled off her and we both just lay there for a while. I then noticed she was asleep. She began to snore gently.

After a while, I fell asleep myself, but was abruptly awakened with her pushing and pulling me. 'Wake up! Wake up. Me feet are cold. Where's your fucking socks?'

'In my fucking shoes.'

She found them and slipped them on. 'You okay?'

'Fine. What time is it?'

'Fuck knows! You have plenty of time.' She snuggled up against me again and her hand crept down to where my awaiting manhood was responding. 'You're fucking amazing,' she said. 'Fuck me again, will you?'

I did, and again we both fell asleep.

Some time later, I was abruptly awakened again. She had got out of bed and run round to 'my side' and was trying to push me over. 'Move!' she said 'Get the fuck over there!'

'What's the fuck up?'

'It's raining and the fucking bed's wet. It's your turn there now.' There was a leak in the roof which let in water when it rained. In other words, when it rained, the bed got wet. Maybe I should have listened to Budgie after all. But then again, as I was feeling randy once more, I knew I was right. I mounted her one final time, and I don't even know if she was asleep before I finished! One thing I did know was I could not sleep with wet feet. I did not want to ride that woman again. In fact, I wanted to get out of the place.

My decision was made. Not wanting to say goodbye, I got up quietly and gathered my clothes. I had it in my mind that I would get dressed on the landing for fear of waking her if she should hear me in the room.

The landing was deserted, as it seemed the rest of the open lobby was. I dressed hurriedly but forgot about my socks, which she had on her feet! But never mind, I just pulled my trollies (trousers) down a bit to cover my ankles and off I went.

What a feeling of relief it was to step out onto the early morning pavement. The rain had stopped, but it was still cold. I breathed in the air and reflected on my night. I was heading for it now. God knows what was in store for me when I finally got on-board!

The canteen outside the dockyard gate, where I had met Budgie only a few hours previous, was still open. I bought a pint of milk and discovered it was 06:15. Time to go back.

When HMS Hermes came into view, once again I was amazed at its size. The tide was in, and the ship had risen against the dockside to an even greater level. The gang way was at a very steep angle, and it would be necessary to use both hands to climb on-board. From the bottom, I could see RPO McSnell. He had seen me approach and was waiting in expectation of my arrival. A smirk was on his face.

'Bastard,' I said, under my breath. I pulled the waistband of my trousers down a little further and began my ascent.

'Not a bad start, Clark,' he bellowed down at me. 'First night ashore and you're adrift. Dear dear.' The end of the gangway was at least six feet above the deck, and some steps were placed at the end to facilitate access down to the Weather Deck. RPO McSnell was more than six feet tall, and the level of his eye was the same as my bare ankles as I stepped off the gangway. His face was a delight to see once I'd flashed my ankle. 'Socks!' he shouted. 'No socks!' He corrected himself. 'Where're your fucking socks? Well? Where the fuck are they?

'Lost them, RPO.'

'Lost them? Lost them? How the fucking hell can you lose your socks?' he screeched at me.

'Dunno.'

'You are adrift and out of the rig of the day. 'His face reddened more as he struggled for words. 'Report to the Reg office at 0800. With fucking socks

4: Number 9 Punishment

So, my first day on Hermes was frantic to say the least. I reported to the reg. office as ordered, but then got it in the neck from the Chief Electrician because I missed the beginning of his meeting of the new ratings in the main electrical workshop. He was further annoyed when I told him I was expected at the Commander's table later on in the day to answer the charges of returning on-board adrift and 'out of the rig of the day'. As my Divisional Chief, he had to attend with me, which pissed him off even more.

We all had to do our joining routine, and whilst it is very convenient to go around the ship together, I was not able to be with the rest of my fellow ship mates. After reporting to the reg. office at 08:00, I then had to attend Officer of the Day's table for the same charges. He would not be able to deal with the severity of the offence so it was a formality that would be passed over for the Commander. Nobody had any patience for us, least of all me, as we were also preparing to go to sea, which imposed additional duties on almost everyone on-board. Normally, we would be involved with testing communications from all points around the ship and also checking outside lighting.

During the Chief Electrician's meeting, we were allocated our normal working departments. I was allocated to the engine rooms and boiler rooms—by all accounts, a very interesting department for a young electrician. I would get to work on motors, generators, starters, speed controllers, automatic voltage regulators, salinometres, as well as all the other mundane stuff of lighting in these compartments and, of course, the bilge lights right in the bowels of the ship amongst all the waste oil and stagnant water. My immediate superior would be PO Harris, who was a very popular bloke, and many people wished for my position. It was all new to me and didn't mean a great deal.

I managed to get my kit stowed in my locker and my kit bag stowed in the kit bag locker in the corner of the mess, and also made up my bed. I got my tool kit stowed in my tool kit locker in the workshop. The others had slept on-board last night, so they were ahead of me on that count. I completed most of my joining routine, but then had to change for the Commander. I left him after he awarded me 6 days' scale and 5 days' nines.

'You were fucking lucky, Clark,' scowled RPO McSnell. 'You fucking won't be next time. I told you I'd be watching you so you better be careful.'

'Fuck off,' I told him under my breath as I walked away from him, knowing my back was towards him and he wouldn't hear.

Six days' scale is a fixed penalty dependent on the amount of time adrift; it means loss of six days' leave and six days' pay. Leave means nothing as we are going to sea. Pay I knew would be hard to lose, but at sea I would spend less. Five days' nines is the punishment for being adrift and being out of the rig of the day, i.e. socks—or a complete lack of them.

In the Navy, punishment, like most things, is assigned a number to denote its format. Number 1, for example, is Death, which is still a penalty in the Navy, which can be metered out to arsonists setting fire to HM dockyards. Number 9s are a mixture of mustering and extra work, all outside normal working hours. First of all, there is a muster at 05:45 and extra work till 06:30. Normal working hours are 08:00 to 16:30, with lunch between 12:00 and 13:15. Men under Number 9 punishment muster at 13:00 and then again at 17:00. Supper would finish by 18:30 and we would muster again at 19:00, and complete two hours' extra work. A final muster would take place at 22:00 and pipe down (lights out) would be at 22:30.

There would be no spare time.

We had to be up early, arranging for our own special wakeup call. We had no opportunity to grab sleep during the day, and to attempt such a thing would be foolhardy as, being so young, once a state of sleep is achieved, the chances of self-awakening are about zero! Many a sentence of 9s has been extended due to a missed muster for this very reason. Also, being so young, tiredness sets in quite easily. Coupled with the additional workload, when considering the additional punishment work was particularly arduous—and for me, it always was from the very beginning—I was a marked man. Marked for the worst jobs.

The worst jobs were always in the Junior Rates galley. This was the biggest galley on-board as it served all Junior Rates. The officers had their own galley, and there was a galley for Senior Rates, albeit much smaller. The worst job was the cleaning of the copper boilers used for cooking the boiled food. Custard was made in these, and the line of scum that followed the level of custard down as it was used got harder and adhered greater to the sides as time went by. One copper full of custard could last for several days so the boiler had several days to form this wonderful job for the boys under nines. It was not beyond the cook's vindictiveness to leave the steam on the boiler, after all was used up, which had the effect of firing the scum into an almost metallic glaze.

Custard was not the only thing. Gravy was made in copper boilers, soups were made in copper boilers, stews were made in copper boilers, a variety of sauces were made in copper boilers, such as was white sauce, chocolate sauce and wonderful viscous cheese sauce. And not to forget rice puddings and semolina. I hung, upside-down, inside every one of these boilers during my time on Hermes. Sometimes, my vomit amalgamated with the glutinous mass swilling around in the bottom. My first 5 days on Number 9 punishment was the most penal punishment I had ever received. There could not be a more vile thing I would ever have to do in my life.

The Hermes sailed out of Portsmouth Harbour as I mustered for the first time outside the regulating office at the 17:00call. McSnell took my name and advised me he had a wonderful job for me later and that the weather forecast was bad! *What the fuck the weather had to do with it?* I didn't know at that point. *Will I be sent outside to do something?* I wondered. I would look forward to that: I'd never been to sea on a ship before so would welcome the opportunity to watch England sail by as we headed north to our exercise area in the North Sea off Northern Scotland.

There were 12 of us at this muster, and one of them was another electrician whom I had seen in the electrical workshop earlier. He had been on the Hermes for more than a year and was about a year older than Fingers. He was a small bloke with really short legs. His body was out of proportion to his leg length, and so he was taller than he should have been had his legs dictated his height. He had dark hair and a long thin nose that ended with a slight swelling; almost like a small cherry on the end of it. His face was smooth, although he had a bit of a shavers shadow on his upper lip and chin where he wielded his razor. I wondered if *he* had ever been called Skin. His shirt tally told me his name was Brendan.

As we were dismissed, he turned to me and said, 'What the fuck you been up to then?'

I was pleased he spoke to me. It seemed I might have a friend. 'Adrift.'

'You were in the fucking Black Cat Café! Yeah, I heard!' He turned away, shaking his head and added, 'How could you fuck that old hag?'

Well, how do I answer that? I wondered. I just shrugged my shoulders in an apologetic motion.

'I heard you paid for her with your socks.' He turned to me and added, 'You're a fucking OD, you are. You know that? A fucking OD.'

There was a pause in our conversation as we walked through the dining room to return to our mess. At the hatch, he turned to me again and said with a smile, 'I heard McSnell blew his fucking top when you came back with no fucking socks on!' He was giggling now. 'I would have loved to see that. Fuck! I would love to have seen that. You are a fucking OD, though.' And with that, he went below.

So already I had a reputation. An OD is short for Ordinary Seaman, but to be called an OD has a more diminutive meaning than that: it's the lowest of the low; the most stupid and the least intelligent.

I walked into our corner of the mess. Budgie, Mick and Max were sat together on the seat made from the two lower bunks of one tier. All these bunks had been converted to seats during the day, but mine, the bottom of three, faced a bulkhead, which didn't lend itself to sitting on sociably. Budgie had pulled his bunk into position so I swung myself onto my bunk amongst jeers of derision.

'Want to borrow some socks, Clarkie?' someone said.

'Been down the sickbay yet?' someone else commented. There was laughter following every remark, which went on for some time until, finally, a mess killick (Leading Hand) came round and told us to keep the noise down. Silence reigned and I ceased to be the centre of attention.

I missed supper, electing to grab an hour's kip with the assurance from Budgie that he would wake me for the 19:00 muster. The ship started to roll gently, which had a soporific effect on me. Coupled with my previous night's lack of sleep, I drifted off to a place of ecstasy, happiness and bliss. I was reliving the flash as I would relive it many times in my life. Budgie's shake came as a rude and unwelcome awakening, and panic instantly set in. Where was I? What was happening? Then, of course, reality. Just enough time for a piss before the reg. office again.

'Clark! Junior Rates galley,' said RPO McSnell.

When everyone had been allocated a work place, we were dismissed and off we went. Four of us went to the Junior Rates galley, and Brendon went in the other direction. I entered the galley and a fat, heavily tattooed, balding, ugly, disgusting, sweating man—who, conveniently, was a cook—led me to my first boiler. Custard! He gave me a spoon and a scrubbing brush.

'Clean the fucker,' he told me.

I looked into it and was appalled. How was it possible to clean it with what I had? I couldn't even reach inside it was that big. There was a quantity of water sloshing around in the bottom that had been poured in for cleaning purposes. Soap bubbles floated about, but it didn't seem to make any impression where it had made contact with the caked-on custard. The roll of the ship caused this motion. One of the other blokes had been allocated one of these boilers to clean, and I watched as he hoisted himself up by placing his foot on the outflow tap of the boiler and grabbed a pipe above it. Next, his head disappeared into the boiler, and he supported himself on his stomach with both arms inside. The motion of his back and buttocks indicated his arms were thrashing about inside in the process of cleaning it. I did the same and, when I assumed the scrubbing position, I found I could reach, just about, to the bottom. My body had blocked most of the light from inside and I was working in gloom.

I was becoming more aware of the rolling of the ship and it seemed my stomach was out of sync with the rest of my body. My inner ears confused my brain, and focusing seemed to become more and more difficult. I dipped the scrubbing brush into the murky water at the bottom and scrubbed the side. Fuck all! Nothing came off! I tried again, but still nothing. *Ah!* I thought. *The spoon! It's a scraper!* I tried this and a small zest of dried custard glaze departed the boiler side. I was on my way.

It wasn't long before I was feeling ill—and I mean *really* ill. I had to get out and stand up straight, yet as soon as I did so the fat, ugly man roared at me to get back to work. I vomited all over my hands but, for fear of the ogre behind me, I kept my head down. Soon the vomiting stopped. It gave way to just retching. Fuck, I was ill. I actually thought I would die.

I must have been halfway through when I was hauled out and fat 'n' ugly took a look inside. 'You dirty moron! You've spewed up! You dirty bastard!' I just looked at him. He must have seen I was on the verge of passing out as he said, 'You can piss off now. Time's up, but you'll finish this fucker tomorrow.' I turned to go. 'Shut the fucking lid!' he bellowed. 'We don't want to smell your fucking spew!' I climbed back up and pulled down the counter balanced lid and secured it.

As I left, he sneered at me. 'Fucking OD.'

I had to return to that boiler the following morning and, during the work session that evening, I finally finished cleaning it. During that session of five days' nines, I cleaned three of those boilers and never went to any other work place. I vomited in every one of them, and each and every time I felt I would die, even just looking inside, knowing I would have to hang there, inverted in the gloom, as the ship rolled from side to side. My arms felt twice their normal size and my muscles felt like sinews of steel wire. But still, I managed to finish my punishment without missing a muster so I felt that was some sort of achievement.

During the musters, I sometimes exchanged words with Brendan. He lived in the other side of the mess, and we Juniors were not allowed around there. His work stations were always the cushy numbers where sometimes they were dismissed after only a few minutes.

I rose early, my first morning of freedom, having become accustomed to rising early. I made a cup of tea and decided to go to the workshop where it would be quiet and I would have some solitude—my substitute for the hiding places I had in the Fens of Forty Foot. Brendon was there when I entered, also drinking tea.

'Can't fucking sleep, eh?' he asked.

Again, I just shrugged my shoulders at him apologetically.

'Don't fucking say much, do you?'

'I guess I'm private a bit,' I said, feeling stupid as soon as I said it.

'Don't worry, you'll be alright,' he said reassuringly. 'You put one over on McSnell,' he added, and then explained, 'He was dying for you to miss a muster and he would have swung for you.'

I was happy Brendan had said that. In fact, it was the way he said it that pleased me more: it was friendly, and not many people had been friendly to me lately.

'I did feel awful the last few days, hanging upside-down in those boilers fucked me up big time,' I explained. 'What about you… Can't you kip?'

'No. I got gut rot again.'

I just looked at him and he knew I didn't understand.

He explained to me that he had a problem with his guts where, from time to time, he had pains of varying severity. Sometimes, he told me, he could not stand and would buckle up on the floor, unable to move at all. He told me one time he had been drinking in The Apple Tree, the first pub outside the dockyard gate, and when he left he was okay but as he passed through the dockyard gate he keeled over in a heap and huddled up behind the big gate. He was there for some time when one of the dockyard coppers came along and kicked him, thinking he was drunk. He had been drinking but he wasn't drunk. Eventually, the copper helped him into the office where he laid out, still doubled-up, on a couch. A Navy ambulance was called and he was carted off to Victory sickbay (HMS Victory, as well as being the Nelsons Flagship, was also the name of the close-by Royal Naval barracks). He said when he got there he was okay, but they kept him in for the night for 'observation'. He told me he had had similar experiences whilst on-board at sea last time, and he said he feared that the medics thought he was just play-acting but, for him, the problem was very real. Said he really thought he might die. The last time he was kept in the sickbay for two days. The trouble was, whilst in sickbay, everything was fine. He said it was a good skive; he'd just lay in bed reading all day. Finally, he was told it was probably a 'rumbling appendicitis'. He was told it was not uncommon for these symptoms to come and go as he had experienced. Should the situation get worse, he may have to have his appendix out. So here he was, suffering again with what he called gut rot. He also said it didn't always manifest itself in such a severe pain but just became an irritation for a day or two.

'Fuck that,' I said. 'I'm sorry.'

'No, it's okay. It'll get sorted no doubt.'

We were then disturbed by others entering the workshop. It was nearing 'Turn To' time, so the workshop would soon fill up.

PO Harris arrived when the workshop was full. He was the last Senior Rate to arrive and was frowned upon by the workshop Chief Petty Officer Mechanician, who was in his office at the corner of the workshop, directly opposite the door; from his vantage point, he could see all the comings and goings. Harry, as we called him, would now direct us on what we would be doing today.

I liked Harry, and I knew he liked me. He liked the antics I got up to before we sailed, but he also liked the way I learned things quickly. I gave him no aggravation, and he knew he could give me a job and it would be done well. Many times, he chose me to help him on bigger, more important jobs. What was more, he was always full of sea stories: he had been in the Navy for years and was known to have been a bit of a rogue himself before he gained a position of responsibility.

The phone on our bench rang and he snatched it up. He didn't say anything before he put it down again. 'Chief wants to see you, Chris,' he told me.

Fuck! I thought, panic instantly rising again. *What have I done now? What had I forgotten?*

I poked my nose round the corner of his office but he didn't look up from the papers he was reading and shuffling about. I stepped inside the door and waited.

'Well, what the fuck's up with you then?' the Chief Mech. scowled at me, frightening me to death.

'I thought you wanted to see me, Chief?'

'What the fuck do I want to see you for? I can fucking see you any time I want!' he answered. 'It's the Chief Elec that wants to see you so you'd better piss off!'

This was more serious: the Chief Electrician was the overall Chief of all the electrical branch. He sat in an office miles away and rarely ever ventured down here. Why on earth would he call for me?

I arrived at his office and he looked up smiling. He invited me in and asked me to sit down.

'Have you sorted yourself out now, lad?' he asked.

I didn't know what he meant but still I thought it best I answered positively. 'Yes, Chief.'

'Well, this has just come down from the reg. office.' He handed me a small chit of paper. 'It looks as if you've caught the short straw, me lad.

You've been copped for communal duties.'

'What does that mean, Chief?' I asked, not knowing whether or not I should panic.

'Most people get a stint during the commission of a ship. In some ways, it's best to get it out of the way early.'

'So, what do I have to do?'

'Well, again, it could be worse, but you've been allocated to the Senior Rates dining room.'

I still didn't know what any of this meant, but felt I couldn't ask again. 'Best thing is to report there now. Ask for the leading Steward there and he will explain things.'

'Okay, Chief.' And then I added, 'Thank you.' Of course, I didn't know where the Senior Rates dining hall was. I went back to the workshop and told Harry. He was disappointed as it meant he would lose me for three months. Three months! I couldn't believe it. He explained briefly I would have to set tables, clean floors, wash dishes. I was devastated. I was an electrician and wanted to do an electrician's work! I felt it was beneath me to do such things. Once again, I felt like crying.

Harry told me where the Senior Rates dining hall was and the quickest way to get there. I found it and asked for the Leading Steward. I waited outside, and then Leading Steward Jenkins appeared. He was tall, red-haired and powerful looking. His arms were muscular with enormous forearms. He could easily have been an athlete. He had a thin face with a long nose, which supported glasses that were so powerful his eyes were magnified to an almost comical effect when viewed straight on.

He looked down at me and said, 'You Clark?'

My first thought was that this was a rather odd thing to ask as my name was clearly displayed on my shirt name tag, which was how I knew his name was Jenkins—because of the same thing. I instantly wondered whether mine had come off or was obscured, and so I looked down to check. It was still there. I looked at him and answered, 'Yes.'

'Now don't come the wise guy with me, boy! McSnell said you were a fucking OD and now I can see why.' He pushed me hard in the chest as he said this, and I realised he had interpreted my looking at my name tag as sarcasm, bordering on piss-taking. It was no good me trying to recover the situation now. I was flying backwards and crashed into a fire extinguisher. Pain shot up my spine and I was able to get my feet beneath me before I fell over completely.

From what he had said, I realised one other thing: he had mentioned McSnell's name, and the Chief Elec had said he had got the chit from the reg. office. It became clear to me, in that moment, that McSnell had 'volunteered' me for this service. I later discovered people are allocated these duties only as a result of their names being drawn from a hat. Once you have done your stint, your name doesn't go back in the hat. But I don't believe for one second my name was ever drawn from the hat. McSnell, the bastard, must have fished it out.

Jenkins grabbed me by the shirt, in the same place he had pushed me, and dragged me towards him, practically lifting me off my feet. He then threw me into the dining hall where my motion was finally halted by a table, loaded with newly cleaned cutlery ready to be put away. All of this went flying. 'You can pick that lot up and wash 'em, then dry the fuckers and stow 'em,' he snarled at me. 'I'll be back in five, and if it's not done you'll get knuckled.' He turned and left through the same door he had just thrown me.

Knuckled was a term meaning a good punching. I knew this guy meant it and he would carry out his threat if I didn't do what he'd demanded of me. I was almost too frightened to be scared.

There were another couple of young Juniors there, one was a Stoker (engine room worker), the other a Junior Radio Operator. They both sprang to my assistance and helped me sort out all the knives and forks. Not much was said during the process, although I was informed Jenkins was a bastard, a prat, a tosser and, most of all, someone not to be messed with. What an impression I had made!

I had managed to avoid the knuckling, for which I was indebted to my two new-found buddies. After that, I discovered the extent of what was necessary for me to insure I never got a knuckling from Jenkins. For me, there was no more the standard routine of call the hands, breakfast, turn to, dinner, turn to, and secure at 16:30, with supper and your own time to do whatever you wished, with movies being shown every other day or so. One day in four would be duty where extra work was necessary depending on what tasks the duty Killick assigned.

There was another guy also allocated to this section and, between the four of us, we had to ensure the tables were set for the meal times of the Senior Rates. We had to clear everything away afterwards, wash everything up and stow it, move all the furniture to one side and scrub the deck, then move it to the other side and scrub the other side of the deck. We then had to reset the tables. Three times a day we had to do this. Additionally, we had to ensure salt was in the salt sellers, pepper in the pepper pots, sugar in the bowls, ketchup in the squeezy bottles, vinegar in their sprinkler bottles, and anything else they might need, including making tea and coffee. Two of us would do the bulk of the work one day and then swap over for the next. It was always a requirement that four of us were there for each meal. We had to take our meals standing up in the small scullery with the steaming, clanking dish-washing machine keeping us company.

It can be seen none of us had the opportunity to spend any great time with the shipmates of our own Mess Deck. We could not get involved in a game of cards or any of the board games that were constantly played, such as Monopoly, Risk, Uckers (special version of Ludo) or any of the many others. There was no chance of dominoes or darts. We would have to get up and go halfway through.

This routine and segregation had an attrition and debilitating effect on my stamina and morale. I was dismayed and became sullen. I knew I could not last for three months. I was deprived of sleep. I had to be in the Senior Rates Dining-hall when my shipmates were in their bunks. It's true we had some time off during those occasions that everyone else were turned-to, but sleep was not a real possibility: mine was a bottom bunk and so was folded away to provide seating during the day. How I longed for a full night's sleep; any sleep without the anguish of waking up at the right time. I lived in permanent fear of Jenkins and his constant threat of being knuckled for being late.

In addition to this, we were doing sea trials. The ship had just undergone a long period of maintenance and was returning to sea with, largely, a new crew. All the systems of the ship had to be tested and put through their paces. The crew had to know where to go when actions stations was sounded and also what to do. As electricians, we had to provide alternative power supplies to various pieces of equipment, vital to the ship's capabilities should we be attacked and damaged. Alternative emergency supply cables had to be run out and tested. We also had to shut down and close off the ventilation system should nuclear, biological or chemical warfare be directed our way.

If action stations should sound during my period of leisure, then leisure was sacrificed. Often—all too often—action stations would be sounded in the middle of the night, which further added to my growing fatigue.

During this period, I was receiving regular mail from Kay. She could always be relied upon for that, and her letters professed her undying love for me and kept me up-to-date with what was happening at home. I replied infrequently. It seemed whenever I mustered the effort to sit down with a pen and paper, there never seemed much to say. I knew I was being selfish, and I realised Kay longed to hear from me, yet it seemed so alien to me.

I did have one pleasant surprise amongst all this, though, and that was when I received a letter with strange, unfamiliar handwriting on the envelope. It was addressed to Chris Clark, HMS Hermes—and that was it. No rate given or official number or mess. It's a good job I was the only Chris Clark on-board! I opened it with anticipation and discovered it was from Dianne from the Victory Pub. It read as follows:

Dear Chris

I hope you don't mind me writing to you, and if I get no reply then I'll know you do and I won't write again. When we met the other night, I thought you were sad to be going away so I thought I'd cheer you up. I hope you are okay and keeping well. I want you to know I enjoyed our game of darts, but it was over too soon. I do hope we can meet again when you get back. I will be thinking of you.

Bye for now.

This letter was a great boost to my ego. It lifted my spirits but did little to fortify my tired body. I replied immediately and informed her of the correct address. I told her it would be good to exchange letters but not to worry if she didn't hear from me during long periods as we were doing sea trials and secret things, and during such times mail was not landed. This was a lie, but I was only paving the way for when the novelty would wear off. I told her I also enjoyed the darts and would like to meet her again. Pretty tame, really, but I didn't know how to express myself further. All I was thinking was, *would there ever be a time when I could get in her underwear?*

After the excitement of Dianne's letter, I quickly returned to my state of tiredness and depression. Everyday was an ordeal to me. When I slept I was frightened of not waking up on time or of being woken up by the Action Stations siren. I wished for a day off from it all—just one day that I could spend in bed, in the quiet. It was then I recalled the conversation I had with Brendon some time ago. If I complained of severe gut rot, then I could get turned in for a couple of days in the sickbay. I would get a full 24 hours' kip, which would sort me out no problem. It seemed the perfect solution, but I was unsure how to effect it. But the answer was simple, really, I told myself: go to the sickbay and complain of stomach pains. I decided I would wait until the following morning when I was due to report to the Senior Rates mess. I would tell the SBA (Sickbay Attendant) I had been awake all night with stomach ache.

5: Elgin

At 05:30 the following morning, I staggered through the ship like a drunkard just about to throw up, my right arm held across my stomach whilst using my left to support me from the bulkheads and fittings. A couple of ratings walked past me, looked, but said nothing. At that time of the morning, not many people were around. I staggered into the sickbay only to find the sickbay office closed. The treatment room was closed. The consulting room was closed and the dispensary was closed. Nobody was around. The double doors to the ward were closed also. I hadn't planned for this. I assumed an SBA would jump up from his seat when he saw my severe condition and help me to a bunk. I was in a dilemma now. If I returned to the Senior Rates dining hall, I would be adrift, and if Jenkins found out, I'd be in the shit big time. I was also scared he'd be violent towards me so I had to stick it out here. I decided to sit on the floor with my back to the sickbay office door and wait. I fell asleep almost immediately. I dreamt of Dianne and nice things. Then I was awakened by the duty SBA returning, just prior to call the hands at 06:30.

He was kicking my feet. 'What the fuck you doing here? Pissed the bed or something?' He was rattling a bunch of keys as he was doing this, trying to locate a key single-handed, carrying a mug of tea in the other. I remembered my ploy and quickly replaced my right arm across my stomach.

'No!' I answered as I tried to get up out of his way. 'I've got bellyache,' I said wincing.

'You'll get fucking bellyache if you don't get out of my fucking way!' he retorted unsympathetically.

I rolled onto my knees and crawled away from the door. I thought it best to stay on the floor at this stage. The SBA opened the office door, switched on the light, and put his mug of tea on the desk. He then got a chair and put it against the bulkhead opposite the door and said, 'Get up off the floor and sit there. Mess that fucking floor up and you'll scrub it.'

I don't know how he would think I would mess the floor up unless he thought I'd be sick, meaning my act was having the right effect. I pulled myself onto the chair and sat doubled over, my right arm still hugging my stomach. I watched him seat himself at the desk, take a swig from his mug, and rifle through some papers.

'So what's up with you, Skin?' he asked, turning to me. He was a small, fat man who had served many years in the Navy. He was covered with tattoos and wore round, rimmed glasses straddling a small button of a nose. His hair line had receded from his forehead, almost to the nape of his neck. His exposed skull was shiny with its baldness, yet two thick bands of black hair were stuck to the sides of his head as if attached there for effect. There was something effeminate about him, which seemed to soften his attitude towards me.

'I've got stomach pains,' I said in a groan. 'I've had them all night and couldn't sleep.'

'You were fucking sleeping alright when I got here! Did the pains just fuck off for a while?'

'No.'

'Well. What did you eat last night?' he asked as if commencing the examination.

'Nothing.'

'Well, that's the fucking problem. You're probably fucking hungry!

Go and get some breakfast inside you and then, hey presto, all will be fucking well,' he said in a dismissive way.

'I don't think so.'

'Oh! So now you're a fucking doctor, are you?' he said, again sarcastic. 'Have you spewed up?'

'No.'

'Have you got the shits?'

'No.'

'When's the last time you had a shit then?'

'Dunno exactly. Sometime yesterday afternoon.'

'Well, there's not much fucking wrong then.' He seemed to satisfy himself with this. 'You duty watch or anything?' he enquired, looking at me.

'No.'

'Should you be somewhere else at this very moment in time?' He studied me.

Fuck! I've been rumbled already. 'I'm a Senior Rates dining room mess man…'

'Ah! Thought so! Want a morning off, is that it?' he butted in. 'Skiving little twat!'

'No!' I said emphatically. 'I really have got gut rot. It hurts just to stand up!' I was beginning to get scared, and this did bring a lump up in my throat, which caused me to catch my breath, which sounded like a muted sob.

He looked at me again and said, 'Go get some brekky and, if it still hurts in a couple of hours, come back.' Once again, he turned to his desk.

So now what do I do? I didn't know what I should do! I didn't know if I should return to the Senior Rates dining hall or not. The SBA said to get some breakfast, so that, I decided, was what I was going to do.

I staggered back through the ship, with more people observing my discomfort. Again, nobody said anything but only looked on. By the time I got to our dining room, the hatches had just opened and breakfast had been served. For the first time in a long time, I queued up and was served a breakfast. I thought it better not to have too much, and so I limited myself to bacon, egg and beans with two toast, but I had forgotten my mug so tea would have to wait. I sat in a corner, facing away from the centre, as I didn't want anyone to sit with me and enquire as to why I was there.

When I had cleared my platter and I was no longer hungry, I collected my things, assumed my painful gait, and deposited the dirty things at the scullery hatchway. I then had to walk back through the dining room to find my way up to the Senior Rates dining hall. This was when I almost bumped into Brendan coming through the doorway with his breakfast. He looked at me with a bit of alarm before smiling. I knew he knew I was faking gut rot to get some time off.

'You are a fucking OD!' he said knowingly. 'A big fucking OD!' And then he went and found a seat, still smiling and shaking his head gently. I doubted he'd ever say anything.

I returned to the Senior Rates dining room and staggered directly into the small scullery. I was told Jenkins had gone looking for me and had been, for a long time, awaiting an excuse to lay into me. I explained the situation and my buddies told me to sit out on the Weather Deck; it was very close to the entrance of the dining hall, they said, and they'd bring me a cup of tea. I did this and was enjoying the early morning sun, although the wind was freezing and the speed of the ship amplified this. I tucked myself in the corner on the deck and was shielded by the boundary of the Weather Deck. Needless to say, I was in fear of the coming confrontation with Jenkins, but I had no option now but to carry on with the scam. *You never know*, I thought to myself, *I might just pull it off.*

I was on the starboard side of the ship, and we were sailing North up the east coast of Scotland, and so all I could see was open sea as I looked out. The sea was grey, bordering on green, and a small swell was running in our direction. The wind whipped the tops off the crests of every wave, causing an angry pattern of chaos to stretch laterally away from me. As I looked astern, I could see the ship's wake, which had spread out some distance from the ship and then followed in a perfectly straight line. This contrasted greatly with the roughness of the sea, and the searing torture the ship had created in it as the giant propellers drove the several thousand tons of steel and men through it. The sky was the same colour as the sea but of a much lighter shade. The sun just about shone through a layer of cloud, which obscured its profile, although it was bright enough. As we ventured North, the sun was low on the horizon to the stern.

Before it happened, I sensed it would. The Weather Deck door burst open, and Jenkins poked his head out into the oncoming wind. 'So, pratt face,' he snarled, 'what you got to fucking say for yourself?' He had been briefed by my buddies in the dining room.

'I've been to the sickbay,' I answered, adding, 'I've got gut problems.'

'They give you a chit?' he asked.

What the fuck's he on about? I wondered. 'No.'

'Then you're fit for duty!' he replied. 'So get the fuck inside!' And with that, he stepped out and reached his enormous arm down to me and grabbed my shirt.

'Please, hooky,' I pleaded, 'I have to go back in about half hour to see the doc,' I lied. I didn't have to go back to see the doc but just to report back with my present situation. It had the desired effect, though. Jenkins released me.

'What's the fuck's up with you then?'

'Don't know. It's just my guts,' I said caressing my midriff with my arm. 'It's agony and I've had no sleep last night.'

'Well, you better get your arse back down the bay!' he said, and with that he turned and went back inside.

Relief flooded me. I knew now I could handle this ordeal as far as dealing with him was concerned.

I finished my tea and then returned to the sickbay. There were four more chairs next to the one I had sat in earlier. The seat in front of the desk in the sickbay office was now occupied by a Petty Officer. I suspected it was his natural position, and the SBA earlier had only usurped the position temporarily. I took a vacant chair and proceeded to feign severe bellyache, moaning occasionally for effect.

Eventually, I was called forward and reported my situation to the Petty Officer, who asked me the same questions and gave me the same responses as the SBA had done earlier, except I was not told to go and have breakfast. 'Shouldn't you be turned to somewhere?' he asked, again suspecting I was skiving out of something.

'No. I work in the Senior Rates dining room and am on free time now till 11:30.'

He looked at me harder, and I knew he was trying to recall if he had seen me there. He seemed satisfied with my answer, and I believe his memory endorsed it.

'Well, you might need a bit of a clear out.' As he said this, he was writing something. He gave me a bit of paper and told me to take it to the dispensary at the end of the short passageway. The door was facing as you walked down the passageway with all the other doors, treatment room, etc., to the left. To the right was a plain bulkhead. The dispensary door was of the stable door style with the bottom half closed and the top half open. Looking at me as I approached was the round-faced SBA I had seen earlier that morning. I gave him the chit of paper, and he turned away from me. He returned with a small glass, as seen in old Western films when the cowboys asked for whisky in saloons. It did not slide down the counter, though, but he passed it to me by hand.

'Drink this. In one go. It'll make you shit. Seems you need a fucking good shit.' He then took the empty glass from me whilst I was wincing at the taste of its acrid contents sliding down my throat. 'Stay close to a bog and if there's no fucking change by noon then come back.'

'Okay,' I said, demonstrating it was too painful for me to say thanks.

By this point, it looked as though I'd be due for a shit soon! I would have to report back to the Senior Rates dining hall by 11:30 so I would have to carry on with the charade when I got there. I didn't quite know what to expect now. Our mess was some way from the nearest toilets so felt it would be foolhardy to lie on my bunk, which would have been a heavenly thing to do right now. I went to the Cable Deck, which was where the anchors are winched up and let go. It's full of chains, shackles and capstans, and things sailor. Not many people use this deck when we are at sea—it's generally too cold as it is open on two sides. Being triangular in shape and the front two sides form part of the bow of the ship, wind and sea can whistle through. When it is rough weather this deck is deemed 'out of bounds' and locked off. I could find little pockets of shelter though where I could hide away from other people and be as close as I could get to the forward heads (toilets).

I huddled up out of the wind and hugged my knees whilst listening to the relentless swish and plunge of the sea as the Hermes ploughed its way through the rolling water. The ship swayed gently, and soon I was drifting off to sleep. I woke with severe cramp in my buttocks having been in that same position for some time now; it was 10:30, and there was a rumbling in my lower tummy. I knew what this would mean, so I made my way down to the heads, remembering to stagger about holding my now genuinely rumbling gut. As I approached, the rumbling became more severe, and I needed to pinch my buttocks together. I ran the final few steps and burst into an empty trap. I had already loosened my trousers and quickly dropped them, with my underpants, as I entered the trap. I pulled down the seat, sat on it, as I simultaneously closed the door and exploded from my rear end. *Fuck my old boots!* I thought. *What's happening?* The sound beneath me was like a fire hose trying to fill a bucket. An enormous splodge of semi liquid interspersed with farts such I have never experienced before. On and on it went until I thought I would turn inside out. Nothing short of an enema for sure, although at that time I didn't know what an enema was! After the first wave, I could feel the next lot coming. It started deep in the pit of my stomach, and I could feel it rumbling round my intestines. I sat upright and could feel it with both my hands now held on my tummy just above the pubic bone. Seconds later, the next loaded hose pipe let rip, although not as savage as the first and not as long-lasting. There followed more, gradually diminishing to little squirts, and finally it seemed to end. Well, I was warned I would shit but this was something different!

After a while, I gently caressed my anus with the rough toilet paper we were given. No tissue for us but government-issued bog roll. I learnt that, if you screwed up some sheets and rolled them into balls, then, when unravelled, they resembled tissue and felt softer. I now felt confident in rising and pulled up my trollies to venture out. I certainly felt weaker for the experience.

I returned to the sickbay at 12:00 and took a position outside the office where the PO still sat. I was the only one there and, after a few moments, the PO looked at me and said, 'Well?'

'My guts still hurt,' I said 'I did have a crap about an hour ago or maybe longer.'

'Was it solid shit that came out?' he asked.

'No, it fucking wasn't,' I answered indignantly. 'Like fucking water, actually!'

'Oh,' said the PO, writing something down. 'You'll be a bit dehydrated now but I don't want you to drink anything, okay?' he said, looking at me. 'And I don't want you to eat anything either, okay?'

'Okay,' I said in expectation for more instructions.

'Come back at 13:00 and I'll get the doctor to take a look at you.'

I left. I supposed I should have gone back to the Senior Rates dining room, but I didn't want the aggravation of a confrontation with Jenkins, and so I just decided to hide away somewhere for half an hour or so. The Hermes was a big ship, and you could disappear quite easily if you wanted to.

I felt I was almost there now; a quick session with the doc and he would have to get me turned in for observation, and then I could have a good kip for 24 hours and make a miraculous recovery. That would give me more than enough energy to last the next six weeks or so of this ridiculous communal duty.

How wrong I was.

The doctor was a Lieutenant with two gold rings on his sleeve and a red ring between them. The red immediately identified him as a doctor. The SBA and the PO were only orderlies of varying abilities, much the same as nurses or assistants in local doctor's surgeries who seem to know what's going on and think they know as much as the doctors themselves.

'Now, lad. What's the problem?' the doc asked, looking at me intently.

'I've got a bellyache that's killing me, Sir,' I whimpered.

'Killing you, eh? Well, I doubt that, but I understand it troubles you.' He spoke with a very clipped, educated accent. We would call it posh. Hoyty toyty, even! Either way, he seemed to be sympathising with me, and I knew he was my ticket to success. 'Now I need to examine you so get yourself undressed to your underpants and lay yourself down on this bed.' He indicated to a bed in the treatment room. I did as I was told, pretending every other movement shot pains around my body. He then proceeded to prod and probe around my abdomen. Things were wrapped around my arm and pumped up, and other things stuck down my throat whilst I was invited to say *Ah*! A cold stethoscope was placed on my chest and back, and I was asked to do a variety of breathing exercises. Finally, he returned to my abdomen and probed further. He managed to make fluid inside my body gurgle with his pushing and probing, and when I heard this I winced as if it was painful. He left the room briefly and, when he returned, he told me to get dressed. I was disappointed. I thought I'd go straight into the ward! It was clear the doctor was a bit puzzled by me. I could tell by his frown and the distant look in his eye.

In the office, the PO asked me to confirm certain details about myself. Date of birth, full name, next of kin, faith, and other details about my medical history. Finally, he said, 'Right, Skin, go back to your mess and relax if you can. Don't eat or drink anything.'

I looked at him and said nothing. My head was spinning.

'Got that?' he bawled.

'Yes, PO!'

'I mean it. Don't eat or drink fuck all! Right?'

'Okay, PO,' I assured him.

'Come back at 16:00,' he ordered.

'Okay, PO,' I said again.

'And don't be fucking late!' he said with emphasis, then added civilly, 'The big doc wants to take a look at you.'

'Okay, PO,' I said for a third time.

At 16:00 I returned, and the Petty Officer told me to get undressed again and wait in the treatment room. I sat on the bed in my underpants and waited. After a few moments, I heard the Petty Officer talking and, by the respectfulness of his language, I knew the doctor had returned. The Lieutenant doctor, who had examined me previously, appeared around the door.

'Hello again,' he said. 'So how are we now?'

The second doctor then appeared. He was a commander and had three gold rings with red rings between. He was a much older man with hair greying at the temples. He reminded me somewhat of my father.

'My stomach still hurts,' I said, answering the first doctor's question.

The Commander had some papers he was reading, and every so often would look up at me. I lowered my eyes and remained still and quiet.

'Right,' the Commander said. I looked up at him and he went on, 'I need to take a quick look at you, so if you can just lie down for me please.'

I stretched out but didn't say anything. I didn't know if I should have feigned pain as I stretched out, but I was lying flat before I could. He probed around my abdomen, as the first doctor had, and eventually made my stomach gurgle again as the first doctor did. When I heard this, I moaned and screwed up my face. He looked up at my face and, patting my stomach, he said, 'It's okay, there'll be no more of that.' He turned to the first doctor and together they stepped out of the treatment room, into the corridor, and spoke in undertones. I couldn't hear but sensed something important was about to happen. I laid still in anticipation.

The Commander came back and told me he needed to do one more test. He told me to take off my underpants and roll over to my left side to face the bulkhead away from the door. So there I was, naked and facing a wall. I had no clue what was happening. I was vulnerable and began to feel frightened. I had a feeling of trepidation that things were getting out of control. I heard someone enter the room and the Commander said, 'Right lad, I want you to pull your knees up to your chest.'

Fucking hell! I thought. *What the fuck's going to happen now?* I did as I was told, feeling more and more vulnerable and all the more frightened. In fact, I was really scared. My breathing was short and hurried, and my chest jerked uncontrollably.

'It's okay,' the doctor said, 'I just need to make one final test.' He was trying to reassure me but failed to do so. Next, he said, 'I need to push something up your bottom. It shouldn't hurt but it may seem a bit uncomfortable.'

Fuck me! Push something up my bottom? Brendon told me nothing of this!

'Please keep still. Here we go.' And with that, something was happening to my rear end that I never want to experience again. He was pushing something inside me that seemed to go up forever. I could feel him moving this thing around and, after a short time, he withdrew it. I thought I would shit myself again as he removed it. I then felt a cooling swab being wiped around my anus and the first doctor said, 'That's it, all done now. You can put your underpants back on.' He then followed the Commander out of the room. I pulled on my underpants and sat on the edge of the bed. I felt humiliated. I had something shoved up my arse, which reminded me of the homosexual we had met on our first night ashore. These people like this sort of thing!

My breathing returned to normal and I considered my position. This must be the end now. Surely they would want to see how things develop from here so I was expecting them to come back and tell me I needed to be admitted to the sickbay for a couple of days' observation.

I was kept waiting.

It seemed an interminable amount of time, and I could hear muffled voices and orders being given and obeyed. The SBA and the Petty Officer were moving past the door in both directions, not running but moving quickly with a real purpose. Nobody said anything to me as they passed nor did they give me a passing glance.

The Petty Officer entered the room and asked me who my best friend was on-board. *Odd question*, I thought. Budgie, I told him, and then corrected this by giving him his proper name—Bird. 'Would you trust him with your locker key?'

'Of course,' I replied, wondering why on earth he would ask me such things.

'Give me your key then.' I rummaged around in my trousers pocket from the pile of my clothes on the floor. Rather dumbfounded, I handed over the key but said nothing. I was in a state of shock, I suppose. Next, the PO returned and asked me to follow him. He led me out of the treatment room, past the main office, and towards the sickbay ward. *This is it!* I thought. *Success!*

'Lie on this,' he instructed, pointing to a steel framed stretcher placed on the floor outside the ward. The stretcher was lined with a thin mattress and had sheets, blankets and a counterpane with a blue anchor on it as we had during our training days. I was not expecting this, but then thought that maybe they had no spare beds in the ward. I laid down and covered myself up with the bed clothes.

'Put yer arms inside, Skin,' he commanded, and he then pulled the blankets up to my chin and reached for retaining straps on either side of the stretcher. I was so surprised, amazed and frightened I said nothing, and only did as ordered. I knew I was looking around with wide enquiring eyes that could easily have betrayed my fear. It was happening too quickly for me to comprehend. The two doctors had gone. To my utter amazement, the plain bulkhead, opposite the doors to the treatment room and office etc., revealed itself to be giant sliding door. It slid to one side, exposing a large doorway leading onto the after-aircraft lift, which was in the down position. The lift was used to take aircraft from the hangar to the Flight Deck and vice versa.

I was engulfed with a blast of cold air streaming in. The icy air was also accompanied with a noise of whirring fans and brumming of tractors manoeuvring aircraft within the hangar and general banging a clanking. Such a contrast to the peace and tranquillity of the sickbay! Four sailors in blue overalls and nylon puffed-up anoraks came rushing in, and each grabbed a corner of the stretcher. I was hoisted up and onto the lift. The lift well was dark and lit only by the huge lights of the hangar, and also some light from the sickbay. As soon as I was on the lift, there was a loud clanging of a bell, which always proceeds a lift movement, and then the lift rose with alarming acceleration and speed. The night sky was an inky blue. I could see stars. It was approaching winter, and although it was early evening, night time had come. The panorama of the sky opened up above me as the lift rose. It came to a jerky halt at the top, sealing off the noise from the hangar below. A new noise replaced it, which was the whizzing of jet engines, and along with this came the smell of aviation fuel stinging my nostrils.

The four sailors carried me forward, but I was facing aft so could not see where I was going. They slowed, turned slightly left and I was transferred, head-first, into a helicopter. The vision of it came over my head as I was pushed inside and slid along the aluminium deck.

The noise was incredible; it was impossible to think, let alone be heard. I could have screamed my head off and nobody would know. I couldn't move as the straps were holding my arms by my sides and my legs were firmly clamped. The four sailors pushed me in and swung me round, and then they receded. A man on-board the helicopter busied himself around the stretcher, clamping it to the deck. He had a helmet on with bulbous ear defenders. He didn't look at me once, but just went about his business in a professional manner. I was impressed.

The outside door slid shut and the noise increased as the engine revs began to multiply. The body of the flying machine vibrated violently as it experienced the passing of a resonant frequency. The whizzing noise rose to a higher pitch, and I felt us being lifted into the air. We were flying away.

Now I was really scared. What the fucking hell had I let myself in for? What had I done? I hadn't a clue what was happening. Nobody had told me anything. I had to think of a way to get out of this mess.

Within a very few minutes, I felt the progress of the helicopter change. I could feel us swinging in the air and descending as the engine revs changed. There was a violent shudder as we landed, and then the engine revs seemed to die. The aircraft underwent the wild vibrations as the resonant frequency again was experienced, then there was a diminishing whirring as the engines were cut. Silence reigned, which seemed sinister and oppressive. I could hear the crackling and staccato of voices on a radio as the ether carried them in, but I could not discern their meaning. The door was slid open, and four men in white medical suits reached in, released the stretcher, and dragged me towards them.

'I can walk,' I said, almost panicking. 'Just let me out.'

'It's okay,' said one of the men, holding his hand out and indicating I should stay where I was. 'You just stay put and we'll have you inside in a jiffy,' he said in a strange Scots accent.

I was carried across an open area and into a building through an old oak door that opened into a long wide passageway with high ceiling. I was being carried head-first, and so I could not see what lay ahead—only what receded. I was placed on the floor and the straps were released.

'I feel okay now,' I said, rather stupidly. 'I've had bellyache all day but I'm fine now,' I added. Nobody took any notice of me. Three of the men left, and the one who spoke earlier told me to get out and jump into a bed on wheels adjacent to where I had been dropped. This I did, and he covered me with a sheet. I was cold but that was the feeling that worried me least. I hadn't a clue where I was or what would be happening to me! I was in a corridor, on a hospital trolley, and I could see two other trolleys in front of me with people on who were sleeping. At least, I assumed they were sleeping. The man told me to lie still and someone would be along soon.

Someone did arrive soon. It was a young woman in the female version of the white medical suit. She was pushing a smaller trolley on which stood a bowl of water and a smaller bowl containing a variety of things.

'I have to give you a shave,' she said, and lifted the sheet and drew it down to my ankles. I looked at her in amazement. She then pulled down the front of my underpants and dragged them down my thighs. She looked at me and said, 'It's alright. It won't take a minute but just be still.'

I was paralysed.

She splodged a dollop of foamy soap on my pubic hair and

proceeded to shave off my pubes with a safety razor. She moved my penis from side to side with a towel in her free hand. I was so embarrassed I did not know what to do. I was leaning back on my elbows, looking between the ceiling, her face and my balding penis. I began to get feelings of arousal, which only increased my embarrassment. *Please don't get a hard on*, I was willing myself desperately, trying to think of things totally unconnected to sex. Finally, she wiped my penis and the surrounding area with a warm, damp cloth, and announced she had finished. I hoisted up my pants and covered myself up again.

The original man came to see me again and told me there was no place on a ward at the moment and so I would have to stay in the corridor until one was found. He gave me a blanket, telling me it wasn't as warm there as on the ward. He told me to relax, gave me a small glass and offered me some tablets, motioning that I should take them. I did without question. 'They will make you sleep,' he said. And they did.

Before I had too long to ponder my position or consider what I should do and how to tell everyone I now felt fine, I was in the land of slumber. I only remember being woken up by another man who said I would only feel a small prick in my arm, and invited me to count to ten. I didn't understand; I was still half-asleep. I couldn't count. The trolley began to move, and I watched the ceiling of the corridor traverse above me until blackness engulfed me once more.

I was dreaming. I was dreaming I was in a warm bed in the corner of a hospital ward and at the foot of my bed was a young girl with a tea trolley. On the top stood a silver urn with a brass tap from which she was dispensing tea into a series of cups. These she placed on a tray next to the urn. She was a beautiful girl of about 18 years old, I guessed. Her hair was reddish with tight curls, which could only have been natural. Her face was white with a splattering of gingery freckles across her nose, which was curved from between the eyebrows to its tip, and then the part between the nostrils sloped back down to the upper part of her upper lip. A turned-up nose. Her eyes were green, although she did not look at me. She was facing me and then stooped down to fish biscuits from a large tin, on the lower shelf of the trolley, which she then placed on plates next to the cups on the top shelf of her trolley. She wore a housecoat made of padded nylon, and the stitching between the padding formed a diamond-shaped pattern. This housecoat splayed open as she bent down, and I was gifted with a wonderful sight of her uncovered pubic bush of red hair. I closed my eyes and drifted out of the dream.

When I awoke, all was dark. I was no longer in the corridor. I looked about me in the gloom as I gathered my senses. I was in a hospital ward for sure. I could see other beds all in a straight line, with the feet facing into the centre of the ward, the heads against the wall on either side, leaving a wide space to walk through the ward. A door was at the end of the natural walkway.

On the opposite side to me, there were windows between the beds. I was in a corner with one door near the foot of my bed. It was closed. At the other end of the ward, another door mirrored mine, which was half-open. A warm glow of light flooded in through the door, but did not penetrate the darkness beyond the first two beds. There was a smell of Domestos in the air, and a sound of gentle snoring, wheezing and occasional coughing. I lifted my head to get a better view, and a shot of agony left my lower belly and ran into my groin. I lay my head back down and probed the area of pain with my two hands. My bald penis felt strange and my hands wandered up from this to the right, where I discovered the culprit. The pain was stinging at my touch, and I could feel wiry bits, which turned out to be stitches. I lifted the covers but could see nothing. It was too dark. Then it hit me: I'd had my appendix removed! But there had been nothing wrong with them! I was only pretending!

Once again, I was plummeted into a state of fear and panic. They must know there was nothing wrong with them when they took them out. What will they say now? *I really think I'm in it now*, I thought to myself. I could not return to sleep. I lay awake with all the permutations of what would happen to me. Would they make me pay for the helicopter flight? What about the operation? Would I have to pay for that also? Jesus Christ! I wished I could turn the clocks back.

I lay there pondering these things for about an hour, or as best I could have guessed, and then a nurse entered the ward and switched on the lights. 'Morning, gentlemen,' she announced as she strolled through, checking each bed and area around to see nobody had fallen out, made a mess or maybe even died. 'It's seven o'clock and it promises to be a wonderful day again!' she added in a cheerful note. She drew back the curtains as she went through, but it was still pitch-black outside. She entered the ward by the door by my bed and exited the one the other end.

People started to wake up. The coughing became louder and more frequent; this was followed by groans and grunts, which increasingly resembled language as men said good morning to their neighbours or even raised their voices to the ones opposite or further down. Some people staggered from their beds and exited through the same door the nurse had done a few moments earlier, shuffling along, adjusting their pyjamas and dressing gowns whilst scraping their homely slippers along the Parquet-tiled floor. Again, I lifted the sheet and saw my scar-to-be; just a thin line of about two inches with six spider-like stitches straddling it, pulling each side of skin together and forming a ridge that was pink with tenderness. I touched it gingerly, and a stinging pain shot deep into my belly. I just lay there, knowing I could never get up to a sitting position.

I saw the nurse re-enter the ward from the far door and walk purposefully up the ward. She stopped at the foot of my bed and said, 'I'm so sorry to have neglected you. I forgot you were here. How are you?' she enquired.

I thought it would be a bit ironic to tell her I had a bad pain in my belly. 'Fine. I think.'

'Yes,' she said. 'You will be a bit sore for a while but we'll let you rest today and then get you about tomorrow.' She spoke with a mellow Scottish accent, not like someone from Glasgow or Edinburgh; she lacked the harsh edge to her tone.

She was a lovely lady—older than my mum and a little rotund, but by no means fat. She did not wobble when she walked and there were no hanging rolls of loose skin from her upper arms or drooping from her chin. She was cheerful, and I guessed she would be cheerful all day long and cheerful every day. I liked her immediately, but it wouldn't last long: she was strict, which caused me some pain.

'Now,' she said, looking at the clipboard at the end of my bed, 'you'll be ready for breakfast as you've had nothing for twenty-four hours.' She looked up and smiled at me, and then came around the bed and drew back the sheets to examine my wound. 'Very nice,' she cooed. 'You'll have a good souvenir to take back to your aircraft carrier!' With that, she spun round and marched off back down the ward, calling over her shoulder that my breakfast would come soon.

Breakfast came and I was propped up so I could eat it. It didn't last long; I was starving and felt immediately better once I had finished. I wondered how long it would be before someone cottoned on to the fact they had removed a perfectly healthy appendix. I wondered if they were checking out the bill before they confronted me. Had they actually taken the thing out or just sewn me back up once seeing everything was okay?

At about nine o'clock, the doctor came round to check on us all. He came in the door by my bed and so attended me first. He asked how I was and had a brief look at my wound. 'That's fine,' he said to me, ruffling my hair as if I was a young child. 'We'll have you back on that ship in no time,' he added. He then turned and went to the next bed.

Well, I thought, *so far so good.*

At 10:00, the door by my bed was thrown open and in came a trolley with a big silver urn on it. It was being pushed by a young girl in a nylon housecoat. I hadn't been dreaming after all: this was the lady from my dreams! I waited in anticipation to be treated to another surprise. Alas, although she went through the same ritual of pouring the tea and preparing the plate of biscuits, her housecoat was securely buttoned, with no secrets to reveal. She came to the side of my bed and placed the cup and plate on my tray. She looked at me and smiled, and I felt her eyes held mine for just a little too long. She was beautiful.

The day passed with no surprises. The doctor visited me again in the afternoon and again confirmed everything was okay. I ate dinner and tea.

I peed in a glass bottle three times, which was a bit embarrassing when having to ask for it and then handing it over full of light orange liquid! Nurse Cheerful brought me some books and Miss Housecoat brought me more tea and biscuits, but nothing more. A porter came to me in the afternoon and gave me my holdall, which Budgie had packed for me. Budgie put my locker key in an envelope with a short note hoping I would have a quick recovery. I sat back and, whilst listening to Desmond Decker rant on about the Israelites, I reflected on the past thirty-six hours. One minute I'm fit, then I pretend to be ill, despite being fit and well, and the next I've been whisked away in a helicopter, carted off to an operating theatre, and mutilated, with nobody at any time telling me what was going on. Apparently, my father had been contacted as his permission had to be obtained before an operation could take place. As I was only 16, I could not give consent. It seems if you cannot give consent but someone else who can does, then it's not necessary to let me know what's going on! Still, I was out of the Senior Rates dining hall and, it seemed, I had got away with it.

The process the next day followed as before. After breakfast, I asked Nurse Cheerful for a bottle and she refused. 'You have to get up and use the toilet properly,' she said.

'I can't get up,' I whimpered.

'Of course you can get up, boy!' she snapped back at me. 'The toilet is down the corridor.' And she wafted her hand in that general direction where the toilet could be found.

Well, there was nothing for it: I had to get up and get myself to the toilet. It took about an hour—an hour of sheer agony. I managed to get into a sitting position on the bed and then swing my legs over the side. My feet would not touch the floor and I dared not jump; I knew that would kill me. I managed to slide one buttock off the bed whilst I leant back and twisted sideways, thus extending the one leg. Once I had this on the floor, I could twist back and slowly slide my weight onto the leg and, eventually, the other foot joined the first on the shiny floor. I stood by the bed like an old man, doubled up from the waist with shoulders hunched forward. I could not straighten up, and therefore had to walk along the length of the ward in this position.

Progress was slow and painful; one wrong step or loss of concentration resulted in the pain pulling all the nerve ends of my lower abdomen, threatening to unzip the surgeon's handy work. I reached the door at the far end of the ward and inched my way around it. I was now in the corridor that stretched out before me to an amazing room at the end, where I could only see glass from floor to ceiling, and beyond that the land rolling away to the sea. The toilet was halfway down this corridor, and as I got nearer I could see more of this room open up before me. It was full of leather-bound settees, where people were sitting in their dressing gowns, reading or talking. I could hear music playing from a radio.

I reached the toilet and managed to perform the act for which I'd struggled so long to achieve. The journey back to my bed was equally as difficult, and ended with me feeling exhausted. It seemed I was drained of all energy, which made the effort even greater. I managed to get into bed but I wasn't central, so just lay there. Nurse Cheerful breezed in and said, 'So, you managed it, then?'

I just looked at her.

'My word you *do* look pale,' she said, showing some concern. She came to me and placed a palm on my forehead. 'Are you in pain?' she enquired.

'I'm in agony.'

'Well, why on earth did you not ask for some painkillers?' she asked indignantly. 'Wait, I'll get you some.' She returned with a couple of pink tablets and gave them to me with a glass of water. 'Don't suffer too much pain, laddie,' she said. 'It'll do you no good.' And then she left.

I discovered I was in Elgin, close to Inverness in the North of Scotland. I was told the building was once a private mansion owned by a local millionaire dignitary. The story goes that his son suffered a mental illness from which he suffered all his life, receiving little or no caring, and so when the millionaire mansion owner died, he bequeathed his mansion to become a hospital for the mentally sick and handicapped. As time went by, another wing was added where general medical care and operations could be performed, such as I had received.

After three days, I had made the journey to the toilet on several occasions and, with the help of the pink tablets, things were a lot easier. I could get in and out of bed quite easily and could walk in a more upright position. The pain was always a constant reminder if I lost concentration and got things wrong. The painkillers did little to allay my fears that the stitches could be ripped out if I fell over or if someone were to bump into me. It really was a case of taking your life into your own hands when venturing to the toilet.

On the fourth day, a doctor came to see me and asked if I wanted to stay for convalescing or be transferred to the Naval Air Station at Lossiemouth a few miles down the road. It was an easy decision for me to make: I would be far better off staying where I was. I didn't have to call anyone Sir and I didn't need to be subjected to the Naval Disciplinary Act. Not only that, there were ladies here and, of course, Miss Housecoat, and so I told him I would prefer to remain here, adding I liked it here. I would have to stay for about another ten days after which I could go. I would then be entitled to some rest and recuperation leave. I just couldn't believe it; not only had I managed to get out of the Senior Rates dining hall, I also would get some rest and recuperation leave, and therefore miss the rest of the sea trials! And it really *did* seem I'd gotten away with it!

I was being rested. I could sleep whenever I wanted and didn't have to do anything. The pain had subsided somewhat, although there was the constant threat of severe pain if I managed to slip up somewhere. I could read whenever I wanted as there was an abundance of books. A library trolley come around the ward each day. I was always in my bed, or nearby for tea and biscuits, where I kept Miss Housecoat under close surveillance. I was informed I could go and sit in the Moray room, as it was known, at the end of the corridor. The first time I ventured down the corridor to the end, I was bewildered to see such a beautiful room. The windows to the front swept from left to right, covering an arc of about 150 degrees. The ceiling—at least 15 feet high—was made from ornate plasterwork cornice, splitting the ceiling into squares of a few yards and each with its own central decorations from which chandeliers were suspended. Bright blues and metallic reds were used for decoration, although the predominant colour was gold. Cherubs, bluebirds, angels and doves flew, entwined in the artwork. The windows gave a most magnificent view of the Moray Firth, with the mountains of the mainland in the distance. Plush leather settees of rich greens and reds were arranged around occasional tables from craftsmen of times gone by. Most of the settees were populated, but not all. On searching for a place to sit, I noticed that many eyes were staring at me; this unnerved me as their stares were unrelenting, wide-eyed yet blank. Many would sit with their knees tucked under their chins, whilst several would rock to and fro. At the most populated table, a couple were playing chequers whilst others watched. The settees around the table were full, and some patients leaned over from the back to observe the game. I found an empty chesterfield, in green, and sat in a corner where I could keep an eye on the interest in the game and also see the rain clouds swirl in from across the sea.

Just as I had settled into a feeling of tranquillity, seduced by the beauty of such a place, there was a loud screech from the game table, followed by an almighty crash as the board, along with all its pieces, was hurled through the air. Almost all the immediate onlookers now joined in the screeching whilst jumping in their seats and slapping their neighbours. Other people in the room were coming out in sympathy and screamed as they rocked. The rocking became more violent and jerky. Eyes gaped wider, crooked teeth were exposed from open mouths, and sinews stood out from the necks as jaws were stretched open to their widest limits. Funnily enough, almost everyone remained in their seats.

Soon, the place was flooded with porters, who went about bringing some calm to this melee. I had had enough; this frightened me, and I feared someone would jump on me and burst my guts open. I have never had any experience of people with mental illness or mental handicap, and I had no idea how to react. To me, they were all fucking nutters and I wanted to be out of the place!

Choosing my moment carefully, I slipped out of the room and went back to my bed. I rang the Call button and soon Nurse Cheerful arrived. 'I've changed my mind,' I told her. 'I'd prefer to go to Lossiemouth for the remainder of the convalescing time.'

'I thought you might,' she said. 'I'll see to things for you. We could do with the bed anyway. We're always overcrowded.'

6: Rosie

I finally achieved my objective by getting into a sickbay bed. It wasn't exactly how I planned it, but it *did* get me some rest—in fact, too much rest! For seven days, I languished in HMA/S Lossiemouth's sickbay. I could get up and play darts with one of the attendants, when he was free, or lounge around reading and watching planes take off and land. The doctor would come in each day and ask how I was doing. Meals were brought to me and the empty trays taken away.

Then the morning came that my stitches were removed and I was told I could leave. I had a bus ticket to Inverness train station and a train ticket to Peterborough. I had to change trains at Aberdeen and also for when I arrived at Edinburgh. I had a warrant for a train ticket from Peterborough to Portsmouth, and I had a leave pass for 24 days' leave for rest and recuperation. I also had a letter from the ship, informing me that the ship would be under sailing orders when I returned. This meant: don't be late as the ship is due to sail! I had only the clothes Budgie packed for me. I had little else, only toilet gear and a book.

I said goodbye to the doctor and sickbay staff and began to walk the long road to the main gate, where I would be able to catch the bus. My scar was sore, and I walked carefully, not wanting to jar my belly. I anticipated the long journey ahead of me and hoped I would not get lost. I trusted everything would be clearly signposted and the station staff would be helpful. I was feeling fine and enjoying the crisp fresh air that was blowing in from the Moray Firth. It wasn't raining, but I feared it may start soon. I went through the main gate and saw a small shelter, with a bench seat, where the bus would stop.

A young girl was seated, and she looked up at me as I approached. 'Hello,' she said.

I looked hard into her face because I recognised her, but had not seen her this close for such a long time. It was the gypsy girl that used to camp at the bottom of Hollow Hill. 'Hello,' I said. I didn't know whether to look away. I couldn't understand why she would be there. I raised my finger to her and continued, 'You're the girl I've seen at Forty Foot.'

'Yes,' she said, 'and you're the boy who spies on us!' She could see this made me uncomfortable, but only smiled at me.

'What are you doing here?' I asked in bewilderment.

'Just checking how you are.'

'What do you mean, checking how *I* am?'

'I heard you had an operation, so thought I'd check you were okay.'

'But how did you know?' I asked, still bewildered.

'Oh,' she said, 'we know everything.' She paused, then went on. 'We are down there.' She pointed down the road towards the sea. 'It's oyster time.'

My eyes followed her finger and there, in the distance, I could make out some caravans. She looked at me again with her soft face. 'I'll see you in Portsmouth in a couple of weeks or so.' She got up and turned away from me.

'Hang on!' I stopped her. 'What's your name?'

'Rosie,' she replied. 'Rosie Lea, as in *tea*.'

'Where will I see you?'

'At the Fun Fair,' she shouted over her shoulder. 'South Sea.' And then she skipped down the road.

I was puzzled by what had just happened; it was very strange that I would see this young girl here and that she would know what had happened to me. I also thought it strange that she would care what would happen to me! I was flattered, and wondered I if ever she would be down in Portsmouth when I was there.

I sat down and waited for my bus.

The train journey towards Aberdeen was wonderfully scenic: a single track line with mountains on one side and the sea on the other. The train trundled on, rocking gently from side to side and weaving in and out of the contours of the land. The train from Aberdeen was more conventional, and sped through the Scottish countryside towards the capital. I took an express train from Edinburgh to London. This rocketed down the track, and Peterborough was the last of only a few stops before London. Kay was there to meet me with her father, who drove us home. It was good to see Kay again, and the thought of being intimate with her again excited me. I was a little concerned because my pubic hair had not grown; it was still stubbly and caused a great deal of irritation. I would be embarrassed if she should see me like that, although she must know I would have been shaved down there.

Kay had taken a few days off work so she could be with me at home during the day. As soon as her parents had left for work, she would come up to my attic room and jump into bed with me. I would jump on top of her, get inside her, shoot my load and roll off her. Then I'd want to get up and do something.

The house was in the small village of Pinchbeck, close to Spalding. There wasn't much to do in Pinchbeck. If you left the house, the best thing that could be done was to re-enter!

My thoughts soon turned to Dianne. She had written to me whilst I was in hospital. She didn't say much, only that she was looking forward to seeing me again when the ship got back. Well, the ship was back. She would have seen Budgie and he would have told her what had happened to me. The memory of Dianne's body lingered in my mind; long shapely legs and big tits. The thought of seeing her again somehow excited me more than being naked in bed with Kay again! I decided I'd return to

Portsmouth as soon as possible.

I told Kay I had to call the ship for joining instructions. I picked up the phone and pretended to dial a number. I then asked for the Chief Electrician. I pretended to speak to him saying, 'Yes, Chief. No, Chief. Of course, Chief. Right away, Chief.' I waited a moment with the receiver pressed to my ear. Kay came into the hall from the kitchen and looked at me with a worried expression. 'Okay, Chief,' I continued 'I'll see you tomorrow then.' And I put down the receiver. I told Kay things had changed and I had to go. She was upset and cried. I had no time or inclination to comfort her. I wanted to be out of there.

I took a bus from Pinchbeck to Spalding. Kay wanted to come with me to Peterborough, but I persuaded her not to. I said goodbye to her, gave her a hug and a kiss, and told her I loved her and promised to write. I then left her and would not see her again for almost a year.

Whilst I was in hospital and in the sickbay, I wasn't spending any money. I would get a room at the Union Jack Club (UJC). I, for sure, would be going nowhere near the ship until my leave ended. If I ran out of money, I was sure my mum would send me some.

Once again, I left a train at Portsmouth station. My first port of call would be the Victory pub. I guessed Budgie might be there, if not someone else from the mess would, and I hoped Dianne would be there above all else.

Sure enough, Dianne was in the corner with her friend, playing darts. Budgie, Max and Don sat at a nearby table. The table had three pint glasses of beer, each about half-full, as well as a packet of cigarettes, two sets of darts and an overflowing ashtray. They laughed and joked together. They did not see me come in. I walked up to the table and said, 'See you're still getting the practice in then!' indicating the darts.

'Clarkie, you old fucker!' Budgie said, genuinely pleased to see me. 'How the fuck are you?'

'Oh, okay,' I told him. 'Still a bit sore, so no fucking about!' And I placed a protective hand on my belly where the scar was.

They all greeted me and asked loads of questions. They were all a bit peeved when I told them I had almost three weeks leave left. 'Who's on?' I asked, motioning towards the darts.

'Resting at the moment,' Budgie said, 'but you can if you want,' and then, looking down at Don, Budgie continued, 'Don's fucking useless.'

'Come on then,' I said. 'Let's give these girls a thrashing!' I then picked up a set of darts.

'Here,' Dianne said as I turned, 'I bet you could use this,' and she handed me a pint of beer she had obviously bought for me.

'Oh, great!' I said. 'You're my hero.'

She looked up at me and said, 'It's good to see you again, Chris.'

I was a little embarrassed. I took the beer and thanked her. 'It's good to see you again, too.'

We played some darts and drank some beer. I explained to Dianne that I was on leave and would be staying at the UJC, and that I would only be going back on-board if my money ran out. 'You can come with me tomorrow then, if you like,' she proposed.

'Oh, yeah? What's happening?'

'It's Saturday and Pompey are at home,' she explained 'I never miss a home match.'

'Ah, sounds a good idea. That should be different,' I confirmed with her.

I noticed that, whenever my beer was finished, she bought me another. I didn't say anything and just let her do it.

I met Dianne the next day, at lunchtime, in the Victory. We went by bus to Fratton Park and settled ourselves near the halfway line. I had not seen a live football match since my grandfather had taken me to watch Peterborough. At that time, I didn't know what was going on and just stood by him, getting cold. Dianne was very loud, cheering on her team. She knew all the players and shouted advice—and a fair amount of abuse!—at them as they ran down the wing in front of us. All the spectators around us knew each other, and they knew Dianne, and she knew them. This little community commented together on the game and state of play. At the final whistle, Portsmouth were beaten and the crowd shuffled out of the ground and dispersed through the narrow streets. Dianne and I walked away holding hands. I wanted to put my arm around her but thought it too forward. I decided to let her take the lead.

'Do you want to come to my house for tea?' Dianne asked cheerfully. I looked at her and she continued, 'Come and meet my mum.'

'Okay. Is it far?'

'Leigh Park. Need to take another bus.'

We walked to another bus stop and waited. A red double-decker arrived and we boarded. Dianne stepped on to the platform, at the back, and proceeded to climb the steps to the Upper-Deck. I was treated to a delightful flash of her thigh as she skipped up the steps. She chose the rear seat, and we sat close to each other. She leaned against me and soon we were kissing. Her mouth was eager on mine; her lips searching mine and her tongue probing around inside. Her hands were squeezing my arms, pulling me closer to her. Finally, she settled for cuddling up next to me with her head resting on my shoulder.

We got off the bus and walked to her house. Her mother took her coat and greeted me cheerfully. 'Dianne's told me a lot about you,' her mother said. I thought that very strange because I had hardly spent any time with her.

'All good, I hope.'

'You look younger than I thought you'd be,' she said as she hung Dianne's coat up. 'You going to stay the night?' she asked expectantly. 'Spare bed's already made up and aired,' she added.

I didn't know what to say. We hadn't discussed anything about this! I also didn't know what Dianne had told her mother or what I was expected to say.

'What you doing tomorrow?' she asked when I didn't reply.

'He's not doing anything tomorrow,' Dianne intervened. 'He'll stay.'

So that was that.

We sat on a sofa and watched TV. Her mother made a meal of fried egg and sausages with chips, which we ate on our laps around the fire whilst watched a programme. Dianne had no brothers or sisters, and her father had left her mother many years before. Dianne sat with her legs curled up and her face against my shoulder. My right hand rested on her thigh, partly touching bare flesh and partly touching the hem line of her short skirt. Her mother sat in an adjacent arm chair, contentedly watching the television. My mind was beginning to wonder if this was how it would be all evening when her mother jumped up and announced, 'Time to put my glad rags on!'

'Bingo night,' Dianne informed me. 'Always goes to bingo on a Saturday night!'

'Oh,' I said, relieved we would get some time on our own. I was beginning to get positive vibes that I might get somewhere with Dianne tonight.

We remained where we were and watched her mother flit in and out of the room, titillating herself in the mirror above the mantelpiece, combing her hair and putting on some lipstick. She left the room again and returned immediately with shoes in her hand. She sat down again and put the shoes on, and admired them from her sitting position. She left the room one more time to return with a coat. She put this on and buttoned the front. A final look in the mirror and then she announced, 'That's it. I'm off.' And then she marched out of the door.

'Bye, Mum,' Dianne said.

'Bye,' I said.

We were now alone with Hawaii 5–0 on the TV. Being so close to Dianne aroused me, and I could not concentrate on the exotic scenery of the show. I caressed her upper arm in an endeavour to turn her attention to me. She seemed content to be close to me. She got up and turned off the light. We were now illuminated by the black-and-white flickering image on the box. She sat next to me again and put both arms around my neck. We kissed passionately, my hands roaming her arms, neck and back. I could not help brushing her breasts as my hands came in front of her. Her breasts were so big they squashed between us. I had to explore these mounds and was allowed to do so through the soft fabric of her blouse. After a while, I was able to get my hand inside and closer to letting them fall free. Dianne would not let me undo her bra, but I was allowed to force my hand inside each cup in turn. Her tits were huge, and my hand squeezed the softness of them. When I realised I would not make any progress in this area, however, I tried to probe her upper thighs. Her legs remained firmly closed, so I had to content myself with her thigh, which was smooth and warm. I did not want to overstep my mark, so was content just to be close to her.

I slept that night in a single bed in a downstairs bedroom. I had visions of her coming to me in the night, but she never did. The following morning, she woke me and sat on the bed, wearing her dressing gown. With no makeup, freckles emerged from the soft skin of her face. Her hair was a mass of cascading red curls. Her green eyes were happy to see me. I told her I would leave soon, as I had to meet someone at Southsea Fun Fair. We arranged to meet the next day in the Victory.

I went to the Fun Fair most days hoping I might see Rosie, but no luck.

Most evenings, I would see Dianne, and afterwards she would take a taxi home. Once the pub closed, we would walk around the back of the buildings on a small road parallel to the Hard. There was some construction going on, and we used to sneak into a partially constructed building, where I would back her up against the wall and we'd kiss goodnight. I would feel her tits, and she would let me undo the bra so they swung free. I always tried to get a hand up her skirt or down the waistband to her most private parts. Eventually, she allowed me to do this. Her pubic hair was fine and downy, and she was always wet inside. She used to touch me, through my trousers, and sometimes I could not restrain myself from shooting my load inside my pants. When things got too hot, she would push me away, adjust her blouse, and we would walk to the taxi rank.

The Fun Fair at Southsea was much like any other: everything was brightly coloured, and music changed from one attraction to the next. Men shouted and women screamed. Kids yelled and babies cried. Stall holders beckoned for pennies. 'Roll up! Roll up!' they would hail. 'Just a shilling for three goes,' displaying the bargain of a life time. Giant teddy bears were up for grabs, as were goldfish and terrible figurines made from chalk and hideously painted. All you had to do was draw a lucky number, throw three darts in a playing card or knock over a pile of tin cans—every opportunity rigged in the favour of the proprietor. The smell of hot dogs hung in the air, along with the sickeningly sweet aroma of candy floss, all supported by the foundation smell of diesel and motor oil.

I was looking for Rosie. I didn´t really know if she was there at all, except she said she would be.

I'd been walking through the fair every other day or so on the off-chance I would bump into her. And in the end, my patience won out when I did just that.

I was watching a girl go by and then, when I faced forward again, there she was. She had seen me and allowed me to almost walk into her. She was smiling broadly, particularly as I had been startled by her sudden presence.

'Oh! Hello,' I said, feeling rather foolish. My hands had come up involuntarily and grabbed her arms to stop myself from knocking her over. I let her go and stepped back. She was still smiling. 'You appeared from nowhere,' I added, excusing myself.

'Yes, I always do.'

'Yes, you do,' I confirmed, nodding my head. We stood looking at each other and, whilst I felt a bit awkward, she seemed to be searching my face and eyes for something lost. It was almost as if she was searching my mind. I returned her gaze, looking deep into the black pools of her eyes, which somehow didn't carry the smile that was set on her lips.

'Have you been here long?' I asked, breaking the spell. 'I mean, in Portsmouth,' I added, my hands waving about me, 'as opposed to the fair.'

'A few days.' Her eyes left mine then, and she looked behind her, as if she thought she was being followed. 'Let's go for a walk a bit,' she said, taking my hand. 'I like to look at the sea.' And with that, we both set off out of the fair.

We walked past the hovercraft slipway, and she asked me about my recovery and scar, and about my journey South from Scotland. I told her everything and how I was hoping I wouldn't have to go back to the

Senior Rates dining hall when I eventually got back on-board. It had been nearly five weeks since I had left the ship, and so I was hoping someone else was doing their stint with communal duties and Jenkins. I was telling Rosie how much I hated it and wanted to get back to proper electrical work. She listened, but I don´t think she was really taking it all in; she hadn't said much, and I didn't know if I should try to put my arm around her or suggest getting some chips or something. Mostly, it was the girls that made a play for me, so I wasn´t very good at going forward. I didn´t know why she wanted to see me again.

'How is your girlfriend?' she asked me suddenly, looking directly into my face. We had stopped walking and were sat on the sea wall, our legs dangling some 30 feet above a stony rubbish-strewn beach.

My first instinct was to look away, but I didn't. I held her gaze whilst I tossed the question around in my mind. How did she know about my girlfriend? Was she referring to Kay, or to Dianne, who I had been seeing a lot of since I left hospital? Was she checking if I had one?

'Do you have lots of girlfriends?' she inquired when I didn't answer. 'They say a sailor has one in every port.'

'I do have a girl,' I said, looking down at my fidgeting hands in my lap.

'The one in Spalding,' she said matter-of-factly before I could say anything to qualify the statement.

I looked at her and my mouth had fallen open. 'We know everything,' she said, answering the question I was about to ask her. 'I know a lot about you, Chris,' she said. 'I have watched you and looked for you.' She was talking as if I should know this. 'I remember the first time we met, when I caught you spying on our caravan.' A smile played on her face. 'In fact, I used to spy on you. You used to go in that old cottage a lot with your friends. You used to talk a load of rubbish about how you were going to be millionaires one day. How you were going to get a motorbike and leave home and travel the world. I remember one time you, and another boy, dyed your hair in there.'

My mouth was agape again.

'You went blonde!' she added, sniggering.

I was dumbfounded! I was totally lost for words. How on earth could she know these things?

'I used to hide upstairs and listen to it all. You lot were too scared to come upstairs. You lot thought it was haunted.'

Now I was embarrassed and feared I was blushing.

'You always said the stairs were rotten as an excuse not to go up! But you were scared.'

There was a moment's silence as we both looked out to sea.

'What do you want to know about my girlfriend for, then,' I asked, feeling hurt, 'if you know so fucking much?'

'Oh, Chris,' she said, reaching out for my hand. 'Don't be mad.' Her hand was warm and soft, and she squeezed mine gently to let me know she was fond of me. 'We were just kids doing what kids do,' she said, as if by explanation.

Rosie then went on to tell me of other vantage points she used to spy from. She used to hide on the opposite bank of the lake, as I had done also when wanting to spy on the rest of my family. She used to bury herself in the undergrowth next to our orchard and watch us fish. She even followed us to the riverbank and the long grass at the bottom of the playing fields.

'Do you fuck your girlfriend, Chris?' she asked, looking deeply into my face.

'What?' I asked in utter amazement. 'What sort of a fucking question is that?'

There was a silence.

'Jesus Christ, Rosie! You're fucking amazing!' I said in bewilderment, shaking my head.

'Will you fuck me, Chris?' she asked flatly.

'What?' I exclaimed again, disbelieving such a question. I looked intently at her, involuntarily shaking my head. I was searching for why she would speak like this and what she really meant. Ordinarily, I'd fuck her at the drop of a hat! She was beautiful and her body delightful! But it all seemed too clinical. Impossible. I was stuck for words and she sensed it.

'My uncles fuck me,' she said. 'My older cousins fuck me,' she continued. 'I know my dad wants to fuck me, but he's too scared of my mum, as is my granddad.'

Again, I looked at her in total disbelief. I was wide-eyed and slack-jawed.

'You could fuck me, Chris,' she declared, as if it was the most natural thing in the world. 'I want you to fuck me. In fact, I need you to fuck me.' And with that she placed a special emphasis on the word *need.* 'Chris,' she said, taking both my hands and sliding closer to me. 'I am different from all your other girlfriends. Different from ordinary people. I'm a traveller.' There was a pause before she continued. 'A gypsy. A Diddycoy. Call it what you want.' When I said nothing she went on. 'Look. My mother is an old woman. She's had nine kids. Three of them died.' She was telling me this purposefully. 'One of my brothers is fucked up. Can't use his arms or legs. Just lays on a bed.' A pause then. 'He can't even talk!' She looked at me with sadness in her eyes. 'My mother never leaves the caravan. Well, hardly ever. Only to hang out the washing or throw the rubbish out. I look into my mother's eyes and they are dead!' She was looking at me again. 'No fucking life in her eyes at all!'

There was another pause whilst I continued to gape into her face.

Rosie turned her head to the sea and tears rolled down her cheeks. She didn't cry or sob. Her face remained calm, but tears rolled over the mounds of her cheeks and dropped from her jaw onto her blouse. Maybe I should cry as well. I didn´t know what to do. I could not take in all she had told me. I wanted to take her in my arms and embrace her. To cuddle her and comfort her. But I couldn't.

After a while, she wiped the tears away with one sweep of the palm of her hand. 'Do you believe me, Chris?' she asked, looking intently at me. She was searching me with her eyes. I held her tear-soaked hand in both of mine and nodded, almost imperceptibly, but enough to give comfort to her. I *did* believe her. But how could someone put up with all that? I had heard of these things happening but thought they were the reserves of newspapers.

'I was 8 years old the first time my uncle came to me. He used to feel me through my clothes, then under them.' She was speaking slowly and deliberately, and her head rocked as she recounted the events. 'He then used to come to my bed and I'd wake up with his hands between my legs.' She stopped and turned to look at me again. 'You know what happens, Chris.' She was searching for agreement.

'I guess so,' I said, taking her hands again.

'Of course, after that, the visits were more regular and his sons would come as well.' She took a deep breath as if relieved she had confided in me.

'Rosie,' I said as soothingly as I could, 'I'm really sorry for you.' Squeezing her hands, I continued, 'I'm so sorry you have had to put up with all this.'

She sniffed and then said, 'Put up… Yes, I've had to put up with it.' She sniffed again, then took a deep breath and continued. 'Do you know how I put up with it, Chris? You helped.'

'Me? How the fuck did I help?' I asked, surprised.

'Because I always pictured it was you doing these things.'

I was about to respond in indignation, but she raised her hand to stop me.

'I couldn't stop what was happening. It happens with our people. I couldn't scream or shout. For the most part, it didn't hurt and I didn´t hate my family for doing it or allowing it.' She paused for breath. 'By thinking it was you, I could lose myself in a fantasy world and,' now she paused again, 'and put up with it.'

'Rosie, I'm fucked if I understand that. I'm really very sorry for you.'

'No,' Rosie said, almost in resignation. 'You wouldn't understand. You never had a mother.'

We sat in silence for a while, and I was trying to digest all she had told me. I was beginning to feel uneasy and really wanted to get away from her. I wouldn't have to think about it then.

Rosie interrupted my thoughts. 'Next year I'll be sixteen. They will find someone for me to marry. Then I'll have kids. Lots of 'em. No doubt they will be fucked by my brothers.' A trembling bottom lip caused her to pause. 'Some of my kids will die. Some always do. I may have kids who are fucked up. Just lying on a bed, and I'll have to feed it, clean it and wipe its arse.' There was a vacant, distant look in her eye as she went on. 'My world will become the inside of a caravan with the daily treat of going outside to hang out washing or dump rubbish. A life of washing, cooking, cleaning and being fucked.' The last word she said with a great deal of distaste. 'My eyes will die just like my mother's.' With that sad note, we again fell into silence.

'Chris, you have been in my mind for as long as I can remember.' She looked at me and the sadness fell from her face. 'I have loved you, in my very own way. That's why I want you to fuck me. Not here and not tonight, but before I disappear into the caravan for the very last time.' There was pleading in her eyes now. 'Will you do that for me, Chris?'

Well, she didn´t have to plead with me too much! I was excited by the very idea of it and could have banged her in any dark corner! I knew she wanted it to be a bit of an event so we would have to wait.

'You know I'm off to sea soon,' I said.

'Of course I do. I know everything. I'll find you when you get back.'

The next morning, I returned on-board. I'd left it to the last minute to enjoy my leave to the fullest extent.

'Cutting it fine,' McSnell greeted me, looking at his watch.

'Couldn't find my socks, RPO.'

'Don't be fucking funny with me, boy!'

'No RPO. I'm not.'

'Get the fuck below and out of my fucking sight.'

I went to the workshop at 6H with the rest of the guys for the 08:00 muster.

'What you doing 'ere?' the Chief Mech. asked me. 'You should be up top.' He was referring to the Senior Rates dining hall. I couldn't believe it! I was convinced I would have been allocated another job after all this time. I felt like crying. I was so sad. I dragged myself back up the ladder and found my way back to the S/R dining hall.

'Oh,' Jenkins greeted me sarcastically, 'the wanderer returns! What's up? You happy to be back?'

'I didn't join the Navy for this.'

'Oh! Didn't join the Navy for what?'

'Setting fucking tables and washing dishes!'

'Well, boy, you do as you're fucking told!'

'Would have joined to be a Steward if I wanted to serve people and wash their fucking plates!'

Jenkins's face reddened as I told him this. 'Well, boy, you do as you're fucking told or you'll get this!' He shook his clenched fist in front of my face.

'Yes, hookey,' I conceded, and turned to the scullery.

I had pushed Jenkins to the limit, and would continue to push him to the limit. It was a dangerous game because he was a big, powerful man, and if he hit me he could do me some real damage. I hated this job and he knew it. I always got the worst aspect of the job and he made sure I did. I had indicated to him that the job was beneath me. I did not learn ohms law and power calculations to be a lackey in a dining room. I had inferred, to him, that that's what I thought he was because he joined to be a Steward.

The Hermes sailed south. We crossed the equator, and I was summoned to be baptised by King Neptune. It is a ritual bestowed on sailors who cross the equator for the first time. I received a certificate to prove it. I endured my work and sulked away my time.

7: Cape Town

Brian Spendler was my new pal. He and I would be going ashore together in Cape Town. Spanner, as he was called, was older than me, and had been around the Far East before and also visited Cape Town on the Hermes during its return voyage. He had a habit of always referring to these times as 'last commish', meaning the last commission. The ship was de-commissioned upon its return when it was then refitted. Upon completion of the refit, it was recommissioned for the next bout of service to the government; there were a few of the crew remaining on-board from the last commission, who always took every opportunity to tell you so. It seemed they were superior to the new crew. When I refer to 'the new crew', I refer mainly to all us lot that came from Collingwood at the same time. In the stoker's Mess Decks, there would be another influx of new stokers from HMS Sultan, intermixed with stokers who also were on the last commish. The same thing would be reflected in the Seaman's messes, and those of the Stewards, Chefs and Communicators.

Spanner was 19 years old, and I was still a Junior of 16 years and a few weeks away from my seventeenth birthday. Spanner was also nicknamed 'Spunky Spendler' because he used to wank a lot. He would handle himself in his top bunk quite unashamedly whilst we played cards, dominoes or some board game. After a while, nobody took much notice. Spanner was a tallish guy but walked with the stoop of an old man. As he strode forward, his head would push forward with every step in much the same way mother hens do when strutting around their chicks. He had dark eyes, dark hair and full lips. He loved to listen to Joan Baez and Bob Dylan. He would listen intently to their songs, straining not to miss any words. He was always trying to understand the songs and read other meanings into the words. He used to smoke a pipe as well, which many people did in those days, but this only seemed to create the image of a much older man. We used to sit and talk for long periods, mainly in an empty switchboard whilst we were writing letters to our respective girlfriends.

I used to write to Kay—very occasionally, however, although she wrote to me nearly every day. Her letters were always full of information about herself and her family, and sometimes included information about my dad. She always ended by telling me how much she loved me and all the things I did to her. These were the bits I used to show Spanner and a selected few of my mess mates. Spanner would receive letters from his girlfriend in Portsmouth. Her name was Mary, and he used to tell me how much he loved her. He didn't know if he would marry her, but he knew he would have to make a decision once the Hermes returned from our current trip. Mind you, that would not be for almost a year. But he did tell me that he couldn't help fucking other women. Spanner also confided in me that Mary was pregnant, which seemed to fill him with more confusion. He told me if he had a son he would name him Harry Michael; then his initials would be HMS.

A couple of days before we arrived in Cape Town, we decided to write a letter home first. We went to the hotel switchboard, which was always empty. We would spend many a long hour in one of the switchboards, our feet on the table as we listened to records playing on a scratchy sounding portable record player. We'd smoke and drink tea or coffee, which we would take turns to get from either the dining room or the main switchboard in the Kilo section. We both had an open writing pad on the table before us, and occasionally we would lean forward to write something. We would both hold our pens hovering above the paper, our heads to one side and our eyes looking upwards for inspiration. Not much was written. I always started *My Darling Kay, I hope you are well.* Then it seemed to dry up a bit. One time, when Spanner went for tea, I looked at his pad and he had written *My Darling Mary, I hope you are well.* When he returned I said, 'I see you start your letters the same way I do.'

'I know,' he said, 'I copied yours when you were getting tea.'

'Hmmm,' I intoned.

I remember thinking for a while, then wrote on my pad.

'What have you put now?' Spanner asked. I looked at him. I picked up my pad and read aloud, 'Today the sea was rough and all flying cancelled. This meant we were able to go on the Flight Deck and fool around. I saw a whale.' I then put down my pad and looked at him.

'That's a fucking lie!' Spanner said in a rising tone of indignation. 'The sea isn't rough! Flying wasn't cancelled! We didn't go on the flight deck and you didn't see no fucking whale!'

'I know. But she don't know that! She just thinks I'm having an exciting life.'

'Exciting life? Exciting fucking life?! What's fucking exciting about this?' He gestured with his hands. 'Five decks down and breathing recycled air.'

'Okay!' I said, trying to calm him down some. 'You put that in your fucking letter to Mary then!' He slumped back in his chair and pouted with his full-sized lower lip.

'Well, I suppose you have to put something,' he said in submission. 'Anyway. It don't make any fucking sense to go on the Flight Deck if the weather's rough and flying is cancelled. It'd be fucking freezing, windy and the deck heaving all over the place.' He paused and looked at me. I was silent—thinking. 'And another thing! There's always a shit-load of whales together! They don't just roam around on their own. They're like humans and like company.'

I was not going to cross out what I had written in my letter and I was not going to start again, so I had to defend my case. 'If I said I saw a shit-load of whales, she wouldn't fucking believe me! And anyway, she would think life was then too fucking exciting!' There was a pause.

'Clarkie,' he said in a calm voice whilst looking straight at me. 'You're fucking barmy.'

I looked down at my pad to give him the impression I was considering what to write next. 'Look, Spanner,' I said, looking back directly at him. 'All Kay really wants to read is the bit I finish off with. The bits between *I hope you are well* and *I love you and miss you and can't wait till next year when I can hold you in my arms again* are only the bits that fill up the letter.'

Spanner was silent.

'Look, for instance, when I show you bits of her letters. I only show you the bits where she tells me I'm the best lover and how nobody does to her what I do and all that shit. I don't read you the shite about her dad and his work and what he brought home and her mother and where they went shopping. It's all a load of crap!'

Spanner looked at me again and said, 'Clarkie, not only are you barmy, but you're a fucking hard bastard.'

I didn't know whether I should be hurt. But now was my turn to pout. 'The fucking whale is staying in!' I said, pointing to my pad with my pen, 'and just the fucking one!'

There was a period of silence between us as we just looked at each other. The Everly Brothers had finished, and there was an irritating regular scratch as the needle jumped over the track as it joins the never-ending circle at the end of the record. This seemed trivial when considering the background noise of all the ventilation fans and other motors forming the theme music of the ship, but it wasn't natural so was irritating.

'Okay, 'said Spanner with resignation. 'You write what you fucking want. She's your fucking girlfriend, not mine.'

I continued my letter with *It's getting late now and so I'll have to go*, and then finished it with, *I love you and miss you and can't wait till next year when I can hold you in my arms again.* Then underneath, *All my love, Chris xxxxxx.*

Spanner was watching as I turned a couple of pages and continued writing. He could see me referring to the first page as I was writing.

'What the fuck you doing?'

'I'm copying the letter so I can send one to Dianne.'

'What?! You writing the same thing to both?'

'Course,' I confirmed. 'Why not?'

'You're unbelievable, you are, Clarkie,' he said, shaking his head.

I then reached for envelopes and wrote out the addresses. He had still not added to his letter. Then he snatched my pad from the table and began to read it.

'Oi, you twat! For fuck sake! Don't fuck it up! I'm not writing it again!'

'I only want to see,' he said, and then gave it me back after reading the contents.

'I'm going to clear things up and go back to the mess. I've had enough.'

'Good idea, I'm nearly finished,' he said whilst writing feverishly. I packed the records and his player away for him, and retrieved all the rubbish we had created. I emptied the ashtray and took the trashcan out to empty it into the one in the main passageway. I had to go out of the switchboard through the stokers' mess then up the steps to the main drag. I left the switchboard door open so when I returned Spanner did not know I had entered. I looked over his shoulder as he was finishing his letter. It read: *My Darling Mary, I hope you are well. Today the sea was rough and all flying cancelled. This meant we were able to go on the Flight Deck and fool around. I saw a whale. It's getting late now so I'll have to go. I love you and miss you and can't wait till next year when I can hold you in my arms again. All my love, Brian xxxxx.*

'You fucking twat!' I said to him, pushing his head forward.

'Well, I had to write something!'

After that, we always composed our letters together and trusted that our respective girlfriends would never meet.

The day we arrived at Cape Town, I was up early. I had the breakfast session in the Senior Rates mess. I was awake and up well before the duty EM was due to shake me. He would have a bit of a problem, as he should receive a signature from me confirming he had woken me. However, that didn't worry me. It was just past five o'clock, and I made my way to the Cable Deck. I wanted to see land. I wanted to see Africa.

As I climbed the ladder from the Capstan Flat, I could feel the cool breeze blowing through the Cable Deck caused by the forward motion of the ship. Hermes was steaming flat out, which was evident by the rumbling running through the ship and the shuddering as its bows crashed against the waves. As I poked my head above the hatch, I could hear the crashing roar of the wake created when 75,000 horse power drives 250,000 tons of steel through undulating water, swelling to 10 feet, at 25 knots. The spray created would be spasmodically blown in and around the Cable Deck, wetting it like the Peterborough pavements on a dank Winter's day. The smell of salt hung in the air. I emerged from the hatch and stood on the heaving deck. As the ship rose, my feet felt heavy and then, when it crashed down, I felt as if I could jump over the moon. There also was a side-to-side rocking motion, which confused the understanding in my brain as to what was happening. The hatch was on the starboard side, and if I was going to see anything of Africa, I needed to be on the port side. In my path would be the two great anchor chains and a variety of other shackles and eye bolts. Walking in such conditions was a sensation in itself; first climbing a hill with a heavy weight, then running freely without total control, and somewhere between all this, I had to hop or jump over the variety of obstacles. I finally crashed into the guard rail strung across on of the deck openings and thanked the lord it had been well-maintained and didn't break.

Looking down at the angry white water caused a dizziness which made me want to jump into it. I looked out over the water and became disappointed. I'm sure I could see land as I searched through the early-morning gloom, but it was so far off and looked only like a dark line on the horizon. I don't really know what I expected to see. I'd never seen a foreign country, except on a day visit to France a long time ago when my mother and Tosh took me to Calais. I stared out for a long time and huddled in a space by the ship's side and some bollards to gain some cover from the wind and spray. I watched as the day began to get brighter. It was a cloudy day, and so I was not able to see the sun rise. It was a waste of time getting up early. I could have stayed in my bunk for at least another half-hour. 'Fuck it all,' I thought, as I stirred from my position and made my way to the Senior Rates dining hall.

Breakfast today was particularly busy, with more people about for Harbour stations, which were due to be called at about 10:00. I was fortunate that I didn't have to be involved with these; they seemed to be another burden on the crew and involved extra men in switchboards, machinery spaces, the multitude of sound-powered phones had to be manned in case normal communications failed and men were standing by for all manner of misadventure. I was increasingly excited as I listened to the chatter about going ashore, and I was particularly interested in hearing of tales of Cape Town from those who had visited before. Cape Town was divided: it seemed there was two of everything; one for the white people and one for the blacks. Bars, train carriages, buses, taxis and even shops had to cater for a divided population. I heard stories of sailors being robbed at knife-point between the city and the docks, and of others accepting rides in cars only to be taken to remote areas and stripped of everything. It seemed a naval uniform was also in demand, as well as your wallet. At this moment, all I knew was that I was going ashore as soon as shore leave was announced. I didn't care about the so-called dangers. To me, these were just part of being a sailor, and I would swagger ashore and be where the action was yet avoiding any direct involvement. Well, that was the plan, anyway.

At 09:45, Harbour Stations were called, and we were just finishing off with cleaning up the dining hall. All the plates had been washed and stowed; knives, forks and spoons cleaned, sorted and placed in their drawers; the decks had all been scrubbed clean and dried, and now we were replacing all the furniture. The next shift of mess-men would take over at 11:00, and we would be free for 24 hours. Normally, when we had finished, we would go to the Weather Deck close to the mess. This was on the starboard side, just forward of the island and below the Flight Deck. There, we would have a fag and drink the last cup of tea before going off-duty, but this Weather Deck was now out-of-bounds due to Harbour Stations, and so we waited in our small scullery whilst Petula Clark pleaded for the sailor to stop his roaming and leave the sea.

As soon as I got away from the Senior Rates dining hall, I went down to the Capstan Flat, where I knew Spanner would be discharging his duty at Harbour Stations. Even if I was glad not to have to do Harbour Station duties, I had a jealousy for some. Spanner had to stand in front of a huge open electrical cabinet that housed a wonderful shiny copper segmented cylindrical drum, along with carbon brushes and woven copper wired conducting tapes, and with all the other cables, contactors and control knobs, not to mention the impressive ammeters and voltmeters. The Capstan Flat was so-called because it housed the machinery to drive the capstan, which was situated above it on the Cable Deck. The machinery consisted of a 'Ward Leonard' drive system. The capstan was powered by electrics, and the mains power of the Hermes was of the Alternating Current, as in the national supply today. Older ships had a Direct Current system which has many advantages over AC. It is not easy to alter the speed of an AC motor, and it is very necessary to vary the speed of a capstan when anchoring or berthing a ship. So, Mr Ward Leonard designed a system that used an AC motor as a primer mover to a DC generator. The AC motor could then run at a constant speed. The DC generator powered a DC motor, which could be speed-controlled easily and effectively. The segmented cylindrical drum of the opened control panel was linked by rod controls to the deck above, where the capstan controller could then operate the capstan on commands from the Cable Deck officer. The capstan controller held a dive wheel, similar to a steering wheel of a car, to effect this control. However, should he be too aggressive in his actions and command the capstan to change speed or direction too quickly, big sparks would fly from the cabinet below with the danger of welding the drum in one certain position. It was Spanner's job to make sure no passer-by got too close to this, and to take the appropriate action if he thought a weld was about to occur.

I wanted to be the one in this position. Spanner was looked upon as someone special because most of the ship's company did not know anything about what was happening. Every time the capstan moved, there would be tremendous whirring sounds from the machinery and the ventilation fans would suck in and blow-out air, causing mini whirlwinds around the compartment. No conversations could be held whilst the machinery was running.

Spanner looked at me when I arrived and raised his eyebrows and nodded his head in greeting. He then grabbed his testicles, gyrating them whilst lowering his eyelids, thrusting out his jaw in a lewd gesture of what his expectations of the night to come would be. Spunky almost always had one thing on his mind. I nodded my head at him and mimicked his jaw movement in acknowledgment.

I knew that, if I stayed with him for some time, I then could use the excuse to go up to the Cable Deck on the pretence of checking things out up there as I would be perceived to be assisting in the running of the capstan machinery. Other than that, there would be no way anyone could get on to a Weather Deck to 'goof'. Goofing was the term used to look around and enjoy the scenery. Entering Harbour was a good time to goof.

I climbed the ladder to the Cable Deck as I had done earlier that morning, and was greeted by one of the most fantastic sights I have ever seen. As mentioned before, the hatch is on the starboard side of the Cable Deck, and the ship was laying up starboard side to. As I mounted the ladder, I could see out of one of the openings of the ship's side, which seemed to be totally blocked off by a blackened glistening wall. My confusion soon gave way to the reality that I was looking at Table Mountain. As I left the hatch and neared the ship's side, there, before me, was the Mountain in all its glory. The top was perfectly flat and so very very immense. The flat surface stretched from Lion's Head to the west to Devil's Peak to the east nearly two miles away, and the whole lot was well over 3,000 feet high. My breath was taken away by the beauty of the sight, and my jaw dropped open. Normally, the top is shrouded in cloud that reaches down towards the city, aptly named the Table Cloth, but today, however, it was clear. So wonderfully clear! At its base is Cape

Town city, although not too much detail could be seen because of the distance we were from it, as well as separated by some stretch of waste ground. We had been warned about this piece of ground and advised not to walk across it at night when returning to the ship: it was a haven for the muggers who would lay in wait for the easy pickings of a drunken sailor.

'What the fuck are you doing, boy!' bellowed the Officer of the Cable Deck. This man was a giant. A Petty Officer of the Seaman's branch with not much between the ears. I never had much respect for the Seaman Department—or the Stewards, for that matter. He was stripped to the waist, and sweat caused his muscles to glisten. His angular jaw was jutted out towards me, and his teeth shone brightly white against his suntanned face. His narrowed eyes were steely as he stepped over the main chain on his journey towards me. 'Get below before I throw you over the fucking side!' The tingling I had in my belly for the beauty of Table Mountain now turned to a rumbling of a soon-to-be-released bowel. I jumped down the hatch, normally a suicidal thing to do, but I had to move quickly. I grabbed the handrail, which slowed my downward decent, but this action caused me to crash into the ladder at the bottom. I landed in a heap but quickly regained my feet and shot past Spanner into the Galley Flat. I turned to see if anyone was coming down the hatch after me but, after a short while, I realised nobody was.

Spanner looked at me in disbelief. I put my hand on my heart to catch my breath and could hear the blood pumping above the noise of the machinery. Spanner then gave me a knowing smile and raised his eyes upwards towards the deck above. I nodded slowly, and so we had communicated to each other what had happened. Spanner reached up to the fan trunking and, from above it, produced a large plastic mug. We all had one. He stretched his arm out to me, waggling the cup in a manner that told me he wanted me to fill it for him.

I took his mug and filled it with tea from the dining room. Tea was almost always available. I had collected mine from the Mess Deck on the way and filled that also. I gave Spanner his tea, and I sat back on a small tool locker to drink mine and be contented with my position. When I finished my tea, I motioned to Spanner that I was leaving. I pointed in the direction of the Galley Flat and also downwards so he knew I was going to our mess. He had to remain in front of the capstan panel until the order came for Harbour Stations to be fallen out.

As I stood over our hatch, the hubbub of noise rose from the space below. The whole mess was filled with excitement: we were going ashore for the first time since leaving Portsmouth some six weeks before. People were in various states of undress; some had showered, some were just about to make the trip to the bathrooms wrapped in towels and carrying dirty knicks and socks to be washed. This was a ritual carried out by everyone on-board every day. Everyone had their own space to hang these smalls, and they could be seen in all locations around the ship. As I entered the main living area, Fingers shouted at me, 'Clarkie, you fucking OD, waste of time, you going ashore? You have to be back at 22:30. You and Budgie the same. Poor fuckers.' He was laughing in ridicule at me. However, his news was indeed news to me. Normally, a Junior has to be back on-board by midnight, so this meant I would be losing two hours. 'Check the fucking noticeboard out,' Fingers added, pointing back the way I had come.

I waved my arm in dismissal of his comments, although I was truly concerned by what he had said. I would check out the noticeboard when I went past it next time. Fingers was larking around with Maxmore. Max was trying to undress and Fingers kept pushing him, especially when Max was only on one foot.

'Fuck off, Twat!' Max would shout at him, but Fingers still persisted. The other side of Fingers was Mick Briggs, who also was getting undressed, but he was allowed to continue without being molested. It would be obvious that Fingers and Briggsy would be going ashore together, but I think Spanner and I would steer clear of them. Budgie would tie-up with Max no doubt. Budgie was not in the mess at the moment, and I assumed he was doing Harbour Station duties somewhere. I had to go and read the noticeboard.

Sure enough, Juniors' leave expired at 22:00. UA's (this meant under age for the TOT) was midnight and G's (G meant you were 20years old and older, and thus qualified for the tot i.e. Grog) at 07:00 the following day. This meant that, if I went ashore with Spanner, which I would, I would have to leave him two hours early to return on-board on time. I would have to arrange to meet Budgie and Max so we could come back together. This news really hacked me off.

'Fucking told you so, Clarkie,' said Fingers as he breezed past me and mounted the ladder on his way to the bathroom.

The time was now 16:00 and liberty men were called to the gangway. A group of us rushed out of the mess, up the ladder and across the dining hall. Up another ladder, then a small passageway, and then we emerged onto the Weather Deck used for the lower deck gang-plank. Other ratings also were emerging at the same time, and there was RPO McSnell to shout orders at us to 'Fall In three deep!' Quickly, three lines of ratings were formed, each line containing 10 ratings and each line directly behind the other. I managed to get in the rear rank, which I thought would make me less conspicuous to McSnell. However, I felt his eyes upon me straight away. The rules of Night Leave were read aloud to us, and we were warned of places not to go, things not to drink, things not to do, and things not to say. We were reminded of the political situation in South Africa, and the fact that the relations with the rest of the world were not so good, and that we were not to embarrass our government by getting into trouble.

Then came the inspection. First the front rank. Normally, a body of men would open order march, which meant the front rank would take two paces forward and the rear rank would take two paces backwards, and then the inspecting office could walk through the ranks inspecting everyone front and back. Due to the confined space, the front rank would be inspected first and then ordered to march off so the next rank could be inspected and so on.

We were all in uniform. We had all pressed our uniforms before we got dressed. Our white fronts would be brilliant white, with a single inverted crease down the front. The collars were to have three creases down the back and creases in the bell bottoms of the trouser legs. If you were tall, then seven creases were needed. If you were short, five would suffice. The cap had to be perfectly white and flat on top like a milk churn lid. The cap tally of gold depicting HMS Hermes was to be turned to the front. Gold branch badges were worn on the right arm. Needless to say, shoes were to be highly polished.

The officer of the watch finally came to me and passed with only a cursory glance. McSnell stood in front of me and reminded me to return on time—with my socks! He pointed to my white front and said, 'No stain today, then?' And I knew if I looked down, that finger would flick up and sear my nose. I looked straight ahead and avoided any eye contact. I felt McSnell was disappointed he could inflict no pain on me.

With the inspection done, the Boson's mate collected all the Station cards, which would be posted in the appropriate pigeon hole and await collection upon return. That was it. With the formalities completed, we then were allowed to descend the gang-plank to dry land—dry African land. It felt good and it felt strange. Here I was, the other side of the world, and about to discover new things. *Very* new things.

8: The Navigators Den

There was some confusion on the jetty as groups of sailors got together to embark on their own 'run ashore'. Spanner grabbed my arm and said, 'Come on.' We turned towards Cape Town and, once again, I was able to relish in the sight of Table Mountain. 'Watch out for snakes,' Spanner told me, but I didn't know if he was joking or not. Regardless, I did keep my head down.

We walked across the area of waste ground and arrived at a road running in front of the city. I could now see the main street of Cape Town with the fountain in the middle. Some groups had already crossed the road and some were still behind us.

'So, what's the plan?' I asked Spanner. We seemed to have broken away from everyone else and were on our own. Neither of us minded this. We were both still smarting from the news about shore leave. Spanner told me that 'Last Commish' he had all night leave and he was only 17 then, so he was hacked off as well. I knew he would not return on-board when I had to, and he knew I knew that. I didn't consider him selfish, but that's just the way it was.

'Well,' Spanner replied with a sigh, 'first of all, we'll find a bar and have a fucking beer.'

I grunted in agreement.

'We won't go to these on the main drag. I remember some smaller ones around the back streets over there.' He waved in the general direction of the right of the big fountain.

District 6 was an area we were told to avoid. It was populated by the black people and it would be very dangerous for white men to go there—even by accident. Looking at the map, I had a mental picture of where District 6 was, and that would be well over to the left of the fountain, as the city began to rise towards the mountain. Therefore, I had no worries about leaving the main drag off to the right.

'Sounds good to me. I aint had a beer since Portsmouth, except a few slugs from someone's can now and again.'

Beer was available on-board if you were over 18, and then you were allowed two cans a day. When these were issued, a ration card was clipped and both cans opened so they could not be stored. Once in a while, I had the privileged of tasting the tot, but rum was a very valuable commodity; it was more valuable than money and was the currency by which favours could be paid. Spanner looked at me, and I felt guilty about what I had said because he had allowed me several slugs of his beer.

'I guess that means I have to buy the first fuckers, then,' I said, quelling his ire.

'And the next bastard,' he added.

We dodged the cars on the main road and made it to the main drag. It was wonderful. The sun was blazing down upon us, and we were on the corner of the wide boulevard of Allderley Street, which ran away from us up toward the mountain itself. The fountain marked the beginning of this street. The fountain was like a jungle, built in a circle with water shooting up from several areas before cascading back to earth. Clouds of mist formed from the spray, and the sunlight split into its spectrum of colours as it passed through causing mini rainbows. This was a truly beautiful addition to the city with its natural magnificent backdrop.

We crossed the road and skirted around the fountain. The noise was incredible. We then crossed the other side of the road and walked up towards the mountain. Sailors were peeling off in groups into different bars, stores and coffee bars. Spanner and I continued on for a while until he stopped me whilst looking down a street to our right. 'This is it,' he said. 'I think.' He rubbed his chin.

'Well, I don't see any bars down there or any lights.' I instantly regretted saying this because it sounded like I was questioning his knowledge and memory.

'I remember going down such a street and then at the end there was like an *S* bend by a square full of garages. I'm sure this is fucking it.'

'Well, let's go and have a look,' I comforted him. 'At least it'll be cooler and out of the sun.'

'Aye, you're right. I'm sure this is fucking it, though.'

He was right. The end of the road opened up to a small square, which had the pavements on three sides running by steel doors, which easily could have been garage doors. We turned left then right, heading away from the square into another street that was narrow, yet full of neon signs advertising a variety of different bars. It was the most exciting thing I had seen in my life. I even began to be a little frightened of what I would see and how I should act! If there would be women there showing too much leg or cleavage, I surely would get such a hard-on I would not know what to do with it!

'Fucking told you so,' said Spanner, rubbing his hands and grinning from ear-to-ear.

The first bar we came to had two doors. We went through the one under a sign of 'Whites Only'. Inside was dark, and I stood slightly behind Spanner. The bar itself was dimly lit, and I could see several people, including sailors in uniform, perched on stools and chatting amongst themselves in a variety of groups. Spanner made his way to a space at the bar, and I followed. He asked the bartender, when he came, for two beers. The bartender produced two bottles of Castle beer, removed the caps, and took the note that Spanner placed on the bar before him. I had given this note to Spanner before we entered. The bartender returned with some change, which Spanner took and looked at. He selected some coins and gave them to me, whilst the rest he put in his pocket. 'That's for the next round, Clarkie,' he said. Well, that was it. We got served, no problem.

I picked up a bottle and took a swig. It was freezing cold, so cold my hand almost stuck to the glass. The liquid burned the back of my throat as my body heat rushed out to equalise the temperature. I looked at Spanner, who was drinking from the bottle quite normally. I decided all was normal and I would not make comment.

By now, my eyes were becoming accustomed to the gloom and I also realised it was a lot cooler in here. I then twigged the place was air-conditioned. I'd never before come across Air Conditioning, except in some of the navigation equipment compartments on-board where the temperature had to be maintained, else the electronics go haywire. There were only men at the bar, and we were not the only sailors in uniform. However, I did recognise some Senior Rates here that could go ashore in civvies; I recognised them from all the time I had spent in their dining room.

Music issued forth from a juke box and The Hollies were singing about walking into a room, which I thought was very apt. Spanner had his bottle to his lips again, and I could see bubbles of air replacing the beer as the liquid slipped down his throat. I was still smarting from my first gulp, but realised I needed to catch up a little, so lifted my bottle and braced myself for the coldness, which wasn't so bad this time.

'Not as good as Tiger,' Spanner said, looking at the bottle in his hand. 'That's the beer you get in Singers.'

'Oh really? Tastes alright to me, though.'

'Yeah. It'll do.' Spanner then went on to explain to me that these bars get full of prostitutes later. Bar girls making a fuss of you so you'll buy them a drink. He told me the drinks were only like sugared water but cost about five times the price of a beer.

'Did you ever fuck any?'

'No. Too much of a rip-off here.'

I didn't know what to say, and so I said nothing. I could feel the alcohol dulling my senses, and that only after a couple of gulps! I had to pace myself somehow or else I'd soon be out the game.

'Singers is different, though. They have brothels there where you can go, and at least you know what you're getting.'

I just looked at him, not daring to speak, really, and knowing he would continue.

'You go in and they all line up. You know how much you have to pay, so you just pick one and away you go.'

I thought to myself that that was a bit clinical. 'Can't be much excitement in that?'

'But, man, wait till you see the women there! Their skin is like velvet. It's heaven to touch,' he added, turning to look at me as he said it.

'How much it cost then?'

'Not much. You have to haggle a bit.'

'Still don't think it's very exciting. Don't think it's for me.'

'Well, you wait till you get there. You'll soon change your fucking mind!' he said with a nod of his head.

'brothels are out-of-bounds for us, though, so what happens if you get caught?' I asked—and it was true: I had heard stories that the Military Police would raid brothels looking for us lot, and *then* we'd be in the shit.

'It's a risk, but our whole life is a risk, man.'

I felt one of Spanner's philosophy of life speeches coming on.

'If you considered the risk in everything, you'd never get out of your fucking bed. May as well stay there and die, man.' He then turned to me and continued. 'In fact, you, Clarkie, is okay because your bunk is on the bottom. Me, I wouldn't even get in mine because mine is the top bunk so think of the risk of getting up there and not falling out all fucking night!' He finished with an emphatic nod of his head. He then finished his beer and asked the barman for two more. Two more Castle beers were produced and their tops removed. Money was exchanged and the barman left us again.

'Wait till you see Bugis Street and the fucking Kai Tais!' he started again.

I had heard of these people. Apparently males undergoing sex changes and apparently in a 'somewhere in-between' phase, who then turn to prostitution to finance the final part of the process, which is surgery to remove the 'man bits' and construct the 'women bits'. The first part of the process is with hormones, which cause breasts to form. They were not very hairy, and so facial hair was not much of a problem. I had seen photographs and, sure enough, they looked female and sexy enough!

Spanner continued, 'I'm telling you: they are fucking gorgeous. I'm telling you, man. Wait till you see them fuckers!'

I was intrigued now and asked, 'Don't tell me people go with them and fuck them!'

'Of course they do! Everyone does!'

'Everyone? No, I don't believe that.'

'I'm telling you, Clarkie. People are falling over themselves to get inside their knickers!'

'How can that be?' I asked 'They still have cocks and bollocks! Why would anyone want to grab hold of that lot?'

'You see, you don't understand, do you?'

'No, I fucking don't.'

'Kai Tais are more feminine than women!' He was holding his hands in front of him, almost in the manner of prayer for added sincerity. Spanner could see me looking at him, and he must have detected that I really thought he had lost his mind. 'Look.' He was now holding a hand up above his head as if to stop traffic. 'A woman is a woman, and she is as feminine as she is. A man has to work hard to be feminine, and when he's pumped full of female hormones, he ends up far more feminine than a woman!' His hand went down to his lap, and he looked at me and waited for signs of the penny dropping.

I looked at him straight. 'So these *men* are more feminine than women?'

'Yes,' he said, clutching his chest as if thankful I had got the message.

'With a cock and bollocks?'

There was a pause as Spanner shook his head then said, 'For fuck sake, it doesn't matter.'

'How can it not matter? How can you fuck anyone with a cock and bollocks, no matter how feminine they are?'

'You don't know they are there! When you are with them, they are women! Fucking sexy women!'

'Spanner, are you telling me that men from ships, *our* ship, for instance, will go there and fuck them?'

'Of course they do.'

'And they pay to fuck them?'

'Of course! Nothing's for free in this world!'

I now had a real problem understanding what Spanner was telling me. The Hermes had a crew of more than two-thousand men. Homosexuality was not tolerated in the Navy, and anyone practicing it was thrown out. But now I was being told it was common knowledge that some ratings were a bit 'dodgy'. The Chief Sickbay Attendant was one, as was one of his assistants. There were some in the fleet air-arm also, but they were associated with the squadrons and so didn't integrate too much with the rest of the crew. Some Stewards, Writers and Chefs also were under suspicion.

As if guessing my line of thought, Spanner stated, 'You don't have to be queer to fuck a Kai Tai, you know.'

'How do they do it then? I asked. 'Doggy fashion like men would do it?'

'No, you fucking idiot.' Spanner turned on me. 'One on top of the other, like a man fucking a woman.'

'Spanner, how can that be? His cock and bollocks would get in the way.'

'For fuck sake, Clark, use your imagination. They keep their knickers on and lay on their backs and hold their legs high, then they just pull their knickers aside, and in you fucking go.'

'Up their arse? I queried.

'Well, of course, up their fucking arse! They don't have a fanny yet!'

There was a pause to digest all this. 'No,' I said. 'Not me. No fucking way,' I continued, shaking my head.

'Clarkie, I'm telling you. You would never know the difference. It's just like a woman. But more feminine,' he concluded.

There was a longer pause whilst I looked at his profile. He was staring into the neck of the beer bottle, which he was grasping in both hands. Presumably to warm it up a little.

'You've done it, haven't you?' I accused 'You've fucking fucked one.' He turned his head to face me and I added, 'You've shagged arse!' I stated, and then went on. 'For fuck sake, Spanner.'

'Chris, it's no big deal, okay?' he said, looking back at his beer. 'But if you tell any bastard, I'll fucking kill you.' He looked at me with menace in his eyes. 'Believe that, Clarkie. I fucking will.'

I could tell he didn't want to talk about it anymore. 'Spanner, I know you're not queer, and I believe you when you say there is something different about them. Of course I'll say nothing. You're my mate. But I can tell you something right now. I'll never put mine up anyone's shitter.' And with that, the subject was closed.

He nodded, and his face relaxed as he returned to staring into his bottle.

There was a bit of an awkward silence for a while, then Spanner finished his beer and told me to drink up. I did, and then he suggested we go next door. I got up off the stool and he put his arm around my shoulder and pulled me tight as we walked out. 'You've got a lot to fucking learn yet, Clarkie,' he said.

The bar next door was similar in design to the one we had just left. Again, we entered through a door marked 'Whites Only', and the bar was opposite the door, running parallel to the front wall. More people were huddled in groups at the bar. These were not so subdued as next door, and the noise level was higher as a result. There were more sailors in this, although none I recognised. They were all older than us and from different branches, as betrayed by their branch badges. Nobody gave us any attention as we entered and made our way to the bar. Consequently, nobody made space for us either. Eventually, we found a small gap, and Spanner pushed his way through and returned with two Castle beers. We found a table by the door and sat down. Looking round, I saw two ladies sauntering towards us.

'Aye up,' said Spanner, 'here we go.'

The first lady arrived at our table and leant forward, placing her two hands between our bottled beer. She was looking at us both in turn, challenging us to maintain eye contact, even though her deep-cut neckline hung forwards, exposing full breasts restrained by a bra struggling to do its job.

'You boys gonna buy us ladies a drink?' she asked, indicating with a toss of her head her friend behind her. Her friend approached the table and stood with her weight on one leg, fingering the hem of her mini skirt. The second lady was younger than the first; taller and altogether more attractive. The hem of her skirt was being hitched up as she twisted the material between her fingers. Her ever increasingly exposed thigh was beautiful. I knew I was staring, and my eyes took in everything.

'Not today,' Spanner said. 'We have no money to buy drinks.' With that, she looked at me and, with one hand, she squeezed her left breast, causing it to swell and undulate.

'What about you, baby boy?' she drooled. 'Buy us a drink and we can go sit in the corner where nobody will see what we are up to. 'Again, she tossed her head to indicate where she meant. 'What do ya say, baby face?'

The truth of the matter was I couldn't speak; I felt as if my face was on fire, and there was a lump in my throat preventing any sound from coming out. My stomach was tingling and my heart thumping against my ribcage. All the blood was going to my face—and to my crotch.

'He's got no money either,' said Spanner, coming to my rescue.

With that, she stood up straight, spun around, and marched off. Her friend let go of her skirt hem, which returned to its normal place. She also stood up straight, turned away from us, and sauntered after her friend.

We looked after the pair of them and remained silent for a while, and then Spanner said, 'Fucking prozzies. God knows what you'd catch if you went with them.'

My heartbeat slowed to a normal rate, my face cooled down, and the pressure went from my loins. I took a long pull on my beer and realised I was getting drunk. My head was spinning, and my vision was wafting in and out of focus. We watched as the ladies periodically approached other men, who seemed to despatch them in much the same. After a while, it was noticeable there were more of these ladies, although none approached us. I had no idea what time it was.

Soon enough, Spanner relieved me of some more money and headed for the bar returning with two more beers. Now I was feeling sick. I folded my arms on the table and laid my head on them before passing out.

From a great distance, I could hear Spanner calling me, and then I could feel him pulling and pushing me.

'Come on, Clarkie!'

He was getting closer. He pulled me to my feet and I tried to stand. I clung to the table for support and opened my eyes. My head felt as if there was a blacksmith at work inside, and I couldn't focus on anything.

'Come-on, Clarkie, for fuck sake!' Spanner persisted. 'We're off!' he added, shaking me in an effort to get me to support myself.

I stood at the table in much the same way as the buxom lady had done previously, but my stance was one of necessity as opposed to allurement. I was now awake. 'Okay, okay, okay,' I said.

'We're going to the Navigators' Den. It's free if you get in before nine.'

I had no comprehension of what he was saying.

'I'll get us a bottle of brandy we can smuggle in. We only have to buy Coke then. They'll never serve us beer in there.' Spanner was saying all of this in great excitement, but my mind was just a blur. He grabbed hold of my arm and led me outside. I was able to walk but needed him to be near.

Once outside, fresh air filled my nostrils. The veins at the back of my head felt as if they would burst, such was the pain there. The blacksmith was still hard at work, trying to get out of my skull. My eyes also weren't working as partners; I had stereophonic vision. The lights hurt me, yet the lights were still there when I closed my eyes; dancing and flashing all over the place. My legs gave way and I slumped to my heels. My head fell forwards to the pavement and I assumed the posture of a Muslim at prayer. Spanner grabbed me by the shoulders and tried to pull me up.

'For fuck sake, Clarkie! Pull yourself together, man.'

I lifted my upper body to a kneeling position, and Spanner took a handful of my hair and lifted my face up to his.

'What the fuck's up with you?' he shouted in my face, then shook my head, inviting an answer.

'I'm alright, I'm alright,' I said. 'I'm alright,' I added for a third time. 'Just let me sit a while.' I rolled to the side and let my legs extend. I sat there watching Spanner walk away, lighting a cigarette. I shuffled around so my back was against the wall, and I leant against it. I rested my head against the wall and looked up to the darkening sky above the buildings opposite. As some moments passed, I discovered my eyes could just about focus. Just a few paces away from where I was slumped, in the direction Spanner had gone, was a bench on the other side of the pavement, close to the road but facing away from the road. I needed to get to that bench, I decided, and so, again, I rolled to the side, drew my knees up, and climbed the wall with my hands until I was in a standing position. With one hand leaning on the wall, I was upright. I turned my back to the wall and looked at the bench. I gently pushed myself away from the wall until my weight was directly above my feet and I could stand unaided. I waited a moment, focusing on the bench, and then strode out towards it. But my legs wouldn't work properly; I couldn't walk. My knees seemed to lift too high yet seemed to buckle under my weight. I went forward and also to the right. I felt as if I was falling, and tried to get my feet beneath me for support. I must have taken about six steps, each one curving away from the bench in a beautiful arc, each one propelling me faster and faster until I crashed into a parked car outside the door of the bar. I was on the correct side of the pavement now, but no nearer the bench. I was once again sitting on the paving slabs with my legs spread before me with my back resting against the parked blue Mercedes. I looked around for Spanner, but I couldn't see him anywhere. I remember being pleased about this, as I didn't want him to witness my actions. I didn't know where he had gone or if he would be returning.

One thing I did know was that I had to get to the bench before he did. I looked up and down the street and, whilst some people were milling about, nobody was paying me any attention. I used the car for support as I once again rose to my feet. I used the car as further support as I took a few steps toward the bench. I was finally able to make my way to the bench without further hiccup. I slumped down and held my head between my hands and supported the lot on my knees. After a while, the pressure in my head seemed to subside, and I could sit up straight and look around. Focusing was erratic, but I was able to take stock of my surroundings fairly clearly.

Spanner was nowhere to be seen. I breathed deeply and slowly. In through the nose, out through the mouth. My stomach reminded me it was having problems also. I could hear rumblings from down there. Firstly, little murmurings of bubbles running around, with bigger grumbles to follow. I decided it was time to stand up. I did so and pressed my calves against the bench for support. I still continued to breathe deeply, and tried to stand up straight with my head held high. I felt it was time to move on, and so walked gingerly in the direction from which we had come and in which Spanner had gone.

It seemed the bubbles that were running around my stomach were reaching the surface and releasing acidic gases. These caught in the back of my throat, carried up with a burping belch. I breathed in deeply and felt air enter my stomach; moments later, this was released in another great burp. I felt this ventilation of the stomach was a good thing, and repeated the exercise several times. Eventually, the erupting gasses were followed by the hot liquid rush of my stomach's contents blasting through my mouth and cascading through the air to land on the pavement in front of me. A second rush came, and liquid was forced up and out of my nose and dripped from my upper lip. A deep retch followed, but there seemed nothing more to expel. I wiped my nose and mouth with my hand, and was disgusted by the smell and texture. As a kid, I always hated being sick, and I felt the same way now.

I walked on, skirting the mess on the pavement. My head was throbbing so badly now; I really thought it would explode. I swore I would never drink alcohol again in my life. I came to another bench and sat down once again. I needed the pain in my head to subside before I could go further. Just being still helped, and once again the pain diminished to a dull throbbing. I opened my eyes and began to contemplate what I should do next, when Spanner appeared from around the corner.

'You okay, Clarkie?' he asked as he came up to me.

'Of course I am,' I lied. 'Just a bit tired, that's all.'

'Fucking tired!' Spanner repeated. 'You're fucking pissed, you little shit.'

'Hang on a minute, pal. Don't forget I had the breakfast shift in the Senior Rates dining hall whilst you still had your fat head down!'

'You sure you're okay?' he asked again. 'I thought you were out for the count.'

'Spanner,' I said, looking at him directly, 'I'm okay, okay?'

'Okay. Here, have a slug of this,' he said, offering me the opened bottle of brandy. 'It'll make you feel better.'

I took the bottle and looked at it. I raised it and smelled the contents. The alcohol stung the back of my nose, causing me to wince. I knew Spanner was looking at me so I put the bottle to my lips and tipped it up. I felt the liquid on my closed lips, but knew I would have to take a swallow to pass the scrutiny of Spanner's eyes. I drew the liquid into my mouth and held it there for a second or two before swallowing it. The brandy burnt my throat, causing it to clamp up, resulting in some of the liquid taking the same path the vomit had taken previously—up through my nose. I am sure some of it found its way into my eyes, as they instantly stung and watered profusely. Some went down and burned its way into my gut. My chest shook with constrictions, and the hairs on the back of my neck stood on end. I swallowed the remaining liquid and felt its fire all the way down to my empty stomach. My face was involuntarily screwed up as if in agony, and my throat heaved an explosive cough. 'Fuck a duck!' I eventually blurted. 'What the fuck is that stuff?'

'Cape Brandy. Best brandy in the world!' he added. 'And fucking cheap! Have another sip,' he invited, as I was still holding the bottle. 'First one's always the worst.'

Again, I looked at the bottle and wondered why he had bought it.

'Go on,' he urged, gesturing with his hand.

Again, I raised the bottle to my lips and allowed the tiniest amount of liquid to enter my mouth. I held it for a moment and then swallowed with trepidation. He was right: the first was definitely the worst. The small amount of liquid slid down with a positive warming effect. It seemed to glow in my stomach and, at the same time, swim in my head. It was like an anaesthetic. The throbbing pain in my head was replaced by numbness. I knew I was still drunk, but I felt happy. It seemed I was in a different place. My feet were on the earth yet my head was up in heaven.

'Come on! Let's go!' He threw down his cigarette butt and ground it into the pavement with his foot.

The Navigators' Den, to me, was like the eighth wonder of the world. We entered up a few steps between two enormous doormen, who looked at us with great interest. I guess it was our uniforms. I was walking quite straight, although my head was still numb and full of a wonderful tranquil feeling. The bottle of brandy was in my sock and covered by the girth of my bell-bottomed trousers. Spanner made me smuggle this in as my part of the deal: he had paid for it as his part. We passed the ticket window, progressed up a few more steps, and entered the Den.

The sight in front of me was unbelievable. The dance floor opened up immediately after the doorway, with a thick piled carpet leading both to the left and right. Beyond the dance floor was a bar, and way off to the right was a lounge area with large, low, comfortable sofas and chairs strategically positioned around low glass-topped tables. Beautiful girls were all over the place. The dance floor, though by no means full, was heaving with rhythmic movement of dancers—dancers in couples or groups of three or four; predominantly girls. Girls in mini skirts, blouses and no bras. Others were dressed in other things, but these did not draw (or even warrant) my attention. To the left was a stage on which was a set of drums and amplifiers scattered around. On the one side was a DJ gyrating behind an array of record players and tape recorders. Behind him was a panel full of switches to control all the lights—lights of all colours; flashing lights, rotating lights and ultraviolet lights that made your teeth shine and showed up every hair on our dark uniform. The Small Faces were singing Itchicoo Park, which boomed around the whole place, making conversation impossible. *What will we touch there?* they sang. *We'll touch the sky.* With this, I looked up to the high ceiling. There was a boat hanging there! The boat was enormous and hanging upside-down so its insides could be seen. It was a fishing boat, and inside were all manner of things: nets, buoys, rods, spars, ropes, chains, anchors, oars, oil skins and sea boots; and then rifles, swords, daggers and pistols. The rest of the ceiling was covered in blue and green sheeting, depicting the sea. Fronds of silky material hung down as weeds, and fish dangled on strings. Hidden fans blew air across these, causing them to swing and undulate, completing the illusion of an overturned fishing boat at sea.

We skirted off to our right, making for the bar. We needed to buy some Coke and get some ice and glasses. I didn't know if my feeling of euphoria was due to this wonderful place or the effects of the alcohol on my head and my empty belly—we had not eaten since we had arrived ashore. Maybe the feeling I had was a combination of all these things.

Spanner propped me against a column, on the edge of the dance floor, and told me to wait whilst he went to the bar. When he returned, he nodded to the lounge section, indicating it would be better to get the brandy out there. Almost all the seats were taken, and we went further away from the dance floor in search of a secure place to retrieve our booze.

'Come and sit with us,' a female voice shouted. 'Hey, you two!'

I heard the calling, but I didn't know where it had come from or who it was directed to; I also saw Spanner looking around. Then, I felt a tug on my arm and looked around to see a beautiful round face looking up at me.

'Me?' I pointed at myself with my other hand, and then realised how ridiculous it was. She was still holding my sleeve. Spanner had seen us, and was pushing me towards them. I half-fell into the seat beside her, and saw Spanner had taken up a position opposite me, next to the other young girl.

'You must be off that big ship from England,' she said excitedly.

I just looked at her in amazement.

'I love your uniforms,' she added.

Still, I could not speak: she was so beautiful and she wanted to be with me!

'Will you sit with us?' she asked, as if reading my thoughts. But I just couldn't find any words.

The music was not so loud here, so it was easy to hear what she said. Were these prozzies, as Spanner would call them? Were we expected to buy them drinks? I didn't know what to do or say. I looked at Spanner, who had his eyes firmly fixed on the other young beauty next to him. I got no message from him. I looked at the girl by his side, who was looking at me as if waiting for an answer. I looked again at the first one; she really was truly beautiful. She had a round face, but her skin was somewhat pock-marked. Her eyes were dark green and they bored into me. Her lips were full and painted in bright red lipstick. Her smile revealed even, white teeth. Her smile began to fade, in disappointment, and the teeth were disappearing. She was moving away from me and then said, raising her eyebrows, 'Don't you want to sit with us?'

'No. I mean, yes. And the *no* was because ....' I stammered then paused, 'I'm sorry. You just took me by surprise.'

'It'd be great to be with you both,' said Spanner, coming to my rescue.

My girl was called Sheila and she was 19 years old, although she looked much younger. The other girl's name was Mary and she, too, was 19. They both had a glass full of what looked like Coke, and they were each eating from a plate of hamburger, chips and salad.

'Do you want a chip?' Sheila asked, gesturing towards the plate.

'No, thanks,' I said, holding up a hand as if to ward off the plate. I really did want a chip, though. In fact, I could have devoured the whole lot in no time!

'What you drinking there?' She nodded towards my glass. I looked at Spanner as if I needed his approval for an answer. The brandy was still in my sock.

'Coke,' I said.

'Oh, that's all we get here. It's so expensive.' Then she looked directly at me, and a cheeky grin came across her face as she went on, 'We smuggled in a bottle of brandy to add to it.' She reached for her handbag. 'Do you want some?' My eyes and Spanner's met, and his drilled into mine as if saying, 'Don't say anything about our brandy'. Spanner pushed our glasses towards her, and she asked me to hold them below the level of the table so she could give us each a shot from her bottle. We all raised our glasses, said cheers, and took a sip.

We spent some time chatting, during which we learned a lot about these girls. Sheila was training to be a bus driver; it was very rare for a lady to be a bus driver, but she was determined it was what she wanted to do. She had to learn all about the 'business' of busses, which included spending time in the booking and ticket offices, as well as learning to be a conductor and taking money from passengers. This only happened within the city. She wanted to progress to coaches, taking people long distances. Mary, on the other hand, was at university studying medicine. Her father was a doctor. She lived in a big house with her parents and her ten-year-old sister.

Sheila asked me if I wanted to dance. *Oh Fuck!* I thought. I didn't know if I could stand, let alone move to the dance floor. I certainly couldn't dance! I could do the twist, but that dance was history now. Then I heard Tom Jones singing about the Green Grass, and knew this was a contact dance. All men liked the contact dances. Sheila said Mary would stay to look after our table and things.

Sheila led me to the floor and then turned towards me and grabbed me—that's the only way I can describe it. One arm went around my neck, the other around my waist, and she pressed herself to me and started to sway with the music. I held her and felt her femininity. She had a narrow back, and it seemed her hips flared out a little, almost disproportionate to her shoulders. I could feel the muscles and tendons at the small of her back, and allowed my hand to descend until I could feel the elastic of her knickers. I went no further. I then explored her shoulder blades and found the strap of her bra. Touching these things excited me, and I knew if I got a hard-on she would feel it—and I was getting a hard-on! She ground her stomach into mine, and I knew she could feel me. She lifted her face to mine, and I looked into it. Her eyes looked far away, and she pulled my face down until we were kissing. Not just kissing—but really snogging. Her tongue was in my mouth, teasing mine and probing my teeth. I was as hard as hard could be, and she was pushing firmly into me.

Then the record changed without the music stopping. Her head was on my shoulder, and my lips played at her slender neck. Her breathing came from deep down, almost like panting. We stayed like this for some time whilst different singers sang of love and love-making. The DJ announced it was time to up the tempo and so, without saying a word, we both agreed it was time to return to our seats. I had to put my hand in my pocket to try to rearrange my bits and save some embarrassment!

When we got back to our table, Mary and Spanner were in a deep lip lock, so it seemed they also were getting on. I sat down and Sheila asked me for her bag. She tapped Mary on the shoulder and said she needed to go to the ladies' room. Mary got her bag, and together they went. Spanner and I looked across the table at each other, both of us wearing the same expression of disbelief and wonder.

'Fucking hell, Clarkie! We're in tonight,' he said. 'These two are essence!'

I was trying to push my receding hard-on into a more comfortable position and answered him, 'I know.' Then, in a different tone, I asked Spanner the time. We both had to be back on-board early—and me even earlier then he!

'Fucking hell, man, we can't leave these two now!'

'So what time is it now?' I asked, again more seriously.

'Chris,' he said apologetically, 'you're already adrift.'

There was a silence between us. He knew the time and wouldn't tell me. He knew the time when I should have left, but he'd chosen not to tell me.

In that moment, my mind was a mixture of so many thoughts and emotions. I knew I was still drunk, very drunk, yet I could think fairly straight. Spanner didn't tell me when I needed to go because he wanted me to be with him—not that he wanted me to be in trouble. He chose me to come ashore with. We liked each other, and he was showing me the ropes. I looked around; the place was more crowded now. I had never been in such a place. Wherever I looked, I saw girls in mini skirts. Some were looking at me. It made me feel attractive and desired. I liked that. Sheila had picked us out and wanted to be with *us*. I knew I could fuck her and, what was more, I knew she wanted me to. I could leave now and run all the way back to the ship, but I would still be adrift. I would still be in the Shetland I still would not be able to come ashore again during this stay in Cape Town. That would mean not fucking Sheila, not enjoying more of this place, and not enjoying more of Cape Town.

The logic of my thinking had almost certainly made up my mind, but then Spanner spoke again. 'Look, Chris, man, let's stay with these two tonight. Let's get our fucking ends away in big style and go back tomorrow and face the music together.'

'We'll both be in the shit, but you won't be in the same shit as me!' I let him digest that thought, then went on, 'McSnell will have a field day with me. You know he hates me and it'll be me hanging out of the galley boilers, scraping away, every fucking time.' I paused. 'Every fucking time!' I repeated again for emphasis. 'At least you have the possibility of library cleaning or some remote bathroom that nobody uses, or some other cushy number!'

The silence between us continued.

'At this moment, I'm in the shit and can't do anything about it.'

Spanner was looking guilty.

'So we may as well make the most of it and fuck 'em all!' I added.

Spanner's face lit up. 'Clarkie, you've still got a lot to learn, but you're learning fast! Let's fuck 'em all together!' He stood up and took my face in his hands and kissed my forehead. 'Now get that bottle out of your sock and I'll get some more Coke.'

The night continued. My head became lighter and lighter, and I bounced off more people as I moved around and tried to dance. There were more and more people coming into the place, and space was getting less. I bumped into Fingers, who had a wide grin on his face.

'Fuck me, Clarkie. You'll be in the shit tomorrow! Budgie and Max left ages ago!'

I just looked at him. In fact, I couldn't even begin to think about constructing a relevant response.

We stayed with Sheila and Mary—or, more importantly, they stayed with us—and, for me, the night turned into an oblivion.

9: First Day on the Run

Somewhere, at the back of my head, I could hear a dog bark. My head was just a throbbing pain on my shoulders. I tried to open my eyes but they were locked shut. My mouth was more than dry. I feared moving my tongue lest it break. I couldn't breathe through my nose. I raised an arm and rubbed the crustiness from my eyes, and morning light flooded my brain. I was in a bright white room. I was lying on my right side and I was looking at a three-drawer chest against the wall with a mirror on top and a small stool in front. *Not really a dressing table,* I thought, as there was no place for the knees when sitting looking at yourself. Next to this piece of furniture was an open door which, because of the tiled floor, I assumed was a bathroom.

I had no idea where I was.

I knew to move my head would mean more pain, and so I decided to remain in this position whilst I explored the feelings across the rest of my body. Surprisingly enough, my stomach seemed okay. I didn't feel sick, and there were no gurgling or other signs of upset. I pushed my feet down so my legs were straight. I looked down at my feet, and beyond I saw a deep red Chesterfield sofa nestled beneath a window, which was flooding the room with light. Next to this was a door, which I assumed led outside. The door was shut. I realised I would have to move my head further to explore further.

At this point, memories from the night before rushed back into my aching brain. An overwhelming feeling of guilt and fear washed over me as I realised I should be back on-board. In fact, I should be back in the Senior Rates dining hall, as I was sure it was still morning! I laid my head back and turned to look at the ceiling. A three-bladed fan was turning slowly and silently. I could feel no disturbance in the air, though. I remembered Sheila, Mary and Spanner, and us having a good time. *So, where are they all now?* I wondered. I then realised I had an enormous hard-on, which was not due to my renewed memory of Sheila, but because I desperately needed a piss. I would have to go.

I swung my feet to the floor and raised my head. The room swung, then settled. I focused on the bathroom door; stood up and stumbled towards it. I peed in the toilet, leaning with one hand against the wall. I looked at myself in the mirror and had difficulty focusing my eyes. My saliva glands, along with my tongue, began to work.

So, where was Spanner? I wondered.

As I left the bathroom, the answer to my most recent thought was revealed. He was sleeping in the same bed. He was curled up in a foetal position, facing the opposite wall to where I was. He was still and very silent. I walked around the bed and determined he was still alive and breathing very shallowly. 'Spanner,' I said in a forced whisper. I didn't mean to whisper, but that's all I could do. I called his name again and shook him gently by the shoulder. He showed no signs of waking. I shook him harder, but still nothing. I didn't know what to do. I felt pathetic. I wanted to be back on-board, where I knew where I was. I wanted to be surrounded by familiar things. *Safe* things.

I stood up and went to the window. Outside was an enormous swimming pool, which looked so beautiful; shimmering blue in the sunlight, cool and inviting. The pool and the surrounding area were enclosed on either side by a high wall, which I could not see over. Opposite was a house—a fucking great, big house! There was an open veranda with swinging chairs and a wooden balustrade. The veranda was covered with a sloping roof with tiles identical to the roof tiles that capped the roof above the row of windows above the balustrade. Gable windows even projected from the roof, indicating at least three storeys. Nobody could be seen. I looked round at Spanner again, just to check he was still there.

On the other side of the room was a dining table with four chairs and, in the far corner, was a sink, drainer and some kitchen cupboards. There was also a fridge. I walked over and opened it. Inside were bottles of beer, bottles of Coke and other soft drinks—no food. I was now reminded by my stomach that I still hadn't eaten—at least not as far as I remembered.

I tried to wake Spanner again, but it was useless. I even turned him on his back, but he was in another land. Our clothes were neatly folded on the dining table. I stood there in my knicks. I decided a shower might help my condition. The shower was in the bath. I turned it on, adjusted the temperature, then sat down and let the water cascade over me. Tepid water raining on my head had a therapeutic effect. Occasionally, I stuck out my tongue and drank in some water, and slowly I began to feel better. I still could remember little from the night before after we had made the decision not to go back on-board.

I dried myself, and again tried in vain to wake Spanner. I pulled on my bell bottoms and white fronts, and decided to go outside to see what I could see. I walked around the pool and determined there was no way out, except through the house. I didn't have enough courage to go into the house, though. I sat on a sun lounger and rested my head in my hands.

'Hello there!'

A lady's voice startled me. I jumped up and spun round. I stumbled and tripped and ended in a kneeling position on the lounger. My head exploded again with the sudden exertion. My mouth had dropped open, and I wanted to wince.

'Oh, I'm sorry,' she said, raising her hands to her head. 'I didn't mean to startle you.' She stepped from the veranda and began to walk towards me. 'Did you sleep well?'

I got to my feet, and then backed away as she approached.

She stopped and, with concern on her face and caution in her voice, said, 'It's okay. I'm not going to hurt you.' And then she smiled again. 'You must be Chris.'

I was still looking at her wide-eyed and opened-mouthed.

'Mary said you were almost unconscious when you got here.'

Well, at least that answered some questions!

She had stopped now some distance in front of me, and put her hands on her hips as she asked again, 'Are you okay?'

I nodded, but knew I would have to speak. 'Yes,' I croaked.

'What about your friend?' When I didn't answer, she continued, 'Your friend Brian? Is he okay?'

'Yes,' I croaked again, and then said, 'He's still asleep.'

'Not surprised. It was very late when you all returned.' She was studying me, and I'm sure she had good reason to. I must have looked like a moron, and I certainly felt like one. 'Mary said you'll be staying for lunch.' She looked at me for confirmation. 'Will you?'

I still could not get my brain into gear. I half-turned and was willing Spanner to come to my aid, but I'm sure he was still in a different world.

'Chris, are you really okay?' Now her head was cocked to one side and she wore an inquisitive look on her face.

'Yes.' Now the croak was leaving my voice. 'I'm sorry. I didn't know where I was.'

She continued to look at me in the same way.

'I think I had too much to drink last night.'

'I am sure you did,' she said, nodding her head with each word for emphasis. 'You shouldn't be drinking at all. You are far too young.'

I regained some composure and just looked at her. I turned my palms towards her, hunched my shoulders, and raised my eyebrows as if to say, 'Well, that's life,' but actually I said nothing.

'Do you want some coffee or tea?' she asked brightly. 'Maybe some toast or something?'

'No,' I replied, shaking my head then regretting it. I desperately needed a hot drink, and toast sounded wonderful 'I'm okay, thanks.'

We stood looking at one another, and I knew she was thinking I was stupid. I guess she contemplated speaking further but, turning away, she said, 'Mary will be back soon.' And as she was walking away she said over her shoulder, 'I'll send her out as soon as she's in.'

I watched her walk back, ascend the steps to the veranda and disappear into the house.

I turned and sat on the lounger again and replaced my head in my hands. I felt low. I felt lower than a snake's belly in a wheel rut. I had heard someone say that and thought it good; the bottom of a wheel rut was lower than the gutter, and a snake's belly would lie flat against it. It was a fitting expression for my depression.

I must have laid back and drifted off to sleep in the warm sunshine. Spanner woke me up some time later. He had showered also and was dressed in his bells and white front.

'How do you feel, Clarkie?' he asked, and I knew he was suffering somewhat.

'I'm okay now, but was fucking rough when I first woke. 'All of a sudden, I felt brighter. Just having Spanner by my side gave me strength, although now I felt terribly guilty again—guilty for the fact I should have been on-board last night. I was also beginning to feel afraid; afraid of what would happen to me when I did get back. I looked at Spanner and he was looking at me; I knew he was feeling the same. We discussed our predicament. We contemplated returning to our ship, and then came up with the same answer as last night—if we go back, we cannot come ashore again during this stay in Cape Town. Therefore, our logic told us to remain ashore until just before the ship sailed. We had no plan what we would do except play it by ear and have a good time. We didn't even worry about money, and we didn't have a lot, especially me.

'So that's it then, Clarkie,' Spanner said with an air of finality. 'We have another five days of freedom before we face the music.'

With that, my heart gave a jolt of fear, which must have shown in my eyes, as Spanner reached across and patted my shoulder in an almost fatherly way.

'Don't worry. They can't hang us.' There were a few moments of silence between us, and then Spanner said in a brightening tone, 'Hey, that Sheila bird was all over you last night. Play your cards right and you could do her.'

I just looked at him as I had no recollection of last night except the way Sheila clung on to me on the dance floor. 'Spanner,' I said, looking at him, 'I was fucking pissed, man. I remember the Navigators' Den, but not leaving.' After a pause I asked, 'Did I just flake out?'

'Not exactly. But you were all over the place. Could hardly stand, man.'

I wanted to know how we got here and, sensing my thoughts, Spanner informed me the girls had arranged, and paid for, a taxi. He continued to tell me how Sheila wanted a goodnight kiss, but I could hardly stand. She left in a bit of a huff. Mary showed us to this room and left us to it. Sailors are always good at getting undressed and folding their uniforms, as we apparently did the night before. Spanner told me he was in love with Mary, and had to fuck her soon. Spanner's girlfriend in Portsmouth was also called Mary, which I though rather strange and somewhat ironic. Maybe he goes for Marys.

'Heyup, man,' Spanner said, slapping me on the knee. 'Here she comes.'

My attention was drawn to the door of the house and the muffled sound of Mary and the other lady talking. They both came out and walked towards us, though Mary was nearing a trot.

'Hello, you two,' she said cheerfully as she approached.

I couldn't believe it, but Spanner was actually blushing. He had gone bright red!

'This is my mum,' she said, reaching out for her as she joined us.

'Hello. You must be Brian?' her Mum said, looking intently at Spanner. 'You have certainly made an impression on my daughter in such a short time,' she added.

'Mum!' Mary scolded her mother, looking at her fiercely.

'Chris and I have already met,' her mother continued, ignoring her daughter's scorn.

'Sheila's coming to have lunch with us,' Mary said, turning to look directly at me. She was a beautiful girl, and no wonder Spanner had got the hots for her. 'She'll be here in about an hour or so.'

'Great,' I responded, not too convincingly.

'Well, you two look remarkably well after the state you were both in last night!' Spanner and I looked at each other and, when we didn't respond, Mary continued, 'Mind you, Sheila and I had had enough!' She then looked at her mother, who frowned at her whilst shaking her head as she began to return to the house.

'The youth of today,' she said wistfully, still shaking her head. 'Your father will be home soon, Mary,' she called as she re-entered the house.

Mary sat down next to Spanner. 'You feeling okay, Brian?'

Spanner glanced at her, almost shyly, and responded, 'I am now. And I'll be better still once I've had some food.'

'You hungry as well, Chris?' Mary asked me.

I was absolutely starving, but just said, 'Yeah, a little,' then added, 'I don't eat much.'

'Well, you're both skinny. But I suppose you make up for it in beer!'

We both looked at each other but said nothing.

'Chris, did you like Sheila?' Mary asked me, looking at me intently.

I returned her gaze, and again was spellbound by her beauty. After a pause, which was bordering on too long, I replied in the affirmative.

'She really likes you,' Mary informed me. 'She'll be here soon, and I know she's looking forward to seeing you not so drunk!'

'Well,' I said, 'it was our first day ashore for such a long time, and this beer here is different than in England.'

'I think it was the brandy that did it!' Mary said, giving me a way out.

'Suppose so.'

'Have you had something this morning?' Mary asked us both, tactfully changing the subject.

'No,' we replied in unison.

Spanner added, 'We have only just got ourselves together really. I could murder a Coke, though.'

'Hang on,' said Mary standing. 'I'll get you both one.' She skipped away in the direction of the house.

We both watched her go, then Spanner turned to me whilst rubbing his scrotum hard and with a screwed-up face agonisingly gasped, 'I have to fuck this fucking girl, you know, Chris, man. She's driving me fucking nuts.' His eyes were rolling as he said it. 'Her fucking mother aint bad either! I could fuck her as well.' He turned to me. 'What do you think, eh?'

I nodded slowly 'What about Mary in Pompey? I thought you were really in love with her?'

'Aye, man, she's fucking miles away,' he answered, looking hurt. 'You have a fucking girlfriend in England as well so you can't fucking talk!' He was still grasping and rubbing his scrotum.

'Yeah. But I don't go on about how much I love her and I'm going to marry her when we get back!'

'Yeah. But you do write to her all the fucking time.'

'No, I fucking don't! I write once every week or two,' I corrected him. 'You should know cos you copy my fucking letters.'

'Well. It's the same fucking thing.'

Mary reappeared from the house with a tray carrying two cans of Coke, two glasses and a jug of ice. We fell silent as she carefully made her way towards us. She sat the tray down on a small table beside us and then announced she was going to help her mum in the kitchen and again skipped away towards the house. Our eyes followed as she disappeared inside. Spanner once again resumed rubbing his knackers, moaning lewdly.

'Come on, you two,' Mary's mother hailed from the doorway. 'Lunch is almost ready. Sheila's here.' With that, she disappeared inside again.

My heart skipped a beat. Sheila had arrived! I didn't know what to say to her and so I started panicking, knowing I didn't have the fuzzy head of alcohol to support me. I really wanted the earth to envelope me.

'Come on, Clarkie! Let's get some scran!' Spanner said, rising and making for the door. 'I'm fucking starving,' he said over his shoulder as he made his way towards the house, expecting me to be behind him.

I had no option but to get up and follow, and I had to do it quickly to hide my fear. I caught up with him as he entered the door to the house. The door opened and I was awestruck with the sight beyond. The room, if you can call it that, was huge. The front door was opposite to this one some thirty feet away. Off to the right of the front door was a staircase sweeping upwards in a semi-circle to a galleried floor above. To our immediate left, again some thirty feet away, was an enormous dining table set for six people, although twelve would have been comfortable dining there. A crystal chandelier hung low above the table. Opposite to the area and left of the front door were three huge Chesterfield sofas of burgundy leather, strategically positioned around a large, low coffee table, and all in front of a grand open fireplace. A spray of dried, exotic flowers sat where a log fire would be in colder weather. The floor was chequered with an array of mats; I say mats but they were so much more. They must have been of the finest quality: Indian, Turkish and Persian, I am sure. Any one of these would have been too big for our lounge at Forty Foot. I am sure my jaw dropped when I saw the house, but I am also sure we must have passed through the place the night before as there was no other access to the back and the area from which we had just come. But still, I had no recollection of it.

I took all of it in within milliseconds, aware of Sheila's presence. She had just taken off a jacket and was hanging it on a row of pegs beneath the stairs. Her back was towards me and she was leaning over a bench, trying to reach the pegs. She wore a white cottony blouse and a flowery coloured skirt of the same material. Her pose accentuated her full hips and buttocks. She had a gorgeous arse, which aroused me.

Straightening up, she turned towards me and a smile filled her small face. 'Hello, Chris,' she said. 'How are you?' When I didn't answer, she continued, 'I hope you feel better than last night.' Her head cocked to one side as she finished speaking.

I had no idea what I had done last night. I don't know if I was bad, embarrassing or offensive, but it seemed it didn't matter to this beautiful young lady. Her eyes were boring into my soul, pleading for some response from me. I was overwhelmed with all the wonderful things I had seen in such a short space of time. I felt out of my depth, not in control, and just wanted to be out of there—if only to take my punishment back on-board. I had to get a grip and tried to play it cool.

'Oh, hello,' I said. 'Yeah, I'm fine now.' I slowly nodded my head, looking away from her and surveying our surroundings. She was still watching me. My eyes came back to hers, which had never left me. Her expression changed, and I detected some disappointment creeping in. I needed to recover the situation and so said apologetically, 'I think I had too much to drink last night. I hope I didn't do anything bad!'

Her face lit-up again, and she came towards me with her hands outstretched. Taking my hands, she said, 'No, no not at all.' She stood close to me now, her face close to mine. 'You were a perfect gentleman. Don't worry about it.'

'Mary, your father is coming up the drive. Let's get to the table,' Mary's mother called. It seemed this was a family of routine: the father came home for lunch and everything had to be ready. It seemed his time was limited before he had to return to work.

Sheila led me to the table, indicating she was a regular visitor to the house and with the licence of freedom. Mary had reached forward and took Spanner's hand, and was leading him to the table as well. Sheila and I sat on the side with our backs against the wall. Spanner and Mary sat opposite, their backs facing the front door. Spaces were laid at either end of the long table for Mary's mother and father.

The table was splendid; an array of cutlery was set out before me, along with glasses, and at the centre were three vases of fresh flowers. I had never sat at such a table ever in my life.

Mary's father entered the house and his wife greeted him at the door, took his jacket from him, and hung it next to Sheila's. He approached the table, rubbing his hands gently. 'Hello there,' he said in a deep rich resonant voice. 'I'm Jeremy.' He had a natural confidence, offering his hand to Spanner.

Spanner took Mary's father's hand and responded, 'Hello.'

'What's your name?' Jeremy asked after a small pause.

'Oh. Brian,' Spanner said, almost blushing.

Jeremy leant forward and gave his daughter a kiss on the cheek. He then walked around the table and extended his hand to me and, having learnt the routine, I took his hand and said, 'Hello, I'm Chris.'

'Pleased to meet you, Chris. In fact, pleased to meet you both, and welcome to our humble home,' he said, extending his arms and smiling broadly. He then leant forward and gave Sheila a kiss on the cheek, and asked. 'How are you, my sweet?' Sheila cooed and said nothing.

Natural Confidence Man took his position at the head of the table, but remained standing. He clasped his hands together and bowed his head. It seemed everyone else bowed their heads except Spanner and I, who just looked at each other across the table. Natural Confidence Man proceeded to give thanks, presumably to God, for the food we were about to enjoy. On completion, we all murmured *Amen*, which was the first time I had said grace since I was at junior school in Forty Foot.

With everyone seated at the table, a small, rotund, black lady emerged from somewhere off to our right. She wore a white dress and tunic, much like a nurse, and carried a silver tray with silver dishes loaded on it. She was followed by two black men wearing dark trousers and crisp white shirts. Each carried a tray similar to the lady. Plates were laid out before us and we were served with a variety of food items: a lump of meat, which Jeremy informed us was wild boar he had hunted in the outback some months before, was served along with vegetables. The serving dishes were left in the centre of the table should we want any more.

Whilst we ate, Jeremy asked about our life on the Hermes with genuine interest. Spanner responded most because he was older and had more experience. Jeremy wanted to know what we did on-board, and I didn't want to tell him I was acting as a waiter for the Senior Rates. I felt uncomfortable. Jeremy was too confident for me. Too intelligent and too well-educated.

I had eaten my food and was invited to help myself to more. I was still hungry, but I declined as I was too embarrassed to serve myself. I was scared I might drop something on the perfectly white tablecloth, and so I decided I'd rather be hungry.

Finally, Jeremy rose and announced he had to return to his surgery.

He left the table and walked across the room with his wife to collect his coat. They spoke in whispers, then his wife reached up and kissed him. 'Bye bye,' he said in the general direction of the table. 'Please come back and see us again whenever you want to.' This invitation was offered to Spanner and I, and we said goodbye in unison, raising our hand as we did. I felt relieved he had gone and wondered what we would do now. I didn't have to wait long, as Mary suggested we go for a walk in the park.

Sheila and I walked hand-in-hand behind Spanner and Mary, who walked in the same manner. Sheila explained more about her job and her ambition to drive long-distance touring coaches. She was fascinated about what we did on the ship and asked if she could pay a visit on-board. I don't think she understood our predicament, but I didn't explain; I simply said it wasn't possible at the moment. She held my hand warmly and clutched my arm with her other hand. She occasionally rubbed her cheek against my shoulder.

We were walking on an incline on the grass with Table Mountain in front of us. We arrived at a plateau and stopped to admire the view. Behind us lay the city, and beyond we could see Hermes by the dockside. It did look magnificent, and I felt proud I was somehow a part of it—quite ironic when you consider I was running away from it! We had stopped by a tree, and Spanner had walked on a little further. Sheila led me to this tree, and I leant against it. Sheila leant against me, and her head fell on my shoulder. I could smell the musk of her hair and feel all the curves of her body against me. She looked into my face and, again, I was captivated by her beautiful dark eyes. I could see more clearly the marks on her cheeks, left by acne, I concluded. There were no signs of any spots or pimples, and it seemed she was now clear of the affliction. I then had a horrible thought: I had seen people on-board, in the showers, who had similar acne scars on their faces. Some still had active pimples and angry red spots with yellow peaks. Most also had these spots on their backs, the back of their necks and buttocks. I wondered if Sheila had these on her back and the cheeks of her ample arse. I tried to look at her neck as she nestled her face against my collarbone. I stroked her head with an excuse to pull the hair to one side and peek more clearly.

She was cooing softly as I did this, thinking I was being affectionate. I was relieved to see the skin of her neck was free from blemishes, although it was much paler, being hidden from the sun most of the time. I ran my hand slowly over her back, inside her jacket and over the soft fabric of her blouse. I could feel her ribs and the knobbly bits of her spine. I could also feel her bra strap and the raised part of the clasp. Fortunately, I could not feel any bumps indicative of spots or boils. My left arm was about her shoulders and it was my right arm inside her jacket doing the exploring. I could see Spanner had assumed a similar position to me, his back against a tree and Mary leaning against him. I let my right hand explore lower to the narrow band of flesh beneath the blouse and before the skirt started. As I touched her flesh, Sheila gave a small shudder and pressed harder against me with a slight thrust of her hips. I knew if I allowed my hand to roam much lower, it would be exposed from the jacket and it could be seen, so I kept it under cover of the jacket.

Sheila lifted her face to mine and there was a faraway look in her eyes. She reached up and pulled my face towards her, and her lips crushed into mine. Her tongue pushed into my mouth, exploring mine, and a soft moaning sound reached my ears from the inside as it travelled through my head. My right hand was now on an upward route and, from the narrow strip of flesh, it continued on the inside of her blouse. Her skin was silky soft. I would bet she had never ever had any imperfection on it. I went higher and let my hand linger over the clasp to her bra. I could feel the hooks and eyes that kept the thing together, and I thought how easy it would be for me to dig my thumbnail behind the overlap of material holding the hooks on one side and, with my first and second fingers, pinch the other side, where the eyes were, and the clasp would be undone and the expanse of her back free. More erotically, her breasts would be free also. But I didn't; it was far too risky.

I reached up higher to her shoulder blades and then up to the nape of her neck. I had a swelling erupting inside my trousers, which I knew she could feel. Her hips were pressing against it. By now, her lips were nibbling at my neck and her heavy breathing was bordering on panting.

Her hands were on my hips, pulling me rhythmically towards her. My hand began to travel down again, and stopped when I reached the waistband of her skirt. I let my fingers slip inside. First one, then another, until most of my hand had disappeared there. My fingers played with the elastic of her knickers. I slid one finger inside this and then another followed. I could feel the crevice between her buttocks and felt the stiffening of the muscles each side of her spine as I massaged this hidden area of flesh.

Her face lifted up to mine again, and she blinked as if in slow motion. Her lips were moist, red and shiny. 'It's a pity it's not dark,' she whispered huskily. It was true. If it was dark, a knee crippler would be a reality.

'Come on, you two,' Mary called across to us, breaking this magical moment. 'Time to go.' This brought us both back to reality.

Sheila jerked her hips away from me and smoothed down the sides of her jacket. I turned away to hide my embarrassing bulge, and thrust my hands into my pockets to sort it out. Spanner's previous comment came to mind as I echoed his feeling that I had to fuck this girl—and soon.

Mary announced she was going to take us to a sports bar so we could play some darts, which sounded like a good idea.

I was getting uncomfortable with the situation with Sheila. I was happy to explore her body in the candid way I was doing it, but her gyrations against me were clear to see for any observer. I didn't want to tell her to stop or draw away from her, but the idea of being observed in a public park with her friend close by took me out of my sphere of comfort. I didn't want her to think I was a prude, and had it been dark then I would be happy—no willing, in fact—to continue in good old Woodstock style.

Sheila and I walked arm-in-arm behind Spanner and Mary. Spanner had his arm about Mary's shoulders, and Mary seemed happy for his closeness. However, she didn't seem so welcoming of his affections whilst he had his back to the tree in the park. Mary was different to Sheila: although they were friends and had been since they were children,

Mary was raised in a Christian, religious family, where the church played a big role in their lives. Mary was probably a virgin, whilst Sheila most probably was not, and sent out clear signals she was available. As I was slipping my fingers down the back of Sheila's knickers, I was looking over her shoulder to where our friends stood, and I could see Mary evading Spanner's advances. She did this in a manner not to offend him, because I felt she genuinely liked him, but rather she 'pecked' him on the cheek, but I knew Spanner wanted more.

I was surprised that Sheila had singled us out the night before: I was three years younger than she; I had a baby face; I didn't need to shave, but did so because I had heard that once you start the facial hair would grow more quickly and abundantly—but not in my case; I had no hair on my legs, and my chest was as smooth and clear as Sheila's unblemished back; I had only recently grown pubic hair, but this was still downy and soft; and I used to wet the bed up until about two years ago.

I had Kay in Spalding, who I thought was a beautiful girl, and over time she had let me feel her tits, put my hand in her knickers, and eventually fuck her. But she was not as beautiful as Sheila. Dianne also let me feel her tits, and they were much bigger than Kay's.

It seemed girls were attracted to me, which I was always surprised about. I was told I had beautiful eyes, and my teeth were straight, clean and white. I was only interested in girls who showed an interest in me. I didn't chase the good-looking ones in competition with all the other boys. If a girl showed interest, then I knew I was on to a good thing. I didn't even care if they were ugly! All I wanted to do was feel their tits outside their clothing. And preferably slide my hands inside their clothing and inside their bras. And of course slip my hand between their thighs up to the very top. Maybe force my hand inside their knickers from any angle to feel pubic hair. But of course, the ultimate goal was to stick my cock into them.

Kay was the best. Kay would get into bed with me naked and she would let me look at her naked. I was always looking to compare her; I wanted to see and feel other tits as I wanted to fuck other girls. I got aroused easily and always felt randy. But I considered myself normal.

We arrived at the sports bar, which was a drab place. There were two dart boards; one at either end of the large square room. Two dishevelled men were playing on the one furthest away. Each man had a dirty homemade cigarette hanging from his mouth, and close to them was a table full of beer bottles, most empty, and these surrounded an ashtray overflowing with dog-ends and ash. The room had several tables, each of steel frame construction with a melamine top. Steel-framed chairs were gathered around each table. Two of these tables were occupied with younger people smoking and drinking either beer or from bottles of Coke. Everyone looked up as we entered and admired our uniforms, and then afterwards paid us little attention.

The counter was a melamine top over a glass-fronted display cabinet. Inside the cabinet. I could see a few bread rolls, a variety of cakes, and some chocolate bars. An old man behind the counter looked upon us expectantly. I looked away as I was not going to buy anything! I walked to the other dart board and inspected the darts; not very good, but they would have to do. Mary ordered and paid for two bottles of Castle beer and two Cokes.

Whilst Spanner and I played darts, we discussed our immediate future. Mary said we could stay again whenever we wanted. The forefront of my mind was where was I going to fuck Sheila. The little house by the swimming pool would be difficult, if not impossible. Sheila lived in a house provided by the bus company, but we didn't speak much about it, so didn't know if it would suit. I told Spanner I didn't like Natural Confidence Man, and he concurred with me, so we really didn't want another encounter with him.

Sheila and Mary must have been thinking along similar lines to ourselves, as Sheila proposed we go to Muizenberg. She said one of her friends had a flat there, and we should make a visit. She said there was a strong possibility we would be able to stay there.

10: Muizenberg

Muizenberg is a seaside town close to Cape Town. It has a large, sweeping, sandy beach, which could be enjoyed by black people as well as whites. It seemed, apart from the streets, this was the only place where the two races could be seen together during this time. The rolling surf of the South Indian Ocean made this an ideal location for surfers.

The promenade had a line of colourful beach huts to facilitate the changing of bathers. People also would store beach chairs, towels and toys in these, much the same as many south-coast resorts in England.

Sheila's friend, Mandy, rented a small terraced house a little way back from the line of colourful beach huts, but in sight of the station clock tower.

It was early evening when we arrived, and we were surprised to see a party in progress. There were three sailors from the ship HMS Dido, which had docked at Simons Town a little way up the coast from Muizenberg. The Dido was on its way back to the UK, having spent several months in the Far East. There were a couple more local guys and some girls. Everyone seemed drunk. Beer bottles were strewn all over the place, along with glasses with varying levels of dark liquid in the bottom. Brandy bottles and Coke cans were also lying around. Ashtrays overflowed and a cloud of smoke hung in the room. Jimmy Hendricks boomed from a single-speaker record player.

We entered the house from the road and stepped into a kitchen area. Mandy was frying hamburgers, and chips sizzled in a deep fat fryer. The smell of burnt fat mingled with cigarette smoke. Mandy greeted us and gave a special hug to Sheila. Spanner and I were given a beer and sent through to the lounge area. We had to pass through no doors, as the lounge was just a large extension of the kitchen. We spoke to the sailors and learned that they, too, were also absent without leave, and had not decided whether or not they were going to return to their ship before it sailed!

There was a small dining table in a corner, and Spanner and I sat surveying the goings-on. Soon, Sheila came to me and told me she and Mary were going out to get some shopping. She had to lean close to me and shout in my ear to make herself heard as the party was so loud. She reassured me she would be back soon. One of the Dido sailors came over to speak with us. He was Welsh and introduced himself as Taff. He told us to get whatever we wanted; beer was in the fridge, along with Coke, and Cape Brandy was all over the place.

We drank our beer and Spanner indicated he was going to find more. Spanner returned with a beaming grin fixed to his face. He carried two opened bottles of beer in one hand and a plate full of freshly fried chips in the other. Piled on top of the chips was a stack of sliced bread. He placed the plate between us and gave me a beer. We both set about making chip butties. Take one slice of bread, cover half of it with chips and then fold it over. A real chip butty would need a thick slice of freshly carved bread, commonly called a 'doorstep', covered in butter. Before folding, tomato ketchup would be poured onto the chips. However, today, there was no butter, no ketchup, and only factory-sliced bread. Nevertheless, we had a feast. We were both so hungry.

We had more beer, and our confidence allowed us to seek out a couple of glasses and fill them with a cocktail of Cape Brandy and Coke. I was happy to remain in my seat by the table because I needed it for support; I was feeling fuzzy headed again.

Taff wobbled his way across to us and asked, 'Wanna try this, boyo?' as he offered us his dirty rolled-up cigarette. 'Fucking good shit.'

Spanner took it and looked at it. He then put it between his lips, whilst still holding it between forefinger and thumb, and inhaled deeply. The end glowed fiery red, and Spanner's cheeks were sucked into his teeth. He removed the cigarette, opened his lips, and sucked air into his lungs, taking down the inhaled smoke with it. He held his breath momentarily and then let out a stream of grey smoke. His eyes seemed to glaze over and he looked at Taff, nodding slowly. Spanner then passed the roll-up to me.

I looked down at it in disgust. It was wet and soggy at one end and dirty brown along its length. I mimicked Spanner's actions and, as I momentarily held my breath, with the smoke held in my lungs, I felt a wave of calm creep up my neck and flood my brain. I exhaled and passed the roll-up on. There, then followed a numbing of my brain. Music didn't seem so loud. My vision was shrouded by a tunnel of fuzziness. My limbs were heavy, and I could not move my arms. I slumped back in the chair and, using all my effort, was able to stop my head from rolling back or flopping onto my chest. Slowly, the paralysis of my brain receded and feeling returned to my limbs. I looked at Spanner, and his head was nodding to the beat of the music and his eyes were closed.

I remember Taff approaching more times, and each time we took our turn with the roll-up. Reality was a distant thing. I had no co-ordination between brain and limbs; my brain simply was not working. If I opened my eyes, nothing made sense. Eventually, blackness overcame me, and soon enough I sank into a deep pit of unconsciousness. I remember the blackness. No feeling—just a silent empty blackness.

The blackness receded with the recovery of my senses. I could hear distant music and people talking. I could feel my arms and legs, and there was a reddish glow at the back of my eyes. I opened my eyes and saw a ceiling. It was off-white and cracked. A lightbulb hung on a wire just to my side. I did not recognise the ceiling or the lightbulb. I did not know where I was, but more to the point, I didn't even care. I closed my eyes again and laid still.

I remembered the blackness and the strange feeling of it. In fact, there was no feeling; only silence. I wiggled my feet. I had no shoes on, and they were not covered. My hands were folded across my chest, and I wiggled my fingers. I opened my eyes again and scanned more of the room without moving my head. I felt fine; I had no pain anywhere. I sat up and discovered I was on a sofa. Spanner was slouched in a lounge chair opposite, his feet propped up on a soft footstool. He was snoring gently. I swung my feet to the floor and rested my elbows on my knees, my head in my hands. I rubbed my head and eyes. I knew I must have passed out as a result of the alcohol and whatever was in the roll-ups. I made a vow to myself, in that moment, never again to smoke that stuff—whatever it was. And I never did.

I stood and stretched. There was a window to my right that looked out towards the garden. Behind me was a door—the only door in the room. I opened it gingerly and peeped through into a lounge.

There were a boy and girl asleep, in an embrace, on the sofa. Taff was asleep on the floor, and the other two from Dido were in the garden, sitting on sun loungers, drinking beer and smoking in the sun.

The toilet was off the kitchen. I found it and emptied my bladder. I did not venture upstairs. I scanned the kitchen for some food and found it in a total mess; there were dirty pots, pans and plates all over the place, and the table was covered with dirty glasses.

I opened the fridge door and saw milk and beer. I took a bottle of beer and opened it. I found some old chips, on a plate, along with a half-eaten hamburger, and ate them for breakfast, swilling them down with the beer. I scavenged around for some more food and took another beer bottle from the fridge and carried it out to the garden. The two Dido guys were drunk and incapable of conversation, although they were talking, shouting and laughing at one another. I sat on a sun lounger at the bottom of the garden, facing the house so I could see what was happening. The sun felt good on my face, and the beer gave me a feeling of contentment. I was dozing.

'Hey, Clarkie,' Spanner said, kicking my feet and bringing me out of my sleep. He gave me another bottle of beer and sat on the lounger beside me. 'You were out of the fucking game last night, man.'

'Don't remember anything after that funny tobacco shite.'

'No, me neither. Well, not much.'

Spanner told me the girls came back, but Mary left as she was disgusted with all the drunkenness and drugs. He told me Sheila stayed and put me to bed on the sofa.

'So what's the plan then?' I asked him.

'We'll fuck off, I guess. Let's see if we can find a bottle of brandy to take with us.'

'So, where shall we go?'

'Dunno, let's get out of here first!'

As I entered the house, Sheila was just coming through from the kitchen. Her eyes lit up when she saw me. 'Well, you seem okay this morning.'

'Hi. I'm sorry about last night.'

'It's okay,' she said, waving her hand in the air.

'I had some of that funny tobacco stuff and I've never had it before. Sent me a bit loco.'

Sheila was shaking her head as she came to me. We embraced each other and I kissed her forehead. She pressed herself against me, which shot a current of desire through me.

'I have to go to work,' she told me with sadness.

'We are leaving also. But I don't know where my shoes are.'

She led me by the hand back to the room I had slept in, and showed me where she had placed them by a chair. We stood inside the door and, again, we grabbed hold of each other. I kicked the door shut and pushed her against the back of the sofa. She wore a dress that resembled an oversized tee-shirt, which hung loosely about her. I could feel every detail of her through the thin material. My hands skimmed over the back of her bra and down her back. She had hitched herself up the back of the sofa, much like a guy would perch on a high bar stool, and wrapped her legs around me. My hand went between her legs, and I could feel her knickers and the softness they were hiding. She was pulling at the front of my trousers, and I helped her. She freed my hard cock and I pulled her knickers to one side. I was inside her with wanton eagerness. *Bang, bang, bang* and then the explosion. She relaxed a little, but I remained inside her, moving slowly. We heard the door open and she jumped to her feet. Her dress immediately fell back into place, and I moved off to the side with my back to the door. I sat on a lounge chair, leaned forward, covering myself as I replaced my shoes.

'Oh! Sorry,' said Spanner as he came in to retrieve his shoes. My belt was still buckled, so he would have noticed no difference from the back.

Sheila left the room, and I finished with my shoes and put myself away. I caught up with her in the kitchen as she was about to leave. I grabbed her arm and we looked at each other. I don't think she was very happy with me, but her face softened. I held her again, and we agreed to write to each other. She then left.

Spanner and I found a bench by the beach in amongst the bathing huts, and proceeded to drink a stolen bottle of Cape Brandy with some Coke we had purchased from a small newspaper shop nearby. We had no glasses, so we had to take a swig from the bottle, then a swig from the can. It wasn't too long before we were both drunk again and talking rubbish.

Spanner asked me my opinion of Mandy, Sheila's friend.

'She's fairly good-looking, I suppose,' I answered.

'So you think she's fairly ugly, then.'

'No. Why do you say that?'

'Well, there must be a degree of ugliness there, else she'd be beautiful!'

'So, Spanner, what you are saying is someone can be beautiful and ugly at the same time?'

'No. If she's ugly, she's ugly. If she's beautiful, she's beautiful. If she's not completely beautiful, then she must be a bit ugly.'

'So, one end of the scale is ugly and the other beautiful. Right?' I was trying to rationalise his theory with my fuzzy mind.

'It's like a wedge. Imagine a long wedge with the thick end to the right and it tapering off to the left.' He was drawing a wedge in the sky as he said this. I nodded. 'Now, imagine another wedge with the thick end to the left tapering off to the right.' I nodded again. 'Now put one wedge on top of the other.'

'And you end up with a long rectangle with a diagonal line.'

'Right. Now, if one wedge is a degree of ugliness and the other a degree of beauty, then unless you are a hundred percent beautiful or a hundred percent ugly, you must have a bit of both.'

'So,' I said with understanding, 'if you are in the middle of the rectangle, you are as equally ugly as you are beautiful.'

'You got it, Clarkie.'

I wanted to ask him how far along the scale you have to be to describe someone as 'fairly good-looking', as I had described Mandy earlier. I realised the brandy was influencing this conversation, so resigned myself to Spanner's philosophy.

It was quickly becoming late evening now, so we took a walk along the beach huts. We tried all the doors and locks. We were looking for a place to spend the night. All the doors were locked tightly shut. We even tried force, but didn't want to cause undue damage. In the end, we gave it up as a bad idea.

We decided we wanted a beer, so counted how much money we had. Not much, but enough for a couple. We decided to go into the Muizenberg Hotel with the idea our uniforms might attract some interest and someone would buy us a beer.

The bar was empty. We sat on bar stools, and Spanner ordered two beers. Fortunately, the bar tender wanted to engage us in conversation, so served us with no problem. After a while, we disclosed our situation to the barman, telling him we were AWOL, and did he know a good place we could spend the night. We also told him we had no money. We even asked if we could sleep in the bar as the soft benches looked inviting. The man began to serve us beer for which we were not paying, which helped things a little. Spanner and Mr Bar Tender started to talk politics, which soon bored me to death, as I knew nothing about the subject. I decided it was too difficult sitting on the barstool and so made the decision to sit in the comfort of a padded bench at a table.

Finally, Mr Bar Tender announced it was time to shut the bar. 'If you really have nowhere to stay, I'll let you have a room for the night.'

We couldn't believe our good fortune!

'You can have breakfast but you'll have to be out by eleven.'

We thanked him and he showed us to a room.

The Muizenberg Hotel was a luxury hotel, and we had our own bathroom. 'I'm going to wash this lot,' Spanner said, ripping off his white fronts. We had worn the same garments since we had come ashore, and so they were in desperate need of washing. We washed our knicks and socks as well, and then showered. Soap, shampoo and deodorants were also provided.

We slept late and only woke when the housekeeping lady knocked on the door. Hurriedly, we dressed and went to the dining room for breakfast. Everything was on offer: eggs—fried, boiled, poached or scrambled, bacon, beans, tomatoes, mushrooms, black pudding, devilled kidneys. There were kippers and smoked haddock. Cereals of all kinds were for the taking. Bread rolls, toast and fried bread. Tea, coffee, orange juice, tomato juice, pineapple juice—the lot! We had a feast.

We returned the key, said thanks once again, and left. We were fed, washed and sober. We had clean clothes, clean shoes, and smelled of cologne.

11: The Spine Surgeon and His Wife

We had decided we had had enough of Muizenberg and that we should return to Cape Town. We hung out our thumbs by the side of the road, and virtually the first car that approached us slowed to a stop by our side. It was a large saloon car, and the nearside window buzzed down. Electric! This impressed us. I'd only ever seen electric car windows in films. The driver was a lady of about thirty years old. She leant across the front passenger seat and peered up at us.

'You two must be going to Cape Town,' she enquired. 'Jump in. It's your lucky day.'

Spanner got in the front and I slipped in behind. As she pulled away, she asked, 'Are you going back to your beautiful ship?'

'No! No, not yet,' Spanner replied, almost a bit too urgently. 'We don't have to be back until tomorrow.'

'Oh. Well, I'm going through the town, so you'll have to let me know when you want to get out.'

The lady introduced herself as Sandra, and a series of questions followed about ourselves and what we did on the ship. We repeated lines we had used many times; with the hope we didn't sound too complacent.

Spanner did most of the talking on our behalf, whilst Sandra threw me glances from her rear-view mirror. Her face was long and thin, and she was very attractive. She was confident, and we guessed she was wealthy. Her nose was on the large size, yet it didn't detract from her beauty. Her pale blue eyes were sharp and bright, and thin dark brows danced above them, enhancing her expressions.

Donovan sang from the radio about a caterpillar. A stupid song—first about a mountain and then no mountain and then a mountain.

The car was luxurious; comfortable, quiet, spacious, and with a smell of leather intermingled with perfume. I caressed the leather seats and wondered how much something like this would cost.

As we approached the city, Sandra asked where we wanted dropping off. We didn't really know, and we had not had the opportunity to think about it. Sandra sensed our indecision and then enquired, 'Do you want to come home with me?' She asked this cheerfully and by way of a solution. 'I can make you some lunch, and I know John would love to meet you two?' The question hung in the air, and Sandra side-glanced at Spanner and peered at me via her mirror.

The thought of more free food was appealing and, looking at the back of Spanner's head, I answered, 'Sounds like a good idea to me,' willing Spanner to acquiesce.

'You sure it's okay?' he said, turning to Sandra.

'Of course I'm sure,' she assured us. 'It'd be great to have you both. You'll have a good time.'

'Okay,' Spanner said finally. 'We have no other plans really.'

As Sandra drove to her house, she explained her husband, John, was a surgeon at the Maimonides Hospital, where the first heart transplant had taken place.

'Is he a heart surgeon?' Spanner asked, as if all surgeons there should be heart surgeons.

'No,' Sandra answered, shaking her head. 'He specialises in spinal surgery.'

'Are you a doctor?' Spanner asked her.

'No. I studied law, but never practised.' After a pause she continued,

'I met John and we married, and he doesn't want me to work. That was five years ago.' It seemed there should be more to be said, but neither of us asked any further.

We drove on, passing the city to our right and the Hermes to our left. Sandra slowed to absorb the view of the ship; a menacing mounting of steel with folded wing fighter planes jutting their pointed noses towards the city. It was a magnificent sight that, once again, stirred some pride within me.

After about an hour, we arrived at Sandra and John's house; a sprawling villa surrounded by big-leafed trees and guarded by high fences with an automatic steel gate. An old black man appeared from the trees and waved at us. Once he had received a return wave from Sandra, he disappeared into the trees from whence he came. The car came to a halt by the steps to the front door, and we all got out. Sandra ascended the steps whilst Spanner and I stretched and took in what we were seeing.

Sandra was tall. She wore a pale blue jumper of fine wool, which hugged her body. She also wore dark blue trousers, which showed off the curvaceous shape of her hips, buttocks and thighs. The trousers flared from the knees into bell-bottoms, which flapped around small open sandals. The eyes of Spanner and I followed every movement she made as she mounted the steps. We watched the muscles in her legs tense and relax as she climbed, and saw the sway of flesh as she moved from one step to the next. She was a very sexy lady.

As she disappeared into the house, Spanner turned to me and, once again, grabbed his scrotum, massaged the handful, and moaned whilst shaking his head. 'I could fuck her, Clarkie,' he murmured to me.

'Come on!' she beckoned from within the house, and so we followed.

The entrance was cool with a marble floor. Off to our right was a large dining table set for six people. Beyond this was a lounge area with two large sofas facing each other across a low glass-topped table. Beyond was an open space with two lounge chairs positioned so the seated could look through the large French windows to a patio area, where the glistening blue water of a swimming pool pleased the eye. To the left of the two lounge chairs was the kitchen. The natural light from the front windows lit the dining table, and light flooded through the French windows to the loungers. Such was the size of the room the light did not penetrate the two sofas, and these sat in a more subdued ambience.

Sandra opened the French windows and invited us to sit on the lounge chairs. 'Do you want a beer?' she asked 'You do drink beer, don't you?' she asked earnestly.

'Yes, please,' we both said in unison.

Things are looking up, I thought to myself, but said nothing.

Sandra placed another small table between the two lounge chairs and disappeared into the kitchen. We sat and she returned with two bottles of Castle beer and two glasses.

'Oh, I'm sorry,' she said apologetically, 'would you prefer wine? I should have asked before.'

'No, this is fine,' we assured her.

'I prefer wine,' she said, and returned to the kitchen to emerge again with a glass of pale liquid in a long-stemmed glass.

We relaxed, sipped our drinks, and answered politely when Sandra asked about England, Hermes, and our girlfriends. She was very easy to talk to. She was rich, sophisticated, educated, yet we were at ease with her. At times, her eyes would bore into mine and fix them for a longer stare. She was a mature woman, and I was hugely attracted to her.

'Have you had a CapeT-bone yet?' she asked us, looking to each of us in turn.

What the fuck is that? I thought. I looked at Spanner, who returned my stare blankly.

It's a steak,' she added. 'Cape Town is famous for them. Look,' she said, 'I can fix us a snack now, and then this evening we can go out and get a steak.' She was looking at us to say something. When we didn't, she continued, 'John would really love to meet you both. We can go out and you can stay here tonight. We have plenty of rooms.'

We shrugged our shoulders, raised our eyebrows, and could think of nothing else to say other than 'Okay'. I think Sandra was looking for more enthusiasm from us, and I detected she was a little disappointed.

'The problem is,' I said rather sheepishly, 'we don't have much money to go out.'

'Money?' she exclaimed 'You don't need money! You're our guests!'

'You sure?' I asked.

'Positive,' she said, closing the subject.

Once again, Sandra went to the kitchen, and Spanner and I exchanged glances and revelled in our good fortune. We knew we were going to get fed and we would end up being pissed again on free beer! This would be our last night, as the next day we had to return to face the music. The ship would sail the following morning, and all shore leave would come to an end the night before. We dare not risk missing the ship, so we decided tonight would have to be our last.

Sandra once again returned with a tray of small sandwiches, sausages on sticks with cheese, slices of pie, and many other things we had never before seen, along with salad. We ate, and Sandra brought us more beer when we needed it.

John came home and breezed into the house. 'Hi, you two,' he greeted us with an outstretched hand. 'I'm John,' he added. Of course we knew what to do now, and so we made our introductions with confidence. John was a big man. He was tall, overweight, partially bald, and much older than his wife. He spoke with a slightly different accent than the rest of the South Africans, but he explained he was an Australian who had served in the Australian Navy. 'So, really, I'm like you guys,' he announced with enthusiasm. 'Glad to see you got a beer! I could use one myself,' he said. 'San, bring us some beer, will ya?'

John told us he had served two years' national service as a seaman. He said he really loved the Navy, but he also wanted to finish his medical studies. He added that he didn't know if he had done the right thing, because now all he does is go from home to the hospital and then back home again. 'Boring,' he said.

Spanner said he wished he had never joined the Navy and that he wanted to get out. Everyone said this, though. Spanner told John he missed his girlfriend in Portsmouth and all he wanted to do was to get out of the Navy so he could marry her. John scoffed at this remark and said the Navy is a wonderful life, and we would have a wonderful future. I didn't really want to get into this argument, so just sat back and enjoyed my beer.

'I'm going for a quick swim,' John announced. 'Do you guys wanna join me? We have plenty of shorts and things for you in the cabana.' He indicated to the little house next to the swimming pool. We declined his offer.

Sandra announced she was going to take a shower and get changed, and asked if we needed anything else. She indicated to the kitchen and invited us to get whatever we wanted. Spanner and I sat in silence. We watched John belly-flop into the pool at one end, breast stroke to the other, then return on his back to where he had entered. He exited the pool using the shiny ladder, then disappeared into the house via a door somewhere off to the left, beyond the kitchen.

Spanner and I succumbed to the tranquillity of the moment, along with the effects of the alcohol and the warm sun beating down upon us through the open French windows. We napped.

'Aye up, Clarkie.' Spanner woke me, banging my knee with his fist.

I sat up and looked around me. Remembering where I was, I could hear Sandra and John talking at the other end of the room, although I could not hear exactly what they were saying. I stood up and checked my balance. I needed a piss—badly. 'Where's the bog?'

'Fucked if I know,' he replied, 'but I fucking need it.'

Sensing our problem, Sandra shouted across to us there was a toilet through the kitchen and another in the cabana by the pool. We sorted ourselves out and returned to the lounge. 'You two ready?' John called to us from near the front door.

'Ready,' I said, and we made our way to them.

Sandra was wearing a red dress; a simple design with thin shoulder straps holding the material above her breasts. The material was gathered in under her breast, and then it seemed to balloon out and hide the curves of her hips and buttocks. The hem, just above the knee, and the dress was light and billowy. Apart from the thin straps, her shoulders were bare, telling the tale she wore no bra. This thought excited me, and I searched the curves of her bosom for further confirmation of this. I looked up to her face, and she was watching me. A small smile played at her lips as her eyes never left mine. I felt blood rush to my face, but held her gaze further.

'Let's go then,' John said, opening the door.

I followed Sandra out, watching the dress float about her.

John took us to a restaurant called The Blue Clog. It was rustic. Inside resembled a log cabin, and the furniture was all made of heavy wood; thick planks and rounded trunk legs. We were shown to a table for four in a booth, with church pew-like benches at each side. I sat by the wall with Sandra next to me. Spanner sat opposite me with John next to him. It was almost as if they were hemming us in.

John ordered and beer came. A man appeared, who introduced himself as the owner and presented us with a bottle of wine. He said he was honoured that he should be visited by English sailors from the warship in the bay. Apparently, we were the first to visit. We thanked him and the wine was poured.

The meal was served on a breadboard-type slab of wood. An enormous T-bone steak surrounded with salad and a slice of pineapple—the latter of which was a strange addition, I had thought at the time. We all tucked in. The meat was succulent. I had never eaten anything like it in my immature life. We ate slowly, which was necessary: the food deserved to be savoured. I followed the example of Sandra and John, as did Spanner. At times, the knives and forks would be laid down and hands were used to gently dab the lips with the serviette, or to take up the wine glass. Sandra would rest her hands in her lap as she continued her conversation with us. This, I thought, was good deportment, as it prevented the possibility of resting the elbows on the table, which I was always brought up to believe was bad manners. Between bouts of eating, I did the same. As Sandra moved her hands, her elbow knocked against mine. She put her hand briefly, and lightly, on my thigh, and apologised. I raised my hand as a sign of no importance, and moved closer to the wall so as to give her more space. Our elbows began to knock again, but not clumsily. The contact was really imperceptible, except for the fact I had moved, and electricity flowed each time she touched me. Then her hand rested on my thigh again. She said nothing. Several times this happened, and then I noticed every time Sandra's hand left the table, it resumed its position on my thigh. The conversation again turned to our girlfriends, and we spoke of Mary and Sheila. Both John and Sandra were asking how far our intimacy had gone, but in a manner that could be construed as joking and just making fun. We had been drinking a lot, so our inhibitions were down. Spanner told them that Mary was religious, and so not promiscuous. He said further that he didn't think she had lost her virginity yet. Spanner went on to tell them about Sheila, and how she was all over me. I felt embarrassed that he should be speaking like that, but I was glad he didn't know what had gone on in her friend's house the other day.

Sandra turned to me and said, 'My word, Chris, that must have been terrible for you.' Her hand was squeezing me gently. 'Did you get turned on?'

I had to brave this out. 'Aw, it happens all the time,' I said, thanks to the fortification of the beer and wine. 'All the girls are after me,' I added, as if I meant it.

John was looking at me with a silly grin on his face.

'And what about you, Brian?' he asked. 'Do you have the same problem with the girls?'

'Yeah,' Brian responded, with the same air of bravado, 'but nothing I can't handle.' This sort of banter continued for a while, all in good humour. John said he wished he was younger, as things are very different now from when he was our age.

'You men are all the same,' Sandra said, almost as a sneer. 'One-track minds,' she added, still massaging my thigh.

It was late when we returned to their house. I was drunk. I could still stand and walk, but I couldn't trust myself to talk, so I stayed silent.

'Who's up for a night-cap?' John asked, overly cheerful.

'I think these boys have had enough for one night!' Sandra said. 'I think we should call it a day. I'm ready for my bed, even if nobody else is!'

Sandra took my hand and led me to the left of the front door and to a small bedroom. It had a single bed. 'This is for you. Will you be alright?' she asked with some concern.

I nodded, turned, slumped on the bed, and began to remove my shoes.

'Goodnight, Chris.' She turned. 'Sleep tight.' I heard her call Spanner and direct him to a room, which I assumed to be next to mine. I heard her wish Spanner goodnight, and then I heard her walk further down the passageway, away from where I was. I heard muffled voices of John and Sandra, and I heard Spanner getting into bed.

I got undressed and into bed. I knew the room would spin, and I hoped I would sleep before the spinning turned to nausea. I was soon in an inky blackness. My head seemed as if it were wrapped in cotton wool. I was floating, and my senses were dulled. My arms and legs had a mild form of pins and needles. Sandra's hand was no longer on my thigh. It was on my chest, her heat flooding into me. I had an erection, and butterflies danced on my manhood and around my lower abdomen. There was a heat there, too, and a hand cupped my testicles. My cock was so hard, I feared it would snap off. I reached down to comfort myself, but my hand didn't feel me. It felt hair. Long hair. It felt a head. My confusion bordered on fear, and it chased the inky blackness away. I wanted to scream, but I could only grunt. The hand from my chest moved up and covered my mouth. And then I realised: it was Sandra's hand—and it was Sandra's head.

My cock was in Sandra's mouth. I was no longer asleep, but I didn't know if I was dreaming. Her head was moving up and down, and her tongue was licking the length of me. I looked down, and she looked up at me. With one finger on her lips she intoned, 'Shhhh. 'She then resumed her business.

It was all too much for me. My feet balled up into fists and my legs shuddered uncontrollably. My stomach muscles bunched, fit to burst. I exploded in her mouth. I erupted gush after gush, with each gush sucked from me. Finally, the cold air hit my penis as she raised her head from it.

She put a finger on my lips and moved up to kiss me through her finger. 'Shhhh,' she said again, and I could smell my liquid on her breath. 'Shhhh,' she said, rising.

She had on a long nightdress that made her look surreal. She took two steps backwards, turned, and glided out the open door. I touched myself there, pinched myself, and had to conclude that it did happen. I listened in the darkness, but heard nothing. I lay awake for a long time, not knowing whether I should feel ashamed. Finally, I drifted back into the comfort of sleep.

I eventually woke from a deep slumber. I had no ill aftereffects of the alcohol. I lay awake for some moments, remembering the events of the previous night. My heart was quickening as again, a feeling of guilt flooded through my mind; mainly about Sandra and what she did to me or, more importantly, what I did to her. I had heard of oral sex, but had no experience either giving or receiving. Whilst I remembered, I was both excited and disgusted. I had mixed feelings about Sandra now. How could she do such things? Putting someone's cock in your mouth, and then swallowing what came out? I'm sure she wouldn't drink piss, and I didn't consider there would be much difference! Why did she do it? But I didn't ask her. I did wonder if she got pleasure from it. I questioned whether she was weird. Things didn't make sense to me. I then asked myself: if she wanted to do it again, would I let her? I guessed I probably would. In fact, I knew I would because I was getting aroused just thinking about it. I wondered if she had done it to Spanner. Had she done it to Spanner before me? I cast the thought from my mind.

Today was the day we would return to the ship. I felt guilty and nervous about that, also. Part of me was looking forward to it, though, just as a way of eliminating the unknown.

'I see you're fucking awake then, Clarkie,' said Spanner cheerfully, breezing into my room. 'Here,' he said, throwing me a pair of shorts and a tee-shirt. 'Put these on, then we can loaf by the pool this morning.' And with that, he left.

I strained my ears for other sounds to determine who was here, but I could hear nothing. I got up, dragged on the shorts, and pulled the tee-shirt over my head.

Spanner was sat by the pool with John, and both looked up as I joined them. It was late morning and the sun shone brightly.

'Hi, Chris,' John said cheerfully. 'How did you sleep?'

A prang of guilt arose in me, and I shot him a quick look, but I couldn't detect any ulterior motive for the question.

'Really well,' I told him.

'There's some cooked bacon in the kitchen for you to make a butty, if you want,' he informed me, and I could see the remnants of such things on the plates before him and Spanner. 'There's juice in the fridge, too,' he shouted after me as I made my way to the kitchen. I wondered where Sandra was and supposed she would be in the kitchen.

'San will be back soon. She's had to pop out for a bit,' John explained, answering my thought question.

I returned with my butty and pulled up a deck chair and joined the two men. I sat in front of them, facing the house. Spanner was telling John about his childhood in Yorkshire, and how it came about that he joined the Navy. I sat in silence, ate my breakfast, and listened. I kept an eye on Spanner to determine if he had been visited the night before, as I had. His eyes gave nothing away, and I was convinced he slept undisturbed.

I heard the front door slam and the faint shout of 'Hello,' followed by 'I'm back.' I don't think John or Spanner heard, but my heart skipped a beat. *What will she say to me?* I wondered. *What will she do?* I felt panic creeping up on me. I would pretend nothing happened, unless she said or did anything.

I saw her walk from the front door towards me. She was carrying two paper shopping bags in her arms, and she turned and entered the kitchen. A few seconds later, she came out of the kitchen and stood in the open French doorway. She wore a white dress, which hung from her shoulders, although it was gathered in at the waist. It floated about her as she moved. Again, no bra. She was beautiful. She stood with one arm raised, resting against the frame, although she was not leaning on it. 'Hi, Chris,' she said to me cheerfully, as John had done earlier. This indicated

Spanner must have been up before she left, because she didn't greet him.

'Hi,' I answered, raising my hand in acknowledgement of her greeting.

'Did you have pleasant dreams?' she enquired, and a smile passed her lips.

John and Spanner had their backs to her, and so didn't notice this.

'I was too tired for dreams,' I told her, to which she raised her eyebrows.

'I slept like a log,' she said, turning as she went back into the kitchen.

The three of us remained outside, swimming, lounging and chatting. Sandra kept coming out with fresh beer and asking if we wanted anything else. I'm sure the 'anything else' was directed at me.

Late in the afternoon, Sandra announced that lunch was ready, and we filed into the house. The dining table had been re-laid with four places. I was directed to a seat facing the front window. John sat next to me, but closer to the wall. Spanner was instructed to sit opposite John, and Sandra would be next to him and opposite me. This table was much bigger than the table we had occupied the night before, and the space between us was much greater. There would be no opportunity of hands-on-thighs today!

Sandra brought a serving trolley from the kitchen, which carried our lunch. She had prepared a fish stew with salad. There also were dishes of new potatoes and vegetables. It looked wonderful, and the smell was even more appetising. We began to eat.

Sitting opposite Sandra meant every time I looked up, I was looking straight at her. There was always a knowing look in her eye, and still she maintained eye contact for long periods. As she worked her knife and fork, I could see the gentle swing of her unharnessed breasts. I studied these, and knew what movements would create the biggest swings. The neckline of her dress was low, but not too low to reveal any cleavage. Sandra knew I was looking at her, I'm sure. Spanner and John were talking cricket, both with knowledge and enthusiasm. Sandra and I did not join in this conversation, due to our ignorance and distaste for the sport. Sandra, again, quizzing me about my girlfriends.

At one point, Sandra stood, reached for the serving spoon of the fish stew, and asked me if I would like a little more, leaning across to me as she did so, and stretching out with the loaded spoon. She placed her left hand on the table for support, as she was determined to serve me and not wait for my answer. The distance between us meant she had to lean low in order to reach me. The front of her dress hung in an arc, and inside the thin material were her breasts, swaying gently. Slightly lighter than the colour of the skin of her arms, each inverted mound was capped off with the darker brown and textured skin of the nipple. Blood shot to my face and to my loins instantaneously. My face went red, I could feel, and my loins hardened. From my peripheral vision, I could see our dining companions were oblivious to my treat—and believe me: it was a treat! Her tits jiggled more as she shook off the load from the spoon. I knew she was looking at me, but I couldn't drag my eyes away at this moment. 'Enough?' she asked.

I looked into her knowing eyes and replied, 'Yes,' then added, 'thank you.' She returned the empty serving spoon to the tray, and then sat. My heart was beating hard, and I was scared someone might hear it. I had to make an adjustment at the front of my shorts.

When all of us were done eating, Spanner was quizzing John as to how he could fake an injury or ailment that would warrant a medical discharge from the Navy. John didn't want to really enter into such a discussion, but Spanner was quite forceful. I remember John saying that a complaint of a back problem could be very difficult to disprove. I wanted to warn Spanner about faking an ailment, but he did not know the truth about my excursion to the hospital in Elgin some weeks beforehand so I decided to say nothing.

Sandra stood and began to gather plates, piling them in front of her. As she leant against the table, her dress material was held tight to her thighs. A dark triangle could be seen nestling at the base of her tummy. At first I thought this to be her knickers, but there was no elastic around her hips. She was looking down at me as she arranged the things on the tray, and continued to clear the table. 'Put these things on the trolley for me, Chris,' she asked, 'and you can help me in the kitchen whilst these two continue their plotting.'

I followed Sandra to the kitchen, pushing the trolley in front of me. Sandra stood at the kitchen sink with her back to me. She busied herself with dirty plates and things. She then turned around and leant her buttock against the edge of the sink. Her feet were slightly apart, and some short distance away from the base of the work units. This was a very provocative pose.

'I caught you looking at my titties, didn't I?' she teased in a husky voice. She looked down to her chest and said again, 'Didn't I?'

I couldn't speak. I didn't know what to say.

She then reached up and pulled the hem of her neckline down, freeing her tits. They both popped out and swayed slightly. She held the hemline under her breasts and gently jiggled them. They jiggled wonderfully. 'Give me your hands, 'she said, reaching out to me.

I took two steps towards her and gave her my hands. She pressed each one flat against each breast. I just stood there.

'Squeeze them gently,' she whispered to me.

I did as she asked, with her hands on top of mine, assisting me.

'You can gyrate your hands as well, like this,' and she moved my hands in circles. I was squeezing and rubbing. 'Can you feel my nipples?' she breathed. 'Can you feel how hard they are?' I could. 'Squeeze the nipple,' she hissed, manoeuvring my hand so the nipple poked up between my thumb and the knuckle of my forefinger. 'Girls like it when boys play with their nipples, Christopher,' she said, breathing heavily. 'Always spend time on a girl's nipples, Chris, baby,' she continued. 'Kiss my nipple, Chris,' she invited, reaching up with her hand and pulling my head down. 'Kiss it, Chris. Kiss it,' she hissed, sucking air in deeply through her teeth. 'Now suck it. Suck it like a baby,' she commanded.

I took the nipple between my lips and sucked it into my mouth. I could feel her back stiffen as I did so. I sucked the hardened nipple between my teeth and bit down gently. Again, she stiffened. I flicked my tongue across the nipple rapidly and her breath quickened.

'Now the other one, Chrissy,' she panted as she moved my head from one to the other. 'That's beautiful, Chrissy,' she hissed. 'Beautiful.

Beautiful. Beautiful'. She continued, 'Do you do this to your girlfriend, Chrissy?' she asked.

I didn't but didn't say anything.

'Chrissy, always spend time on a woman's breasts,' she affirmed. 'All the doors will open then.' She then took my right hand and guided it down to that secret area at the base of the tummy. 'Feel this,' she invited. 'Don't grab it. Just rub it gently.' Her hand was again on mine, pressing my hand onto her pubic bone. I could feel her pubic hair underneath the material of her dress. Her fingers pushed my fingers down to the crevice normally protected by the closed legs. 'Just rub it gently, Christopher.' There was huskiness in her voice again. 'You have to find the spot, Christopher.' She continued taking my index finger and working it into the top of the crevice. 'There,' she whispered, stiffening. 'Can you feel it? Always find the clitoris, Chris. Always find the clitoris. Massage it gently.' Her eyes were rolling in their sockets and her head was thrown back, her face up to the ceiling. Her right hand reached up to my shoulder, and she pushed me down. 'Look,' she commanded. 'Kneel,' she demanded further, and as I knelt before her she pulled up her dress with both hands and tucked it behind her buttocks, trapping the material against the sink unit.

There, in front of my eyes, was the most perfect hairy triangle. I had never seen one so close.

She reached down with her right hand and, with her fingers, parted the skin of her vagina where the crevice started at the top. 'See that?' she hissed. I did: she had opened a small hood that revealed a tiny pimple of a button. It resembled a minute head of a penis. As she pulled the skin apart, she tapped the button with her middle finger. 'See that, Chrissy? That's my fucking clit. That's what you have to find.' She was breathing hard now. Drawing in sharp breaths through her teeth, she said, 'Lick it, Chris! Lick it!'

She wanted me to lick it! She wanted me to lick where she pisses from! I was excited, but also appalled, bordering on disgusted.

'Lick it!' she said again, pressing my head into her.

I could smell her. The scent of a woman is indescribable. I stuck out my tongue and tasted her. She stiffened again as I touched her. I played with her clitoris, with my tongue, as I had played with her nipples earlier.

'Suck it, Chris,' she urged. 'Suck my fucking clit.'

She was pulling my head down hard now in jerky motions, banging my nose into her pubic bone. She was going crazy, and I didn't know if I should be afraid or not.

'Yes,' she hissed. 'Yes, Chris.' She began to shudder 'Yes. Yes. Fucking yes!'

I thought she was having a seizure. She shuddered more and more, and then seemed to relax some. She took my head between her hands and lifted my face. She let her buttock slip down the kitchen cupboard doors until she was on her haunches in front of me.

'You made me come, Chris,' she sighed with a faraway look in her eyes. 'My first orgasm in years.' She reached out and released me from my shorts. She stroked my cock, and it responded by spitting my juices all over her rumpled up dress. 'My my,' she cooed. 'You were ready!'

We both stood and she let her dress fall back into place. A quick flick of the neckline hem and her tits were back inside, hidden from view. I pulled up the waistline of my shorts and my tee-shirt fell back into place. We were decent again.

'Chris,' - she spoke to me over her shoulder as she renewed her efforts with the washing up - 'always spend time on your girlfriend's tits. Remember that. Never go downstairs first. Girls don't like that. Never grab them downstairs and don't force your fingers inside. Find the clit, Chris. Find the clit and give the girl an orgasm.' She turned towards me and looked at me. 'Don't come too quick, Chris.' She paused. 'Make sure she comes first.' She turned back to her work. 'Make sure she comes first.'

I was still watching her and had said nothing. My mind was full of new information. New sensations.

'Remember this, Christopher,' she said, turning again to look at me. 'Make a girl laugh and give her orgasms, and she will love you forever.'

I nodded my head, and promised I'd try.

I left Sandra in the kitchen, and noticed Spanner and John were still scheming. John was telling Spanner that there is all manner of dermatitis that could be induced with a variety of substances, which would baffle doctors. John said a colleague of his had gained a medical discharge from the Australian Navy because of open sores in his armpits. These had been self-induced by rubbing carbolic soap there after showering. Spanner showed great interest, and hardly paid any attention to me.

Whilst John and Spanner continued their exchange of information, I retrieved a beer from the kitchen. Sandra smiled at me as I did so. 'You okay, Chris?' she asked in a dreamy voice.

'Sandra,' I replied looking at her, 'I'm really fine.' I nodded my head as I spoke. I knew we would have to go soon, so I went outside to enjoy a moment of tranquillity.

Well, I thought, *girls like their tits being played with, do they?* Who'd have thought it? I thought tits were for babies and men's curiosity. Maybe I should tell Spanner. Maybe he could get somewhere with Mary - *if* he spent some time with her tits first. Nobody had ever mentioned a clitoris to me before. I heard people boasting about the girls they had fucked with some describing what they did, and nobody had ever mentioned one! Nobody ever mentioned the clit! *Well, I fucking know now!* I thought. *I'd seen one! I've touched one and tasted one!* It is a fact Sandra seemed to go berserk when I was fiddling with it. I realised I now knew all about oral sex; I'd done it and had it done to me. I must admit, whilst I was lapping away at Sandra's clit, I did have an enormous sense of power; power of giving her pleasure and causing her to lose control. And what about orgasms! Never in my life have I heard of a woman having an orgasm! I thought that was a men-only preserve!

The other day, I fucked Sheila on a couch. I didn't play with her tits. I didn't spend time on her tits at all. I had a good feel around, but that was to satisfy my curiosity. All I really wanted to do was stick my cock inside her, which I did. She didn't have an orgasm. She never complained. I never found her clit. Well, that's not surprising as, up until about half an hour ago, I never knew they existed.

I felt sorry for Sheila because she really had the hots for me. It would have been easy for me to spend some time in the right areas and do a good job for her. Play with her nipples. Find the clit. Give her an orgasm. But how the fuck was I to know? She must have thought I was a moron.

I thought back to Kay. I knew she loved me, but she had never had an orgasm. I never spent time with her tits. I just fucked her. I'm sure it would have been the same with Dianne in Portsmouth, if I would have had the opportunity. A quick 'in and out' and away we go. I made a promise to myself that, when I got back to England, I would give both these girls an orgasm before putting my cock inside them.

12: Cells

John and Sandra gave us a lift back to the ship. Sandra drove and stopped in front of the gangway. The car was dwarfed by the size of the vessel, and I knew both John and Sandra were mesmerised by the size and noise of the thing. Sitting in the front, they both leaned forward to look up the side to the Flight Deck and island towering above us. I also leaned forward to look better out of the side window, but only to see who was in attendance at the end of the gang-plank. I was looking for McSnell or any other reg. staff, but I could see only the on-duty Bosun's Mate, who was looking down at the car with a puzzled look on his face.

We were both a bit drunk, but I felt I could walk straight, so didn't really worry about a charge of 'drunk on-board'. We were adrift and well and truly in the shit. That shit would hit the fan shortly after climbing that gang-plank. Spanner and I looked at each other, and knowingly rolled our eyes to the heavens as we shared the same thoughts.

Both front doors opened, and John and Sandra got out and gawped at the ship, Sandra with her hands on her hips and John with interlocking fingers at the back of his head. We opened our doors and alighted from either side of the car. After a short time, whilst our hosts surveyed our ship, Spanner said, 'We have to go now.'

They both turned to us, and now their hands reached out to us. John, who was closest to me, held out his hand, took mine and, then held it with both of his. 'It's been a pleasure meeting you, Chris. I wish you luck in all you do.'

Then he let me go and turned to Spanner.

I mumbled 'Thanks' to his back as he was outstretching his arms to Spanner.

Sandra stood in front of me and took my hands in hers. She looked deep into my eyes. Whilst gently shaking my hands, she said, 'Always remember what I told you.'

'I will,' I answered, nodding my head.

'You'll be a beautiful man one day,' she said, then stepped close to me and embraced me. I looked over her shoulder and could see John doing the same to Spanner. Again, I could feel arousal within me with the closeness of this woman. She then pulled back. 'Good luck,' she said, then turned quickly and got back in the car.

John let go of Spanner and walked to the car. 'Good luck to you both,' he said, and waved. The door closed and the car slowly moved off. We waved and watched them drift away.

'Fuck me, Clarkie,' Spanner said, taking a big breath. 'Here we fucking go.' He pushed me forward to the gangway. I ascended, pulling myself up the incline with my hands on the guard rails. The Bosun's Mate studied us without expression. I think I must have had a supercilious grin on my face, because I was feeling quite devilish. The Bosun's Mate moved towards the station card pigeon hole box, ready to give us our station cards.

I approached him and could hear Spanner jump down to the deck from the gang-plank. 'Clark,' I said to the Bosun's Mate, and he turned to the box. The pigeon hole on the top row, third from the left, had a big C above it. It housed a few cards, which the man removed. He looked through them and then repeated the process, almost like counting playing cards. He turned and looked at Spanner, raising his head in a question.

'Spendler,' Spanner said, and he again looked in the C box before moving his hands down and retrieving the cards from the S box. With both sets of cards in his hands, he searched through them again.

'Clark and Spendler,' he said, as if asking for confirmation. 'ID cards.' I then noticed to the left of the box was a board with six photographs. Each was a blown-up version of our ID card photos—and we were amongst them. I elbowed Spanner and nodded towards them. The heading on the board was 'Wanted for Desertion'. We both thought this was rather funny. The guy was trying to find our station cards, and next to the box we were on the Wanted list.

'When did you go ashore?' he asked.

'Can't remember,' I said.

'Earlier,' Spanner said. We were on the verge of giggling.

'What, today?' he asked.

'Can't remember,' I answered again.

Spanner followed with, 'Earlier.'

We sniggered at this, and he turned to look at us with a menacing expression. 'Don't play the prat with me cos I'll drop you as soon as, look at you. The pair of you.' He was threatening to administer violence to us both.

I could hear a group of ratings climbing up the gangway, and they jumped down and crowded around the Bosun's Mate.

'Hold your fucking horses, you lot!' he shouted. 'Make a line and shut your gobs'. He told us to stand to the side, which we did, right next to the 'Wanted' board. He proceeded to find and retrieve the station cards for the group of returnees, then looked at us again. He still had all the C cards and S cards in his hand, along with our ID cards. Re-examining them, he asked, 'Did you put your cards in when you went ashore?'

'Can't remember.'

Following my lead, Spanner said, 'Earlier.' And with that, we could not stop giggling. The man looked up in surprised confusion. He couldn't understand why we were acting in this stupid way.

'Clark and Spendler,' he said, as a hurt expression came over his face. He had finally twigged as he glanced at the board and saw our photos there. 'Fucking ODs, the pair of you,' he said, and reached for a telephone. A few seconds later, he spoke into the mouthpiece. 'Got Clark and Spendler here.' A second later, he put down the phone without saying anything further. 'Stand over there,' he commanded, and shoved us hard into the corner of the Weather Deck away from the ship's side and gang-plank.

Shortly afterwards, RPO McSnell eased through the watertight door leading from forward and jumped down to the deck with his large, highly polished boots. He was followed by Leading Regulator Thorn—Pricky Thorn, he was called, and nobody liked him, either. McSnell was smiling as he approached me, but the smiled turned to a grin, and then a snarl. He grabbed me by the collar and jerked me forward with such violence I was thrown across the deck.

'You drunk, Clark?' he asked.

'No, RPO,' I grovelled. 'No, I promise,' I grovelled further.

'Well, get the fuck up!' he bellowed, and grabbed my collar again, jerking me up, propelling me to the same hatch he had bounded through earlier. He shoved me through, causing me to trip and sprawl out face-down on the other side. He helped me up by my collar again and impelled me forward once more. He then pulled me violently to my right and round to a hatch and ladder-way to the next deck down—to 4 Deck, the main thoroughfare of the ship. He threw me down, and I managed to fend my face and head off the rim of the hatch in front of me with my hands and get my legs under me enough to break my fall. I scrambled up quickly and rushed for the door, which now faced me. I didn't know where he was taking me, but the only other door at the bottom of this ladder led to the Royal Marines mess, and I guessed that would not be my destination. I quickly went through the door in front of me, which led into the dining room. I knew the next door to my left took me to the canteen flat, where the regulating office was located. I assumed this would be our destination. McSnell caught up with me again as I was about to go through this left-hand door. Grabbing my collar, he jerked me back and then forward into the dining room. He frog-marched me at arm's length into the centre of the dining room, and then turned forward. There were many people in the dining room, but all fell to silence when they saw what was happening. Holding me, McSnell stopped and waited for Spanner to fall in line behind us. Pricky was holding him by his shoulder and urging him forward. The dining hall comprised two watertight sections, namely E and F; we were in F, and McSnell thrust me forward and pushed me through the watertight door to E section. I slipped and caught my shin on the lower rim. Pain shot up my leg, but I contained the yell that wanted to escape. We were now above our mess, but he thrust me through the next watertight door into D section—the galley flat. Next into C, the capstan machinery flat, then round to B section, the bathroom flat. My mind was confused. I was fuzzy from the beers I had drunk earlier. I was scared of McSnell and feared he would do me serious damage. I then realised the ships cells were on 5A Deck, so there was just one more door to go through, but immediately through it there was a hatch and ladder leading down to the next deck.

The final door was to our right, meaning McSnell could not push me through as fast or as violently as if we were going straight. I had to be careful. I grabbed the right-hand side of the door as he forced me through, and managed to get my leg on the top step of the ladder before he was fully behind me. I jumped down to the deck below, which ordinarily would be a stupid thing to do, but at least I was in control and felt I was limiting the damage I would suffer. I scrambled to my feet and dived into one of the cells, and stood with my back against the bulkhead opposite the door.

McSnell did not immediately follow; he waited for his colleague to appear at the top of the hatch and then said breathlessly, 'Well done, Thorn,' adding, 'throw that idiot down to me.' Pricky pushed Spanner, but he was already on the ladder with one hand on the guard rail. He descended rapidly, yet safely. McSnell was waiting for him, and grabbed him by the front of his tunic before throwing him backwards into the adjacent cell to me. I heard Spanner fall and grunt. I heard his cell door slam shut and the bolt go home.

McSnell appeared at my cell door. He looked at me menacingly and breathing hard. 'The Hermes don't need idiots like you,' he snarled, 'nor does the fucking Navy,' he added, wagging his finger at me. 'You need to grow up, boy,' he said, then turned away. The door slammed and the bolt slid home. I heard him tell Prickly that he would have to stay until a cell sentry could be appointed. 'Don't let them out. Don't let them talk. And don't open their fucking doors!' There was a pause then McSnell added, 'I mean it, Thorn. You do as I tell you.' Then silence.

I pressed my palms hard against the bulkhead and felt reassured by the strength of my support. My heart raced. My breath came in short gasps and my head throbbed. But my mind was clear.

As I was frog-marched past the capstan machinery flat, I had noticed the machinery was not running and nobody was there as they should be had Harbour Stations been ordered. This meant we were not due to go to sea for a little while, although I thought the ship was sailing today. I didn't quite understand why we were thrown in the cells as we were.

McSnell really frightened me. He could have caused some serious damage to me if I had hit my head on any one of the hatches, and as it was I already had a great lump forming on my shin, which throbbed as it grew. I had made up my mind: I would do something to Snell to cause him problems. I would have to think about this carefully, as he would not have to know it was me. He would kill me if he did.

I had never been in one of these cells before. I had used the bathroom opposite a few times. Normally, we used the bathroom on the deck above, but it was only small. If you turned up for a shower and it was crowded, you could then descend to this deck and use 5A bathroom. It was much bigger than 4B, but 4B was always the favourite. It was at those times that I had used this bathroom that I had passed by. There were four of them in a line on the port side of centre. Behind these, almost under the ladder leading down, was the PTI's (Physical Training Instructor's) office. In fact, this could have been another cell but just used for his purpose. The cell was about eight feet long by about four feet wide. A wooden bunk was on the centre of the forward bulkhead, which left about a foot at either end. The door was solid, with just a spy hole and a sliding cover on the outside. Above the door was a light behind a thick Perspex cover. The bunk had its own built-in wooden pillow—nothing more than a raised section on the end closest to the door.

All was quiet; I could hear nothing from the cell next door, where Spanner was being held, nor could I hear anything from outside where Pricky was guarding. There was the constant hum and throb of the ship's ventilation and machinery systems. The background noise would prevent any sound from permeating down from the deck above. People would pass the top of the hatch to enter 4B bathroom, and also the large heads (toilets) on the port side.

Maintaining the same position, against the bulkhead, I tried to anticipate what actions would follow. We only had the clothes we had returned in. At some stage, the disciplinary process would kick in. First would be the Officer-of-the-Day(OOD) table, who would pass us over the Commanders Table. He would, undoubtedly, pass us over the Captain's Table. It may be a couple of days before we would see the Captain, and I doubted we would see the Commander today. However, the OOD could be arranged quite quickly. We would have to be in the dress of the day for any formalities so, at some stage, we would have to go to the mess or get gear brought to us.

I have heard of people being thrown in cells if they return on-board drunk, but a medic has to see them first to determine they were drunk and not suffering any other problems, such as with Brendan and his gut rot problem. I suspected we were here for safe-keeping. And another thing: I knew we would be celebrities when we returned to the mess, and I suspected no-one wanted the crew to be detracted from the serious business of getting the ship ready for sea. Furthermore, it could be that the authorities would think we might make another run for it before the ship had taken sail.

I knew it would be pointless being angry or demanding to be let out. Pricky would expect us to ask to go to the toilet, but we would not be allowed. He was also scared of McSnell, and his orders were quite unequivocal. I would relax and wait. I inspected my damaged shin, which had trickled some blood. An angry blue bulge was growing. I lay on the bunk, resting my head on the hard pillow.

I had lots of things to think about. My first run ashore in a foreign place had been epic. It was the first stop on an almost year-long journey around the Far East and Australia. I knew I had to behave myself, else I would not see the end. My mind drifted to Jenkins, and I knew I had caused him problems. My absence from the team would cause him to take my place initially, and then get someone else in. Maybe he would have declared he didn't want me back. That would be a blessing.

I heard someone descend the ladder and an exchange of chat between Pricky and the Chief Elec., whose voice I recognised. I heard the spy hole cover being slid across and, after, the bolt being withdrawn.

'Stand to attention, Clark!' Pricky bellowed as he opened the door. I jumped off the bunk and did as ordered at the foot of the bunk. Pricky held the door open and the elderly, seasoned Chief Electrician stood looking at me with his piercing, pale blue eyes. He wore his uniform-black trousers with a crisp white shirt, black tie with the golden insignia of a Chief Petty Officer. No hat covered his balding pate, bordered with short white hair swept back from his temples. He held a clipboard in front of him, close to his extended waistline.

'Relax, lad,' he said, in an almost sad and exasperated voice. 'Are you okay?' he added, looking at me carefully. I didn't realise he was trying to determine if it was safe for him to enter the cell. He didn't know if I was drunk or violent. I relaxed from the attention position. My chest deflated and head came forward. My arms and feet remained fixed. 'Sit down.' He motioned to the bunk, and he drew up a chair and sat at the door. I guess he felt safer there. 'Now, what's the problem, lad?' he asked, and waited for me to answer.

I thought hard. I didn't know what he meant. I didn't have a problem. I didn't like working in the Senior Rates dining room, but I don't think that was the kind of answer he was fishing for.

'You know you are in serious trouble, lad?' he went on when I didn't answer him.

'Yes, Chief,' I said, more into my hands held in front of me than to his face.

'At least you came back. Do you realise had the Police or Naval Patrol picked you up, you would have been charged with desertion?'

I turned to look at him squarely now.

'And that would have been the end or your Naval career.' He paused for me to digest that. 'A court martial,' he went on, 'a spell in DQs (Detention Quarters) and a dishonourable discharge!'

I was still looking at him, but my mouth had dropped open. My heart began to race again. I was beginning to be frightened.

'Is that what you want, lad?' he asked, but before I could answer, he went on, 'because if that's what you fucking want, I can arrange it. Believe me, I can fucking arrange it!'

I *did* believe him. His fatherly demeanour had gone, and he was looking at me wide-eyed, awaiting my response. 'No, Chief,' I said, falteringly. My bottom lip was quivering as I said again weakly, 'No, Chief,' then added, 'No, Chief. I don't want that.'

'So what were you fucking thinking of then?' he asked. 'What were you fucking doing, gallivanting all over South Africa,' he said, waving his hand around, 'when you should have been here? So, tell me what the fucking problem is.'

I still didn't have a problem, except I knew it would be the end of the world if I was kicked out of the Navy.

'Why did you do it?' he asked, and I could tell he was getting annoyed with me. I didn't want him to be annoyed with me, because I really liked the Chief Elec. I knew he was a powerful but fair man. Above all else, he seemed to understand lots of things. 'There has to be a fucking reason,' he said, pleading with me. 'I can't help you if I don't know why.'

At that very moment, I knew my whole career was in jeopardy. I needed this man's help but, more importantly, I needed him on my side. 'The problem, Chief,' I started, and he leaned towards me to capture what I was about to say, 'the problem was I was having a good time, and then realised I was adrift.'

He studied me hard.

'I knew that if I returned on-board, I would be in the shit and not be able to go ashore again in Cape Town.'

His eyes softened, and he drew in a deep breath.

At that moment, I knew I had explained enough. I knew he understood. I knew he would have joined the Navy when he was fifteen and I knew he had also been a Junior Electrical Mechanic. I didn't know if he had done the same as me, but he would have had the same temptations.

'Clark, lad,' he said, resuming his fatherly wisdom, 'you have to be very careful. You are a bright lad, and could go a long way in this Navy.' I was looking at him intently as he continued. 'You are also young, and you could fuck it all up if you're not careful.'

The Chief Electrician explained the OOD Table would be arranged once we were at sea. I had to stay in the cell until we had departed and Harbour Stations had been stood down. We then would be allowed to the mess, where we would have to get into the rig of the day and sort out our gear. Commander's and Captain's Tables would be the following day.

I laid back on the bunk and heard the Chief Elec. enter Spanner's cell, and the muffled tone of their voices. I guess Spanner was telling him a similar story. No room for fabrication—it was true.

When the tannoy came over, instructing the ship's company to fall out from Harbour Stations, our cell doors were opened. Pricky was still there and told us to return to our mess, change into the rig of the day, and await instructions for our meeting with the Officer of the Day. Spanner and I exchanged sheepish looks, and then smiled a little at each other. I know we were both gaining strength from one another. We marched into the mess, and were immediately met with a hail of cheers and hoots of derision. Endless questions followed of where we had been, what we had done and why we hadn't returned. We also were warned we were in for it—as if we didn't know. We were told to report to the Chief Electrician's office to meet with our Divisional Officer, prior to seeing the OOD.

The format of attending the OOD Disciplinary Table was the same as always, as was the Commander's and Captain's Tables. Accused men would muster by the regulating office, and the routine would be read out to them. We would be inspected for correct dress and cleanliness of shoes, etc. Any deficiencies would only add to the charges already in abeyance.

We were finally escorted to the Quarterdeck where a makeshift courtroom would be set up, which consisted of only a podium, behind which the trying officer would stand. All accused would fall-in in line to one side. We could see our divisional Senior Rates and Divisional Officers mulling around with the regulating staff, shuffling and exchanging pieces of paper.

Eventually, we would be called to attention, and the OOD would step through the door from the ward-room and take his position behind the podium. We then would be stood at ease. Pieces of paper would be placed before the OOD, and a Ratings name would be called. The rating would answer, 'Yes, Sir!' and then would stand to attention before marching off to halt on a line on the deck, indicated by a regulator—and today, this was RPO McSnell. The Regulator would order 'Off Caps!' and the offender's right hand would whip across the front of his torso, up, and grab his cap from the left side. A pause of two marching paces would follow, then the hat would be whipped off his head, and held by the right thigh. Another Regulator, normally the Master at Arms (the Chief Petty Officer of Regulators), would read out the offence and ask how you plead. Everyone had to plead Guilty. The OOD then would determine whether or not he could deal with the offence or if it needed to be passed over to the Commander at a similar hearing, but of higher authority.

Eventually, the procedures led us to the Captain's Disciplinary Table. The Captain was a tall man with a long podgy complexioned face. Loose skin hung in bags from under his eyes. His bottom lip protruded beyond the upper, and skin hung from under his chin, like the plucked neck of a chicken. He leaned forward with his hand on either side of the podium, and explained to me that the Navy was a necessary fighting force for the defence of our nation. The Navy had a rich history of traditions, rituals and successes, all achieved by the loyalty, professionalism and discipline of the men who served on its ships. He went on to explain how the Royal Navy is held in high esteem in all countries around the world, and that he was proud to command a ship such as HMS Hermes. He further stated that he could not afford for the name of the ship, or that of the Navy, to be tarnished by members of its crew that could not uphold the necessary levels of discipline, loyalty and professionalism. Whilst he explained this to me, his head rotated from left to right, his eyes only resting upon my face periodically. He looked up and down, left and right, and sometimes at me.

Finally, he looked directly at me and explained, 'You are at the beginning of what could be a very long career serving your country in the Royal Navy.' He looked at me directly with his bloodshot blue eyes and continued. 'We have just had our first port of call in a long commission, which will take us to many countries around the world.' He paused. 'If you are going to be with us until we return to Portsmouth, you have to adopt the same loyalties and professionalism, and be disciplined.' He stood up straight now, and I had to tilt my neck to see his full height. 'It must be seen,' he said, in a raised voice, 'that there is no tolerance for ratings who disregard these principles.'

There was another pause as the Master-at-Arms passed him a card. Looking at this, he turned to me again, and said, 'You are sentenced to twenty-one days' cells, with additional work duty.'

Almost immediately, the MAA barked, 'On Caps! About turn! Quick march!'

And that was it.

I now sat on the bunk in the same cell I had occupied the day before. I had a holdall next to me, which I had packed previously with a spare set of Number 8s, clean underpants and socks, a notepad for writing letters, toilet bag, towel and a book—Micky Spillane's' My Gun is Quick. We were ordered to pack this after visiting the Commander's Table, so we knew what to expect. We were also allowed one blanket.

The door was closed. I knew Spanner was next door, and there would be a cell sentry outside. A cell sentry was a necessary thing, just in case we had a problem—just in case we had a heart attack, fit or stroke, for example. They were there for our safety. The trouble was the cell sentries were selected from our own mess. They are people we lived, worked and played with but, for them, this was an additional duty. They were all pissed off they had this extra duty imposed upon them. Four ratings would take turns sitting for periods of four hours on the wooden seat of a steel-framed chair, in the space between the cells and 5A bathroom and heads. These bathrooms were now out-of-bounds to the rest of the crew, so there was no passing traffic acting as a diversion for the sentries. They were instructed not to talk to us, and only open the cell doors at predetermined times.

We were awakened before 'Call the Hands', and allowed into the bathroom to wash, shave, and use the toilets. We attended the early morning muster of men under punishment, and allocated our points of extra work—the Junior Rates Galley for me and Spanner. It was preordained by McSnell that that was where our additional work duties would be carried out. On completion of this thirty-minute spell, we were allowed to have our breakfast. A table was set aside for our sole use. We would sit with the sentry whilst others looked on, giggling and pointing at us. Derogatory remarks would be levelled at us as people passed, much for the benefit of other onlookers. After breakfast, it was back to the cell, which had to be scrubbed out. All the cleaning gear—buckets, mops, cloths and detergents—were stowed in the bathroom opposite. Thirty minutes were allocated for this evolution, and then we were locked-up until midday. The doors were opened at noon and we were led up to the galley, where we collected our meal and resumed our position at our allocated table. Immediately afterwards, we would return to our cells, and the door would be locked. At 18:00, the doors opened again, and we returned to the galley and dining room for the evening meal, returning to the cell after another thirty minutes. At 20:00, we had to muster with men under punishment and for our work detail. Two hours were spent cleaning the boilers in the Junior Rates Galley then, at 22:00, it was back to the cell, where we could use the bathroom to shower before being locked-up for the night.

The first few days were the worst. We felt awkward with the sentries. They resented their duties, and held us responsible for the imposition. We needed the good will of these people, but it was difficult to ask for anything. We allowed them to do their duties without giving them the complication of asking favours. I soon read my book and swapped Mickey Spillane with Spanners' James Hadley Chase.

Things began to relax a little. The cell sentries were also bored. They had to sit there for four hours at a time, so to talk with us was a diversion for them, and helped to pass the time. We were visited by the Chief Electrician, who asked about our welfare and who gave permission for us to be allowed to use the bathroom outside the times when the cell doors were normally opened. This allowed us to interact more with each other and the sentries. It backfired a bit because the Middle (midnight to 04:00) and Morning (04:00 to 08:00) watches were the worst for the sentries; they had to stay awake whilst we slept, so they would welcome any diversion during these watches. Sleeping, for us, was not so easy. If you were tired, then sleep came easily, but all too soon, the hardness of the bunk with its wooden pillow forced you awake. But we could also sleep in the morning, after breakfast, and in the afternoons, after lunch. As such, we discovered the Middle and Morning watches were good opportunities to make amends with the sentries. We swapped books with them, and from then on, always had access to different authors and titles.

The regulating staff paid us visits only during working hours. They would reinforce the duties of the sentries: 'Don't talk to them and don't let them out,' they would be told. They would never make their way so far forward in the middle of the night.

Soon, we got into a routine where we could sit in our cells, with the doors slightly opened, and chat with the sentries. I could sit on the head of my bunk with my feet on the threshold of the door and chat, face-to-face, with the sentry. Spanner would be doing the same, but I could not see him because his door opened towards my cell so he was hidden, from me, behind it.

We looked forward to certain highlights of the day. Scrubbing out the cell was an enjoyable task that took up a great deal of time, but we could not prolong it beyond the allocated time, or the sentries would be in trouble. Meal times were always anticipated, and even hanging upside-down in the boilers gave a certain relief. Showers were taken with relish, and time was taken to thoroughly wash our underpants and socks every night. Normally, overalls, Number 8s, sheets, and towels would be sent to the on-board Chinese laundry, but not during this period. We would wash our Number 8sby hand, and we got permission for the sentries to bring us an iron and ironing board so we could always look clean and tidy. We were spending more time out of our cells, now expanding into the bathroom flat and bathroom. We always made sure we were in our cells during working hours with the cell door shut, just in case the reg. staff paid a visit.

During these moments out of the cell, when Spanner and I were together alone, we were able to snatch bits of conversation about our spell 'on the run', and the way we were treated when we returned. We were both repentant. We knew it was a stupid thing for us to do, and the consequence could have been a lot worse. However, we took a bravado attitude towards it, and made a public display of a cavalier attitude. We revelled in the notoriety of being 'bad boys' and 'dare devils'. We knew the people who called us idiots, ODs and stupid actually felt a little envy that they could not be so daring or anti-establishment as we had demonstrated.

Spanner, whilst frustrated that he was not able to get inside the knickers of Mary, told me he was glad, in a way because he had still remained faithful to his girlfriend Mary in Portsmouth. So, he had remained faithful by default. He knew I had fucked Sheila, but he didn't know what really happened between Sandra and I, and I felt it best not to say anything. It was such an incredible occurrence that I didn't think he'd believe me for one moment. Spanner was in a dilemma because he said he was in love with Mary Cape Town, as well! He said they had agreed to write to each other and meet up again on our way back to Portsmouth. He was very insistent that I keep in contact with Sheila, so it would make it easy for him to resume his relationship with Mary Cape Town when we returned. He still lived in high expectation of having his way with her.

My seventeenth birthday came and went. Nobody knew, and I didn't say anything.

It was one early morning that we sat at the doors of our cells, our writing pads on our knees and biros at the ready, to author a letter to our beloveds. Don Donessy was on watch, chewing gum as he habitually did, and reading a well-thumbed paperback. He paid us little attention.

'*My Dearest Darling Mary,*' Spanner read aloud. '*I hope you are keeping well,*' he continued. I waited in anticipation for him to continue. Finally, 'I bet you put the same, Clarkie.' I didn't answer. 'Well. What else you put?' he enquired, knowing I had started the same.

'*Thanks for all your letters,*' I answered,

'That's good,' he said, and I knew he was adding it to his page.

'*I hope you got my postcard,*' I continued reading from my pad.

'I can't put that. I didn't send a postcard.'

'Nor did I,' I confided, 'but she don't know that.'

'You're a fucking bastard, Clark,' he told me indignantly. 'You know that? A fucking bastard!'

I couldn't help but chuckle. 'Why? She doesn't know I didn't send one, and if she did know then she would think I don't think about her. This way, she thinks I do think about her, and so she loves me more,' I said, with satisfaction.

'So what happens when she don't get the fucking postcard?' Spanner asked, almost triumphantly.

'Lost in the post.'

'You're a fucking bastard, Clark. You really are,' he repeated, but I knew he was adding it to his letter. 'So what you saying about cells and all that?'

'Not saying anything. Too much aggravation,' I explained. 'If you tell 'em about the cells, you have to tell 'em about being on the run, and then about lots of other things.' I knew Spanner was digesting this. 'Best not to say anything. I just said Cape Town was a nice place, but we were only allowed ashore a couple of times, and that I had to be back on-board early, so only had time to walk around the streets and shops and things.' I knew Spanner was thinking on this and he'd have to agree it as being the best option. After some moments 'silence, I announced I was finished.

'So what else did you say then?' Spanner asked.

'Only that the weather was good. We were on our way to Singapore but couldn't go to the Flight Deck because they were flying every day.'

After a short pause, Spanner said, 'I hate writing letters.'

A few more days passed, and we learned of the arrival date for Singapore. It was the same day we completed our punishment. I had already been informed I had to report for duty at the Senior Rates dining hall to resume my duties there. It seemed I would get no respite from it until I'd done my time there. I was not looking forward to it at all. Spanner was already planning his run ashore. For me, it seemed an additional punishment heaped on as an extension to this.

13: Singapore

The Thursday we arrived in Singapore started the same for us. We scrubbed out our cell, but had the knowing satisfaction that this was the last time we were going to do it. We were due to return to our mess at midday. We engaged Mick Briggs, our cell sentry, in conversation about pending runs ashore, to extend the time we had before he locked us up again. The ship was already nearing the jetty, and we could hear all the activity taking place on the Cable Deck above us. Mick was excited about going ashore, and was planning to go with Spanner, along with a few others, as Spanner had been there before and was going to lead them to the best places.

Spanner told us he really wanted to remain faithful to Mary in Portsmouth, and he felt real guilt about being with Mary in Cape Town, although nothing really happened between them. He always told me about the women in the Far East and all about their silky soft skin. 'Like fucking velvet,' he repeated to me. A mist seemed to form over his eyes as he recalled previous visits. 'Be careful of the women, Mick,' he said, prolonging the conversation. 'They are all on the fucking game and you could easily catch something.' Mick looked at him with the familiar sideways tilt of his head. 'Some of them are fucking Kai Tais,' he added, 'and you won't know the difference until you get your hand in their knickers and discover Mr. Toggle and Two!', referring to the male genitalia. Spanner was nodding his head for emphasis, and then slipped me a sideways glance as a warning not to say anything about our conversation in a Cape Town bar. I just returned his gaze but he knew I was remembering. 'It's so easy to get led astray, and before you know it, you're on top of one.' Spanner was already rubbing his crotch. 'Anyway! I had a fucking good jerk off this morning to ensure I won't be randy ashore.' He was looking at Mick again now. 'No urge with an empty sack,' he continued, and then turned to attend to the cleaning gear we had used. Mick and I exchanged a glance as we both thought, *'Well, we'll see'*.

RPO McSnell clunked down the ladder at five-to-twelve. 'Right, you two wankers,' he bellowed, 'time to return to reality. Holiday time over.' He unbolted our doors and threw them open. I stood in the middle of the cell, clutching my few things: blanket, toilet gear, book, writing pad, and pen. 'Get all your fucking gear together,' McSnell bellowed further and stopped as he saw I had already done this. 'Go straight to your mess,' he instructed, with authority. 'And you,' indicating me with the point of his chin, 'get changed and report to the Senior Rates dining hall. You have a shit-load of washing-up to do.' He moved aside which indicated I could pass. I did, fearing I'd get a boot up the backside, or some other abuse but, thankfully, nothing.

We returned to the mess and were greeted with cheers and a barrage of questions, accompanied by hearty slaps on the back and ruffling of the hair. I went straight to my bunk. Budgie was lying on his, above mine, and he turned to greet me. 'Hi, mate. Welcome back.'

There was a lot of fondness in the message. 'Cheers. Have to fucking go to the SR's dining room now. Fucking pisses me off,' I replied as I ripped off my shirt and replaced it with the dining hall white tee-shirt. 'Have a good run ashore,' I told him as I ducked out of the mess.

Jenkins was waiting for me as I arrived. 'You're fucking late,' he sneered at me menacingly. 'You should have been here at ten!' He raised his eyebrows as he announced this.

'I only got out the cell at twelve, and got here as soon as I could. Go and ask McSnell if you don't believe me.'

'Don't be cocky with me, boy. Get in that fucking scullery, and get to work. You've got some catching up to do.'

The colleagues I had worked with before had all gone. They had all done their three months, and were now engaged in their own professions. This depressed me, as there seemed no end to when I could get on with mine. It seemed I was doomed to set tables, clear plates away, wash dishes, scrub floors, and polish silver.

The three new people were a junior stoker, about the same age as me, a youngish Radio Operator, and a more senior (by years) seaman. For the latter, he seemed to enjoy this role. For me, all I had ever seen seamen do was paint. They'd chip off old paint and then put on new. First an orange, then finish off with either green for decks, grey for bulkheads, or black for fittings, like clamps or bolts, etc. Determined would not like to be a seaman at all.

I had to resign myself to doing this job until someone said I had done enough. I realised getting in the shit would not help the situation. I would try, from this day on, not to be angry or depressed about my situation, but would accept it, keep my nose clean, and then someone else would replace me. I accepted I would be victimized and would get the worst jobs. I accepted I would not get any privileges, and I resolved myself not to be 'smart' with my superiors. I briefly thought of going to see Chief Elec. and plead with him to see if I could get off this role. I felt Chief Elec. was a kind and just man, but I also knew he was not soft, and no fool. I felt I would have to win some respect from him if I was ever going to get any favours from him. Maybe I shouldn't go ashore with Spanner so much. Spanner was a bit of a loose cannon, who would get depressed about certain things, like Mary in Portsmouth, and then, through a drunken haze, do crazy things. I was easily led, and so I would follow. In a way, I revelled in the notoriety of the thing of being bad. Spanner would also get a short circuit between brain and bollocks, and fall in love with the first female who he fancied. In fact, if they showed him any attention, that was enough. It also seemed resembling a female was enough.

My shift would finish tomorrow at 11:00, when I would be free to go ashore. All my Mess Deck buddies would be working, so if I went ashore, I'd be going on my own. I didn't know anyone else, and the idea of being on my own somehow gave me comfort in my resolve to be 'good'. Maybe I could meet up with Budgie later. He was a sensible person, who if I would have listened to, would not have gotten myself into trouble the last time in Portsmouth.

My day passed slowly. After the evening meal and cleaning up, Jenkins allowed us to go. I checked out the Weather Deck before I went below. It was dark, and I could only see lights of the jetty and other ships. It was very warm and humid. All of a sudden, I was very tired.

I went to the mess, which was unusually empty and quiet; only the duty watch were on-board, and most of them were engaged in their duties in various parts of the ship. A couple of people were around, but they were lying on their bunks, either smoking or reading or both. No-one paid me any attention, so I just got undressed and into my bunk. It would be normal to shower, but there was no-one to see I didn't, and I was too tired.

I was awakened by the duty EM at 05:30. 'Welcome back, Chris,' he said. It was one of the Senior guys from the other side of the mess—Pedlar Palmer. He didn't drink, smoke or chase women. He didn't go ashore much, and if he did it would only be to see the sights. 'Sign here, mate,' he said, offering me the clipboard and pen. I scribbled my name, and he left. I had slept almost undisturbed. I recalled some guys coming back from shore, which I guess must have been after midnight, even though they didn't make much noise.

I got up, showered, and went up to the Weather Deck adjacent to the SR's dining room. It was still dark, still warm, and still humid. I lingered for a while and then entered my work station with a couple of minutes to spare. Breakfast came and went. The Senior Rates came and went. Jenkins came, issued orders, and went. 11:00 came, and then we left: twenty-four hours off. What a relief.

I went back onto the Weather Deck and saw the dockyard in daylight. Nothing very special: lots of low-lying buildings of timber construction; small, Chinese-looking dockyard workers in straw hats and wearing flip-flops with skinny bowed legs sticking out of khaki coloured shorts. It was even hotter than the night before; very hazy and humid. I was disappointed not to see the sun blazing down. Beyond the buildings, I could see rich green palm leaves covering the hills, gently rising away to the distance.

I returned to the Mess Deck to, again, find it empty. Everyone was at their place of duty. This suited me, as I was content with my own company. I had a plan. I would shower, dress and go ashore. Spanner, and others, had given me a good idea of the dockyard and how to get out. Get off the ship, turn right, follow the main road and as you approach the main gate, you will see the dockyard canteen on the left. Opposite the main gate, on a small hill, is Aggie Weston's - sanctuary for sailors; cheap beer, cheap food, swimming pool, snooker room, darts and accommodation if you needed it. Turn left for Sembawang village and right for Terror Barracks. Singapore City was a taxi ride away, with a good stopping-off place of Ne-soon. Another taxi ride could take you to Johor Bahru (JB) over the causeway to Malaysia.

When I was ready, I left a quick note on Budgie's bunk, telling him I'd meet him at Aggie's whenever he got ashore; I said I'd either be around the pool or in the snooker room. With that, I left. I took a route that bypassed the regulating office. The last person I needed to see was McSnell. I posted my station card in the pigeon hole as the Bosun's Mate looked on. I mounted the gangway, walked its length and then jumped on to the island of Singapore.

I quickly walked away from the ship without looking back. I was scared someone would be there, beckoning me to come back. Just a bit of paranoia, I suppose.

The sun shone brightly now, burning down on my head. Heat radiated up from the burned concrete, and the soles of my shoes became distinctly hotter. The last dockyard I walked through was Portsmouth; there, the ground was tarmac black. Here, the white concrete reflected the brightness of the sun, causing my eyes to squint. Here, tarmac would melt. I now knew why all the Chinese wear those funny straw hats.

I soon came upon the dockyard canteen, and, as I approached, I heard the bawdy singing of a group of sailors having a good time. I had no plan of whether I should enter this establishment or not. I didn't know if I could enter. I was now seventeen but still looked about fourteen. I didn't know if it was like a pub in England, where you had to be eighteen or not. In fact, I didn't know a lot, to look through the windows meant leaving the concrete, which had now turned into a path crossing a stretch of thick leaved grass. I certainly was not going to venture onto that for fear of disturbing dangerous spiders or snakes.

The entrance was away from the road, and as I skirted the building, I could hear more clearly the chorus of a shanty song:

Dinah, Dinah, show us your leg, show us your leg, show us your leg, Dinah, Dinah, show us your leg, a yard above your knee.

Having arrived at the entrance, I could see into the voluminous bar. The floor was full of steel-framed tables and chairs with no padding. The floor was white marble tiles, and brown, dirty fan blades whirled lazily from the ceiling, wafting the warm air towards them. A long bar ran the whole length of the building, although all the activity seemed to be at the end nearest the door, where I stood. At the far end, a group of shanty singers sat around a circle of tables, which had been strategically placed for that purpose, like King Arthurs around a table. Sailors of all shapes and sizes sat around in various states of inebriation; some with beards, some with big fat bellies, some old, some young, many tattooed, but all red-faced and sweating. They were having a great time singing their songs. One guy stood up to sing a verse:

Rich girls ride a limousine; poor girls ride a truck. The only ride that Dinah gets is when she gets a fuck.

Then they all join in heartily with the chorus again:

Dinah, Dinah, show us your leg…

I see the barman; another small Chinese man with skinny, bony arms with bulging veins, holding a hosepipe and directing it over a tray of glasses, filling them rapidly and moving the end of the pipe from one glass to the next without stopping the flow. The tray also is awash with beer. When the glasses are full, the sailor, this side of the counter, slides the tray along, where another skinny, yellow man takes some paper money from him and gives him a few coins in return. The sailor then carries the tray to the group of populated tables.

The small man looked over at me and shouted, 'Yu wan tiga bea?' I looked at his expectant face as he held up the hosepipe which he was pinching between his finger and thumb to stop the flow of beer. The man was asking if I wanted a beer. I wanted to ask how much it was, but couldn't speak. He had taken me by surprise. 'Yu wan big bea or smaw bea?' he shouted again.

Then, from the other end of the room, a fat-bellied sailor with a shiny black beard bellowed at me. 'Hey, skin! Get your arse over here and give us a song.' I was like a rabbit caught in the headlights of a car, frozen to the spot.

'Sing, you fucker!' someone else shouted.

Then a chant started: 'Sing! Sing! Sing!' Beer glasses began to be banged on the table in time to the chant. My heart was thumping against the side of my ribcage so hard it hurt. My breath came in short pants. I was scared stiff. 'Sing! Sing! Or show your ring!' the chant continued. Now all attention was on me. The whole crowd joined the chant: 'We've seen your ring, so sing, you bastard, sing!' I just raised my arm, shook my head, and turned away. It took all my willpower not to run. At my back I could hear roars of laughter. I wondered if one day, I would be able to sit amongst such a crowd and join in as one. I wondered if ever I would be able to learn those songs. As I retraced my steps to the main road, I heard the roar of laughter subside and someone began the next verse of *Dinah*:

Rich girl used a brassier, and the poor girl uses string, but Dinah didn't use fuck all, she let her titties swing.

The road soon led through the main gate and there stood Aggie Weston's, atop the small mound, as I had been told. Inside, the entrance was like a hotel reception with an open side, leading out to the swimming pool opposite. No-one seemed to notice when I entered, and no-one paid me any attention, so I marched straight across, towards the swimming pool. It looked beautifully inviting; a cool blue, and a faint smell of chlorine. Water slapped against the underside of the overhanging paving slabs that surrounded the pool. Only one person was enjoying the water. I could see the bald head of a man breast stroking his way the length of the pool. He did this effortlessly and hardly disturbing the water as he went. Nat King Cole sang from the tannoy system in the same effortless manner, recanting a story of a Nightingale in Berkeley square. It made me remember when I bought my first record. I was given a record token, and was discussing with my mother which record I should exchange it for. She suggested, 'a nice Nat King Cole song.' I opted for *Glad All Over* by Dave Clark Five. However, on this occasion, I must concede: Nat King Cole is more fitting.

I could see the snooker room to my right, so decided to check it out. There were two tables, both occupied by groups of players, who were smoking and drinking beer. Not much was being said, and only then in hushed tones. Concentration hung in the air. The only real sound was the crisp click when two or more balls collided. I watched, but was not too impressed with the standard of play.

Next to this room was the bar. Some people sat on stools; others sat on tables around the small room. The marble-tiled floor was covered with woven raffia mats. Nat King Cole was also singing in this bar. A Chinese man, similar-looking to the barman in the dockyard canteen, stood behind the bar; however, this one wore a clean white shirt and black bow tie. He was looking at me as he polished a glass.

I had a problem: I had no money… Well, I had very little money. When you are in cells, you lose your pay also. That means three weeks without pay. Other people would have been saving their pay whilst we were at sea, and so would be able to have a good blow-out ashore. Today was Friday, and the next payday would be Thursday next week. Paydays are every two weeks, so next week I would receive one week's pay. Three pounds bloody ten (£3.50 in today's language)! I would get a pay rise for reaching17 years, but it would not take effect for a month or so. I didn't know if this guy would serve me a beer if I asked him, or if he would embarrass me by asking for an ID card. I decided not to bother and save my coins.

I turned around and could see a large grassed area the other side of the pool. Some deckchairs were positioned randomly, and there were also towels strategically placed on the ground with small deposits of clothes, sunglasses, books, packs of cigarettes, etc. I decided to select a chair and relax in the sun. I took off my shirt and sat back with my face towards the sky. The sun came and went. Increasingly, the haziness returned. It was still hot, and the humidity caused beads of perspiration to form on my upper lip. More people arrived, and the pool got noisier as more people splashed about inside it. More people were looking for deckchairs, so I was determined not to move.

Late in the afternoon, Budgie arrived with Don; a fine pair! Budgie's ginger hair seemed to be more ginger now, as his face seemed to be more red. He had obviously spent some time in the sun. During the three weeks at sea, there must have been ample time to meander up and down the Flight Deck or to loaf around on many of the open Weather Decks, taking in the sun's rays. Don's blonde hair was even paler, and his face positively pink. Both had served time as Cell Sentry for Spanner and I, but the light in the bathroom flat had not revealed this change in them. As much as I wanted to laugh, it was good to see them both.

'Now you can buy us a beer for all that extra duty you put us through,' Budgie said heartily, thumping my shoulder as he said it.

'And me too,' Don added, thumping the other shoulder.

'You have to get them then, Budge; you look older than me,' I responded, paying him the compliment. I gave him all the money I had and off he went.

'You still writing to that Janet bird in Cape Town?' I asked Don.

'Yeah,' he responded in his slow, Northern drawl. Everything about Don was slow. 'She says Sheila is going to organize a big party for when we go back there.'

'Fuck me,' I said, 'that's six months away! Anything can happen in that time.' Janet was a friend of Sheila. I had seen her once; she was beautiful, and I was amazed Don could trap it. 'Did you shag it?' I asked, digging him in the side with my elbow. He slowly turned his head towards me and looked at me without saying anything. 'Did you?' I asked again. He lowered his eyes and slowly turned away.

'Nearly,' he said, 'but I fucking will next time.'

Budgie returned with three beers. Tiger - Beer in large bottles - with three small glasses. It was cold and tasted good; it was my first beer since Cape Town, and it fuzzed my brain.

Budgie had been ashore the night before and had ventured into Sembawang village. He told me you could get an eggy banjo really cheap. An eggy banjo is just fried eggs, fried in a wok, made into a sandwich with a long French stick. 'Sounds good to me,' I said encouragingly. I told Budgie I had no money, but he said he'd treat me.

The following days, many things happened. We were scheduled to visit Hong Kong next, but an announcement was made that we had been diverted to Sydney, Australia, and that we would visit Hong Kong after that. A visit to Sydney came as a surprise to us all and I, for one, was very excited about it. We would sail next Friday—the day after payday.

The young stoker who was in my shift was called Quinn, and I only ever knew him by his nickname, Mighty. He was about my age, smaller and quite weedy. When he walked, his hips were not level, almost as if one leg was longer than the other, but that was not the case. He had very dark hair and thick eyebrows, which hung over large, round eyes. Dark bum-fluff grew on his upper lip, much the same as mine, but I shaved mine off, hoping it would turn into whiskers. He had pimples, not many, but they were angry red with whitish heads, just ready for squeezing. He came from Bristol.

Mighty was a good boy. He had never been in trouble, neither in the Navy nor at his school, and never at home. Nothing seemed to bother him. He passed through his training without any great problems. He was never top of the class, and had to study each section to guarantee a pass. He could cope with all the physical things but excelled at nothing. He told me he had never had a girlfriend; I did not tell him that that did not surprise me. During the moments when we could relax a little, when Jenkins was not around, we would chat, and he would tell me interesting things about where we were. He would read the history of places we visited and, whilst history was not my favourite subject at school (in fact, I hated it), I found these chats very compelling. He told me stories of how Singapore came to be such an important Naval base; how the land was cleared; how the Japanese came; and a variety of other things.

He had no desire to go out and get drunk; he had never been drunk. He had never been with a woman, and would never enter a strip club or brothel. He was not homosexual either. He was happy although not very adventurous.

He told me about Raffles, the hotel, and how one time a tiger was found sleeping beneath the snooker table. When I showed such interest, he asked me if I would go with him to see Raffles Hotel. Thursday was payday and we were off, so we said we'd go together. He was very pleased. For me, I felt I would not get into trouble going ashore with Mighty on our last night.

So, for the next few days, I lead the quiet life. I mainly went ashore by myself, walking to Aggie's and spending time by the pool. I walked to Sembawang and found another route back to the ship via another dockyard gate close to the village. I worked hard in the dining room, focusing my attention there. Doing so made me feel content, and made me relax more easily during my time off. I didn't have any confrontations with Jenkins, and he intimidated me less.

Because of my schedule, I was out of the mess when my colleagues were there, and when they were at work, or ashore, I had the mess pretty much to myself. I saw very little of Spanner. When he was on-board, he was mainly, sleeping or hungover and sleeping. I didn't want to disturb him.

I didn't go to Singapore City because I couldn't afford it. We were due to visit again some months later so I would be in a better position. My seventeenth birthday would mean my pay was set to increase by nearly 50% so, relatively speaking, I would be rich.

Thursday arrived. At 10:00, I left the SR's dining room and at 11:00, I queued up for my pay. A line was formed in accordance with your ship's Book Number, and the Assistant Writer would call your name out when it was your turn. At the command, you marched two paces, stopped to attention, saluted the paying officer with your right hand, and he would announce your pay and deposit it in your outstretched left hand. 'Three pounds, ten shillings,' he said, looking up from his sitting position as he placed the sum in my hand. It was the smallest amount he had handed out. He must have wondered what I had done to receive so little. As always, the regulating staff was in attendance just to make sure all went well and to check the state of your dress, cleanliness of your shoes and length of hair. I grasped the three green notes and the one brown one in my left hand, smartly turned to the left, and marched off, past the leering eyes of McSnell. 'Don't spend it all at once,' he sneered as I passed him.

'No danger of that, PO,' I answered him politely. 'I still have plenty left from Cape Town.' I knew this infuriated him, but I was gone by the time he recovered. I should never have done that, but I couldn't resist it.

I met up with Mighty, and we shared a taxi together to the city. I didn't realise that Raffles was so close to the Union Jack Club (UJC). In fact, it was just opposite: the UJC was similar to Aggie Weston's, a club for sailors to provide leisure and recreation. I heard it was the starting place for a run ashore. Beer was cheap, so everyone would get tanked up before wandering off down the dingy back allies leading to Bugis Street. I wanted to go in, but Mighty was excited about the building on the other side of the road.

We sat in the foyer of the Raffles Hotel in wicker chairs beneath a ceiling fan, slowly turning directing warm, smoke laden air down towards us. Smartly-dressed waiters cruised around in white jackets, black trousers, and a tea towel over the arm carrying a tray. One came to our table and raised his chin in a question of what we would order. 'Can I have lemonade?' I asked, trying to be confident. In reality, I was nervous: I dare not ask for a beer here.

'The same for me,' Mighty said in a lame voice when the waiter's chin was directed towards him. I was watching Mighty as he surveyed this place. There was a glint in his eye as he scoured all the old paintings and photographs on the walls. Then, he leaned forwards and his lit-up face turned to me. 'There's the snooker table,' he said, pointing excitedly. The waiter returned with a jug of light-coloured liquid and ice cubes chinking on the sides, slices of lemon positioned on the edge. He placed the jug and a glass each in front of us. He picked up the jug and poured some liquid into each glass, then repositioning it. He stood up, nodded a bow towards us, turned, and walked away. 'He forgot to ask us for our money,' Mighty said in bewilderment.

'No,' I said, 'I don't think so. We ask for the bill before we leave.'

We both commented on the lemonade, thinking it would come in a bottle. This was prepared especially for us and, no doubt, we would pay handsomely for it. We both had a good look around and peered under the snooker table, just in case, and then returned to our table. After a while, the waiter returned and asked if we needed anything else.

'How much is it?' I asked.

'I'll just get your bill,' he said, turning away. I announced to Mighty I needed the toilet and marched off towards them. I made sure I enjoyed all the grandness of them, lingering whilst I admired the ornate tilework, colourful murals and intricate wrought iron work around the basins. I lavished the supplied soap onto my hands, relishing in its creaminess. I waited for a second for the water to turn hot before rinsing it off. When I finished, I looked at my reflection in the mirror and smoothed down my hair. Good enough. I turned and left. When I returned to our table, it was clean and all the chairs empty. Mighty was by the door.

'We have to pay,' I said to him, trying to fake concern.

'I already did, Chris. You can get the next one.'

'Oh, okay. Thanks.' He didn't realise I had just manipulated him into paying.

'Chris?' He turned to me as we left the hotel. 'I want to take a walk down the waterfront.' Struggling to retrieve something from his pocket, he added, 'I think it would be very interesting.' His eyes grew larger as he produced a map. Almost offering me the map, he added, with a perceptible nod of his head, 'do you want to come with me?'

I looked at him for a moment and I saw some of the brightness of his eyes disappear as he knew I was going to decline. 'Well,' I said, matter-of-factly, 'I'm going to check this place out.' I gestured with my arm to the UJC opposite. 'I hear they have an enormous six-track scalextrics there.' He looked across the road. 'Could be fun,' I added, trying to entice him. He looked away and towards the waterfront.

'Naw,' he said with resignation. 'It's getting dark soon, and I don't want to miss this opportunity.' He was looking at me again now.

'Okay, mate. I'll see you tomorrow, then.' He waved and took off. I watched his lopsided gait jostle down the street. It almost seemed his back was crooked.

The UJC had everything: a large swimming pool, snooker tables, bars, restaurants, lounges with TVs and, of course, an enormous scalextrics layout. I was watching the racers, and it was clear some cars were faster and some racers better than others. There was one guy boasting he was the best, and taking bets he could beat anyone. Strangely enough, his car did not seem to be as fast as the others. I saw him with his thumb pressed all the way down on the controller, yet he never went fast enough to come off the track. No skill was needed with this car. I watched as he took on bets and, sure enough, his opponent would spin off the track or mysteriously slow-down in certain sections. Invariably, he would win. Stakes were not high, so no-one took it too seriously. If you raced against him, you also had to contend with the other players; their cars could spin off and crash into yours, and you've lost. People came and went, put their money in a machine and their track became live. Whizz around the track a few times and, by the time you get the hang of it, time's up and you have to feed the machine again. Mr Win Bets was badgering a guy to race him for money. I had been watching this guy, and he was good; I saw him navigate his car round the circuit several times at good speed, and never spinning off. Finally, the guy agreed to a one-dollar bet; twice around the track. The cars were brought to the start line, and off they went. The opponent sped ahead and led, until the long curve and back straight opposite the starting line. His car slowed almost to a stop and spurted forwards in jerks. Mr Win Bet's car trundled past. The challenger's car recovered, and on the next lap overtook his rival, and, again, in the same place, the same thing occurred.

Mr Win Bets was making a lot of noise, cheering, jeering and urging people to look at his pathetic opponent. All eyes were on the spluttering car as it was overtaken again. I was looking closely at Mr Win Bets as he cast a sideways glance to a man by the track, but close to him. He was standing, and seemed to be leaning on the track for support as he, too, jeered at the faltering car. Then, I noticed his hand was on the electrified track of the opponent's car. In his hand was a coin with which he was shorting out the track. Once his friend's car came around the final bend, the man sat down and, miraculously, the opponent's car regained its power but, alas, too late. Mr Win Bets won the dollar, and I learned a new trick.

I watched this scam for some time, but no-one else noticed what was going on. Mr Win Bets won quite a few dollars.

'Clarkie!' a voice boomed behind me and, before I could turn, a flat palm slapped me between my shoulder blades, causing me to stumble forwards. 'What the fuck are you doing here?' Spanner added. 'Where the fuck you *been*?'

I recovered, and any annoyance that was welling up inside me vanished when I realised who it was. I was genuinely pleased to see him. 'Hello, mate,' I said, 'How ya doin'?'

'Fucking great, mate. Here, have a swig of this,' he said, offering me his beer.

'Cheers.' I took a swig.

'Don't play this game,' he said, nodding towards the track. 'It's a fucking rip-off. Those fucking machines eat all your money.' Then, gesturing towards Mr Win Bets, 'and then that arsehole will take the rest. Never bet against that arsehole, he always fucking wins.'

We moved away from the track and stood by the balcony overlooking the swimming pool. 'I hear you've been bagging off, then,' I said.

Spanner looked at me a little hurt. 'Well, fuck it,' he said in resignation. 'You fucking have to, don't you?'

'So what about Mary, then? Thought you wanted to be faithful.'

'For fuck sake, Clarkie. You my fucking dad now?' There was a challenge in his tone.

'No,' I said, turning my attention to the blue water of the pool. 'I knew you wouldn't anyway.'

'Wouldn't what?'

'Stay faithful.'

'Ah, fuck it. She's in Pompey, and that's a fucking long way away,' he said in finality.

After a pause, I asked, 'So, was it in some bag shanty then?'

'I told you, these women here are fucking gorgeous. Can't fucking help it, man.'

'But you had a jerk off in the morning so you wouldn't feel randy ashore,' I reminded him.

'Yeah, didn't work.' Then, after a while, he confessed, 'I had another jerk off in the shower, just before I went ashore—just to make sure.'

'Fuck my 'ole boots. Two fucking jerk-offs, and you still go ashore and shag.' I was shaking my head in disbelief.

'Clarkie?'

'What?'

'It was so fucking good, man, that when I got back to my bunk on-board, I had to have another jerk-off just thinking about it.' I looked at him in amazement. I could think of nothing to say.

I was still thinking of a suitable reply when Spanner leant towards me, bumped my shoulder with his and, with an impish look in his eye, asked, 'Do you want to come and see her?' I had a thousand things I wanted to say and ask, but could say nothing. I could not prioritize my thoughts into words. 'It's just round the corner from here.'

'You're going to fuck her again, then.'

'Fucking right I am. It's our last night. Fucking *got* to, man,' he answered. 'You can pick one as well. Empty your fucking sack before we go to sea again.'

The thought for just shagging a prostitute did not turn me on. The thought of paying for it turned me on less. I had fucked that old woman in Portsmouth, but there was something erotic about that. In fact, it was incredibly erotic. I had jerked myself off many times thinking about it. I had fucked Sheila over the back of a sofa - a quick in-and-out with no fucking about. Not very erotic. I could have fucked Rosie that night in Southsea Fun Fair if I wanted to be mercenary about it, and that wouldn't have been very erotic, either. Sandra told me different: spend time on the tits; make 'em laugh; make 'em have an orgasm. Mind you, then she said they will love you forever. Well, I suppose love comes into it at some stage.

'Naw, I don't think so.'

'Aw, come on, man! It'll be fucking great!' he urged enthusiastically. I didn't want to go to a brothel and pay to fuck a prostitute. I had never been inside a brothel, yet I was intrigued to know what goes on there, apart from all the fucking. I was thinking I may go along with him, just to see what the routine is, and then I could wait for him to empty his sack—again. I was about to offer this to him as a compromise when he said, 'Aw, come on, man! I'll buy you a beer.' *Fuck me*, I thought. *I almost blew a beer here.* 'I'll buy you two beers,' he added, when I didn't answer immediately.

'Two beers?'

'Two beers.'

'Pints?' I checked dubiously.

'Pints,' he assured me. Well, that was a result.

'Okay. But we have to be on-board for midnight,' I cautioned him. 'Right?' I pushed for the answer.

'Of course. If we don't, they throw away the key next time.'

We sat and drank two beers each. We chatted about several things. Spanner told me that Fingers had also met a friend of Sheila's in Cape Town, who he had shagged. Fingers shags anything. Her name was Maggie, and she was nicknamed Maggie Steaming because she was always drunk. Anyway, she told Fingers a big party will be arranged for when we return. Finally, Spanner stood up and said, 'Let's go.' I stood, but wobbled. I followed Spanner.

We walked in mainly silence and I was taken in by the bright lights, narrow streets, and the wonderful strange aromas of food cooking, incense, and charcoal burning. Finally, Spanner turned to me and said,

'This is it.' He ducked into a small narrow doorway. Inside opened up to a surprisingly large room, which was dimly lit with red lamps. On one side was a raised platform, and opposite were a couple of straight-backed chairs, seemingly not built for comfort.

An old woman screamed a greeting to Spanner as she ran over to embrace him. 'Yu wan fukifuki with same girh?' she asked, then, without waiting for an answer, 'Yeh, you ahways wan same girh.' This woman was thick around the midriff, her face full of wrinkles, her mouth half-full of teeth, many of which were black. She looked at me and said, 'Yu wan fukifuki? Waih here. I get girhs.' She shouted a command, and about twenty girls appeared from the end of the room and lined up on the platform. They giggled a little, and tried to look shy. They were all dressed in kimonos with a slit to allow a lot of leg to be seen. 'Wish won yu wan?' the woman asked me, indicating with her arm the assembled ladies.

I held up my hands. 'None. No fucky for me. I'll just wait for my friend.' There was a lot of noise and high-pitched squeaks and squeals. 'Do they have a toilet here?' I asked Spanner. 'I'm bursting for a piss.'

'Yeah,' he shrugged, pointing to the end of the room. 'Back there.'

'I need pissy piss,' I said to the old lady as I went in the direction of Spanner's pointing hand.

The woman said, 'Yuh pissi pissi,' waving her hand in the same direction. A curtain covered the doorway, and I brushed it aside and went through. The next room was much smaller, and in front of me was a naked young girl with her back to me. She stood on a tiled floor with one leg up and her foot on the rim of a basin. She had a hosepipe in her hand, the end of which she was holding up her fanny. Water was gushing from inside her. I froze just inside the doorway. She looked over her shoulder at me, but continued with what she was doing with the hosepipe. Then, she stood up and turned towards me. 'Wah yu wan?' she asked, and the hose was still gushing water. She was small and young. It was impossible to guess her age. She had small conical breast, so small gravity didn't affect their shape. The nipples were large by comparison and very dark; shiny, dark and puffy. She was thin; skinny stick-like, arms by her side. She was not emaciated. You could not see her ribs, but her hips were bony. Her pubic hair was jet-black, but not in a triangle. It was shaped like a thin, vertical rectangle and comprising straight hairs. It resembled a tailless mouse disappearing between her legs. There was a gap at the top of her legs, even though the knees were almost touching. Skinny thighs led down to skinny, bony knees. Her body was overly long for the length of her legs. Her face was round with a crop of jet-black hair tied on top. Narrow, slanting, black eyes bore into mine. Her nose was just two nostrils in the middle of her face, and goofy, crooked teeth prevented her lips coming together. She was fucking ugly! 'Wah yu wan?' she asked again, her voice raised voice.

'Pissi piss.'

'Yu cahn pissi piss therh.' She pointed to her right. The 'toilet' was a hole in the ground, a foot plate either side. She was looking at me as I tried to get my cock out. I wanted her to go away.

All of a sudden, there was a loud crash from the room I was in earlier. The old woman screamed unintelligible orders, and I could hear all the other girls squealing at a higher pitch. I could hear people running and the girl by my side dropped the hose and disappeared. I turned to leave by the same way I came in, just as the curtain was thrown open and a Royal Navy shore patrolman stood in my way. He held his hand up and commanded, 'Stop!' I did, frozen with fear. 'Hold your hands out!' he commanded further. I did so. 'You got an ID card?'

'Yes,' I quivered.

'Give it to me!' I handed it to him and he put it in his pocket. 'You'll get it back in a minute. Now follow me!' He led me outside and told me to get in the back of the waiting shore patrol van. Inside, there were already three more guys.

'Fucking vice squad,' one of the guys said. There were three patrol men, and altogether they brought out nine men, Spanner not amongst them. Some of the guys had to finish getting dressed as they got in the van.

We drove off, no-one saying anything over the rev of the engine. I wondered where we were going, and what would happen to us. I was frightened, and feared for my future.

We were taken to HMS Terror Barracks, and put in separate cells. *Once again alone in a cell*, I thought despondently. I felt low, lower than a snake's belly in a wheel rut. Soon, I was called for and taken to an office where an old civilian man was sat behind a desk. He explained I was there because I had been caught in a brothel, and that brothels are out-of-bounds to all Naval ratings and so, as such, I had committed an offence against the Naval Disciplinary Act. Furthermore, should it be confirmed I had contracted a Venereal Disease, I could be further charged with making myself unfit for duty. I would therefore be required to give blood and urine samples. If the blood, or indeed urine samples, contained excess amounts of alcohol, I could be charged with being drunk. If that was the case with me, then I would be further charged with drinking under the legal age. I tried to explain I had done nothing, but was told to shut up.

A urine sample was easy; I was bursting. However, I had to wait for ages for someone to come along and take a blood sample, after which I would have to wait for the results, and they would be forwarded to my ship.

I was returned to the Hermes at about 02:00. I suppose I could also be charged with being adrift. The Bosun's Mate noted the time of my arrival, and explained my station card had been passed to the Regulating Office and I was to report there at 08:00.

So, I was to leave Singapore as I had left South Africa and indeed, the first time from Portsmouth—in the shit

.

14: South to Aussie

At 08:00, I reported to the regulating office, as ordered. McSnell was in conversation with the Master-at-Arms (MAA) and the rest of the staff at their chairs at a communal desk. I waited at the door. McSnell had seen me, but continued with his discussions. I knocked on the door, and all eyes turned towards me. 'Wait outside!' the puffy-faced MAA said. I watched people come and go to the NAFFI shop opposite. This would soon be closed, as Harbour Stations were about to be announced and people were stocking up. Everyone glanced at me, knowing I had done something wrong—why else would someone be waiting outside the regulating office?

Eventually, I was summoned by McSnell, who informed me a report had been submitted by the RN Singapore Shore Patrol Vice section. McSnell was not being mean to me because of where we were. I was glad the MAA was around. 'Why were you found in a brothel last night?' he asked me.

Instinctively, I replied, 'Because I was there when the Patrol came.' I instantly wished I had rephrased this, as it sounded antagonistic. It infuriated McSnell, I could see.

'Okay,' he said slowly, keeping his cool, 'and why were you in there?'

'Well, I needed to go to the toilet.'

'You went to a brothel to go to the toilet,' McSnell confirmed sarcastically.

'Yes.'

'Who were you with?' he demanded. I looked up at him and lied. 'I was on my own.'

He turned and walked to the desk and shuffled some papers, buying time. 'First bloke I know that went to a brothel for a piss,' he mumbled to the staff around the desk, who all sniggered at his comment.

He turned back to me with more paper in his hand and announced, 'You are going to be charged.' He looked down at the papers and carried on: 'How many charges you will face is not yet clear. The Chief Electrician wants to see you in his office at 09:00. Come back here afterwards.' He now looked at me. 'Is that clear?'

'Yes.'

'Right, get out of here!' was his way of dismissal.

When Chief Elec. saw me at his office door, he immediately rose from his desk chair and came towards me. He gently took my shoulder and steered me to the door of the switchboard opposite. Opening the door, he said, 'It's more private in here.' We went inside, and he motioned for me to sit at the small square table, and he sat opposite. 'Now, lad,' he began; then paused, uncertain. 'Tell me, were you with Spendler last night?' He leaned on his elbows and looked intently at me with those piercing blue eyes.

I had seen Spanner that morning, and he told me when I went for a piss, he went upstairs with his whore. He had only just got there when the commotion started. The woman told him to get under the bed, and she stood by the door. The patrolman just looked inside and moved on. Some guys were caught because they were bagging off or undressed; he waited till it was all quiet, and then left. He then found out I had been taken; I told him not to worry, and that I wouldn't say anything. I didn't want to lie to the Chief Elec., and I didn't want to get Spanner in the shit, so I answered truthfully: 'I went ashore with JMEM Quinn, who is on the same shift as me. He wanted to see Raffles Hotel.'

'And?' His eyebrows rose as he wanted me to continue.

'We had a lemonade there, and afterwards he wanted to walk by the waterfront. I wanted to go in the UJC, so we split up.'

'Then what?'

'Well, I watched the scalextrics for a long time, and then decided to go for a walk,' I told him. He said nothing, expecting me to continue. 'I found myself in an area of narrow streets and bright lights. I needed to go to the toilet, so I went through this door thinking it was a bar. Once inside, I saw loads of girls, and an old woman asked me if I wanted to fuck one. I told her I needed to piss, and she showed me through the back.' I paused, but Chief Elec. wanted me to continue. 'That's when all hell broke loose and the patrolman got me. And that's it,' I said, before adding, 'I was then taken to Terror Barracks.'

The Chief Elec. sat back in his chair and took a deep breath. He exhaled and leaned forward once again. 'When you went through the door and saw all those girls, didn't you realise you were in a brothel and not a bar?'

'Chief, they all looked the same to me.' Again, he was looking directly at me. I continued: 'There were girls in every doorway. I have never been into a brothel before in my life. I never went into any other bar there either. I didn't know if I was in a brothel or a bar. I wouldn't know how to tell the difference. All I knew was I needed a piss.'

The Chief Elec. once again sat back in his chair, sighing deeply. 'You know; this doesn't look very good.' He paused, and it was my turn to say nothing. 'That McSnell hates you, and he probably has the right to.' Again, he paused, and again, I said nothing. 'He wants to charge you with everything, including being adrift, which is an aggravated offence because the ship is under sailing orders.'

'But Chief…!'

'I know you were in custody, but technically, he *is* right.' The Chief Elec. interlocked his fingers and twiddled his thumbs, and again looked intently at me. 'You happy on the Hermes?' he asked in a quiet voice. I did not know how to respond to this question, yet somehow I knew my answer would be very important. I knew further a one-word answer would do me no good.

'Chief,' I answered earnestly, 'I hate working in the Senior Rates dining room. I accept that some people have to do it…' I looked up at his expressionless face and then continued, '…I accept some people have to do it for a three-month period.' His expression didn't change. 'I have done more than three months, even though it has been interrupted by being in hospital and being in cells, but all-in-all, I have done more than three months.' Again no change of expression. 'It seems to me I am being punished; punished for having my appendix out, and punished for being in cells. 'Furthermore,' - and now I was beginning to feel I was on dodgy ground, - 'I feel victimised for being given the job in the first place.' The Chief Elec. exhaled and shifted in his seat—almost uncomfortably. 'So, to answer your question, Chief, I would be very happy on Hermes if I could go with all my mess mates at 08:00 to muster in the electrical workshop, exercise the theory taught me at Collingwood, and then reunite with them all at 16:30 in the mess and join in the recreation, comradeship, and banter.' I felt the senior man opposite me was about to speak, but before he did, I added, 'That would make me happy on Hermes.'

'Wait here,' he said, rising from his seat. As he reached the door, he turned and asked if I wanted a cup of tea. He said he'd arrange one for me.

It was more than an hour before he returned, which had now made me adrift for my duty in the Senior Rates dining hall. I had telephoned them and told them, so there would be no surprises when I eventually got there.

'Well,' said the chief, sitting down again, 'I read all the reports. Almost no alcohol in the blood, some in the urine, and no sign of infectious diseases.' He looked up at me and continued. 'The patrolman confirms he found you in the toilet, and the Mama San confirms you didn't want to fuck, but only piss.' He looked at me again, and then informed me, 'The shore patrol does not want to charge you, which is a good thing. However, the Master-at-Arms does.' *That really meant McSnell does*, I thought. He continued. 'You will be charged with visiting a location designated out-of-bounds by ship's standing orders. Sorry to say, you'll probably get three days 'nines. Believe me, it could have been worse. 'I did believe him, and I also believed he had a lot to do with the shore patrol dropping charges. I really was very grateful to this man before me. 'Okay, that's it. You better get back to the dining hall,' he said, letting me out of the switchboard. 'But before you do, just come in the office.' I followed him in, and he sat on his desk. He drew a piece of paper towards him and wrote something on it. He handed it to me and said, 'Fill the rest of this in.' I looked at it, and it was a request form. It's a form we use for requesting things: leave, new badges, afternoons off, permission to grow a beard, permission to shave a beard off; in fact, just about everything! In the request section, he had written, *For a job change out of rotation.* 'Do it now, and let me have it,' he added, turning his attention back to his desk. I could hardly write; such was my happiness. I couldn't believe I would be getting out of that dining hall and away from Jenkins. I filled in the boxes for my name, rate, official number, ship's Book Number, and signed it. The Chief Electrician took it from me, cautioned, 'No guarantees, but I'll do my best.'

'Thank you, Chief,' I said cheerfully, and bounded up the ladder to the main deck.

We sailed, and the Officer of the Day's disciplinary table was a formality, as was the Commanders table. He was able to deal with this case, and proceeded to lecture me on the dangers of being with prostitutes and how my health could be ruined. I could become impotent, blind, brain-damaged, or suffer paralysis. He also lectured me on the value of Ship's Standing Orders, reminding me that they were direct orders from the captain because he had signed them, and so I should feel myself lucky I was not facing a charge of direct disobedience which, he went on, carries a very severe penalty. Finally, he stopped, stood upright, and announced, 'Five days' Number Nine punishment.'

Almost immediately, the MAA bellowed, 'On Caps! Right turn! Quick march!'

So back to the familiar routine: musters and extra work. I had to work around my duties in the SR's dining hall, which was an added complication, but five days was nothing.

Needless to say, for my two hours extra evening work, I was despatched to the Junior Rates Galley. 'You still in cells?' the Killick Chef asked me as I arrived on the first day.

'Nah. Nines now.' I went straight to the first empty boiler, selected my spoon for scraping, climbed up on the pipes, and dived in.

On Monday morning, almost halfway through my latest stint of punishment, I received a message to report to the Electrical office. Could this be the really good news I was waiting for? I dared not get my hopes up, but there was a distinct skip to my step as I walked on the main deck from E section to P. Echo to Papa. I surfed down the ladder and presented myself to the Chief Electrician's Assistant. He was Leading Electrical Mechanic Williams; Bungey, we called him. He smoked heavily, and always had a fag on the go. He was always smart, his Number 8s always clean, and freshly pressed, shoes always shiny. He worked in an office, so never got dirty. 'Hello, Skin,' he greeted me. I hated being called Skin. Bungey always had a permanent smile, which revealed large white front teeth. 'Good news for you,' he beamed. '08:00 tomorrow, report to the Chief Mech. in 6H workshop.'

'Yes!' I said, punching the air in triumph. I was elated. 'What section?' I asked, referring to what electrical section I would be joining.

'Air Conditioning and Ventilation,' he informed me. It really didn't matter. I was out of the SR's dining room, and was on Cloud Nine. I was on shift upstairs today, but this would be my last. I returned to the SR's dining room, where Jenkins demanded to know where I had been. 'Had to go to the Electrical Office,' I informed him, then, immediately continued. 'Ask the chief of all the Electricians, Chief Wepner, if you don't believe me.'

'Huh,' he sneered, 'probably in the shit again.' I said nothing. He didn't know yet, and I was not going to tell him.

Later in the day, before I left to do my stint in the Junior Rates Galley, Jenkins told me not to be late for breakfast the next day. 'I'm not coming,' I told him.

He looked at me menacingly. 'What did you say?' he hissed threateningly.

'I'm not coming.' Jenkins was getting redder in his already reddish face. 'I have a job change. Did nobody tell you?' Jenkins was furious. And my attitude was making him worse. 'My time here is done.' Mighty and Mr Older Seaman were looking on, also surprised by my news. 'I have to go to the reg. office now.' I knew he wanted to thump me; he had always wanted to thump me. I turned my back on him and left. I knew his eyes would be bulging behind the thick lenses of his glasses, and yet I didn't care.

The next day was a new phase in my life: I was to resume work as an electrician. After my extra work, I joined my buddies making the trip from our mess, along the passageway to H section, down two flights of stairs (passing the Stokers' mess), to the workshop flat. The workshop was directly in front of the ladder. The electrical stores were behind it, and between them was a compartment housing the ship's gyroscopes and navigation systems.

The workshop was a large space. Immediately opposite the door was a small office, where the Chief Mechanician sat at a desk facing the door. He could see everyone who came and went. To the right, at the end of the workshop, was a bench with a grinder and drill mounted upon it. Either side of the workspace ran benches the full length of the workshop. Each Electrical section had a designated length of bench. Next to the office was the Engine Rooms and Boiler Rooms (Ers and Brs) section. Next to that, and stretching to the end, was my new section Air Conditioning. Opposite was Domestics, which dealt with lighting, sockets and galley equipment—not a very interesting section. Finally, there was the Switchboard section that dealt with power generation and power conversion.

The Chief Mech. saw me enter the workshop, and beckoned me with his finger to enter his office. He didn't say anything, but once inside his small office, he pointed to a chair with the same finger, indicating I should sit, to which I did.

The Chief Mech. was a short man. He was also a very senior man.

Not as senior as Chief Wepner (the Chief Elec.) and not as old either, but not far off. He had a round face, in fact a round head, with very little hair on top. The hair to the sides was mostly grey, but very curly, and his complexion was craggy from scars and from old acne problems. His lips were full and shiny and his smile, when he did smile, was lopsided. His eyes were small with wrinkled eyelids, and when he stood, he was round. He had a large belly, which buckled in with the tightness of his belt at his waistline. Clothes didn't hang on him well.

I sat in silence whilst he wrote, his eyes flicking up as he did so, monitoring the people entering the workshop.

At precisely 08:00, he got up and left the office, but stood by the door. 'Good morning, men,' he bellowed.

I was surprised to hear a response of, 'Good morning, Chief,' in unison from all the ratings there.

'We have a new member joining us today.' He was beckoning me with his hand. I stepped through the door. 'JEM Clark,' he announced. There followed some jeering and words of ridicule as I was introduced. He led me down the length of the workshop, and stopped me before another Chief Petty Officer. 'This is CPO Hurst,' he introduced me. 'He's your new boss.'

'Hello, lad,' CPO Hurst said, patting me on the shoulder warmly. 'I guess you know Parky,' he added, indicating to LEM Parkinberg. I nodded yes.

The Chief Mech. left me there and strolled back to his office, telling each section certain maintenance targets had to be met, and a variety of other things I didn't really understand; in actual fact, it was just a briefing he gave everyday. Once finished, everyone huddled in their own sections, and things began to get done.

The Air Conditioning plants were scattered all over the ship. They tended to be small compartments, housing motors with compressors, pumps, and controllers. The compartments, which were deep down in the ship, were always clean, though noisy. Access to them was always a long, straight ladder down a vertical shaft. The fans were mainly housed in compartments between 3 deck and the Flight Deck. This meant we could roam all over the ship and always have an excuse for being where we were. Parky was a good person. He was about 23 years old and came from Burnley, and spoke with a heavy Lancashire accent. He was blonde-haired with pinkish coloured skin, which turned a funny yellowy-brown colour when he tanned. He was very knowledgeable and wanted to become a Mechanician. This meant completing a two year technicians' course, but you had to be recommended for this. Therefore, it meant keeping your nose clean, working hard, and impressing people.

I learned a lot from Parky about our trade. He also introduced me to cryptic crosswords and showed me the secrets of the clues; he knew all the tricks of the trade. 'If you walk around the ship with a handful of rags, no-one will ever ask what you are doing,' he informed me. I found this to be true.

CPO Hurst, who everyone called Jeff, didn't do much. Technically, he was very knowledgeable but, when everything was okay, there was very little to do. Most days started off with 'Rounds'. Parky showed me: we systematically visited every compartment and visually checked the equipment. We would listen for strange noises and look for leaks of oil, grease, or water. Electricians always carried a long screwdriver; it was about fourteen inches long, and was called a Long Black. Originally, they were black, but the one I was issued with had a yellow handle and red insulation on its long blade. The tip of the blade was placed on a bearing housing, and the handle pressed against your ear. If there was any defect with the bearing, the rumbling could be clearly heard. So, 'Rounds' also consisted of listening to all these bearings.

Generally, in the mornings after the Chief Mech. had given his little talk, Jeff would turn to me and just say, 'Rounds.' So off I went. It didn't take long before I was doing these on my own; I learned Jeff would go back to his mess and read and drink coffee. He was a Chief Petty Officer, so no-one questioned what he did. Parky would disappear and reappear from time-to-time in the workshop. It was never good to be in the workshop with nothing to do—a job will always be found for you. Routine maintenance had to be carried out on all machinery throughout the ship; maintenance cards would be issued, and you just followed the instructions. The maintenance I was entrusted with mainly consisted of isolating the machinery, opening covers, inspecting for general condition, such as tightness of terminals, and clean and blow-out. Using special test equipment check electrical resistance of earth straps and insulation resistance. Parky showed me for the first few pieces of machinery. I asked him what 'clean and blow-out' meant. I didn't know to what extent you should clean the inside of an electrical starter box. Parky showed me his 'Mk1 cleaner', as he put it. It was just a small paintbrush. He would make a couple of brush strokes on the inside base of the box. 'That's it,' he said. He explained further, 'I, and you, will, in the future, have to sign to say we have completed all the tasks detailed on this maintenance card.' He tapped the card as he said it. 'So,' he said, showing me his brush, 'I have cleaned.'

'What about blow-out?' I asked; I was thinking it was necessary to get some kind of reverse vacuum cleaner of something.

'Watch and learn,' he answered. He took a deep breath and blew around the panel, much the same as someone would blowing out birthday candles. 'That's it,' he said, 'clean and blow-out. Tick it off, he said.' I remembered that, and always had a clean paintbrush in my tool box. I taught this to my subordinates later in my career; I always thought that the term 'clean and blow-out' to be rather vague and lacking actual detail, but it remained the same for the whole time I was in the Navy.

For this period, nothing very exciting was happening, but I was pleased to be part of the Electrical section, just like the rest of the guys in the mess. During this time, Spanner was part of the Domestic section, and I used to meet up with him in various 'secret' locations around the ship, and just chat and do nothing.

It was announced that five days' station leave would be given in Australia, and also in Singapore, for the next visit. You could choose which one you preferred, but you couldn't take both.

This became a good topic of conversation in the mess. You could not just go ashore and come back five days later. There were some options: you could go to a disused army camp (there was a list), go on some sailing trips or on an expedition (Exped); there were also other things associated with schools and animal reserves.

There was a guy, who was a friend of Spanner's, who used to come and sit in our section of the mess. His name was Jacklyn, and he came from the Senior side of the mess. He was about twenty or twenty-one years old. Needless to say, he was called Jackie. Jackie was a bit of a frightening guy for me; he was renowned for wanting to fight when he was drunk. He was a powerful, muscular man, and although he was not enormous, he had good muscular definition. He had light brown, curly hair, and his eyes were always bright with eyebrows raised, almost as if he was surprised all the time. He was always ready for a laugh, and I quite liked listening to him. I don't think he was super-intelligent, as he would say some daft things at times. I didn't speak with him much, because I was scared he would take a disliking to me, and then I could be in trouble. Anyway, this guy had the idea of going on Exped. He said one of his friends was one of the ship Physical Training Instructors (PTI), and they had the responsibility of looking after all the Exped gear. Mainly, that means camping equipment, tents, sleeping bags, etc. Jackie was very excited about it, and asked who'd be interested; Spanner was the first to speak. 'So, what does that mean? We get all this gear and follow the fucking PTI to Ayres Rock?' Everyone sniggered at the thought of this.

'No,' Jackie reassured him, 'we just get the gear and go where we want.'

'So we get the fucking gear and we go to Ayres rock.'

'No, Spanner, for fuck's sake,' Jackie said. 'We tell them we are going up the Blue Mountains or something, and *then* we go where we want.' Jackie looked around the table.

He looked at me as if inviting my opinion. I didn't want to offend this guy; I wanted him to be my friend, really, so I said, 'Well, sounds like a good idea.'

Mike Ward was sat with us. He was from Birmingham, about nineteen years old and was with us at Collingwood. He was a quiet sort of guy, but not a loner; he was a follower, not a leader. He asked, 'Can you really get the gear, and will they really let us go?' It was a good question.

'Sure I fucking can.'

Mike then proposed, 'Well, go and ask and find out exactly what we need to do. Then we'll know where we're at.'

'Right.' Jackie said. 'Who wants to go then?' Spanner said he was interested; I followed Spanner. Mike said he'd be interested in principle. 'We need six, Jackie said.'

'Budgie might go,' I suggested.

Fingers was sat there and said, 'I think you're fucking crazy. I'm going to Frazers Hill next time in Singers.' Nobody dared say anything against Fingers because he was powerful, and could lash out if you weren't careful.

There was a bit of silence. 'Okay,' Jackie said. 'I'll get some real fucking info. Tomorrow.' He was looking at me as he said this.

'Okay, mate,' I said. 'I'll ask Budgie.'

I spoke with Budgie and he said it could be fun to go camping, but he wasn't into rock-climbing or hiking all day long with a heavy load on his back. I assured him I was not into that either. He thought Don might be interested in camping as well.

That evening, after supper, we sat around our table in the mess, waiting for Jackie. Soon, he came breezing in with a big smile on his face and waving a piece of paper. 'No fucking problems, men,' he announced, plonking the paper on the desk, which turned out to be a map. In fact, there were *several* maps. 'Look,' he said, shuffling the maps. 'We tell everyone we are going here,' he said, pointing to a spot on the map. 'Katoomba,' he announced proudly. We were all looking at him, and he continued. 'Katoomba is like a base camp to the Blue Mountains. People come from all over the world, camp there, then go off hiking.' None of us said anything but just looked at him, the map, and at each other. 'If we tell the PTI and everyone else that we are going there to do some fucking hiking, then we can get all the camping gear.' Jackie was looking for some sort of reaction from us. 'For fucking *free*!'

Mike Ward was the first to speak. 'So, where do we go, then?'

'Anywhere,' Jackie replied.

'We wanna be by a river,' Spanner said. 'At least then we have water, a toilet, a swimming pool, washing machine, and a place to fish.' There were a few giggles, but I was impressed; what Spanner said made sense.

'We need to be close to a town as well, so we can buy food,' I chipped in.

'We need some fucking pubs as well,' Donessy added.

We were all looking at the map without paying too much attention to it. Jackie had the solution. 'Turn this map over; I'll go out and you lot spin it around. I'll come back and stick a pin in it, and then let's see where we fucking end up.'

'You watch,' said Budgie, 'we'll end up in the fucking sea.' We cleared the table and spread a map of New South Wales upside-down on it with Sydney in the middle.

Mick said, 'I'll go get him.' Mick made Jackie cover his eyes with one hand and then led him into the mess and stopped him in front of the table.

Jackie had a dart in his hand. 'Ready?' he asked.

'Ready,' we all confirmed.

He raised the dart in his fist and stabbed it down on the table. All our eyes followed the arc of his arm, and were fixated on the point in the map. Jackie uncovered his eyes and said, 'Got you, you bastard.' We turned the map over and we all leaned forward to look. *It seems a long way from Sydney* was my first thought.

'Newcastle!' someone said.

'It's a fucking long way from Sydney,' I said. On closer inspection, the point of the dart pierced a town called Hexham.

'Hexham,' Jackie said. 'That's it, then.' We were all straining to see the map in greater detail. Sure enough, the small town of Hexham had a hole in it.

'See! See!' said Spanner excitedly. 'See!' he said again, stabbing the map with his finger. 'There's a fucking *river*.' It was true; a river ran nearby.

'And a railway line,' I said. Everyone looked again.

'That's it, then.' Jackie repeated. 'Are we all in?' We all agreed in unison.

We all submitted our request forms for *Station Leave in Sydney as Promulgated*, and Jackie reserved all the camping gear.

I finished my latest spell of punishment and settled down to 'normal' life on Hermes. I wandered around the Air Conditioning plants every day, and found several places to loaf and waste time. Whilst it was great to be out of the SR's dining hall, life had a deal of boredom to it now. We spoke a lot about our forthcoming camping trip, and we all looked forward to it. I looked forward to spending some of my extra pay!

15: Sydney Australia

Harbour Stations were sounded a 07:00, and immediately, men filed out of the mess en-route to their designated Harbour Station position. Mine was Kilo switchboard. There were six switchboards about the ship, and Kilo was the main one. Kilo switchboard was always manned; the others remained empty, unless something out-of-the-ordinary was happening, such as Harbour Stations, Action Stations, close-down for NBCD (Nuclear, Biological, Chemical Defence), or if we had an emergency on-board like fire or flood, etc. I just had to sit around and wait to be told to do something. Hopefully nothing would happen.

Spanner was on-duty today, so could not go ashore. He was pretty pissed off about that, but it happens to everyone. Someone has to be on-duty first night in; I'd planned to go ashore with Budgie, Don and Max. We intended to go over the bridge to Luna Park, where they had a giant wooden rollercoaster.

Tomorrow, we would get our gear and set off on our trip. During the last few days, we had been putting all our equipment together: tents, sleeping bags, cooking utensils, stoves, survival ration pack and also, much to Spanner's delight, fishing lines and hooks; we even had matches! We had to check it all and sign for acceptance. It would be checked when we returned it, and any shortcomings would have to be paid for. The plan was to hike to the railway station, through Sydney City, and get a train to Hexham. There, we would find a suitable place to make camp. At this stage, there was no other plan.

Kilo switchboard was on 5 Deck, Section K. Once down the ladder from 4 Deck, you stood in Kilo switchboard flat. From here, you had access to the switchboard, on the starboard side, some stores on the portside, and forward of the switchboard was the ships laundry. This laundry was run by a team of Chinese, and it was here they lived and worked. You would bring a load of dirty laundry, Number 8s shirts and trousers, overalls, bedding, and towels. They would mark them, wash them and iron them, and the cost was very little. The process was on-going for twenty-four hours, but always some Chinese could be seen sleeping and some eating. They slept in any space they could find, even just on the hard deck next to their machinery, which buzzed, whirred and whined. Someone would prepare their food in the corner of the laundry, which mainly consisted of noodles and rice, which they would eat out of stainless steel bowls with chopsticks. Generally, they would sit in Kilo flat and eat their food, hunched in small groups on their haunches. I watched as they ate, and occasionally one would look up at me and smile, offering the bowl to me to try. I always declined, although it always looked good, and smelled delicious.

I was a particular favourite of the Chinese because, on leaving Singapore, we took on a band of tailors' and a band of cobblers. The tailors' made their 'factory' on 5 Deck underneath the galley; the cobblers camped on 6 Deck beneath our mess.

They needed electricity for their machines and lights, and I helped provide this for them. I ran cables from fuse boxes and sockets. Everything was of a temporary nature, because when we returned to Singapore, they would disembark, and all the wiring removed. Everyone on-board had at least one suit made to measure by them, and everyone on-board had at least one pair of shoes made to measure. Shirts could also be tailored to your exact requirements and styles. The workmanship was fantastic, and very cheap. I accumulated a wardrobe of made-to-measure suits, shirts and shoes. However, my work for supplying the electrical power was not given for nothing; the Chinese had access to beer and would drink beer in the evenings. They thanked me with beer; not only that I could go to them from time-to-time, and buy beer. They really didn't like doing this, but I explained I could not buy beer on-board as I was too young. If I bought beer, or they gave me beer, I would mostly sit with them while I drank it. I could not really take it back to the mess as too many eyes would be upon me, and I could end up in the shit because of someone's vindictiveness. Sitting with the Chinese cemented our relationship, and I guess that's why the guy opposite, chop-sticking his way through his noodles, smiled at me.

After a couple of hours, we were dismissed from Harbour Stations, and so could return to our normal places of duty. Parky had told me in the past that part of our duty as being members of the Air Conditioning section was to check the outside atmosphere. This was his way of 'legalising' us being on the Flight Deck, or on the Weather Deck of the island, if flying was in progress, or any other Weather Deck, for that matter. Up in the island was a perfect spot to see the aircraft being catapulted off the front end as we sailed into the wind at full power; more excitingly was to see the aircraft coming in to land, especially the jets. The ship could be tossing around some, and the aircraft would approach on a diagonal line in alignment with the angle deck; the approach 'runway' was angled to provide an exit path for the aircraft, if their trailing hook failed to grab one of the three arrester cables stretched across the deck. Before aircraft carriers had angled decks, too many planes crashed into the island; it was a wonderful sight to see a squadron of aircraft land on-board. As soon as one was safely down, it was towed to the very front of the Flight Deck. The arrester wires would be reset, and the next would roar in. As one landed, you could see the next taking up position in the flight path. If one would miss an arrester wire, a flair would be fired, telling the pilot to power up and go around again. The jets would roar with ferocious noise, and it would climb back into the sky and join the back of the queue of the landing planes.

I met Parky in the Electrical workshop, as arranged, and together we set off to do 'Rounds'. Parky had friends all over the ship, and today he took me to some of his Fleet Air Arm friends, who worked from a small workshop at the aft end of the island. The Fleet Air Arm were the crew that dealt with the aircraft and flying manoeuvres. We called them Waffoos. Generally, they didn't go to sea much, as they could only go to sea on Aircraft Carriers, although more and more Destroyers and Frigates were carrying helicopters, so they had more opportunity. The ship's company and Waffoos didn't get on very well with each other and each, pretty much, kept to their own. The guys in the small workshop aft of the island were like the seamen of the ship's company: they were responsible to the deck fitments associated with flying, such as arrester gear, catapults, landing sites, etc. The guy Parky introduced me to was called Taff; needless to say, a Welsh man. He was old, at least thirty, with a big pot-belly, full of tattoos and an extremely dark suntan from working most days in the open air. He was a leading hand, a killick, and led a team of subordinates from his workshop.

'Hiya, Skin,' he said, 'how's your bum for spots?' The man frightened me, and I didn't really know what to say to him.

Parky put his arm around my shoulders, rocking me off-balance. 'Clarkie's a good 'un,' Parky told Taff. 'He's my winger.'

'Right, Skin,' he said, as a note of acceptance, 'you want some of Taff's Limers, I suppose? 'Taff always had a big container of Limers ready. Lime was traditionally given to sailors to stop scurvy; obviously the modern diet negated this necessity, but tins of powdered lime were issued to all messes. Just add water was all that was necessary, so the instructions said; however, it was very difficult to turn the powder into a drink, which was palatable. The powder was difficult to dilute; it was strong and very bitter. Taff had his solution: he would mix a quantity of this powder with sugar, and dilute it with boiling water. When the powder went into solution, cold water was added, and the end result was Limers like you'd never tasted before. You could drink it without grimacing, and it tasted good.

Parky had already told me about this, so I was waiting with

anticipation. 'Yes, please,' I said cheerfully, knowing Taff had accepted me.

'Here, Skin,' he said, handing me a pint of the light green liquid.

I thanked him and took the glass in two hands. It was cold, and the slightly acidic taste cut through your thirst. It was refreshing. We walked around the island on to the Flight Deck and we got our first proper view of Sydney. Once again, a magnificent sight greeted us: Sydney Harbour bridge, a replica of the one spanning the Tyne in Newcastle; in front of it, the opera house gleaming white in the sun; the radical structure reminded me of giant parrot beaks stuck in the ground. We walked to the edge of the Flight Deck and looked out into the harbour. It was full of sailing boats and speedboats darting this way and that. The sails of the sailing boats bellowed out, full of wind, which caused the boats to list under their strain. Closer to us, bikini-clad girls in smaller craft waved at us with upturned faces, relishing at the hoots and catcalls the sailors were directing their way.

'They'll be in for some cock tonight,' Parky said as he finished his drink. 'Come on!' he said, turning to go. Reluctantly, I followed, and we retuned our glasses to Taff. We said our farewells and returned below.

Later Budgie, Don and Max mounted the gang-plank, skipped along its length, and jumped off the end onto Australia. I followed suit and the four of us ambled away from the Hermes. Outside the dockyard gate, we found a taxi and told the driver to take us to Luna Park. As he drove, we surveyed the neighbourhood; not very exciting. We went over the bridge, where we could see the Hermes beyond the opera house alongside the harbour wall. It looked rather magnificent, and a familiar feeling of pride welled up inside of me again. I said nothing, but thought the others felt the same way.

Luna Park was a disaster. The Big Dipper was closed for maintenance, and the rest was just like Southsea Fun Fair. Although bigger, many of the attractions were closed down, and so we wandered around whilst Budgie and I talked about our trip, starting tomorrow. We both looked forward to spending a few nights away from the ship; we decided to go, but couldn't decide *where* to go. Max wanted to go into the city; Budgie and I preferred to stay closer to the dockyard. I certainly didn't want to go someplace where I could land in trouble. Don said nothing, really; he was pretty relaxed about it. Finally, we decided to split up. Don went with Max, and Budgie and I took a taxi and told the driver to drop us off at a bar close to the dockyard.

The drinking age limit in Australia was twenty-one, although there was talk of it being reduced to twenty. We had no chance. We were seventeen and both looked younger. The inside of the bar was very bare; no decorations on the walls, and the lights were bulbs on the ends of cables. No bar stools; a few tables, but not so many chairs. The floorboards were littered with rubbish and cigarette ends, and in some places soaking wet where beer had been spilled. The bar was large but not full; about twenty men stood in small groups drinking, smoking, shouting and laughing. No women were in sight. The men at the bar were drinking beer from small glasses, and refilling the glasses from a jug; away from the bar, I could see some younger men who were only like us: boys, really. They were also drinking beer.

'Right,' I said to Budgie, 'let's just go up there and ask for a jug, like them.'

'Well,' Budgie replied, 'they can only tell us to fuck off.'

We marched up to the bar. The barman looked at us, as if questioning us. 'A jug like that,' I said, pointing to the jug in front of the men next to us. He looked at it and then back to me. Looking directly at me, his arm reached under the bar, and he placed a jug in front of us. 'Like this?' he asked.

I was thinking of saying with some beer in it, but he may respond by just putting a drop in. 'Yeah,' I said, 'but full of beer.'

'You fucking Pommies?' he asked, Pommies being the derogatory name for the British. It comes from when we used to send our prisoners out there to serve time; their shirts were marked P.O.M.E., standing for Prisoner of Mother England.

'Yeah.'

'You off that fucking big ship that came in today? 'he asked, still looking intently at me.

'Yeah,' I repeated for the third time, and nodded again.

'It's a fucking pitcher,' he said, picking up the jug and shaking it in front of me, 'and what you want is a fucking pitcher of beer.' He paused, waiting for an answer. Before I could respond, he went on. 'That right, mate?' He then turned, walked down the bar, and began to fill the jug. 'Here,' he said as he placed the jug of beer on the bar. 'A fucking pitcher of Australian beer on the fucking house for you pair of fucking Pommies. The first fucking Pommies I've seen in this bar from that fucking ship.' He reached under the bar and came up with two small glasses, which he placed on either side of the jug. We couldn't believe our luck; not only does he serve us, but he gives us the beer for free.

'So, Budge,' I said, 'it's not a jug; it's a *pitcher*.'

Budgie thought for a moment, and then asked, 'Is it a pitcher or a fucking pitcher?' We both smiled at this. We drank the beer and again talked of what was to come in the next few days. When we finished, we decided we couldn't just walk out, but had to buy another beer, as if to say thanks. We were both feeling the effects, but decided we were close enough to the dockyard not to get into trouble. The barman looked at us and Budgie raised his arm. 'Can we have another pitcher of beer, please?' he asked, with an emphasis on the word *pitcher*.

'So, you want another fucking pitcher of beer, do you, mate?' And before we could say anything, he continued. 'No fucking worries, mate.' He took the jug and refilled it, returning and placing the beer in front of us. 'Now,' he said, 'whose round is it now?' We didn't quite understand what he meant. As if reading our minds, he asked, 'Who would have paid for the first fucking pitcher if it were not on the fucking house?' he clarified.

'I would,' I said.

'Oh,' he said, and now turned to Budgie. 'You better have this fucker on the house as well, then. Then you're fucking even.' With that, he resumed his position in the centre of the bar. We drank the beer, and time passed; we were getting drunk, but we could both still talk and walk. We decided to go back on-board. We both waved a *thank you* to the barman, who waved back. 'Tell your fucking friends to come and see us here,' he shouted to us, 'and tell them to bring their fucking money with them. Can't afford to fucking give beer away to you fucking Pommies all the time.' We waved again in acquiescence.

The next day, we emerged from the train station at Hexham with our rucksacks on our backs. True to form, there was a bar almost opposite, which we made for. The inside was similar to the one by the dockyard: it was smaller, and had more chairs with the tables; no decorations on the walls or behind the bar, and no women. We made for an empty table by the wall, and piled our rucksacks on the floor close by. Jackie and Mike went to the bar and came back with two pitchers of beer and six small glasses. 'Cheers, fellas.' Jackie raised his glass in a toast.

'Cheers,' we said in unison, chinking our glasses together and drinking.

On closer examination of the people in the bar, many had bags and holdalls, and some of which were of a military nature. We got into a conversation with a guy on the table next to us; he was about the same age as Jackie, and was in the Australian Army. He was about to return to Vietnam for another turn of duty there; he was interested to know what we intended, and soon realised we were, in effect, on holiday. I don't think he liked the idea of us being military men, but not having any responsibility; I knew we had to be careful what we said, as this guy was looking for a fight. The Vietnam war was raging at the time, and many American lives were being lost. I didn't know that Australia was involved. We turned our attention to other people, and eventually found a local person, who was not waiting for a train. He told us of a location, by a weir, where we could make camp; it was more than an hour's hike outside the town, and we had two options of getting there: we could go via a regular road, or by a farm track, which ran parallel to it. He said he would lead us to the farm track, if we wished. He led us through the streets of Hexham to the track he referred to.

'Right, mate,' he said to Jackie, 'just follow this until you see a disused railway bridge.' He pointed. 'A fucking big pile of rusted steel, really. Can't fucking miss it, mate,' he added, bidding us farewell.

We saw the bridge long before we got there, and the man was right:

it was a big, ugly mass of rusted steel. It looked as if two electricity pylons had collapsed onto one another. There was not much evidence of a railway track; all the sleepers had been removed. We got to the weir and looked about us: one side of the weir was a freshwater river. It was not very wide, and water did not flow very fast; the water must have passed the weir by some underground valve system, as the level was much lower than the weir itself. The other side was where the bridge crossed: the river here was much wider and, we suspected, much deeper. It was also saltwater. Further downstream the salty river, we could see a road bridge and traffic; beyond that, there was a much larger, newer bridge which carried a motorway across the river, which would have been very much wider there. The traffic could be heard, but it was not offensive. By the side of the river, almost under the bridge, a large grass clearing was surrounded by bushes; this would be our campsite. On the edge of this was an abandoned American Ford car; it was enormous and the bonnet, boot and roof were dented in, as if kids had run over it. We surveyed our campsite and had to trample the grass down to make a clearing. We soon had the tents up; we also intended to light a fire to burn during the night to keep wild animals away, but decided it was too dangerous as the grass was too dry. If the wind blew any sparks or embers away, then we could have a serious problem. We would use our camping stoves for cooking and use them by the riverbank, where we would be able to control things better.

Spanner and I shared a tent; Don and Budgie shared, as did Mike and Jackie. We had to have some rules, so we sat down and talked about it. We had no food except for the emergency rations we brought with us; we decided two men would go into the town each day to buy food for that day. Those two guys would stay in camp that evening, whilst the other four went into the town. We then drew straws: Spanner and I would have to stay at the camp for the first night; the next day, Budgie and Don would go and do the shopping run. Jackie and Mike would shop the following day, and then it would be our turn. It was late in the afternoon, and the other four were eager to get off. We told them to go, and we would organise things further. They left, excitedly tripping off down the farm track as the sun began to lose its heat with its aspect in the sky.

Spanner and I were both keen to do some fishing, with high expectation of catching fist to eat. We checked our lines and hooks; we had some lead weights, but no floats. I told Spanner about my first experience of fishing, where my brother and I had only poles; in fact, they were clothes line props. We had line, hooks and weights, and used a cork, from a bottle, for a float. I said we could cut a branch for a rod, and then look for something for a float.

We checked out the car and, in the boot, under a rotten mat, we discovered a rusty old tool kit. It comprised a few rusty spanners and a couple of screwdrivers; there was also a tyre lever and a jack. The seats were leather and, although cracked, in reasonable condition. With the tools, we took out the seats and carried them back to our campsite. The front seat was like the back seat; a bench seat. When we removed them, we had four cushioned seats, which we arranged in the space around our tents. They made comfortable loungers.

The car had also been a place for parties: empty beer cans were all over the place, along with empty beer bottles; and then I discovered an empty wine bottle. 'Look at this,' I said to Spanner, excitedly holding the bottle up for him to see.

'So?'

'It's a wine bottle.'

'Yeah,' he said, 'a fucking empty wine bottle.'

'Where there's an empty wine bottle, there must be a fucking cork,' I said. Spanner looked at me, and I could see the penny drop. He joined me by the side of the car, and we searched through all the empty containers; sure enough, we found corks. We found lots of corks.

We soon sorted out our rods. Bait we found under stone; always under a big stone, you can find worms, along with all manner of insects. We dragged one of the car seats down to the riverbank and we sat, side-by-side, and began to fish. When the sun went down, mosquitoes came out to play, and the only bite we got was from them. We packed up and went to our tent; we had paraffin lamps, but decided not to use these in the tents for fear of knocking them over, so we were reduced to torches. What we did bring with us was an abundant supply of batteries. We got into our sleeping bags and read. We heard the others come back, but they made little noise.

We slept well, and the following day, Spanner and I awoke to hunger. We did not eat last night, and we now had the option of waiting, or tucking into the survival food. We said we'd wait.

The other four had hangovers. We could hear them moaning in their tents, giggling and swearing at each other. Spanner and I took a camping stove to the riverbank and began to boil water for tea. It was still early, but the sun was high in the sky and burned down upon us.

Jackie emerged from his tent, but his blue eyes were not so bright this morning. His curly hair looked like a tangled mop on his head. Immediately, he nagged Budgie and Don to go and get food. Eventually, they sorted themselves out; we all gave them some money and off they trekked down the track.

Spanner and I resumed our position by the riverbank. A tabby stray cat observed us from close quarters. Spanner pulled in a small fish. 'Give it to the cat,' I said. He unhooked it and did as I said. The fish flapped about a bit, but finally the cat plonked a paw on it to steady it, then bit its head off. It continued to devour the entire thing.

Budgie and Don returned with bacon, sausages, tins of beans, bread, butter, cornflakes, and milk. From his rucksack, Don also pulled a twenty-four can case of Foster's lager. Jackie made a suggestion that we only drink three cans each, which will leave extra beer for the two guys who remain behind. We all agreed.

With a belly full of bacon, bangers, beans and beer, I crawled into the tent for a siesta. After a couple of hours, we were getting ready to go to town: me, Spanner, Jackie and Mike. We went from one bar to the next. I was soon drunk, and life was a blur; I made it my goal not to fall over and not to be sick. I remember staggering back down the farm track, in the dark, bouncing between Spanner and Jackie. They kept me on my feet.

The next morning, Spanner and I sat by the river with our fishing poles stretching out from us in the warm morning sun. The traffic from the road was a dull drone, yet the small insects made a greater noise about us. Sun glistened from the small ripples on the water as we both eagerly watched our cork floats, tossing our thoughts around our minds. We had had some success this morning, both landing two small roach: the first we put on the riverbank behind us, and it wasn't long before the tabby stray came, sniffed it, licked it, then hunched up beside it and ate it. Tabby was later joined by two other strays, a black one and a ginger one, who both sat in the sun, like us, waiting for the next fish. They didn't sit together; they were not social. The three were behind us, out of reach, and each well-distanced from the other. We gave them the fish in turn, and they never fought over them. The morning was tranquil and calm.

'Wouldn't want to be a fish,' Spanner murmured. 'Eh, Clarkie?' His comments interrupted my thoughts, and it took me some time to digest what he had said. He continued, 'Can't talk. They don't have a tongue, you know.'

I looked at Spanner and he was staring at his broken cork, as if mesmerised. 'Can't hear either,' I said. 'Don't have any fucking ears.'

'Maybe that's why they don't talk,' said Spanner. After a while he said, 'No good talking if no-one's listening.'

'Don't have a nose either, so can't smell.'

Spanner turned to look at me and asked sincerely, 'Who the fuck would want to be a fish?' He turned back to the cork, and after some moments said, 'They say a shark can smell blood in the sea from miles off.'

'So does a shark have a nose then?' I responded. 'I can't see that. How can you smell underwater?'

'Dunno,' Spanner said adding, 'but that's what they say.'

'Tell me this then, Spanner,' I demanded, 'how does a fish see where it's going?'

'For fuck's sake, Clarkie, fish *do* have eyes, ya know,' he told me, as if I was stupid.

'I know they have eyes, but they are on the side of its head.' Spanner thought about this. I continued, 'That means they can only look to the side.' I could see Spanner still thinking. 'Look, it's like me and my brother when we were riding in my dad's car.' Spanner was looking directly at me, so I continued. 'We sit in the back and I look out of one window and my brother looks out of the other. We both see what we pass, but we cannot see where we are going.'

'Maybe you're right,' Spanner conceded.

We were disturbed by Don approaching. He had just woken and staggered from his tent. He was smoking a cigarette as he sauntered towards us, one hand in his pocket, the other cupping the cigarette. Sucking on it occasionally, he would exhale through his nose and mouth as he squinted with is left eye. As he reached us, I confronted him. 'Spanner reckons he wouldn't want to be a fish.' Don looked at Spanner and took another drag.

Spanner said, as if in explanation, 'No fucking tongue, so can't speak. No fucking ears, so can't hear, and they can only look sideways.'

Don looked up at the bridge, and then to the road. He swung around and looked at the cats momentarily. After a while he said, 'Don't have any fucking bollocks either, so can't fuck.'

'That's another fucking reason,' Spanner confirmed, nodding his head.

'I'd rather be a cat,' said Don. We all looked around at the cats. They were relaxed again after a moment of tension when Don arrived. Tabby was sat upright licking its paws after devouring his second fish; Blackie laid looking at us like the giant sphinx; and Ginger had rolled onto his back, offering its belly to the warm sun. 'Cats have a good life; just laze around in the sun all day, sleeping and eating and they fuck when they want to.' Spanner and I contemplated Don's preference over being a fish.

'Not all cats have a good life,' Spanner said, and then by way of explanation, 'some are skinny fuckers that can't find food, and some have their tails cut off by cruel gangs of kids.' Spanner, again, was earnestly watching his float. 'And some fuckers get chased by dogs.'

'I tell you what,' I said, 'being a rabbit is better.' Spanner turned to me, waiting for me to continue. 'Rabbits only eat, sleep and fuck, and not necessarily in that order.'

'Yeah,' Spanner said, 'but they get run over also.'

'Cats get run over as well, you know,' I told him, 'and human fucking beings.'

There was a pause. 'Fish don't get run over,' Don announced.

'And another thing,' I continued 'you never see a skinny rabbit like you see skinny cats.'

There was a moment's silence, which was broken by Don. 'You never see a skinny fish,' he said.

We all thought about this for a while, and finally Spanner said, 'Still wouldn't want to be a fucking fish.'

Jackie and Mike returned from the town with another case of beer, more bacon, bangers, beans, and also some steak. We had another feast on the riverbank, followed by a siesta. That evening followed a similar pattern to the first: just a blur.

The following morning, I opened my eyes to see what looked like a pile of mashed potato on my pillow. Pain hammered in my skull, trying to break through my forehead. There was a rancid, pungent smell in the air. I reached up and pushed the 'mashed potato' away; it disintegrated. I raised my head to discover Spanner had changed his sleeping bag around. His head was now towards the exit flaps of the tent. I raised myself on one elbow and felt moisture in the sleeping bag. There were small bits of sodden food all over the place. 'Spanner,' I croaked.

'You dirty bastard, Clarkie,' he snarled at me.

'What's up?'

'You… you piss head,' he snarled again. 'Spewing all over the place last night.' I looked around, and he was right. There was vomit all over my side of the tent and my sleeping bag.

I apologised profusely, but it didn't seem to change his mood. Fortunately, I missed his sleeping bag, as I must have been facing away from him when I vacated the contents of my stomach. Spanner crawled out of the tent and told me to sort it out. I took his sleeping bag out and checked it. It was clean. I took all the other items out of the tent and put clean things on one car seat, and all the others in a pile. My vomit splashed my rucksack, torch and some books, but nothing of Spanner's—fortunately. I rolled my sleeping-bag up, and cleaned the tent ground sheet with it. I took it down to the river, and threw it in to soak. I cleaned the ground sheet and all the other contaminated items using my towel. I left the tent flaps fully open to let the inside dry. I then jumped in the river and washed the sleeping bag as best I could; I washed my towel as well. The river water worked wonders for my hangover: I felt refreshed when I had done. I spread the sodden sleeping bag on the roof of the old car and my towel on the bonnet. I knew the sun and the heat of the metal would soon dry them. I returned to the riverbank, where the rest of the guys were boiling water for tea with the camp stove and eating cornflakes. The cornflakes were dry, as we had no milk; we had powdered milk for tea. 'What's up,' Jackie jeered, 'can't hold your beer?'

'No,' I said, 'it wasn't the beer. Must have been something I ate,' I added. They all mocked me, but that was to be expected.

Other than my drying towel and sleeping bag, I put all the other items into our now-dry and fresh-smelling tent. Spanner looked in and said, 'Well, it needed a fucking good sort-out, anyway.' With that, I knew his temper had subsided with me. 'Come on, Clarkie boy,' he chirped cheerfully, 'our turn for the shopping.' We took our empty rucksacks and trundled off down the farm track. We went into the first bar we came to, and Spanner told me to get the beer in. I could not refuse nor argue. I boldly went up to the bar and told the barman, 'A fucking pitcher of beer, mate.' In Australia, I discovered, you cannot use the word 'pitcher' without preceding it with the word 'fucking'. Plus, everyone is called 'mate'.

'No worries, fella,' he answered. He didn't call me 'mate'!

We drank the beer, and Spanner got another. We drank that, then left the bar bound more towards the town centre, where the supermarket could be found. Hexham was a small place, and we had only discovered four bars. The town had a small supermarket and a cluster of other shops further towards the town square. Traditional shops: butchers', bakers', ironmongers', grocery store, and some clothes shops. We found another bar, and I was despatched to get the beer. This bar had a darts board, and a couple of guys were playing. We watched, and soon, they asked if we wanted to play. We joined them, but it was difficult for me to focus, as the beer was taking its effect. Spanner engaged them in conversation about their involvement in Vietnam; Spanner knew a lot more about what was happening around the world than I did, so I just shut up, listened, and played my darts. Spanner was also telling them about our camping expedition and how we took it in turns to come into the town to buy food, and today was our turn. 'Well, you've fucking missed it, mate,' one of the guys said. He went on to say, 'Today is Thursday! Everything shuts here at two o'clock!'

'Everything?' Spanner asked

'Everything, mate,' the guy confirmed. 'Half-day closing.'

Spanner and I looked at each other. There was a look of horror on his face. 'Fuck my'ole boots!' Spanner exclaimed. 'So where can we get food?'

'Can't get food anywhere, mate,' he replied. 'Fucking told you, mate. Half-day fucking closing.' Spanner sat down and poured out the last of the beer from the pitcher to our glasses. I could see he was worried. I sat down with him and picked up my glass. He drank his beer and plonked the glass on the table.

'We have to think about this, Clarkie,' he said to me. I nodded but said nothing. 'We'll have another fucking pitcher to help us,' he said, standing and taking the empty pitcher to the bar.

We continued talking and playing darts until the beer was finished. I was drunk again, and needed full concentration on keeping on my feet and keeping what was in my belly *in* my belly. I had no confidence in talking, so tried not to. 'Let's see what we can find,' said Spanner, and I followed him out. We made our way to the town square. The supermarket was shut, the butchers' was shut, the bakers' was shut, as was everything. We stopped by the ironmongers', and I was leaning against the window, pretending to look at what was offered by this shut shop. 'Hey, Clarkie! Look! Look! Look!' Spanner exclaimed excitedly. I thought he had found a shop which was open. Next to the ironmongers was a pet shop, and in the window were two small kittens, rolling around with each other. Spanner was tapping the window to call their attention, and they stopped their frolicking and looked at Spanner with big blue eyes and wobbly heads. One was pure black with longish fur; the other was a mishmash of colours. It was a cross between a tortoiseshell and a tabby, and had a mangled-up tail. 'Ah, man, they're fucking beautiful,' he said. 'Poor fuckers,' he added with great emotion. 'I'm going to buy them,' he announced. I have learned that once Spanner sets his mind on something, then it has to be. Fortunately, the shop was shut, so I didn't have to try to dissuade him. He scanned the window and the closed door. The door had several notices advertising puppies for sale, dog kennels for sale, fish for sale, amongst many more. There was also a sign declaring when the shop would be open, and, thankfully, not until tomorrow morning. 'Look!' Spanner said, pointing to a sign which read '*For emergency Veterinary services, ring the bell*', and an arrow pointing to the bell by the side of the door. Before I could stop him, Spanner had his thumb on the button. No sound could be heard, but he repeatedly pushed the bell.

'Spanner! What the fuck are you doing?'

'I'm going to buy these kittens,' he told me firmly.

'But the place is shut,' I pleaded.

Just then, an upstairs window opened and a head popped out. 'What's the panic?' a lady's voice shouted down to us. We stepped back from the door and looked up. I almost fell over, and had to stagger backwards to keep my feet.

'I want to buy these two kittens,' Spanner said, pointing to the window.

'Come back tomorrow morning,' the lady said. 'They'll still be there.'

'No! No!' Spanner said desperately. 'We won't be here tomorrow!'

'Wait,' the lady said, and disappeared, closing the window after her.

'Don't tell me you are really going to buy 'em,' I checked.

'I have to,' he said earnestly. 'It's cruel to leave them like that.' There must have been a thousand and one reasons why he should not buy these kittens, but I could hardly talk, let alone reason with him.

'Well, what are you going to do with them?' I asked.

'Keep them!' he said, as if that was the final answer.

'But you can't keep them on-board.'

'Why not? People have kept loads of animals on-board ships.'

'Not on the Hermes, and not cats either,' I reminded him.

'I'm going to have 'em,' Spanner said, just as the lights went on inside and the door opened.

'Come in,' the lady beckoned, turning to go behind the serving counter.

I grabbed Spanner's arm. 'Just buy the black one. The other one is fucking ugly.'

'If I don't take the ugly one as well, then no-one will buy it,' he said, pulling his arm free. 'Anyway, they may be siblings or something, so they have to stay together.' He went inside. The smell of animals along with animal food, birds, rodents and the shit from their cages that wafted through the open door into my face nearly made me puke. It stopped me dead, and I returned to the street.

It seemed like an eternity, but finally Spanner emerged from the shop with a large cardboard box and a beaming grin on his face.

We made our way down the track, Spanner coo-cooing into the box, and me desperately trying to walk straight. We had no food and no beer for the boys; we would *not* be popular. I feared that Jackie may lose his temper, and who could say what would happen? When we got to the campsite, I went directly to the old Ford to check on my sleeping bag and towel, almost dry. I turned them over and just wasted time. I could hear excited voices from the campsite, and Spanner was giving as much as he got. I approached the furore. 'What the fuck?' Jackie asked me, with arms outstretched.

'Half-day closing,' I told him matter-of-factly.

'Well, why didn't you go shopping before they closed?' he asked menacingly.

'We didn't know it was half-day closing,' I shrugged. 'Did you know?' I asked. He didn't say anything.

'Fucking pet shop was open, though!' Jackie announced to no-one in particular.

'Look,' Spanner said, calling everyone's attention 'If it was half-day closing yesterday, you wouldn't be able to buy food either.' Nobody said anything. Spanner continued, 'Don't tell me you didn't go and have a few beers first.' Everyone knew Spanner was right. 'The pet shop was a vets', so that's why it opened,' he said, by way of explanation. The heat left the argument, which was replaced by frostiness. Spanner went to the tent with the kittens. I got a fishing pole and sat on the car seat by the river.

'Come on! Let's fuck off,' Jackie announced to the others, and they soon trekked off down the track for town.

My drunkenness was wearing off. I sat peacefully with my pole and, looking around, I saw I had company. The tabby stray was sat behind me in expectation. As the sun sank lower in the sky, I raised myself from the seat. The cat looked at me and realised its wait was in vain, so crept away. I retrieved the sleeping bag and towel, both of which were dry and warm. Spanner was in his bag with the two kittens.

The next morning, four of us woke with hangovers and two with hunger pains. We replaced the car seats in the Ford and packed our camp away into our respective rucksacks. Spanner placed the cats in the box, and we set off back to the bar by the station. We got back on-board late in the evening and no-one knew Spanner had two cats with him. However, it didn't take long before people in the mess did. He tried to contain them to his bunk and their box, but soon, they were venturing all over the place. The killick of the mess spoke to him and told him to get rid of them. Spanner said he would ask for official permission to keep them on-board. He submitted an official request form to this effect. Needless to say, it was denied. The Chief Elec. came to the mess to speak to Spanner personally; he was kind, and said he understood why he would want to keep the cats, but explained that there was no room for such animals on-board in today's modern Navy. He told Spanner that he must find another home for them, before we sailed, or they would be just left ashore where they, no doubt, would join the band of stray dockyard cats.

The day before we sailed, Max, Fingers, and Mick Briggs had gained permission to bring on-board some young ladies they had met and been trying to further their relationship with, such that they could explore the insides of their underclothes. They thought bringing the ladies on-board and showing them around would induce them to allow this to happen; they even cleaned the mess especially for their visit. They came to the mess, and the girls could not contain the excitement of being on such a war ship. The boys had given them a good tour of the Quarterdeck, Flight Deck, hangars, Cable Deck… even the cells that housed Spanner and I on our trip to Singapore. They were taken to the workshops, switchboards and galley. They felt sure that tonight would be the night.

Spanner was on his top bunk when they arrived, and I saw that familiar expression on his face as they sat, two on the bunk beneath him and the other opposite. Max, Mick and Fingers huddled amongst them. Spanner climbed down and joined them around the table. Beer was produced, and a little party had started. Talk soon got around to Spanner's kittens, and he fished the box down to show them. They fell in love with them. 'You can have them,' Spanner said. There was an excited discussion of 'no, we have nowhere to keep them' or 'no, we have no-one to look after them'. Spanner explained that a new home had to be found before we sailed. The excitement continued and the discussion changed to, 'Well, we could keep them in such-and-such-a-place' and 'this person or other could help us'. Spanner then informed them that should no home be found, then they would be just let loose at the bottom of the gangway. This information was received with some horror, and finally a more positive note ran through the conversation: 'We have to have them' and 'we must find a way to keep them'. It seemed a good solution. It was learned that later that evening, the three girls, and their friends, were having a party in one of their flats, as a thank you and farewell to our three friends. Needless to say, Spanner got himself invited. I was on-duty so had to remain on board.

16: Hong Kong

The next day, we sailed out of Sydney Harbour. Again, I sat in Kilo switchboard flat for Harbour Stations and watched the Chinese laundry workers eat their food. We were going to sea, and I was not in the shit. *Well, that's something to celebrate*, I thought. As I awoke this morning, I could hear Fingers and Mick complaining bitterly to Spanner: it seemed giving the cats to the girls was the worst thing. I understood that all night, at the party, the girls were only interested in the kittens, and spent all their time and attention with them. Any hope Max, Mick and Fingers had of getting their end away disappeared as the box of cats disappeared from the Hermes. It made me smile.

Our next destination would be Hong Kong. From when I first joined the Navy, it seemed that every sailor went to Singapore and Hong Kong, and it looked as though I would follow suit.

Occasionally, it was necessary to replenish fuel and stores, and this was generally done at sea. Commonly called RAS (Replenishment at Sea), a tanker would steam a parallel path to Hermes, on the starboard side, and a line thrown across to haul in several reinforced pipes. These would be clamped onto flanges on the ship's deck, oil, diesel and aviation fuel would flow. A freighter would steam along the port side;

ropes thrown across and a jack stay transfer line set up. Pallets of goods, from the freighter, would be sent across and landed on the forward aircraft hangar, which would be in the down position, i.e. hangar level. The pallets were swiftly broken down, and the contents sent down chutes and along roller conveyors to their respective stores below. Almost always, the conveyors were set up through both Junior Rates dining halls. Beer was the favourite to be brought on-board; the beer store was below our mess on 7 Deck. So chutes were set over our access ladder, the access ladder for the flat below where the Chinese shoe factory was, and a length of conveyor to take the cases from the bottom of one ladder to the top of the next. Needless to say, no access could be gained to our mess during this evolution, except from an Air Conditioning access shaft, which was accessed by an open hatch adjacent to the door, linking the forward and aft dining halls. The hatch was normally left open, and there was an access door from the shaft into our mess. Everyone was devising ways of steeling beer during a RAS. Leading hands were strategically placed along the conveyors, to ensure all goods remained on the conveyor. However, stuff always went missing; for instance, if the right person was stationed by the door as the conveyor passed through the dining hall linking door, he could quite easily pick up a case of beer and throw it down the Air Conditioning compartment access hatch to a guy waiting by the access door to our mess. This would then rapidly be broken open and the cans secreted away in the mess; all it needed was a little distraction for the Leading Hand, who was patrolling that area. In addition to the leading hands, the regulating staff were also part of the vigilance. On one occasion, I was told to observe the cases as they came down the chute into our mess from the dining hall. Pricky Thorn, the Leading Regulator, was standing guard in this area. I was told to linger here, which would catch the eye of Pricky, as he knew I was an opportunist and might fancy my chances. I set up an ironing board and ironed some clothes; the NAAFI staff also were present because the beer belonged to them. To make things comfortable, one would make a stack of about five cases to sit on. He would have a bag of rags at his feet that the cases would crash into as they came, free-fall, down the chute; he would then pick up the case, place it on the conveyor, where it would go to his colleague at the top of the hatch down to 6 Deck. He, too, would make a stack of about five cases to sit on. He would take the case off the conveyor and place it on the chute going down, all-in-all a slick operation. It was nearly impossible to steal a case from this part of the line; however, this time, when all the cases were loaded and no more were coming down, the order was given to dismantle the conveyor line. The five cases forming the stack for the NAAFI guy at the bottom of the ladder were placed on the conveyor and sent to his colleague, who transferred them to the chute. He then got up and started to dismantle the stack he was sitting on, taking each one and placing it on the chute. When he got to the last, he was in for a surprise: this case was different. It was not full! The side of the case had been cut open, and eight cans removed. Pricky was aghast; his jaw dropped. He looked at me, and I just raised my eyebrows at him and hunched my shoulders. He flew round to the Senior section of the mess, but nothing was happening. Some guys were playing cards or lay on their bunks reading and smoking; no-one even paid Pricky any attention. Whilst I had been keeping the attention of Pricky at the bottom of the ladder, he did not wander from his station to other parts of the mess, which he normally did. My friends removed a shoe locker from under the bunk opposite to where the NAAFI guy had made his stack; he was then able to crawl into this space and reach under the lockers to the bottom case of beer. Carefully, he cut away the side, extracted some cans and, replaced them with empties. During the next RAS, a board was placed against the lockers, and the stack of beer cases, to prevent this happening again.

During the three weeks' voyage, Parky and I continued to do 'Rounds', with occasional trips to the Flight Deck to see Taff and get a pint of Limers. Parky often disappeared on his own, and I asked him where he would go. Normally, the mess was out-of-bounds during normal working hours, unless you were a Watch Keeper, or had some other duty, like I had had in the Senior Rates dining hall. To be caught in the mess could be a big problem.

Parky took me into some of the ventilation spaces. No-one ever went into these places except us, and only then to do planned maintenance on the fan motors; they were generally too noisy. To carry out planned maintenance, it was necessary to turn the fan off and isolate the supply. Needless to say, the compartment, supplied by the fan, would get hot during this period; therefore, care had to be taken when the maintenance was planned. Parky told me of one special place he knew, and made me swear never to tell anyone: it was a small ventilation compartment with only one fan in it. Access to it was from a Weather Deck aft on the port side. 'This is it,' Parky told me, patting the door clips, 'and this is the starter,' he continued, patting and electrical box next to the door. We could hear the loud whirring of the fan, and knew it would be almost unbearable if you opened the door. Parky pressed the 'stop' button on the box, and the whirring changed pitch with the frequency of the slowing fan. Eventually, it stopped. 'This fan is one of the fans that supply the steering gear compartment,' Parky told me. The steering gear compartment was way down on 8 Deck and just about as aft as you could get. This was an un-manned compartment, except for Harbour Stations and emergencies. This compartment was so deep in the ship and so far away from the boiler rooms that it never got hot. 'No-one notices if this fan is off,' Parky explained, 'because no-one is in that compartment to complain.' He then opened the door, and we let ourselves in. He switched on a light and closed the door. 'This is it,' he announced. I was not impressed, and thought why I had come here. 'See that?' he said, pointing to a corner. I followed his finger; all I could see was a sack or rags. 'That's no ordinary sack of rags,' Parky informed me, and he pulled it out and unfolded it. 'It's my daytime pit,' meaning his daytime bed. He made a few more adjustments, and then laid out on it. 'I can come here and get my head down anytime I like,' he announced. Well, it did look comfortable enough.

'There's one of these in Nine Sierra as well,' I informed him, referring to the Air Conditioning plant on Nine Deck S section.

'That's not a pit,' Parky informed me matter-of-factly, 'it's a beer catcher.' He could see I was having a problem understanding this, so he went on. 'Sometimes when we RAS, the NAAFI have to fill up the store back aft. It's mainly for the Grunters,' he explained. The Grunters are what we called the officers. We called them Pigs, and Grunter was just a progression of that. Pallets are taken from the side lift and across to the back end of the hangar where they get broken down; chutes are set up by the starboard ladder, and then conveyors take it round to the store.' He paused whilst I listened. 'The conveyors pass the access shaft for Nine Sierra. 'The access shaft was a vertical shaft, about one yard square in cross section, that descended from 4 Deck to 9Deck. Looking over the hatch was a daunting sight, and real care had to be taken climbing the ladder. I was told never to hold the rungs of the ladder with your hands; rungs are for feet, I was told. Feet get oily, and the oil can be transferred to the rungs, which make them slippery to hold. Always hold a ladder by the vertical risers. I never forgot that. Parky went on to explain that during a RAS, someone would go the Air Conditioning space and place the sack of rags on the floor at the bottom of the shaft. As the beer cases flowed (at an opportune moment, when the leading hands were distracted), one would be taken from the conveyor and dropped down the shaft. Care had to be taken to release the case in the middle of the shaft to ensure a vertical fall; it would be no good bouncing off the sides of the shaft as it fell, as the case would break open, cans would burst, but more dangerously, a lot of noise would be generated, drawing the attention of the guard. Executed correctly, the case would land and be cushioned by the sack of rags. The guy in the machinery space would retrieve the case and hide it, retrieve the sack, close the door, and ascend the ladder. A party would be held later.

Turning our attention back to this ventilation space, I asked, 'What happens if someone comes?'

'If they move just one clip off, I'm awake,' he said. There were six clips on the door in all, so I had to accept that would be the case. 'If anyone does come—and no fucker has come yet—I tell them I am investigating why the fan has stopped.'

'What happens if they just start the fan?' I asked.

'Can't.' He showed me an isolating switch inside the door. 'I fitted that. Won't find that on any 'As Fitted' drawings.' Well, that was it. Parky had got it worked out. His own little hideaway. 'Chris,' he said solemnly, 'on a big ship, there's always a place to hide.' I nodded as this fact was pointed out to me. 'Now, don't you ever come looking for me here, and don't tell any fucker.'

'No,' I said, shaking my head, 'never.'

It was easy for us in the Air Condition section. There was only the three of us: the chief, who just went back to his mess after the morning muster, Parky, the Leading Hand, and me. My problem was to keep out of sight. I hadn't found a place to safely sleep during the day, but at least now I had an objective: I would begin to explore Hermes more thoroughly.

Rumour had it that job changes would be announced before we left Hong Kong. I thought about this, and considered I might be left where I was, as I had only been on the section for a few weeks. I was happy to explore the ship with a handful of rags, and, sure enough, no-one asked me where I was going or what I was doing. I wasn't doing much electrical work, but I really didn't *want* to work.

The day before we arrived in Hong Kong, I returned to the mess, and on my bunk I found a chit, summoning me to the regulating office at once. It was signed and over stamped by the MAA. My heart quickened. Had I forgotten to do something? Should I be somewhere else? Had I missed a duty watch muster? All these thoughts passed through my mind, but I could think of no reason why they needed to see me. I checked my shoes, did up the top button of my shirt, checked myself in the mirror, grabbed my best hat and polished my shoes on the back of my trousers. *Here we fucking go*, I thought as I climbed the ladder from the mess.

Inside the regulating office, Pricky Thorn sat behind a desk facing the door—a place McSnell normally occupied, I noticed. There was one other Leading Regulator sat to one side. No-one else was there, and the MAA's office was empty. I knocked on the door; Pricky looked up at me and beckoned me in. I gave him the chit that was left on my bunk; he took a piece of paper from the desk and handed it to me. I looked at it and it informed me I had been selected for Ceremonial Guard duty. This was an awful thing to do: it meant getting dressed up in Whites (Number 6 uniform) and standing at the bottom of the Quarterdeck gang-plank with a rifle, and having to salute when Officers came, or left, the ship. 'Why me?' I asked.

'Your name came out of the hat,' he said simply, as if it was a lottery.

'Yeah,' I sneered. 'I bet that was fucking McSnell's hat.'

Pricky jumped up and stormed around the desk. I did not fear Pricky as I feared McSnell: Pricky was not the violent type; he was just officious. I stood still. 'I could have you for insubordination for that, Clark,' he threatened. Although there was a witness, it would be difficult to prove it was disrespectful. I didn't want to push Pricky or antagonise him. At that very moment, I knew I would seek revenge for this: I would think of something to enjoy revenge against both Leading Regulator Thorn and Regulating Petty Officer McSnell. Each dog has its day, and I will have mine. 'Report to the Quarterdeck,' he ordered. I turned to leave. 'And get your fucking hair cut!' he barked after me.

Hong Kong is a small island close to mainland China. The sea channel leading in is dotted with small islands, all green and hilly. The day we arrived, the sky was hazy grey and the sea deep blue in colour; Chinese Junks criss-crossed the water with their high sterns and dull-red sails like enormous dorsal fins of scaly fish., and the smell of incense hung in the warm humid air.

As it transpired, Ceremonial Guard Duty was not as bad as I first thought: there were six of us who had drawn the short straw. They were from other branches, which I didn't know much about, although I knew Mighty, a stoker and Jenkins, who was a Leading Steward. I knew several cooks from my time in their galley; I found it quite remarkable that, of the five other guys, three I recognised from punishment musters.

All of us had to be on the Flight Deck at 06:30 each morning to form a Ceremonial Guard for Colours. Colours was a ceremony of raising the White Ensign flag at the stern of the ship; the Officer of the Day would be there saluting with his sword; we would salute with our rifles. The GI (Gunnery Instructor—a Chief Petty Office) would bark the orders, and salute with his hand; the marine band would play *God Save the Queen,* and not salute at all.

During the day, we had to do a two-hour stint at the end of the gangway. Mostly stood at ease with feet apart, the butt of the rifle by the right foot and it slanting forwards and held by your hand, where the wooden furniture ends halfway up the barrel. When an Officer approached, you snapped smartly to attention: feet together, rifle upright by your right leg, and head up; next the salute with the right hand, propelling the rifle upwards with the smallest movement of the hand possible. At the same time, the left hand comes across your body to catch the rifle, where the right hand was holding it, and the rifle is also caught with the right hand at the trigger grip. Wait two marching paces, and then smartly bring the rifle out in front of you, so that your right hand is at the height of your chest; the rifle is vertical and the fingers of the left hand pointing straight along the barrel where it gripped it earlier. Keep the rifle close to the body. Wait two marching paces; the final movement: take the rifle down vertically with the right arm, the left hand, once again, gripping the rifle and the left elbow out to the side with forearm parallel to the deck. Simultaneously, the right foot moves backwards, and rests at an angle of about 45 degrees, with its instep close to the heel of the left foot. The officer should return your salute. To return to the Attention position, move the rifle to the right side of the body and down, releasing the grip of the right hand and repositioning the grip beneath the left hand. The left arm will be across the body and left hand gripping the rifle as before. With this movement, the rifle butt should be close, but not touching, the deck. Simultaneously, bring the left foot back to normal; the right elbow will be flexed and pointing to the rear. Wait two marching paces. Finally, release the rifle with the left hand, and bring the left arm smartly to the side of the body. Gently lower the rifle with the right hand so its butt rests upon the ground; when you are ready, you can resume the At Ease position. Extend the right arm straight, allowing the rifle to slant forwards again. At the same time, move the left leg away from the right. Wait two marching paces and relax.

Only one guard was required during the evening, just in case any VIPs came on-board. We were in Hong Kong for five days, and I was the lucky one that didn't have to stay on-board. Every other day, we finished at lunchtime and could go ashore; otherwise, we had to wait until 18:00.

Another band of Chinese came on-board and set up a cold drinks' market on the Cable Deck. Several wooden barrels, cut in half, were filled with water and ice and cooled a myriad of bottles containing fruit juices, flavoured milk and fizzy drinks. Each morning, the Cable Deck was full of crew members getting their hangover cure. My favourite was a banana-milk flavoured drink. They ran out quickly, but I was always early going there immediately after we finished on the Flight Deck.

The first night in Hong Kong, I went ashore with Budgie. We stopped off at the China Fleet Club: this was to Hong Kong what the UJC and Aggie's were to Singapore. The China Fleet Club had a bowling alley and we wanted to check it out; we decided to see if we could get a beer, so I complimented Budgie again by saying he looked older than me. The compliment worked, as he went off to the bar and came back with two ice-cold glasses of San Miguel beer. After that, we wandered down Lockhart Road: it was full of life and bright, colourful lights, much the same as the area Spanner took me to in Singapore, when I was nabbed by the vice squad. We had heard about the tailors here, so were keen to investigate. We were told they can make a suit to your exact requirements in about six hours. Sure enough, we found tailors; in fact, they found us. They would pour out of their stores as we passed, imploring us to go inside and be measured. We said we would return the next day. We ventured in a few bars, and immediately were confronted by beautiful girls ushering us to a side-booth, where they professed their dying love for us and asked us if we would buy them a drink. We both liked the attention, but we liked our money more, so declined. After a while, the girls got fed up and moved away. We tried a few more places with similar results. We decided to come ashore the next day, as we were both off at midday, and go directly to a tailor for measuring. We returned on-board well before midnight. We were not drunk, we did not lose our money, and we did not get into trouble. That's called a 'quiet run ashore'.

At about 06:00 the next day, I was waiting in my Number 6uniform for fall-in time for ceremonial guard. The sun was rising, an enormous red ball lifting over the horizon, chasing away the darkness. The underside of the clouds turning magnificent shades of scarlet, crimson and ruby, and the red ball disappeared from view behind the clouds as the light intensified. Soon, the sun was a bright yellow ball seen through the clouds, and its heat began to turn the morning dew into rising mist from trees and grass. Today, I was glad to be up early.

At 12:45, we allowed a tailor to coax Budgie and I off Lockhart Road and into his tailors' shop. I selected some material from samples he showed me; Budgie chose the same. He measured us each in turn and then asked about the design. I told him I wanted parallel trousers; drainpipe trousers were well and truly in the past. Bell bottoms, whilst very hippy were becoming a thing of the past. Young people were wearing single-breasted jackets with four buttons; however, four buttons would never be used. It was cool to just button the top two, and let the rest of the jacket flow open at the front. I told the tailor just to give me two buttons, but to position these where the top two buttons would be if I had ordered four buttons. Normally, two buttons would be positioned low, giving a long 'vee' at the jacket front. Eventually, I made the tailor understand my requirement with regard to buttons. I only wanted one vent at the back, as the tailor normally provided two. I told him I wanted only one, and it should start at the small of my back; this made it a very long vent, which, again, caused a bit of an argument with the tailor and I. We agreed there should be flaps on the pockets; he suggested a small ticket pocket above the right-side pocket which was traditional, but I told him I wanted a small ticket pocket on the left-hand side and two, one above the other, above the pocket on the right-hand side. The man thought I had gone nuts. He explained to produce these two extra ticket pockets would be very difficult, and make the price considerably higher. He suggested just the one ticket pocket, as normal, but just dummy flaps for the others, which I agreed. Budgie ordered the same design.

We returned two hours later, and the man produced the beginnings of our suits. I tried the jacket on, and he fussed about me with his chalk and pins; we discussed the position of the two buttons, and I adjusted them to a higher position. The buttons were only pinned on, so it was easy to move them, which the tailor did tut-tutting and shaking his head as he did so. With the button position correct, I instructed him to cut more material away from the sides of the jacket, so it flared open from the bottom button. Finally, I was satisfied. Budgie gave similar instructions, and we were asked to return at 19:00 to collect our suits.

I could not have been more pleased with the finished result. The material was a light brown colour, which would complement the light brown boots I had made for me on-board. We decided to return on-board so as not to damage or lose our garments. We stopped off at the China Fleet Club, where it was my turn to buy the beer; another quiet run ashore.

The next morning, I entered the mess just as my buddies were waking and climbing from their pits. I was fresh and was ready for breakfast; I had to stay in my white suit as I would be required at the Quarterdeck gangway later.

I looked at Spanner in his top bunk, who was looking at me with road map red eyes. 'Bad fucking night last night,' he declared to me.

'Pissed?'

'No,' he answered, but I knew he was. 'Some chinky bastards stole my fucking ID card.'

'Shit! Really?'

'Yeah. Fucking loads of 'em.' He tried to raise himself. 'Fucking kids, really.' He was now sitting with his head ducked beneath the ventilation trunking. 'Just fucking surrounded me,' he said, 'pushing, pulling, screaming and shouting, and then they just fucked off.' He looked at me, held his hands up. 'When I checked, no fucking ID card.'

'Money in it?' I asked. An ID card is held in a plastic transparent wallet, and it's normal to carry paper money in the non-photo side. Saves carrying a bulky wallet.

'Yeah.'

'Much?'

'Enough,' he answered, deflated. Losing an ID card is an offence—even if it's stolen. Normally, it's punished by three days'9s.

I waited for Spanner to shower and get dressed, and then we went to breakfast together. 'Got to see McSnell soon,' he announced in a demoralised tone. We both knew he would be in for it from McSnell; he would love the fact that he could write a charge sheet out for Spanner, and he would do all he could to get an increased punishment for him. 'Officer of the Days table, then,' he said.

'Listen,' I said, trying to comfort him, 'the OOD cannot deal with this. He would have to pass it over to Commander's table, and the Commander will not see anyone whilst we are alongside here.' Spanner looked up at me. 'The Commander will wait till we get to sea, and then deal with all the offenders in one go.'

'Makes no difference,' Spanner said. 'Got no money to go ashore anymore.'

'Listen, Spanner,' I told him, 'go and see McSnell; think of Mary in Portsmouth as he rants and raves at you, and when he's finished, ask for another ID card.' Spanner was still looking at me. 'He *has* to give you a new one. Then we can go ashore tonight, even if you do get OOD's table.'

'Got no money.'

'For fuck's sake, Spanner! I'll buy you a few beers.' He looked up at me, and his eyes brightened.

'Yeah,' he said, 'you owe me a few fucking beers anyway.' And that's about all the thanks he could muster. I knew he was grateful though, and it was true: I did owe him a few beers.

At 19:30, both Spanner and I posted our station cards as Pricky Thorn looked on. 'Don't be late,' he warned us sarcastically.

'At least we're going ashore,' Spanner retorted, drawing reference to the fact Pricky was on-duty and had to stay on-board. We knew that riled Pricky.

We had a couple in the China Fleet Club, and then wandered down to Lockhart Road. We went from bar to bar, enjoying the attention off the girls and getting a little more drunk as the night progressed. Then, as I was beginning to think we should make our way back, Spanner grabbed my arm. 'That's one of them little fuckers there,' he said, pointing to a Chinese kid of about twelve years old, who stood in an alley lined with stalls selling cheap lighters, cameras, and watches. To me, all the stalls looked the same, as did all the alleys and all the kids. Spanner marched off down the alley and grabbed the kid by the neck, shouting, 'Where's my fucking money?' Several things happened at once: I screamed at Spanner to let the kid go; the kid screamed a high-pitched scream. It seemed the whole population of Hong Kong descended upon Spanner; I'm sure people came out of the walls, up through the streets and down from the sky. The noise was tremendous. I tried to get to Spanner, but everyone was pushing and pulling. I was doing the same; it seemed no-one was throwing punches or kicking. I fought my way to Spanner and pulled his arm, trying to drag him away. It was like trying to get off a crowded tube train onto a crowded platform. The kid had been taken away. I pulled Spanner with one hand, and held the other hand high, shouting, 'It's okay! It's okay.' The crowd backed off a little, and I was able to get Spanner moving back towards the main road. The crowd followed menacingly, remonstrating with their arms and shouting at Spanner. I got between Spanner and the crowd and with my two hands held high, palms facing them, I repeated, 'It's okay! It's okay. It's okay,' whilst moving backwards. The crowd stopped when they got to the end of the alley. We turned and moved off; my heart was thumping in my chest like never before. I was out of breath and breathing hard. Anyone of those guys could have pulled a knife, and the story could have been a whole lot different. I was furious with Spanner, but of a greater emotion was my bewilderment at why he should do such a thing. We stopped outside a bar, some distance from the alley, to regain our breath and composure. 'What the fucking hell was all that about?'

'I'm fucking telling you, man, he was one of them from last night,' he said emphatically.

It was pointless saying anything. The best thing to do was to get back on-board. 'Come on,' I said, beckoning him inside, 'one for the road and back on-board.'

It was safer going ashore with Budgie. We bought another suit each, and one day took the ferry across to Kowloon on the mainland side of Hong Kong.

Job changes were announced and, to my disappointment, I was transferred to the Domestic section. There were three EMs on this section, and the section leader was a petty Officer Electrician called Windiranks. Windiranks, of course, got the nickname Windy and, more derogatory, Windywanks. Nobody liked Windy too much; he was too officious, insisting we call him PO. He was skinny, although he always threatened to 'fill people in', meaning beat them up. He had no charisma and no sense of humour. Max was on this section with me along with a tall, lanky guy called Mortiman.

17: Bunk Light

The first morning after we sailed from Hong Kong, we mustered at our new positions in the Six Hotel Electrical workshop. The Domestic section was to the immediate right once through the door; Parky was still with the Air Conditioning section and his new EM was EM Jones. He was one of the more senior EMs, and lived in the Senior side of the mess. He was a Scotsman who came from Perthshire, and was small and quiet. Apart from the nickname of Jonah, he was sometimes referred to as Gorbals after the district in Glasgow. I suspected he didn't like being called Gorbals.

The Chief Mech. came out, dead on 08:00, and said he hoped we all had a good time in Hong Kong, and that we would all enjoy our new sections. He handed a bundle of maintenance cards to the section leaders, and then disappeared into his office.

Windy took his bundle and jumped up to sit on the bench whilst he shuffled through them. He made one pile by his left thigh, and one by his right. He crossed his short, spindly legs, and swung his feet as a child might. If we did not need to wear overalls, then we could wear shorts as the dress of the day was Tropical—shorts, sandals, and Number 8 shirt. Shorts on Windy made his legs look more ridiculous.

The Ers. and Brs. (engine rooms and boiler room) section all wore overalls and steaming boots as Parky and I had in the Air Conditioning section. The Domestic section would take us into Mess Decks and the wardroom, so a more appropriate dress was required. The work was cleaner, and so no need to get changed for meals, which could be construed as being an advantage with this section.

Windy jumped off the bench, picked up the cards, and turned towards us. 'Right,' he said, 'get this lot done as soon as you can.' He started handing us each a reduced bundle of cards. We each studied our card: at the top would be the equipment the card referred to; underneath, a grid of squares for signatures and dates as to when the work was completed; on the reverse of the card would be a description of the work to be done—just the same as before in the Air Conditioning section. I looked at a card, and this was referring to a lighting circuit Number 3 in 5F Mess Deck. Instructions for the three monthly-routines were: one, check all light fittings for tightness of connections; two, check insulation resistance is greater than 1Meg Ohm.; three, check lighting tubes for general condition (tubes with blackened ends should be replaced); four, functionally check unit (ensure tubes strike within three attempts of the starter—if not, replace); five, visually check condition of diffuser and replace as necessary; six, check all fittings and wiring for integrity. I noticed there was no instruction for 'clean and blow-out'. Once all the tasks have been completed, you need to sign and write the date in the next available box on the front of the card; then return it to the section leader. To carry out this work, it would be necessary to isolate the circuit. To isolate the circuit, you would need to know where the appropriate fuse box is. Some pieces of equipment have this information printed on them; lighting circuits should carry this information on the switch. However, this is not always the case; sometimes, it would be necessary to refer to the As Fitted drawings to locate the panel. The instructions on this particular card are quite simple: no brain-teasers here. As with everything, there could be hidden problems: the information on the switch could be missing, or even wrong. The circuit could be in a watch-keeper's mess, where it would be suicidal to start switching on lights when the watch-keepers are sleeping.

I am aware it is common practise for some guys to take these cards away, sign and date them without even looking at the subject matter. It could be argued that's a good option; Budgie was on this section before, and he told me that one time, he tried to take a diffuser off a light, but the threaded bolt and retainer had ceased. He used too much force, and the retainer sheared off. The diffuser then dropped down at one end; there was no option but to remove the whole fitting to the workshop for repair. The light fitting is bolted to 'U' shaped resilient mounts, the problem being that the retaining bolts have been painted so many times, it is very easy for the retaining nuts and bolt to bind-up, resulting in a sheared bolt. This happened to Budgie, and he couldn't get the fitting free from one of the 'U' mounts. The solution was to undo the mount where it is secured to the deck-head; sure enough, this securing stud also sheared. A new stud had to be welded to the deck-head so the fitting, once refurbished in the workshop, could be replaced. Welding, of this nature, is only done in refits or maintenance periods in Harbour. So, in an endeavour to carry out 'Preventative Maintenance', a light fitting was put out of service for the duration of the whole trip. This is a classic case of 'if it works, leave it alone'. Budgie also got a bad reputation for this: the light fitting was in a Stokers' mess, and several people saw him struggle with it. Ultimately, when it had to be removed and never replaced, Budgie became known as 'Fuck it up Bird'.

I could do what many had done before me: just sign the cards and return them; in the meantime, just kill some time walking around the ship with a bunch of rags in my hand. I don't know if anyone would ever check up on whether the maintenance has been done or not; I had never heard of anyone getting in the shit for just signing the cards.

Some of the other cards referred to portable socket circuits, sockets where portable equipment, such as irons, kettles, table lamps and the like, can be plugged in. Some of the routines call for the cover to be removed, and the inside switching mechanism inspected and lubricated. The covers were secured with four screws; a flat-bladed screwdriver is necessary to remove the screws. I looked at several sockets around the ship, and the slot in the screw heads was full of paint - old paint, at that. These covers had not been removed for a long time. I looked at the card again, and saw that the periodicity for removal of the cover was Annual; it was dated a year ago, and signed, although the signature was more of a scribble. I found the socket circuit my card referred to, and the retaining screws of the socket covers were full of old paint. The slot was filled with pain, such that the surface only dimpled down a little where the slot was. I doubt that this cover has ever been removed. I looked at the socket's fixtures to the bulk-head; a threaded stud would be welded to the bulkhead and holed flanges, forming part of the socket body, would pass over the studs. A washer was then placed over the stud, followed by a retaining nut; once the nut was secured tightly, a length of stud, about ¼ inch, would stand proud. Everything was painted. Then, everything gets painted again and again; the nut and the exposed threaded stud were caked in it. To hope the nut could unscrew all the way up over the stud would be a lottery; the excessive build-up of paint would have to be removed first. It could be that someone, like Budgie, came to this socket, tried to undo the lid, but damaged a screw head, which makes it impossible to extract. The socket would then have to be removed to the workshop for repair. Whilst attempting to remove the retaining nuts, these become ceased because of the build-up of paint, and so the studs are sheared. End result: one socket out of commission for the rest of the commission. In my mind, I was building a good case for just signing off the cards.

Whilst I was in front of this socket, I decided to experiment: I placed one corner of the blade of my screwdriver where the slot of the screw would be; I then hit the blade with my pliers, and the blade dug into the slot and ran along it, taking out all the paint. I did this again in the other direction, and then I had a perfectly clean screw head slot. I positioned my screwdriver, pressed hard, and tried to turn it anticlockwise; the screw resisted but then submitted. It was then easy to remove. I repeated this with the other three with the same pleasing results; the four retaining screws were free, but the cover remained firmly in position. I had to lever it open with my screwdriver, and it popped off into the air and over my head, landing behind me. I was now the first person to look inside this socket since the man who had made the electrical connections during initial installation.

I felt pleased with myself; I felt so pleased with myself, I smiled. I looked inside the socket, and it looked like new. I checked the connections for tightness and they were tight; I could see some excess petroleum jelly around the mechanism, so I smoothed this into the articulated parts so I could safely say I inspected and lubricated the mechanism.

The lighting circuit in 5F Mess Deck was in the Seaman's mess next to ours. I wanted to look at the lights there; all lighting switches are together, close to the entrance hatch. I found Number 3 and switched it off whilst I looked over the top of the lockers to where the lights were. The Seaman's mess is large, about the same size as our mess. I could see the area where the lights had gone out, so went to investigate: there were six lights in all that were out. Each interspaced by a working light, so light was afforded to the area, although one circuit was out. The diffusers let the light through and dispersed it around; it was only possible to tell that both tubes were on or not on a working light. It couldn't be determined if the tubes were blackened with the diffusers in place; this meant that the very least thing needed would be to remove the diffusers. These were retained by two round, knurled edge discs, similar in size to chequers counters. No tool should be necessary to remove them; these light fittings were universal around the ship. They would be the same as those in our mess, yet here I was, in another mess, scrutinising light fittings for the very first time. I got a chair and reached up to one in a passageway; carefully, I released the knurled retainers and removed the diffuser. I learned it did not just drop off; it had to manoeuvred over the tubes. Move to one side slightly, and one side would be clear of the tube to drop; move to the other side to clear the other tube. I then had the diffuser in my hand: it was dirty, but all intact. Everything looked okay. I didn't touch anything, and so replaced the diffuser; I left the mess, turning the circuit back on as I did so.

I decided I would not just sign off the cards as, obviously, people had done so. I had learned a lot from Parky: he taught me the 'clean and blow-out' trick, although it wasn't a trick; Parky was showing me his interpretation of the procedure. It was an interpretation that no-one could argue with; not only that, I saw he was being responsible in carrying out the procedures. I wanted to be responsible as well. With regard to the tubes, I would not change them if they were black. How black do they need to be? Just a bit black or a lot black? If they worked, they were okay; I would not count how many strikes it took to flash the tubes. If the starters worked, I would leave them; if anyone were to pick me up on these points and discover blackened tubes, I would say they were okay when I checked them. Same with the starters.

The biggest thing I learned that day was it was very easy to mess things up completely, just by doing your job. I am sure, and maybe Budgie will agree, that had he been more careful and applied a little more thought to his problem light-fitting in the Stokers' mess, he may have been able to resolve the issue, saving the light fitting and with his reputation intact. The other thing I learned was it seemed to be okay to take something out of service, because things cease up or break. I went to the mess to find Mort.

Mortiman was at least six feet and four inches tall, although he was also lanky. He had narrow shoulders and narrow hips for his size; he was quite muscular, though with big hands. He had fair, gingerish hair, as well as on his arms and legs. He was athletic, and a keen rugby player. He spoke with no accent and with perfect diction, just like a Toff. 'How many cards you got then, Mort?' I asked him.

'Enough,' he said, holding them up. 'Want some?' He tossed them on the table in front of us.

'Anything interesting?'

'Don't know. Haven't looked.'

I picked them up and sifted through them. I found one I was looking for: Lighting Circuits in the Steward's mess. I swapped it with one of mine; Mort didn't seem no notice. He was not interested.

I was looking for something similar for the RPO's mess, but he didn't have it. I went round to where Max's bunk was and found him lazing about, smoking a cigarette. John Lennon was singing *Hey Jude* from the ship's sound reproduction system. Max was singing with him:

'nah nah nah nah, n nah naaah, nah n nah naaah, hey Jude...'

'Hi, mate,' I said, slumping next to him 'How's it going?'

Another couple of *nah*'s, then he stopped. 'Alright, mate,' he said, sitting more upright.

'What you think of Domestics, then?'

'Piece o' piss. And you?'

'Well, we'll see.' I waited whilst he did a few more *nah*'s, then asked him, 'Done any cards yet?'

'No,' he said dismissively, then added, 'Don't think I will. Just sign the fuckers, like everyone else.'

'Have you checked them? Might be something else other than lights and sockets.'

'*You* fucking check them,' he said indignantly, and he reached down, retrieved them from his tool bag, and tossed them on my lap. I looked through them, but nothing for the RPO's mess.

'Nah,' I confirmed, 'only lights and sockets.' I sat with him awhile and then went to my own bunk.

So, now I had a legitimate reason to enter the Steward's mess. I wanted to see where Jenkins laid his head to sleep and spent his leisure time; I wanted to do something to him to make him feel uncomfortable. I did not know what I would do, but I knew two things: first, it should not cause hardship or discomfort to others; and two, I must not be caught doing it, the second thing being the most important.

Spanner entered the mess, cursing and swearing. He was in a foul mood. 'Fucking bastard, Reggies,' he snarled. I didn't know if I should answer or not. There were other people in the mess who also fell silent. 'I always get the fucking galley!' he said. 'Upside fucking down in a burnt boiler of tapioca for two hours. 'He was ripping off his dirty shirt and getting his things ready for a shower. Spanner had got five days'9s for losing his ID card; he blamed McSnell for that.

'You know why you got the galley?' I asked him from my bunk.

'Fucking McSnell bastard,' he was mumbling through his teeth.

'It's because I'm not under pun,' I told him. 'If I were there, it would be me in the galley for sure.' Spanner said nothing, but continued to prepare for his shower. 'You can count on that,' I added as he grabbed his towel and made for the bathrooms.

After the muster in the workshop the following morning, I made for the Steward's mess. I knew where the mess was, but had never been inside. The mess was small, only twelve bunks arranged in two rows of three tiers facing each other, only like one of the many sections in our mess. Between the bunks, on the after bulkhead, were two full length wardrobes. The lockers were on the forward bulkhead as you came into the space created by the bunks. A table and four chairs were positioned in the centre of the mess. No-one was in the mess, which didn't help my cause. I wanted to find out which bunk belonged to Jenkins. I guessed it would be one of the top bunks; during the daytime, the middle bunk is lowered and forms a backrest to a seat, similar to a settee. The bottom bunk forms the seat itself. That means if you have either middle or bottom bunks, you have to stow your bedding away, and your bunk disappears into seating. All Senior people have a top bunk, as this can be left as it is all the time; it is only necessary to arrange the blankets and pillow neatly. I stood at the entrance corner of the mess and considered which bunk I would have if I had the choice. I had two options: the top bunk, on the side of the entrance, close to the after bulkhead; this would be the most difficult to see by someone entering the mess. I was picturing a situation where I could be skiving off work and deciding to get my head down in the bunk space. I could get on the edge of the bunk and not be visible by a cursory glance of someone entering the mess to see if it was clear. I don't think I would ever do this, because to be caught in such a situation would invite the wrath of the Regulating staff. No, Parky had taught me there are other places, safer places, to find to take a daytime nap. Strategically, the best bunk would be the one opposite the entrance—the one at the top in the far corner. I wanted to investigate, but didn't want to be caught in the mess doing nothing. I took out the maintenance card, found the circuit switch, and switched off a circuit of lights. Half the lights in the mess went out. There were eight fittings in all, and four were now off. I placed a chair beneath the one closest to what I thought would be Jenkins' bunk, and removed the diffuser. I placed the diffuser on the table and then moved the chair so I could see onto the bunk. Nothing revealing was to be seen; then I noticed, on the side of the wardrobe, adjacent to the bunk, there had been fixed a small shelf. It had been made of wood and was really quite intricate; there was a shelf with a cup-holder cut into it. A clean ashtray was on the shelf, but nothing more. There was a smaller shelf underneath with a paperback book on it; I could not see the title. Extending up from the shelf was a wooden backboard with a mirror attached to it, and above were two pigeon-hole type pockets. I could see some opened letters in these pockets, and so I lifted one and could see the address. It started *Leading Steward Jenkins*. I was right; this was his bunk. I quickly replaced the diffuser and left the mess. No-one saw me, which was the way I liked it.

I had it in mind to deny Jenkins the use of his bunk light. I could easily mess it up, but he could then get a new one or someone else to repair it. New ones were like gold dust, and someone would have to give Father Rudge a lot of rum for one. Father Rudge was the Killick of the mess. His daytime job was Electrical Storeman; we called him Father because he was old, perhaps nearly forty. He had a big, bushy, black beard flecked with grey, and a potbelly. Because of his age and longevity in the Navy, he commanded respect. Senior people would ask him for things when they could quite easily demand them. If you needed a favour, you paid for it in rum, beer or cigarettes; he had to maintain a level of stock in the store and he could not ask too much when it was time to replenish the store. Items in great demand were termed 'Attractive' items, and a typical one would be torch batteries. If you needed torch batteries, you needed to go to the store when Father was not smoking, not sitting down, not drinking tea, and not sleeping; if you could catch him awake and on his feet, you would ask politely for two new torch batteries. You would have to have the old ones ready to give him to prove you needed them, and also produce your torch. Further, it was necessary to explain why you needed a torch. So many people had purchased battery operated appliances, particularly record players and radios, let alone the multitude of electronic toys, which were available in the Far East, which all needed batteries. Many people needed a torch for reading at night because their bunk lights didn't work.

I considered the best I could achieve would be to make it uncomfortable for Jenkins. I had to somehow do something so his bunk light would not function always; I had to somehow create an intermittent fault.

Don had a problem with his bunk light; he could be heard at night cursing and swearing at it and thumping it. Don was a Radio Electrical Mechanic; whilst he was taught basic electrics and electrical theory, he spent more time learning radio theory and modules of frequency generators, transmitters and receivers. Whilst we learned circuits, how to read them and fault find on them, he learned blocks; we learned terminals and cables and he learned wiring looms with plugs and sockets. I guess Don didn't have the confidence to open up the bunk light and investigate what the problem was. 'What's the problem with your bunk light then, Don?' I asked him one morning.

'Fucking thing,' he said, waving his arm in the air.

'I could get you a new one, maybe,' I teased him.

'Really?' he said, looking at me in expectation.

'Cost you a can,' I said, referring to beer raising my eyebrows as I said it.

'A new one?'

'A brand-new one,' I confirmed.

'You're on,' he said, extending his hand for me to shake, and so consolidate the deal. Now, a plan was forming: I could not go to Father Rudge and ask for a new bunk light. If he had any left in the store, I would be the very last person he would give it to. I was still a Junior; I had no beer or rum to offer.

I needed to get an officer to report his bunk light defective. In that way, I could condemn it, and get the officer to sign a stores requisition form, and so get a new one. I assumed all bunk lights would be the same design. If not, then I would have to resort to Plan B; trouble was, at this moment, I had no such plan.

During normal working hours, if someone had an electrical problem, it would be reported to the office in the electrical workshop. Anyone could receive this call. The problem would be logged in a book, giving details of the problem and who reported it. A defect report would be raised and handed to the Section Leader responsible for the equipment. The Section Leader would give the report to one of his team, who would attend to the defect. Outside, normal working hours all defects were reported to Kilo switchboard. The defect would be logged and passed to the duty EM, who would investigate the problem. If he could fix the problem, he would; if he could not, then it would be passed to the electrical workshop the following morning. Serious defects were treated differently; Section Leaders were dragged out of their beds, if necessary.

The officers didn't have a mess; they had a wardroom. The wardroom had a dining room, bar and lounge. The officers could eat there, drink there and socialise there, although they did not sleep there; Officers had their own individual cabins. All cabins were the same except for the Senior Officers such as Commanders and the Captain. I had seen inside one of these cabins, and was impressed by their luxury: all the bulkheads were wooden panelled; opposite the door would be a large wardrobe, with drawers to the side. To the left of the door would be the bed, with the head of the bed close to the door, and to the right of the door would be a desk and chair. All the units were fitted and fixed in much the same as a caravan's furniture would be. Thick pile carpet was on the floor. I needed to check if their bunk lights were the same as all others. I took my tool bag, with maintenance cards visible on the top, and I carried a load of rags in my right hand. I set off aft and pretended I was looking for something around the corridors of the officer's cabins. I was hoping I could see a door open so I could see inside; no such luck. I noticed the bulkheads had a large amount of wiring; lots of individual cables running down from the central cable tray above the passageways. Cables ran down and through the bulkheads either side of the door and at different levels. One cable could go into a small junction box, and then branch off in different ways.

I decided I needed to befriend Windy, as I needed Windy to be on my side. I wouldn't creep around him, but wanted to make sure I wasn't cheeky to him, and let him know I could be reliable. There was more to this section than lights and sockets, and I wanted to be involved in more interesting things.

The next morning, after the Chief Mech. had said his piece, Windy asked us how were getting on. Mort slinked away, and said, 'Fine,' over his shoulder as he went out the door.

Max said, 'Getting into it now,' as he gathered his things together. Neither wanted to speak to Windy. Max followed Mort out the door.

'PO,' I asked, 'what happens when we have done all these cards?'

'You get another lot to do.'

'What about all the galley equipment?' I asked. 'Who does that?'

Windy turned to look at me. 'We can't do much in the galley while they are cooking.' He was looking at me as if I had asked a dumb question.

'They don't cook for twenty-four hours,' I replied, 'and they don't use all the equipment all the time.'

'We normally wait till we are in harbour; then the workload in the galley is less, as lots of people are ashore,' Windy explained.

'But PO,' I started, 'if we could do some, then we wouldn't have to do so much when we get alongside.'

I could see Windy was thinking about what I had said. I could also see that just to sign off the cards was a pretty acceptable thing for Windy: he was only really interested in getting the cards back signed. He could then give them all back to the Chief Mech. and say, 'All done, Chief', and take the credit for accomplishment. I didn't have much respect for Petty Officer Windybank, and I don't think many people did either.

Time went by, and I progressed through my pile of cards. I opened up all the sockets and I removed all the diffusers. I came across several fittings that needed new tubes, and discovered further damage could be done to a light fitting just by changing a tube. The wiring insulation became brittle, as did the tube connectors and starter sockets. It really was very easy to cause damage just by doing maintenance. There really is something to be said for just signing off the cards.

I eventually found out the reason for all the wiring on the bulkheads by the officer's cabins. These were cables to the cabin light, desk light, bunk light, and socket. The cables were run in this fashion because the cabins were wood-panelled, and should there be a problem with the wiring, then it can be fixed without the wood-panelling being damaged. This made my plan very much easier.

The next time I was duty EM, I went to the officer's accommodation and removed a fuse for the lighting in the passageway. I replaced a good fuse with a blown one. I returned to Kilo switchboard and waited for the call to come. Sure enough, the phone rang, and a Steward reported that the lights were out. The switchboard watch-keeper logged the defect and sent me off to investigate. I went to the passage in question, and I had already selected the officer who would sign my requisition for a new bunk light. Facing a door of a cabin, one cable passed through the bulkhead above the door. This cable came from a small, round junction box at the very top of the bulkhead. This box also fed a cable to the right that went through the bulkhead at about head height; this was for the desk light. Another cable went to the left and through the bulkhead at a lower level; this was for the bunk light. One cable came from the main cable tray and ran down and through the bulkhead at about chest height on the right-hand side; this would be the supply to the socket. I removed the cover from the junction box and disconnected one wire that ran to the bunk light. I wrapped some insulation tape around the bare conductor and tucked it away inside the box. I then replaced the cover. I replaced the fuse for the passageway lights and then left.

I returned to the switchboard and signed off the defect as having been repaired. *Defective starter causing circuit fuse to blow*, I gave as the reason. I then waited for the bunk light defect to be reported. It was not reported that evening, nor during the night. The duty EM has to sleep on a mattress behind the switchboard, so as to be close at hand, should any emergency arise. The defect was not reported during the night either.

I showered early and put on a clean pair of shorts and clean Number 8 shirt. I checked my sandals for cleanliness and had breakfast before heading to the workshop early. I had spoken often with Windy, and we had chatted in a friendly manner; he could see I was keen to learn, and I think he found that strange as no-one liked the Domestics section. I felt I was gaining his confidence and also respect, as I displayed a deal of responsibility.

As the Chief Mech. was winding up his usual morning chat, Lieutenant Commander Flannigan entered the workshop. The Chief Mech. straighten up and shouted, 'Attention in the workshop!' We all stood to attention smartly. Lt/Cdr Flannigan was the Electrical Engineering Officer. He was in charge of all the ratings, and officers, in the Electrical sections.

'Relax, men,' Flannigan said in his rich, booming voice. 'As you were.'

We all relaxed. Flannigan was as tall as Mortiman, and he towered over the short, rotund frame of the Chief Mechanician. Flannigan looked down at the chief and said, 'Send an EM to my cabin to fix my bunk light, if you would be so kind, Chief. Bloody thing is out.'

'Certainly, Sir,' the chief acknowledged. Windy had relaxed, leaning back against the bench. Max and Mort were shuffling tools around in their tool bags, having turned their backs on Flannigan. I stood next to Windy: clean, fresh and smiling. 'Petty Officer Windybank!' the chief barked.

'Yes, Chief!' Windy replied, straightening up.

'Send EM Clark to Lt/Cdr's Flannigan's cabin to fix the bunk light,' he ordered.

'Yes, Chief!' Windy said again. He didn't need to say anything to me; I picked up my tool bag and away I went. I had a broad grin on my face as I exited the workshop.

'Clark!'

Flannigan balled after me, which stopped me in my tracks. I turned my head towards him. 'See the Steward for the key,' he said. 'He'll let you in.'

'Yes, Sir,' I acknowledged, and continued on my way.

I was relieved to see the bunk light was exactly the same as all the others. I reached up to the junction box and took out the other wire to the bunk light, thereby totally isolating it. I removed the cover and released the screws securing it to the wall; I then released the cables from their terminals and there, in my hand, was a perfectly good bunk light.

The next step was the stores requisition. I had already got one and filled it in, complete with the store's part number of the light. Lt/Cdr Flannigan had an office next to the Electrical office at 5P flat. His door was open and he sat behind his desk, facing the door. Two very much younger Lieutenants were seated opposite him, one I recognised as a mechanical engineering officer. As I approached the door, he saw me and looked up. 'What is it, Clark?' he asked authoritatively, beckoning me in as he did so.

'We think it best to replace your bunk light, Sir,' I said. I said 'we' because I wanted him to think I had conferred with others about it, and it was not just my decision alone. I stepped into the office and offered the requisition form. 'Can you authorise this requisition? Then there will be no problem with the stores.' I extended my arm fully.

He took the piece of paper and placed it in front of him and read it. 'I suppose it's that damn Father Rudge that wants this, eh?' he said to me as he signed it.

'Yes, Sir,' I said meekly, not believing my luck.

'Better have one of these as well, then,' he said, taking a rubber stamp, inking it and crashing it down on his signature. He handed it back to me.

'Thank you, Sir,' I said as I left.

The Electrical store, outside the Electrical workshop, had a stable door. If Father Rudge was in the top half, the door would be open. The bottom half had a small shelf on top, where spare broken bits were placed, and a discussion would take place as to whether Father Rudge had the part in stock. I placed the requisition form on this shelf and waited. There was sufficient space the other side of the door for Father Rudge to stand; no-one else was ever allowed in this store. Behind Father Rudge would be the end of two back-to-back racks of shelves. It was impossible to see what these shelves contained. They could be accessed by going round to the left, or round to the right. To the right-hand side, Father Rudge had a desk, where he would sit. I could see his back now as he sat at this desk. He could see me because he had a mirror strategically placed in front of him, much like the rear-view mirror of a car. However, he did not acknowledge me or stir from his position. I waited a little longer. 'Excuse me, Father?' I called.

'Wait!' he bellowed. I waited. I could not see what he was doing. It seemed to me he was doing nothing.

'I need a new bunk light,' I told him.

'No fucking chance,' he informed me, still sitting where he was. 'Unless it's for the fucking skipper.'

'Not the skipper,' I confirmed. I waited for some response. No response. 'Flannigan,' I said, and instantly he spun in his chair to look at me.

'I suppose you'll have a requisition, then, Skin?' he challenged.

'Yes, I do. Signed by Flannigan.' He rose from his chair and took the form. 'And stamped by him as well,' I added triumphantly.

He reached into his pocket and extracted a pipe, which he placed beneath the nicotine-stained moustache of his beard. 'See your mate's been in the shit again,' Father said in a friendly tone. He was referring to Spanner, of course.

'Yeah,' I said. 'Lost his fucking ID card.'

'What's this I hear about you being caught in a bag shanty?' he asked. 'Went in with 'ole Spunky, I heard.'

'I only went in for a piss.'

'Yeah, that's what they say,' he said, as if recalling. 'You went in for a piss and came out fucked, and 'ole Spunky went in for a fuck and came out pissed.' Now he was chuckling at his own joke. He disappeared around the corner and came back with a white cardboard carton, which he placed on the shelf of the door. He went round to his desk and came back with a book. He wrote in the book, offered it to me, pointing at a place on the page and said, 'Sign there, Skin.'

I signed picked up my box. 'Thanks.'

'Only bloke I've ever met who goes into a bag shanty for a piss,' he said, shaking his head and chuckling more. 'Go on, piss off,' he said, by way of dismissal.

I quickly returned to the wardroom, fitted the new bunk light, and reconnected it. Everything worked perfectly—much the same as it did less than twelve hours previously. I then went to our mess to change out Don's bunk light. The less people who were aware of what was going on, the better. If word got back to Father Rudge that I gave Don a new bunk light, I may be in a sticky situation. I promised Don a brand-new light, but this was not. However, it looked new, and I would show him the box and wrappings to ensure I got my beer. I was very careful how I removed the old light. I wanted to preserve its intermittent fault, and investigate how this was happening. At lunchtime, I showed Don his new bunk light. His eyes lit up, and he was genuinely pleased. 'Don't say a fucking word to anyone,' I told him. 'If Father Rudge finds out, he may confiscate it. I'll dispose of these,' I added, showing him the new box and installation instructions, etc.

'Cheers, pal,' he told me. 'I'll see you tonight.' This meant tonight, he would give me my can of beer.

I had to wait until late evening before I could investigate Don's old bunk light fitting. I didn't want to be seen doing this, and in the evening, the workshop would be desolate. The bunk light consisted of a pygmy bulb, bulb holder and switch. At the base of the bulb holder were two spring-loaded pins, which pressed against the connections on the bulb base. One of these springs was broken, which meant there was no pressure on one of the connections. The pins pointed downwards, so gravity will keep it extended. That's why the light worked, but any vibration could cause the connection to be broken. The pin could jump around, randomly making connection. The corresponding connection on the base of the bulb was blackened and roughened due to spasmodic arcing of the bad connection. The older the bulb got, the worse the problem got. I assumed that if I put a new bulb in, the light would appear to work as normal. It would begin to fail as someone made their beds or got in and out of bed. Any vibration could cause it to go out as any vibration could cause it to come back on. Hence, Don banging and thumping the thing all the time. My plan was to change the insides of Jenkins' fitting with that of Don's. In that way, Don's frustration would be transferred to Jenkins, and no-one else in the Steward's mess would suffer. I would have the satisfaction of knowing I had caused Jenkins to suffer. The only problem now was how to do it. I could wait until the next issue of maintenance cards, but there could be no guarantee that the next issue would include anything in the Steward's mess. I could just go in during the day, when no-one is there, but if I got caught, I'd be in the shit—big time. Or I could cause a failure and go in for repair. The last option was the best. Again, I waited until I was Duty EM. At the end of the working day, I removed a fuse for the bunk lights in the Steward's mess and replaced it with a blown one. I waited in the switchboard for the defect to be reported. I didn't have to wait long. One of the Stewards wanted to lounge on his bunk and read. I was despatched to investigate the repair. I went into the mess. Jenkins was there. 'What the fuck do you want?' Jenkins asked me in a threatening manner. 'You should knock before you come in here.'

I ignored him. 'Came to fix your bunk lights,' I said. He didn't know they were out. He had only just entered the mess himself. He remonstrated with one of the Junior Stewards for not telling him. I asked for all bunk lights to be turned on. Six worked and six didn't. I went away and played a trick. I took out the old fuse and replaced a new fuse in the holder. I gingerly put the fuse in position and wiggled it about. This caused some sparking, and I knew the lights would be flashing on and off. I took out both fuses to isolate the circuit. 'Something is wrong with one of the fittings,' I said. 'I need to check them.' I placed my tool bag on the table and fiddled with my tools. I took the cover off one fitting and then another. I reached up to Jenkins' bunk.

'Mind my fucking things up there,' he said. I took the cover from his light and removed the bulb. 'You see, Clark,' he sneered again, 'you are a servant as well.' I turned to look at him. 'You think it's only Stewards that are servants, don't you?' I said nothing. 'You see,' he went on, 'we report a problem and you come running.' He paused for a while. 'To serve us,' he added triumphantly.

'Only because you can't do it yourself.'

'I don't need to,' he said. 'I have you to serve me.' Jenkins thought he was being clever. He turned with his nose in the air and left the mess. I had Don's old fitting in my hand, which brought a smile to my face. I exchanged it for the one in Jenkins's unit. I put a new bulb in and replaced the cover. I replaced one screw with one I had doctored earlier. I had used a hack saw to increase the depth of the screwdriver slot. This was now very weak. I put some adhesive compound, used by the engineers to lock in bolts on machinery, on the threads, and screwed it into place. I tightened the other three and gently tightened the last. I replaced the covers on the other two fittings, put all the switches on the off position, and replaced the fuses with good ones. I first reached up to Jenkins' bunk and gingerly switched it on. The light came on. I tried it a few times and it was perfect. I tested the others and, of course, they all worked. Jenkins was not in the mess, but the other guys thanked me, and I left. I was confident this light would continue to work for some days or weeks before the first failure. He would tap it and the light would come back on. With the first failure, the first little pitting and blackening would come on the base of the lamp. As time would pass, failures would occur more often; the little taps would become slaps. Pitting and blackening greater causing failures more regular. Slaps would turn to thumps and Jenkins would be pissed off, big time.

18: Okinawa

HMS Hermes dropped anchor off Okinawa in the Pacific Ocean. Okinawa is a Japanese Island, which is home to an American military base. The base was used for Rest and Recuperation of the Americans serving in Vietnam. We would spend a few days here, and we could go ashore. We were advised to remain in the base camp and not venture into the nearby villages.

The more senior guys in the mess were celebrating that it was 'Trap a Yank' time. This means go ashore, befriend an American, and they will buy all the drinks. You didn't have to like them, but just tolerate them, and they'd buy all the drinks and most things else you would need. They would also give you most things you asked for, such as Zippo lighters, belt buckles, uniform caps, and jackets. It seemed all we had to do was talk; they loved the British accent.

I was still on Ceremonial Guard Duty, but because we were not alongside, our services were not required. This was a relief to me. We had to take a boat to the shore. These left the ship every half hour or so, and the same for returning at the end of the evening. Budgie and I decided to go together and see what we could find. We got ready and waited in line for the first Liberty Boat. We had to climb down, scrambling nets to get on-board the boat, which bobbed around at our feet. Timing was essential as to when you launched yourself from the net to the boat. The ride ashore was a pleasant change. The boat undulated as it ploughed through the water towards the shore. The Hermes changed from a towering cliff face of metal to a sinister, grey warship with dark, shiny aircraft on its flat-deck as we got further away and could appreciate the perspective better. The sun shone brightly, high in the clear sky. The sea was a deep blue with a long swell running. The sun glistened from small ripples as they broke at the crest of their waves. The wake behind the boat was a milky, swirling whiteness of turbulent, angry water.

The Liberty Boat berthed at a pontoon, where we all scrambled off. The jetty was lined with Yanks in all manner of uniforms. We were in civilian clothes, and casual, at that. They greeted us with hoots and howls and whistles. We went up the gangway, and the greetings continued. 'Hiya, fellas,' they'd shout. 'Wanna beer, I bet.'

'Get some pussy later, hey, guys?' some called. We were directed to their social club. The air-conditioned atmosphere inside was a great contrast to the warm, humid air out. We were ushered into the main bar area, which was cavernous: the ceiling was high but looked low, such was the vastness of its unsupported area. Many people crowded around the bar, eager to get a drink. We turned to the windows that looked out to sea: they stretched the whole length of the room and from floor to ceiling. We could see Hermes majestically sitting in the bay. Lots of low tables were about us with plush lounge chairs surrounding them, such a contrast to the bars in Australia. We stood in the middle of the bar, just taking it all in, when we heard from behind, 'You fellas okay?' We turned to face the voice. There were two men stood in front of us: it was Don Quixote and Sancho. I could hardly believe my eyes. One was at least as tall as Mortiman and skinny as a rake; the other about five feet, whichever way you measured him. 'I'm Don,' he said, extending his skinny arm. I wanted to say 'I know', but was still in shock. 'Don Williams,' he added, 'from Massachusetts. 'I took his bony hand. It was cold and lifeless in mine. *The man's a wimp*, I thought.

'Hello,' I said. 'I'm Chris.' I thought I should add I'm from Forty Foot, but didn't think it was fitting. I let go of his hand, and he turned to Budgie, repeating his greeting.

Sancho Panza reached his stub of an arm up to me saying, 'Hi, I'm Sam Patcho from Illinois.' Before I could answer, he added, 'Mighty pleased to meet you.'

'Hello. I'm Chris.' His hand was small and sweaty, and he seemed to wipe some of the sweat on mine before he let my hand go. I wiped my hand on my trousers. Normally, when you look at two guys in front you, your eyes go from left to right. In this instance, they went up and down.

'You guys wan' a beer?' Don asked in an excited voice of expectation. He was looking from Budgie to me and back again, as if willing us to say yes.

'Yes please,' we said in unison, nodding enthusiastically.

'Come on,' Sam said, 'let's relax.' He indicated to a vacant table nearby, and Don turned towards the bar.

Sam sat forward in his chair, leaning his elbows on his knees. I guess it's the only way his feet would reach the floor. He asked lots of questions about the Hermes and what we did on-board. He was genuinely interested, and our answers were received with *wow*s and *ooh*s of wonderment. Don returned with a tray of beer and a small bowl of peanuts. Budgie and I were impressed with the peanuts; it was a detail to which we were not accustomed to. Don repeated Sam's questions, and responded as Sam had. Don also sat forward in his chair, and as he leant forward, his knees where close to his shoulders. As we drank the beer, we began to learn a bit about Don Quixote and Sancho Panza. They were both in the US Army, and had both been wounded in Vietnam. Don's squad got hit by a grenade attack. Two of his buddies died, and he got fragments of the grenade in his legs. He rolled up his trouser legs to show us. His skinny legs had deep red and purple scars on his calves and thighs. Some were small whilst some were the size of half-crowns. 'Nearly a pound of metal, the docs took out of these,' he said, slapping his thighs. 'Luckily none hit the knees, else I may have had a problem.' He started rubbing his knees. Budgie and I were shocked at the horrible sight of his legs. It must have been reflected in our faces, as Don quickly went on to say, 'Hey, fellas, this is nothing. I'm really one of the lucky guys.' He readjusted his trousers, covering his legs.

We both instinctively turned to Sam. 'I got it in the butt,' he announced, almost shyly. 'Forgive me if I don't show you the scar.' He grinned. 'I only got one bit, but it was a big motherfucker. God-damn thing embedded itself in my hip bone.' Budgie and I were looking at him, unable to speak. We were wide-eyed, and I had to make a big effort to keep my mouth closed, lest my jaw drop open. 'Motherfucking doctors lifted me off the operating table, trying to pull the darn thing out!' he informed us. 'Eventually had to use a hammer and chisel and chip my fucking butt bone away.'

The two of them had been there for about three months recovering from their unfortunate experiences. Shortly, they would be honourably discharged from the Army and sent back home. They would each receive a Purple Heart Medal for being injured in battle. Budgie and I were humbled by their accounts of what happened to them, and to many other people there. Both Don and Sam could not emphasise enough that they were the lucky ones. As we chatted, Don kept calling over a Japanese girl and ordering more beer. This girl wore a kimono, which clung tight to her body. The garment reached down to her ankles but a slit at the side, which revealed her leg up to her thigh. As she bent forward to place the glasses of beer from the tray to the table, a full length of nylon clad leg was on show. An electric shock travelled through my body and tingled my testicles. My cock stiffened and strained against my clothing. My mind imagined what lay behind the rest of the kimono. Her face was not as round as most of the Chinese women I had encountered in the past. Hers was longer, with high cheekbones that caused the cheeks to lose their fullness. Her eyes were not slits but rounded, although tapered to the outside, giving the classic almond shape. She had beautifully-shaped, delicate lips, which remained closed. I knew she knew I was scrutinising her. As she placed the last glass, I directly thanked her. Her eyes narrowed into a smile, and her hand went up quickly to cover her mouth as the smile dragged her lips apart. Her head went down in a bow to hide her face, and she backed away. She turned, and I watched her arse wiggle as she went.

We referred to all these oriental women as Chinese, but of course they are not. There are different races, and generally, we considered them all to be the same. The ugly girl I saw naked in the brothel in Singapore would be Malaysian; in Hong Kong, it would be true to refer to them as Chinese. However, the features are very much the same. This girl was Japanese. I wanted to see more Japanese because she was beautiful.

'We should go to the village later,' Don said as he watched my eyes follow the waitress away.

'Got to be back on the jetty by midnight,' I told him.

'Midnight!' Don exclaimed. 'God-damn party don't start 'till midnight, man!'

We felt embarrassed, and it must have shown because Sam immediately jumped in. 'Aw, we can take 'em to Sally's,' he said. 'At least they can see some titties before they go back.'

'Sure,' Don said, 'we'll do that.'

We had drunk several beers now, and I was feeling the effects. I was still talking okay, but was worried about standing, as I didn't want to show myself up. 'You wanna bowl?' Don asked us excitedly. Again, he was leaning forward, looking from me to Budgie and back, willing us to say yes. 'We got a bowling alley here.,' he informed us. 'Twenty-four motherfucking lanes.'

'Yeah,' I said, 'great idea.' We played, but I was no good. The action of bowling almost caused me to lose balance due to the amount of beer I had inside me. Don was good. He could spin a ball and start it off down one side of the alley and cause it to come across the lane, always striking the lead pin. Although he was tall and skinny, his action was fluid and rhythmic. Sam was more staccato, but he held his own against Don.

'You wanna race cars?' Don asked us as excitedly as he did before. 'We got scalextrics! Eight motherfucking tracks.'

The layout was similar to that of the UJC in Singapore. There were only a handful of guys around. Two were racing and the others looking.

The atmosphere was tense, as all eyes followed the two cars around the track. They sped like lightening down the straights, and whizzed around the bends. Speed control was crucial on this track, and the two guys were good at it.

Finally, one of the guys jumped up with his arms in the air. 'World Champion!' he declared triumphantly, hooting a cheering his victory. The loser pulled a note from his pocket and passed it to the 'World Champion'.

'They are racing for ten dollars,' Don informed us. 'You any good at this?'

'I'm not, but Budgie is,' I told him. Budgie looked at me in amazement.

'Do you wanna take on the Champ?' he asked Budgie.

'Let's have a practice first and we'll see,' I said.

Budgie looked at me in amazement. 'I'm not betting no ten fucking dollars!' he hissed at me.

'Budgie,' I said to him. He looked at me. 'Trust me.' It seemed it was now practice time: everyone was having a go. We had our turn, and it was really easy to spin off the track. These cars were really fast.

We were having fun when Mr World Champion announced, 'I have a challenger! I have a challenger!' His arms were raised, indicating everyone should stop and clear the track. The challenger went and stood by the Champ, and a coin was tossed. The few people around the table were giving loud encouragement to both racers. If you won the toss, you could choose which cars would be used, and the other guy which tracks you had to use. This seemed to be a fair arrangement. The cars were placed on the track; someone counted down and started the race. The first twice round the track would win. Mr World Champion soon got into an early lead and was first home on the first lap. The challenger, in an endeavour to catch up, accelerated too long on the long straight, and flew off at the next bend. There were hoots of derision from the few onlookers, and the Champ, once again, jumped in the air with raised arms chanting, 'World Champion! World Champion!'

'Can you keep the car on the track?' I asked Budgie. He looked at me, puzzled. 'Can you go round and keep the car on the track?' I asked again.

'Well, yeah.'

'That's all you need to do,' I said. 'My mate will challenge you!' I shouted. There was silence.

'Fuck off, Chris, for fuck's sake.' Budgie was trying to pull my arm down.

'Listen, you just go around and keep your car on the track, and you *will* win.' He looked at me in bewilderment. 'If you lose, I will pay.'

'Okay,' Budgie said in submission.

'If you spin off the track, you pay.' I added. Budgie and I went forward, and I tossed a coin for the World Champion. Cars and tracks were chosen and cars placed on the starting line. The starting line was on a small straight. Half a yard later was the first ninety-degree turn into the longest straight. It was important to start slow, and to safely get around the first bend. I moved off to the right, away from the flow of the race. As the countdown started, I used the coin to short out the track of the World Champion's car.

'Go! Go! Go!' the starter screamed, and Budgie's car lurched forward and safely navigated the first bend. The World Champion's car did not move. 'Motherfucker!' the World Campion screamed at his car. He looked from the car to the controller in his hand. His thumb was pumping up and down on the controller. 'Motherfucker!' he screamed again, looking at the controller with his thumb fully pressing the plunger. He began to shake it. I released the coin from the track and his car shot forwards, straight over the first bend and bounced off the wall. 'Motherfucker!' he screamed for a third time. There were hoots of laughter from the audience, and they were on their feet watching Budgie's car.

'Slow down, slow down,' they all urged Budgie. They just wanted him to complete the two laps.

'Fucking told you, Budgie,' I said to him triumphantly.

'Chris, that was amazing,' Don said to me, patting me on my back. I wondered if he had seen what I did. 'Budgie is so lucky!'

The ex-World Champion picked up his car and scrutinised it. He watched as Budgie guided his car around the track at a snail's pace. Everyone was cheering Budgie on: 'Not too fast, not too fast.' When Budgie's car passed the line for the second time, there was a genuine roar of triumph from the crowd. Through all the cheering and laughter, the ex-World Champ could still be heard cursing, 'Motherfucker! Motherfucker!'

After the race, Budgie looked at me, and I held the coin up for him to see. 'Lucky coin, eh, Budge?' I said with a smile on my face. Budgie didn't even know what I had done. Mr Ex-World Champion replaced the car on the track and set it in motion. It worked fine. 'Cock-sucker motherfucker!' he cursed. 'Would you believe that son of a bitch?' He shook his head. 'Hey, man,' he added as he turned to Budgie, 'you gotta give me another shot.' He handed Budgie ten dollars. 'Make it twenty this time, eh, man?' he offered.

'You sure about this?' I said to him.

'Hell yes I am, man!' he assured me.

'Okay, Budge, let's go.' Budgie just shrugged his shoulders and turned back to the track.

'Chris, are you sure about this, man?' Don cautioned me. 'That guy is really good, and Budgie just got lucky.'

'It's okay,' I told him. 'Just this one.' Just to rub it in to the Ex-World Champ, I said, 'How about we just swap cars and tracks?'

'What, you want him,' he pointed to Budgie, 'to use this piece of shit?' He pointed to the car.

'Well, it does make it fair, then,' I said, and I knew he thought I was stupid. The controllers were swapped, and the cars placed on the starting line. Someone started the countdown whilst I hovered the coin over the Ex-World Champ's track.

'Go! Go! Go!' the starter said, and off they went. Budgie gingerly took the first bend, but by then Mr Ex-World Champion was halfway down the long straight. I waited until it was time for him to slow down and then shorted out his track. His car came to a stop.

'Go, you motherfucker!' He screamed at his car. Budgie caught up to him and trundled round the bend. 'Go! Go! Go! You motherfucker son of a bitch!' he screamed, holding his controller in front of him with his thumb pressing the plunger fully. I released my coin, and again his car shot forward, off the track, and on to the floor. Again, the onlookers were on their feet, screaming and laughing. Again, they urged Budgie to slow down.

'Slow. Slow. Slow', they chanted.

'I don't fucking believe it, man,' Don said by my side. Budgie did his job and brought the car home safely to tremendous cheers.

'Limey bastards,' Ex-World Champ said as he gave me twenty dollars, then brushed past me and left.

'How did you do that then, Clark?' Budgie asked. I showed him the coin again.

'Lucky coin,' I said.

We had consumed several beers and had not paid for any. We were never prompted to pay, so we didn't. We had just gained ourselves fifteen dollars each, so we felt rich. 'Let's go to the village,' I said to Don and Sam, 'and we'll buy you a beer.'

'We'll go to the village, but you are not buying any beer,' Don told me.

'You are our guests,' Sam added.

Don and Sam took us to the village. They paid for the taxi there. They paid for a hamburger. They paid for all the beer. They paid for drinks, for the bar girls, whilst they sat with us and let us feel their tits, and they paid for the taxi back to the base. We staggered down the jetty with a belly full of beer and pockets full of zippo lighters, belt buckles and a variety of uniform badges. We had both successfully, 'Trapped a Yank'.

The next morning, HMS Hermes hauled up its anchor, turned around, and set off for Singapore again. Tragedy befell us: A Gannet aircraft failed to catch an arrester wire, and failed to increase power. It ran off the end of the angle deck and crashed into the sea. Three days later, the port wing off another Gannet aircraft became unlatched, as it was being catapulted off the ship. The aircraft heeled over, crashed into the sea and was run over by the ship. Three men lost their lives. There was an air of sadness within the ship, but life soon returned to normal.

It wasn't long before the bunk light on Jenkins' bed began to fail. It would go out, he would bang it, and it would come back on. Soon, this got too monotonous, and he reported it as a defect; I saw the entry in the defect book. I didn't want to be the one who attended this defect because I knew what was going to happen. The defect report was given to Windy, and I made a big show of telling him how I was planning to change a load of fluorescent tubes in the Junior Rates dining room. The defect was given to Max, who mumbled something about, 'Fucking Stewards' as he got his tool bag ready.

After lunch, I lay on my bunk, smoking and relaxing after my meal. 'Hey, that Jenkins has got it in for you, Clarkie,' Max shouted across to me from his bunk. 'Says you fucked up his bunk light.' I wanted to ask how he got on. 'Says it was alright before you started fucking around with it.'

'Did you fix it for him then?'

'No,' he said, 'fucking screw sheared and couldn't get the cover off.'

'So what did you do?'

'Well, nothing. If the cover won't come off, can't get into it.'

'What did you tell him, then?' I enquired.

'Said he'd have to wait till we got back to Pompey,' he told me. I didn't say anything. 'He's not very pleased. He reckons it's all your fault and he's going to get you.'

Well, we will see, I thought to myself. It seemed my mission was accomplished. I had caused Jenkins to have some frustration, which gave me a sense of pleasure. I knew he would continue to use the light, and the situation would get worse; he would have to bang the thing more often to keep it on. He would not be able to enjoy his books so much under these conditions.

19: Kai Tais and Christmas

The same haziness hung over Singapore; it was hot and humid. It was as if we had never been away. Fingers and his circle of buddies were excited about their station leave. They would travel, by train, to Fraser's Hill, close to Kuala Lumpur. They would be staying at a disused army camp. It seemed a big difference from the venue where we had spent our station leave in Hexham.

We had a new EM join direct from Collingwood. He had flown to Singapore, and was waiting for the ship to arrive. His name was Bob Walkinson, and he came from Scunthorpe. He was not so tall, but broad across the shoulders. He had done a lot of boxing training, and was quite fit-looking. He was nineteen years old and had tattoos, which he obtained before he joined the navy. He had a red rose tattooed on his right arm with a banner across it, in which held his girlfriend's name was held. Above the rose, he had tattooed *New Castle Brown Ale*, and everyone thought this strange, to say the least. I got on well with Bob, and he confided in me that he had changed his girlfriend, and so the tattooed name was redundant. He planned to go ashore sometime to have the ex-girlfriend's name and *New Castle Brown Ale* obliterated.

The Chinese tailors and shoe-makers packed up their things and left the ship. I dismantled all the light fittings and wiring. I discovered four of them had acquired bunk lights. I had no idea where they got these, or who from. I took all the wiring and light fittings to the Electrical workshop and threw them in a box under the bench, which contained 'handy spares'. I kept the bunk lights in my personal locker; I would trade these for rum and beer at some stage. All the Chinks said goodbye to me and handed me a bag full of beer. Whilst I was grateful, I now had a problem of where I would stow all this beer. There were thirteen cans in the bag. It could be dangerous to keep it in my locker as, from time-to-time, random locker searches were carried out. I could not drink so many cans all at once, else I'd be staggering around the ship like a drunken bum. I was sure there was not a place on-board Hermes that I could hide these, and that place not be known to the reg. staff or the Chief Electrician. These people were senior and experienced. It was their job to know these places and seek out contraband. However, they did not search these places every time. It would be impossible. They knew beer went missing during a RAS, and they knew basically where it would be, so they hedged their bets and narrowed down their searches. Whilst they found some beer, they never found it all. A bag of thirteen cans of beer was quite large, and I could not just walk around the ship with it and hope no-one would suspect what I had. It was quite normal to carry a pillowcase stuffed with laundry, though, provided you were making for the laundry in Kilo switchboard flat. I got a bundle of laundry together and wrapped the beer within it. I explained to one of the laundry Chinks that his friends had given me this beer, but I couldn't keep it. They knew I was not allowed beer, and that I was rewarded in beer for the favours I had done for their friends, the tailors and shoe-makers. I asked him to keep these for me, and I would come for one or two from time-to-time. He understood and agreed.

I was still on special duties as Ceremonial Guard. Almost every morning, I had to be up for Colours at 06:30. As time went by, I got used to this. I would be awake when the duty EM came around to shake me with his clipboard and torch in his hand. I'd run to the bathroom and shower. I'd dress in my Number 6 uniform—in the dark—and make my way to the Flight Deck. We would wait inside the Flight Deck door of the island, smoking and waiting to be summoned by the GI. We swapped stories and it transpired that all my colleagues on special duty of Ceremonial Guard had been under punishment at some stage or other, and we all felt we had been victimised by McSnell. We had all won the same lottery.

The two-hour stints we had to do at the end of the gangway became less of a chore. I was fascinated by the variety of people who came to and from the ship via the after-gangway. From time-to-time, ladies would be invited on-board. A car would stop in front of the gangway, and out would step a picture of elegance: a lady in a dress. Sometimes, the flash of leg was tantalising. The lady would stand, adjusting the hang of her dress and titillate her hair. When ready, she would move forward with her escort. If he was a Naval officer, I would snap to attention and present arms, with the rifle, in salute. Up two three, up two three, down; and snap my right boot behind the left to finalise the salute. This always impressed the ladies. They would stand in front of me, large-eyed and smiling in wonderment. The escort would return my salute, and I would snap the rifle down and return to attention. Down two three, down two three, and the rifle would be back by my side.

Sometimes, there would be afternoon cocktail parties on the Quarterdeck or wardroom, and the number of beautiful ladies streaming passed would be a wonderful sight. If you had the spell of duty when the party was winding up, the sight was not so wonderful: some of the ladies would be drunk. They'd stagger down the gangway, almost twisting their ankles as they stepped from it in wobbly stiletto heels, their escorts supporting them by a firm grip of their arm near the armpit, their hair not so tidy now. They would then be bundled into waiting cars in very undignified manners.

During quiet times, I took to bringing myself to attention, bringing the rifle to the Slope Arms position. This is where the left forearm is parallel to the deck, with the elbow locked to the side of the body. The rifle is held in the hand and resting on the left shoulder. I would then turn right and quick-march ten paces, about turn, return, and then continue ten paces in the other direction, where I would about turn once again and then march ten paces back to the gangway. Halt, turn to the left, and then bring myself back to attention with the rifle by my side. Moments later, I would assume the At Ease position. Moments after the first time I did this, I heard someone descend the gangway. It was the Officer of the Watch (OOW). I was aware of him standing by my side. 'What's your name, lad?' he asked in a quiet voice. He had a Norfolk accent.

'Clark, Sir,' I answered.

'Why did you do that, Clark?' he asked. I felt like saying 'do what, Sir?', but knew that would lead me to trouble. This young officer was not being hostile.

'I was beginning to think I might faint, Sir,' I said, trying to gain his sympathy. 'I just wanted to get the blood moving, Sir.'

'You feel okay now, Clark?'

'Yes, Sir,' I replied.

'Good,' he said. 'Don't do it more than once every fifteen minutes. 'I heard him mount the gangway once again. I had to smile to myself. I think my routine impressed him. Repeating this routine brought some pleasant relief to a very boring duty.

With this special duty, it did mean I could get off ashore most days at midday, if I wanted to. Most of my friends could not, except for weekends and some special circumstances. I mostly took advantage of this privilege by going to Aggie Western's, and lounging by the pool. I was not spending any money, and to laze out by the pool was a much better pastime than hanging around the mess on-board. I always enjoyed the stroll from the ship through the dockyard on my own. I always looked towards the dockyard canteen as I passed, but never ventured in. The memory of last time stuck in my mind. Most people from the mess would start their run ashore from here, so by about 17:00, my mess mates would be arriving. The general routine would be to swim, relax and then start drinking beer. Whilst most people had a plan for their evening, the plan could change, and often did, dependent upon the number of beers consumed. Budgie and I would be content to hang around for a while and then wander off, down to Sembawang Village for an eggy banjo, and back on-board. Spanner, after a few beers, always wanted to go to Bugis Street. Just the thought of it would be enough for him to grab his scrotum and grind it, thrusting his chin forward and groaning with a lewd look in his eye. I had never been there. I got close last time, but then got into trouble. I knew I must go, because everyone does.

We would be in Singapore for several weeks now, and would spend Christmas here. Weekend leave was available, if you were not on-duty watch. The normal duty roster would mean you were required to stay on-board every other weekend. The Ceremonial Guard was not required at weekends, which was another advantage. The coming weekend, I had booked to share a room with Budgie at Aggie's. Spanner had booked to share a room with Don. Max was looking for someone to share with him. I told Spanner I would go to Singapore City and Bugis Street with him on Friday—the first day of our first weekend off.

The first Friday came, and Budgie and I checked into our room at Aggie's. It was great to see and lay on a proper bed, and we both did so, enjoying the comfort and space. It would be our home for the next three nights. 'What you reckon about Bugis Street tonight, then, Budge?'

'Dunno,' he answered, thinking about it. 'Ain't going near none of them Kai Tais.'

'No, me neither,' I assured him. 'You watch Spanner, though. Can't leave the fuckers alone.' It was still early in the afternoon. Budgie had got away early, and we were the first to get here. 'Let's go to the UJC,' I suggested enthusiastically to Budgie. 'We can meet up with the rest there. 'We took a taxi. We arrived at the UJC and bought a Tiger beer at the bar. We carried the beer to the scalextrics track, and watched. The place was crowded, unlike the club in Okinawa. I showed Budgie a coin. 'Remember the lucky coin,' I said. He nodded. 'Look at the red car.' I pointed over to the far side of the track. The car was whizzing down the long straight on the outside lane. I shorted the track out, and it stopped. Budgie looked at me, and then noticed what I had done. I released the coin, and the car continued its course. A surprised, knowing look came over Budgies face.

'You could have got us killed, you fucking moron,' Budgie said.

'No. All eyes were on the other side of the track from me.' Budgie was not looking happy. 'Relax. We won thirty dollars!'

'I ain't doing it here, though,' he said, and turned away. We walked to the balcony overlooking the pool.

'There's a guy here that does it,' I told him. 'I saw it last time.' Budgie said nothing. I think he was frightened I may want him to repeat his performance as in Okinawa. 'Too many people here, though,' I said, and he relaxed a little.

The bar was filling up. In one corner, tables had been brought together and a 'sing-song' had started.

Sambo was a lazy coon, used to sleep in the afternoon, so tired was he…

The gathering reminded me of the episode in the dockyard canteen. They looked similar: mostly pot-bellied, bearded, tattooed, rubicund and sweating. They went into the chorus:

Arsehole rules the Navy, arsehole rules the Navy, arsehole rules the Navy, but you'll get no arsehole here.

At the opposite corner of the bar, there were a couple of dart boards with some guys playing. 'Come on!' Budgie beckoned me. 'Let's give 'em a game.' We played darts and drank another bottle of Tiger each. We were enjoying ourselves and passing time. We were not getting drunk and nor spending too much money. We were content.

We were both keeping our eye open in the bar for the rest of our mess mates to arrive. Mortiman was the first I saw. He was towering above Spanner and Max. Don sauntered behind. They went to the bar, bought a beer, and then selected a table not too far from us. I guess they, too, didn't want to be too close to the shanty singers, lest they get roped in to singing a song. We finished our current game, got another bottle of Tiger, and went to join them. We talked, laughed and joked, smoked, and drank more beer. People kept reminding me where the toilets were, should I need to go, clearly drawing reference to the last time I was in this area. Spanner was professing he knew where all the best women were, and seemed eager for someone to take interest, so he could go off and get his end away. Our table was getting more noisy. More beer was spilled on the table and floor, and the ashtrays overflowed. It was getting late, and time to move on.

Budgie and I went down the stairs, through the front door, and were met by the dark, sweet-smelling, humid air of the night. The front of the Raffles Hotel was floodlit, and looked resplendent. Trishaw drivers were touting for our business. We watched as Spanner and Max got into one. Mort and Don got into another, looking ridiculous, and the driver struggled to get the machine moving. They went off into the dark night, urging the driver to go faster. To our right, we heard a faint cry of help. We looked at each other, wondering what it could be. We edged our way to the end of front wall of the UJC building; next to it was a small building, similar to a garage. A large door faced the road. There was a small gap between the two buildings, yet there was a chain-link fence surrounding the garage. This meant the fence passed between the two buildings with a greater gap on the garage side. There was almost no space between the fence and the end wall of the UJC. There was a man sandwiched between the fence and the UJC. His back was pressed up against the wall, and his face was popping through the diamonds formed by the woven wires of the fence. 'Help,' he whimpered again as he saw us look at him. Budgie and I just looked at each other again with open mouths. We were both wondering how on earth this guy could have got in there. 'I'm stuck,' the man said.

'How did you get in?' I asked, thinking that maybe he had come from the other side of the building, trying to get to the road.

'I was hiding,' he said, and I could detect an American accent. His hand was reaching out to me. Reaching in, I was just able to grab it, but he couldn't grip me; he had no strength. I had to reach in further, so I could grab his wrist and so my hand would not slip off so readily. As I pulled, he cried out in pain.

'Are you okay?' I asked, beginning to be worried.

'Stuck,' he said. I pulled harder, and his upper torso moved towards me. I pulled and he toppled to the side. His head and shoulders were free from the vice grip of the fence and wall, but he was lying on his side. Both Budgie and I grabbed hold of his arm and pulled. He moaned, but we were able to drag him clear of the crevice. Once free, he rolled onto his back, still moaning. 'Thanks, man,' he said.

Again I asked him, 'Are you okay? 'He looked up at me and nodded. His face was red and scratched, but I could see no serious wound. He raised his head, and I helped him into a sitting position. He leaned forwards and pushed his head down, as if stretching his back. This movement was accompanied by moans and groans. With his hands, he tried to shuffle around. We helped him turn so his back was towards the wall. He sat there with his back against the UJC, and drew his knees up. He folded his arms on his knees and rested his head on his arms. 'Do you think you need a doctor, or something?' I asked him.

After a while, he raised his face to us, shaking his head. 'Gee, thanks, you guys.' He took a deep breath. He tried to get up and we helped him, his legs violently shaking. 'Let me get you two a beer,' he said, and placed an arm around both our shoulders. We went back into the UJC and sat at the same table as before, which had now been cleaned. He called to a waiter to bring three beers. He told us he was drunk, and two Australian army guys were chasing him, so he went into the gap to hide. He said he forced his way in, and saw the two guys pass without seeing him. He decided to wait a while, and then fell asleep. I guess he meant passed out.

'When was that?' I asked.

He looked at me and about the bar, then declared, 'Dunno, but it was still light.' It had been dark for about three hours now, so he must have been there for some time. His name was Jake, and he was returning to the States from Vietnam. He was staying with about twenty other American GI's in Terror Barracks. He didn't tell us why he was running from the Aussies, and we didn't press him too much on the issue. 'What are you fellas doing tonight?' he asked us.

'Off to Bugis Street. Our mates have already gone.'

'It's early yet,' Jake said, and ordered another beer for us all.

'This place is nearly closing,' I told him, in reply to his remark of it being early.

'Yeah, but Bugis Street is only waking up,' he said with a knowing smile, pushing my knee as he said it. 'It's not far. Let's have this, and we'll go.' Over and over, Jake told us how grateful he was that we rescued him. He said we saved his life, and that the rest of the night was on him. Budgie and I looked at each other and I'm sure he was thinking, as I was, we'd trapped a Yank again.

Jake led us through the narrow streets towards Bugis Street. Brightly-lit facades invited us in to dimly-lit bars. Street girls touted for business, and pimps offered all manner of women; beautiful women, young women, and old women—even two women at once. If you refused all these, they would make one last attempt and enquire if you wanted a young boy. The guy would then chase you down the street and ask if you wanted a dirty photo or a blue movie. Finally, he would give up and return to his previous place.

Ultimately, we turned a corner and we had arrived. To go to Bugis Street meant to go to the end of Bugis Street, where there was a small square. At the far side of the square was an old toilet block. The square had numerous wooded tables with bench seats attached, much the same as garden furniture. Opposite the toilet block were a small number of market stall-type bars serving beer and food. The whole area was full. No empty table existed. Chinese waiters and waitresses shuffled around on worn-out flip-flops, carrying trays full of beer bottles from the bar and trays full of empty beer bottles back to the bar. It seemed the glasses remained on the tables and never got washed. Prostitutes were intermingling with the crowd; I saw them being provocative to prospective customers; raising their short skirts, revealing thigh and a glimpse of their underwear. They would push their breasts up, and then embrace the man. Their hands would encircle the man's back and shoulders and then caress his buttocks. In reality, they were searching for the wallet, normally kept in the back pocket, and try to relieve the man of it. Many men lost their wallets, money, and ID cards to this trick. I was lucky: it was one of the first things I saw, so when I was approached, I enjoyed the show and attention, but made sure I kept my belongings. Jake went to a stall and returned with three bottles of Tiger and three glasses. 'Motherfucking Kai Tais,' Jake said, indicating the prostitutes. I was now confused. I did not know if they were women or men. 'You can always tell the difference. The Kai Tais are beautiful,' he said 'and the women, well, they're just ugly, cock-sucking whores.'

I remember what Spanner had told me: he said the Kai Tais were more feminine than women. I could see what he meant. The so-called 'women' I was looking at were very beautiful, sensual and feminine. They certainly had real tits; no cleavage of that depth could be produced by a man's chest. And I meant a proper man. Compared to the bar girls we had passed on our way here, the 'ladies' of Bugis Street were infinitely better manicured and dressed. If you looked hard, there were some tell-tale signs: women do not have pronounced Adam's apples as men do; men's hands, generally, are bigger, and women have wider hips and fuller arses. As they approached me, I scrutinised these features, and concluded I had initially been duped: they were men. Another tell-tale sign is when they spoke: some ladies have husky voices, but it was a common trait with these, and a dead giveaway. They were all Kai Tais, men in various stages of transgender. They were without gender; unusual, and somewhat strange to my mind. Just then, two men appeared on the top of the toilet block. A roar went up from the crowd, and the two men raised their arms in appreciation. A group of the crowd started to sing:

Haul 'em down, you Zulu warrior, haul 'em down, you Zulu chief…

More of the crowd joined in with the chorus:

Hoy da zimba zimba zimba, hoy da zimba zimba zay.

The two guys started to undress, and tried to be sexy and sensual as a striptease artist would accompanied by the stripper theme. However, these were service men, soldiers and sailors, and more attuned to running a field gun than turning other men on. They were also drunk. They looked clumsy and in danger of falling off the roof at any moment.

Haul 'em down, you Zulu warrior, the song continued, *haul'em down, you Zulu chief.*

Now, the alternate chorus began:

Chief, chief, chief…

The chorus was chanted as the Zulus would chant before they went into battle. Indeed, the song originated with the Zulu tribe. A shirt was divested and waved around in the air, encouraging the chanting more. The crowd obliged:

Hoy da zimba zimba zimba, hoy da zimba zimba zay.

Belt buckles were unclipped, and belts extracted from their hoops.

Haul 'em down…

Trousers were unzipped.

…you Zulu chief, chief, chief…

Turning to the crowd, the two dropped their trousers to their ankles and raised their arms as the crowd roared with excitement.

Haul 'em down, you Zulu warrior…

The chant continued with an increase level of volume. A newspaper was thrown up to them, and they took a page each. The pages were rolled into two long tubes, and these were waved for the crowd to see.

Hoy da zimba zimba zimba, hoy da zimba zimba zay.

The two men bent over, showing their arses to the onlookers. They then inserted one end of the rolled-up newspaper in the crack of their arse. *….you Zulu chief, chief, chief…*

The two danced around to the delight of the chanting crowd. A lighter was produced, and the pages were ignited. They danced more vigorously, and the flame flickered behind them. The cadence of the chanting increased:

Chief, chief, chief, chief, chief, chief…

As the flames grew bigger, the pages grew shorter and, in a well-timed manoeuvre, the two men came to the front of the toilet roof with their backs to the crowd, and bent forward once again. The crowd then threw the contents of the beer glasses towards the two men. Everything got soaked, the men, their clothes, but more importantly, the two fires were extinguished. The singing turned into hoots of joy, cheering and applause. All joined in clapping and whistling. We had just witnessed the Dance of the Flaming Arsehole.

'You cock-sucking Limies are crazy,' Jake said to me, shaking his head. 'You know that.' The two men struggled to find their clothes and get dressed. They were soaked in beer. Beer was brought to them and placed on a table in front of them. They would not need to buy any more beer that night.

I whispered in Budgies ear, 'At least we don't have to do that to get free beer.' Budgie nodded in agreement.

As the bewitching hour approached, I noticed the crowd had grown. Local people had joined, as did ex.pat civilians. People who not only wanted to see the antics of drunken servicemen, but were waiting in anticipation for the parade of the Kai Tais. Normally, just after midnight, they would make their way into the city from outlying villages and, as if by magic, they would appear out of the shadows. Kai Tais and transvestites in beautiful, colourful, flamboyant attire would sexily slink amongst the crowd. They'd select a man, sit on his knee, and invite him to buy a drink for them. The man would be allowed to caress the leg and thigh, and even peek down a blouse or front of a dress. Some Kai Tais would pull open their blouses, revealing their ample breasts, and allow them to be fondled. That's when I noticed another distinguishing trait of Kai Tais; they all had small nipples. A woman's nipple has a much larger diameter than a man's.

As the night progressed, Jake bought us more beer, and we all got more drunk. We found a free table and slumped down at it. We watched as Kai Tais wandered off between the buildings in dark shadows with a man in tow, the man with his arm about the waist and standing close. Some moments later, they would return, this time the Kai Tai leading, the man trailing whilst adjusting his trouser zip and belt, and with a broad smile on his face. He'd just bought a jerk-off or a blow job. The Kai Tai would go looking for other customers whilst the man went looking for another beer. Some Kai Tais would take their men in a taxi, and off they would go. The Kai Tai would return some time later, having been fucked in the arse, and emptied her purse to a safe place in her flat. The man would wake up there later, wander off back to his ship, or be thrown out when the Kai Tai brought another customer back for the same service.

We lingered and watched as the crowd thinned. The Chinese staff were able to collect the empty beer bottles and glasses, which were not broken. They swept up all the broken glass, and rats came out of the storm drains to help clean up all the food that had been dropped on the ground. It was time to go.

The next day, we slept late and ventured out by the pool late in the afternoon. We met Mort and Don, and told them of our rescue of Jake and him buying drinks all night. He told us that Spanner was beside himself with wanton-lust ogling the Kai Tais. I can imagine how Spanner would be. They then said that some time later, they had lost Spanner and Max. I think we all knew what happened to them.

Christmas came and went. Some colourful streamers were strung across the Junior Rates dining hall in an endeavour to embrace the Christmas spirit. A Christmas tree was erected in the foyer of Aggie Western's, with colourful lights flickering on and off. The chef on-board produced a traditional Christmas dinner, which was wonderful. I returned to the mess afterwards and laid on my bunk, feeling satisfied and full.

I ventured down Bugis Street several times after that to witness the spectacle there. Someone would always climb onto the toilet block to perform the Dance of the Flaming Arsehole, and sometimes as many as four guys would perform together. Often, there would be fights: it seemed the Australians were always ready to do battle. Chairs would be thrown, tables overturned, glass broken, and people scattered. I don't think anyone got seriously injured; I just made sure I steered well clear of it. I got to know my way around the narrow streets, and could always get back to the UJC. I even went into the dockyard canteen. One evening, I met Parky in Sembawang Village and walked back to the dockyard with him. He planned to call into the canteen there to have the last couple of drinks before returning on-board. The place was crowded. As before, a spindly, sinewy Chink was filling trays full of glasses with Tiger beer gushing from a hose. As the guy at the front to the queue took his tray away, another guy would join the queue at the back. Next to the Chink with the hosepipe was another Chink, filling smaller glasses from a large aluminium jug. The liquid reminded me of Taff's Limers. Parky got an empty tray and took two full glasses from Mr Hosepipe; after placing them on the tray, he slid it along and took two glasses, placing them beside our beers. 'JC's,' he turned to tell me. He slid the tray further, and gave some money to the next Chink in line. 'You can get the next ones,' he said over his shoulder. We sat at an empty table close to the door, and he gave me one big glass and one small one. He picked up the small glass, raised it to me and said, 'Cheers.' I picked up mine and did the same. We both took a sip.

'JC,' Parky told me, indicating the glass. 'John Collins. Whisky and lemon juice.'

'Oh,' I said. I was a bit worried: I was not used to drinking spirits such as whisky. I had already had a load of beer, and knew I had to be up early. I could only taste the lemon juice, so thought that maybe it wouldn't affect me so much. I was wrong. We had a couple more, and I was gone. My head felt fuzzy; my binocular vision had gone. I could see two images, and these were out of focus; not only that, they would not keep still. My spirit seemed to have been transported to another world. Images came and went.

At 06:00, my early morning call came. Normally, a clipboard is thrust under your nose, and a torch illuminates where you have to sign to confirm the duty EM has done his job; this morning, my feet were being pulled, being jerked hard. A torch was shone in my face. Brendan's Irish brogue told me, 'Get up, you fucking OD, and clean this shit up.' He swung the torch beam to the floor, which illuminated a pool of vomit. 'Put your fucking bunk light on,' he ordered. I reached up and did as he said. 'Now don't you go back to sleep.' He jerked my feet again. He left mumbling under his breath, 'Fucking OD.' There was a jackhammer in my head and a whirlpool in my gut. The smell of my vomit invited me to add to it. I didn't know what to do first: I had to clean up this mess before Call the Hands was piped, and other people began to get up. I had to get dressed in my Number 6 uniform, and report to the Flight Deck by 06:30. I also had to vomit again; I could feel it coming. I got out of my bunk and put a towel around me. I lurched out of the mess with a bucket in hand, and made for the bathrooms. Whilst the bucket was filling, I puked into the toilet bowl. I returned to the mess and began to clean the floor. It *was* a mess; liquid vomit had run under the boot lockers, which had to be removed to clean properly. Kneeling down in my condition was a killer. I retched into the bucket and thought my head would explode. I had to return to the bathrooms twice more to get clean water. Finally, the floor was clean, and I had added some disinfectant to the last bucket of water so the smell of vomit had gone. I thought a shower would help my condition, and so I placed the bucket by the shower, in case I needed to vomit. I let the water cascade into my face, hoping it would bring back some normality, which it didn't. I sat down and let the water crash down on my head; I didn't know if this was making the pounding inside go away or not. My stomach muscles hurt from retching, but it seemed I didn't need to do that anymore. Panic suddenly hit me: I should be on the Flight Deck. I didn't know what the time was, so quickly returned to the mess. Too late; it was 06:35, which meant I was late! I had missed the muster! I was in the shit—again. Panic filled my entire body.

I got dressed, went for breakfast, returned to the mess, and waited to be summoned to the reg. office. I didn't have to wait long. 'I fucking knew I'd get you sooner or later, Clark,' McSnell sneered at me in triumph. 'OOD's table at 10:00. Don't be late!'

I turned to leave, and Pricky Thorn called after me, 'And get your fucking hair cut!'

The officer of the day asked me why I had missed the muster. There was something strange about his voice. 'I'm sorry, Sir, but I was sick,' I informed him. 'I was in the bathroom being sick, Sir.'

McSnell seemed to be unable to keep his thoughts to himself any longer. 'You know the routine, Clark. If you're sick, and can't do your duty, you get a chit from the sickbay.'

'Once I had been sick, I was okay,' I said, 'No good going to the sickbay when the problem is over.'

'Did you tell this to RPO McSnell this morning, Clark?' the OOD asked me. There was a Norfolk accent; this was the same officer that allowed me to march up and down at the end of the gangway.

'No, Sir! RPO McSnell didn't ask me, Sir. He just told me to be here for 10:00, Sir.' I didn't tell him what he really said to me, though.

'Sir, JEM Clark has a history of disobedience, and has had to be disciplined on a number of occasions,' McSnell interrupted again, and offered my record card to the OOD for his examination. 'Clark should be passed to the Commanders table for punishment, Sir.'

The OOD did not take the card, only looked at McSnell. 'I will pass this case over to the Commander, if I see fit.' McSnell's jaw almost dropped. 'I have read your report, RPO McSnell,' he continued, 'and I will thank you not to interrupt us again.' McSnell now clenched his jaw. 'Is that clear?'

'Yes, Sir,' McSnell replied. I could not believe what was happening here.

'How many times have you been sick since you have been on the Hermes?' the East Anglia OOD asked me.

'Only once before, when I had to have my appendix out, Sir. That was during trials in the North Sea.'

'More than a year ago, then?'

'Yes, Sir.'

'And how many times have you missed a muster for Ceremonial Guard duty?' he asked.

'Never, Sir.'

'How many times have you missed any muster since you have been on Hermes?'

'This is the first time I have missed any muster, Sir,' I told him sincerely. The OOD looked at me hard, and I returned his stare. There was a long pause.

'I am going to give you the benefit of the doubt.' Another pause. 'Case dismissed!' he declared.

I could not believe what had just happened. I wanted to burst out laughing; punch the air and jump for joy. I had to wait for the order On Caps, but it seemed McSnell was paralysed. Finally, the order came, and I marched away.

'Report to the Regulating Office, Clark,' McSnell barked after me, 'and wait for me there.'

After all the formalities of the OOD's table, McSnell returned to the reg. office, where I was waiting. 'Inside!' he ordered, flicking his head towards the door. I stepped through the door, and he followed. He closed the door, which, was a very strange thing to do: I had very rarely ever seen this door closed. 'Stand there!' he ordered, pointing to a spot on the deck in front of his desk. Pricky and another Leading Regulator were sat at the other desk. I could not see if the MAA was in his office or not. McSnell moved around the desk, and sat down, resting his chin on his hands. 'You trying to make me look a fool, Clark?' he coolly asked me, but I could see he was fuming.

'No, RPO. I am not trying to make you look a fool, RPO.'

'Don't be clever with me, Clark,' he cautioned.

'No, RPO. I won't be clever with you, RPO.' I could see now he was beginning to get really mad.

'Shut it, boy,' he hissed through clenched teeth.

'Shutting it now, RPO,' I replied. I could see my responses were making him absolutely furious.

'Get the fuck out of my sight!' he barked at me in frustration.

'Yes, RPO,' I said as I turned to go. I wanted to add 'getting the fuck out of your sight now, RPO', but thought it too provocative.

'I told you to get a fucking haircut, Clark,' Pricky barked at me before I could open the door.

'NAAFI barbers not open yet, Leading Regulator,' I informed him. 'Not open till tomorrow, Leading Regulator.'

'Well, get it cut tomorrow,' he said.

'I will, Leading Regulator,' I replied. McSnell knew I was taking the piss; he jumped from his chair and came around the desk, standing close to me.

'Shut your fucking gob, Clark, before I put my fist in it,' he hissed at me. I opened the door further, so people standing in the NAAFI shop queue could see us. I looked at him with my lips tightly shut, yet with a half-smile on them. I turned and left him fuming after me as I went.

I remembered my resolve to get both Pricky and McSnell, and I would. I had a plan

20: Vengeance is Sweet

One of the responsibilities of our section was Upper-Deck lighting. When we were in Harbour, floodlights were rigged to illuminate the island at night. Large lights were suspended out on poles from the ship's side, and secured with guide wires. I had not been involved with this before, as I had been part of the Ceremonial Guard. The lights had been dismounted prior to us sailing from Singapore and taken to the Electrical workshop to be checked before stowing away ready for the next use, which would be Freemantle, Australia. We all took great care with our checks, and maintenance because should there be a problem, it was up to us to stay behind until the lights performed correctly. None of us wanted to miss valuable shore time, especially first night in. Everything was cleaned, and the cables neatly coiled and tied up. These lights were stowed in a small store in S section, so we had to carry them up to 4Deck and then along the main drag to S section. The store was off a small passageway that went from the main drag to a ladder, up to the hangar on the starboard side. It was this ladder that the beer came down, when the after-store was being replenished. The roller conveyor went past the store door, past the hatch to the long ladder, down to the Air Conditioning plant then, turning aft on the main drag, to the wardroom store. The discovery of this small storeroom was crucial to my plan.

I inspected the hatch to the shaft down to the Air Conditioning plant, and found it to be like most of the others around the ship. It was a daunting sight peering over the edge of the hatch; the ladder extended down for five decks into, what seemed, an almost bottomless pit. The hatch, when shut, would be watertight, and capable of withstanding great pressures from either side. The hatch was mostly left open. It was only closed in cases of emergency, i.e. fire, flooding, risk of collision or being under attack. The hatch was hinged open and secured in the open position by a steel bracket and spring-loaded latch. Just lift the latch, and the hatch would be free to swing closed. However, it was necessary to support the hatch, as it was so heavy that to just let it drop may well cause damage to the hatch, the seal, or the rim of the shaft. Once the hatch was shut, it would be secured in that positing with eight screw clips. The clips would be swung up from their securing bracket, and the threaded bar located in a cleat in the hatch. A large 'wing nut' would then be screwed down to tighten on the cleat, and so clamp the hatch firmly onto its seal. Two clips were on each side of the square hatch. Access was still possible through the hatch via a manhole door. This was elliptical in shape, with the largest diameter sufficient in size for a man's shoulders to pass. This had two lever clips, which would secure it, and which could be operated from either side. So, if you were caught in the machinery space, when the hatch was shut, you could still get out using this small manhole door.

In the centre of the manhole cover was a 'test plug'. The 'test plug' was a hollow, threaded bolt of about two inches in diameter, with a solid hexagonal bolt head on the top. Its purpose was to facilitate testing the state of the compartment the other side of the hatch; after an incident of fire, flood or collision, it would not be known what existed the other side of the hatch. The fire may still be raging, it may be flooded, or it could be pressurised from an explosion. The 'test plug' could be unscrewed carefully. After about two or three turns, a small hole would be uncovered in the thread of the screw. This hole would extend to the hollow part of the bolt, and so there would be a path for air to travel. If there was a fire, smoke would issue from this hole; if it was flooded, water would spurt out; and if it was pressurised, a loud hissing would be heard. It must be remembered partial flooding would cause pressurisation also. I checked the 'test plug' on this hatch, and it was free to move as it should be.

Next, I needed an iron tubular bar, similar to a length of scaffold pole, of about three feet long, and a bucket; these items were easily found. I also needed a large funnel; maybe not so easy to find.

After we had stowed all the Upper-Deck lighting, we returned to the workshop, where Windy was sorting through the next lot of planned maintenance cards. He gave some to Max and some to Mort, and off they went with tool bags swinging by their sides.

'Well, young man,' Windy said to me, 'let's go and see how much of this we can do.' He marched out the door, expecting me to follow him, which I did. 'To the galley,' he said, as if leading an army into battle. It seemed my conversation with Windy earlier had got him thinking. At the galley, Windy asked to speak to the PO Cook, and he came to sit with us at an empty table in the Junior Rates dining hall. After mealtimes, the cooks often came and sat at these tables for a rest, drink tea, and smoke cigarettes.

'Smudge!' the PO cook called out, and a cook from the next table turned to face him. It was the fat, heavily-tattooed, balding, ugly, disgusting, sweating man, who first put me to work in the galley when we left Portsmouth. 'Get us some tea, will you?' said the PO Cook. 'Three cups.' Smudge looked at me with disdain as he rose from his seat. I didn't look at him. He returned with three mugs of tea, and placed them in front of us. It was clear which mug was meant for who. Windy had placed the maintenance cards on the table, and shuffling them about as he selected one, and discussed it with the PO Cook. I dragged some of these cards towards myself, showing interest in what was happening. I had to move the cups to make space. As I moved them, I swapped mine for Windy's, so if Mr Fat and Ugly had spat in it, then I was not going to swallow it.

It transpired that if we were careful with our timing and liaised with the galley staff beforehand, equipment in the galley would be freed up for us for maintenance. The PO Cook called over the Senior Leading Cook, and explained the situation to him. I knew the Leading Cook from boiler cleaning; he was always civil to me, and never ridiculed me. We agreed that Windy or I could let him know what equipment we required and he would let us know when it could be freed up if, indeed, it *could* be freed up. No work could be carried out whilst meals were being served for about an hour beforehand. The following day, we could start, after breakfast, with one of the ovens and one of the mixers.

The next day, Windy and I went to the galley, and Windy instructed me what to do. He just looked on whilst he led me through the procedures. I was now working with more sophisticated control equipment that had a greater importance than bunk lights or kettle sockets; common faults on this equipment would be heating element and thermostat failures. Switches would always take a bashing, and so be prone to failure. Many of the indicating lights did not work, which was a frustrating for the cooks, but they seemed to tolerate it. Over the next couple of weeks, we had worked through a lot of equipment in the galley, and the cooks were beginning to see the benefits. Many switches were replaced, and many indicating lights were telling the cooks what was happening, so they had to guess less. I was also doing more work on my own. I was the only EM who worked on galley equipment; Mort and Max didn't seem interested.

One morning, after our morning muster, Jenkins stormed into the workshop. 'That fucking idiot fucked my bunk light up!' he said in anger, pointing to me. Max disappeared, as it was he that sheared off the screw head and didn't want to be blamed for it.

'What's the problem?' Windy asked him, putting on his most authoritative voice.

'I had no problems with my bunk light till that fucking idiot started messing about with it!' Again, he stabbed his finger in my direction. The Chief Mech. quietly stepped out of his office and stood before Jenkins.

'Who the fucking hell do you think you are, coming in to my workshop without being invited?' he boomed at Jenkins, who turned his attention to the Chief Petty Officer. With his red face and eyes popping behind the thick lenses of his glasses, it was clear he was fighting for words to say. 'You fucking knock on the door when you come here, and wait to be invited in,' the Chief Mech. boomed again. The powerful figure of Jenkins towered above the rotund frame of the Chief Mechanician. 'Is that clear?' the chief demanded.

'Yes, Chief,' Jenkins said meekly.

'Now, what's the problem?' the Chief Mech. asked calmly. Again, Jenkins pointed at me, 'That fucking idiot…'

Before he could finish, the Chief Mech. boomed again. 'That is *no* idiot!'

Jenkins looked down at the Chief with his mouth open.

'*That* is EM Clark! We don't have idiots here!'

Jenkins was now lost for words completely. His rage would not allow him to speak.

The Chief Mech. continued calmly again. 'You will do well to apologise to EM Clark,' and with that, he waited for a response.

Jenkins looked from the Chief Mech. to me and back again.

'Leading Hand,' the Chief Mech. said again, and repeated, 'you will do well to apologise to EM Clark.'

There was absolute silence in the workshop now, and all eyes were on Jenkins. Jenkins looked into my face and looked defeated. He looked at my chest and uttered, 'I'm sorry.'

'Now,' the Chief Mech. asked, 'what's the problem with your bunk light?'

Jenkins turned to the Chief Mech. again and, after a small pause for composure, said, 'It keeps flashing on and off. I think it's dangerous.'

'Ah!' the Chief Mech. said, 'So you think it's dangerous, do you?' Sarcasm dripped from his voice.

'Yes, Chief.'

The chief of the workshop turned to me and ordered, 'Clark! Go to the Steward's mess and remove the bunk light on Jenkins's bunk.' I looked at him in surprise. 'It's dangerous,' he added. 'Also, strip out the wiring back to the first junction box, and then all the danger will be removed.'

'Yes, Chief,' I acknowledged, and began getting my tools together. I could not look at Jenkins; his jaw had dropped further, and his face even redder.

'And you may go,' the chief said to Jenkins as he turned to go back into his office.

Max could not get the cover off Jenkins' bunk light, because a screw head had sheared after I had weakened it, which he hadn't known I'd done. Because Max could not get the cover off, he could not remove the fitting, as the securing screws are under the cover, and so he left it. When I got to the fitting, it was easy to break the other side of the screw head by forcing a screwdriver down underneath it. The cover came off easily, and it was also easy for me to remove the fitting. The Chief Mech. had ordered me to remove the wiring, because he didn't want Jenkins to get someone else to rig up a temporary light for him, as I had done for the Chinese tailors and shoemakers. Jenkins returned to his mess just as I was finishing with the cable. He didn't say anything; he was too angry.

'Not your fucking servant now, eh?' I said to him. He lunged at me and grabbed my shirt front, and shoved me back into the doors of the wardrobe, almost lifting me off the floor. He was snorting through his nose, much like a horse would do. 'Touch me, Jenkins,' I said, 'and I'll have that hook off your arm.' A hook is a colloquial term for an anchor, which is the insignia of rank for a Leading Hand. The badge is worn on the sleeve of the upper-left arm. He knew I would. He knew if I returned to the workshop, bruised or bleeding, and reported him for violence, the Chief Mechanician would march him straight to the Regulating Office. No witness would be required; enough people had seen the exchange in the workshop earlier. My word would carry the greater weight. I knew he would let me go, but just then, another Steward could be heard descending the steps into the mess. He now had no option: he threw me to one side onto a bottom bunk. I got up, straightened my shirt, put my tools in my tool bag along with the bunk light fitting and the piece of cable. I had the fuses in my hand ready for replacement in the panel. As I got halfway up the ladder, at a safe position I knew I could escape from, I called back to him, 'Oh, by the way, I accept your apology. 'I then shot out of the mess because I was sure he was after me.

It was time now for Hermes to replenish oil, fuel, and general stores, including beer. This evolution was crucial for my plan; I had acquired a bucket, which I had placed in the Upper-Deck lighting store in S section cross passage. I visited this store at about three or four times a day to piss in the bucket; I kept a spare Perspex light cover on top of this, and weighted it down with a cardboard box of light fittings. The purpose of the cover was to keep the contents inside when the sea was rough and to reduce the smell coming from the bucket. No-one would come into this store whilst we were at sea except us, and only then just before we got alongside.

During the RAS, I was curious to see what happened with the after-store replenishment. I wandered aft to where the roller conveyor turned ninety degrees by the ladder shaft to the Air Conditioning space. I was surprised to see Leading Regulator Thorn standing guard at this corner. I think this was the first time I was pleased to see him; it certainly would help with my plan. I stopped by the conveyor, and listened to the whizzing sound as each case of beer was pushed around the bend. 'Move it, Clark!' Pricky said to me.

'I have to go down there,' I said, pointing down the shaft. I ducked under the conveyor and climbed onto the ladder, standing with my head at the same level as the conveyor. I slipped my right arm through the loops of my tool bag and pulled them up to my shoulder, forcing the bag to be on my back. I then had two hands free to descend the ladder, which was necessary to be able to climb and descend this long ladder safely. I had no right to go into the compartment below, as I was no longer on that section, but Pricky wouldn't know this; I was just planting a memory. A few moments later, I ascended the ladder and popped my head above the conveyor, watching cases of beer flow past. I regained my breath, climbed out of the shaft, and ducked under the conveyor. I took the tool bag off my shoulder and put it on the floor to make sure my tools were aligned orderly and not sticking out; in actual fact, I was showing Pricky there was nothing else in the bag. He was watching me intently.

The day after the RAS would be the day. After breakfast was finished, the shutters came down on the galley serving counters, and the aluminium trays were removed. The surface was wiped down, and then, I was allowed access. Today, I was to do maintenance on the black heaters of the serving counters; they were called black heaters because they never glowed red like most electrical heaters do; heaters were positioned above the counters to keep the food that was being served warm. Also, there were heaters below the counter to keep the cupboard warm, where more cooked food could be kept waiting for immediate use. Underneath the serving counter, on the outside of the galley, there were covers that allowed access to terminals of the heaters. I took covers off the heaters above the counter, and left them on the counter. I took covers off the terminals under the counter on the outside, and left these propped against the closed shutters. I took covers off the elements in the cupboard under the counter and left these on the floor of the galley. The serving hatches were on a cross passage that stretched from the port side of the ship to the starboard side. The galley was in 'D' section and there were two watertight doors that allowed the dinners to carry their food into E section where the dining hall was. Most of the galley staff were drinking tea at a table in the Junior Rates dining hall, but two cooks were working in the galley, preparing food. I had to go in and out of the galley many times, and I made sure the two cooks saw me come and go. I told them it was a pain in the arse crawling under the counter from one side, then going around outside to get access to the other. I also traversed the passage across the ship, because the fuse box was at the end of the passage on the starboard side. I whistled loudly as I passed the watertight doors, and, occasionally, a cook would look up and wonder what I was doing. I think my whistling was annoying them—which it was meant to do; I had set the scene. Maintenance of the black heaters was not my prime objective in the galley this morning; I was creating an alibi. The cooks got used to me coming and going into the galley and also traversing the cross passage by the serving hatches. If I was going to do this, then now would have to be the time. I had everything ready; it wasn't fool-proof, but I considered the risks small and worth it. My heart was beating fast, and I had a guilty feeling. But, nonetheless, I would do it.

I went up the ladder at the end of the passage on the starboard side. This brought me to 3Deck. A passage ran from the Cable Deck to the Quarterdeck each side of the hangar on this deck. The passage would alternate from an enclosed passage to an open Weather Deck. Each time you passed from an enclosed section to an open section, or vice versa, a watertight door had to be opened and closed behind you. These doors were held shut with one clip only, so it didn't take so long to get through. I arrived at the trunking to S Air Conditioning unit, and descended to the bottom. I checked inside the machinery space; sure enough, no-one was there. I closed the door using all clips; this would be unusual. I then reached up above the lagged pipe-work that exited the compartment and passed through the shaft. I had hidden my iron bar there previously. I took the bar and placed it over a clip lever, and forced the lever using the mechanical advantage of the bar. It would be impossible to open this door just by hand; not even two people would be able to do it. I forced two clips shut in this fashion. I hid the bar again and went back up the ladder and removed the 'test plug', then putting this on the deck behind the hatch. Next, I went into the store and removed the box from the makeshift lid of my bucket. I reached behind the stowed lights and retrieved a galvanised funnel I had acquired from the galley some days previous.

The next step would be no turning back.

I had a ball bearing in my pocket, about the size of a marble. I checked to see it was there. I went to the next section—R—and into the switchboard. I knew no-one would be here at this time of day, but to be sure, I checked behind each switchboard. During the evenings, people come to write letters or read in peace and quiet. I picked up the telephone and dialled the reg. office. My heart was pumping anew. I was breathless, my breaths coming out in ragged gasps. 'Regulating Office,

Leading Regulator Thorn speaking.' *Fuck!* I thought. Now I was panicking. I put the ball bearing in my mouth and pinched my nose. I knew when I spoke no-one would recognise my voice.

'There's a party going on in Nine Sierra Air Conditioning plant. Able seaman Jones is there with stoker Robinson and EM Clark,' I mumbled nasally. 'They're drinking beer.' With that, I slammed the phone down. *Fuck!* I thought again. *That's it!* I went back to the little storeroom, and waited. I assumed McSnell would come. If Pricky told him I was there, then I was sure he would come. After the last episode with McSnell, I'm sure he'd do anything to get me again.

It didn't take long, and I couldn't believe my luck; both McSnell and Thorn arrived at the top of the hatch. I peered through a crack in the door; the door was shut, but by pushing at the top, a crack would open enough to see through. McSnell stepped on to the ladder and looked up to Pricky, who was about to follow. McSnell raised a finger to his pursed lips, and started to descend the long journey to the bottom; Pricky climbed in afterwards, and also began his descent. The veins in my neck pulsated with adrenalin. I opened the door and crept to the side of the trunking, and looked both ways. I went back to the store, and got the bucket and funnel before placing them beside the trunking. Our tool kits consisted of a small mirror, much the same as dentists use, for looking at the backs of panels, etc. I used this to look down the shaft. McSnell had just reached the bottom, and Pricky was about to join him. I took another look in the main passage—still all clear. *This is it*, I thought. I moved to the side of the hatch, careful not to stand over it where I could be seen, should they look up. I released the latch of the hatch, and let it fall forwards. I caught it and lowered it carefully so I did not clip it. I expected a shout from below, but none came; the shaft was adequately lit, and deep enough that they didn't know what was happening. I quickly placed the tapered end of the funnel in the hole left by the 'test plug'; I knew it fitted perfectly because I had tried it earlier. I picked up the bucket and began to pour the contents in the funnel; I knew I had to take care and not overfill it. It would take time to run through the tapered end. I could have easily thrown the contents of the bucket down the shaft, but then most would have hit the sides and run down the bulkheads; with this method, a stream of liquid would fall vertically in the centre of the shaft. As it gained speed, the stream would be broken up and fall like rain, covering the whole area of the floor. Now, I could hear some muffled shouts from below; they were not loud enough to raise alarm, and I expected these cries. The liquid disappeared quicker than expected, and in no time, less than ten seconds, two gallons of piss had rained down on McSnell and Pricky. I removed the funnel, and placed it in the bucket. I then locked the store door and climbed the ladder back to 3Deck. The first Weather Deck I came to, I threw the bucket and funnel over the side into the sea. I made my way forward and down the ladder in D section, back to the galley. I was a little breathless, but somehow elated. I went into the galley and asked if I could open the shutters of the serving hatches. I didn't need them open, but I wanted to make sure there was continuity of being seen and not being seen.

I had done it! I had planned it, and it had worked to perfection! I got both Pricky and McSnell. They would not know it was me, but they would suspect. I was confident my alibi was sound.

I knew now I must discipline myself: I must keep clear of the reg. office, as I always did, and not tell anyone what had happened. I must keep away from Sierra Air Conditioning space. Someone would find the 'test plug' and replace it, and some beefy stoker would open the Air Conditioning space door with a hammer, or something. I finished up with my work in the galley. I replaced all the covers and packed my tools away. It was approaching 10:00, and I returned to the workshop to sign off my cards. At 10:15, I went to the mess for Stand Easy. Stand Easy was the term of a morning or afternoon tea break. An enormous pot of tea would be made, and mess members would return to their lockers, retrieve their mugs, and fill them from the pot. We would sit around the mess, socialising whilst we drank our tea. At 10:30, the mess would be cleared again and we'd all return to work. No mention of McSnell or Thorn had been heard during this time.

I returned to the workshop and got some more maintenance cards; I needed to be busy to take my mind off the morning's events. The thought of what I had done kept bringing a smile to my face, and I was full of wonder as to the reaction of McSnell and Thorn. I was also filled with anxiety: not knowing anything was a killer. I was checking the lights on 2Deck in the passageways around the Senior Rates messes. This was close to their dining hall, where I had laboured so much. I decided to go to the Weather Deck on the starboard side, where we used to drink tea and coffee, and smoke during periods of rest. Jenkins was no longer in charge of the Senior Rates dining hall crew; he got a job change as well, and was working in the wardroom, so there was no danger of bumping into him. I pushed the door open, and a stiff wind hit my face. I had to hold the door tightly, lest it be blown out of my hands and crash open against its stop. To my surprise, Jackie was there, sat on the deck with his knees drawn up. He was leaning against the small bulkhead that you would normally rest your elbows on whilst looking out to sea; he was sheltered from the wind there. 'Hey, Clarkie,' he greeted me. Jackie was doing his spell in my old job. As always, Jackie had a broad smile, and his bright blue eyes sparkled through a mop of curly hair that had flopped forward over his forehead.

'Hello mate, how's it going?' I said as I sat down beside him.

'Hear you had a bit of a do with McSnell,' Jackie said. My heart sank. Did he know something? Had I been seen? 'He was fucking pissed off with that OOD, I'm sure.'

Relief ran through my body; Jackie was referring to my missed guard muster. 'Well,' I said matter-of-factly, 'some you win...' We both thought about it for a moment. 'He really was pissed off, though.' I confirmed to him. We chatted some more before he said he had to go. I had some more time to kill before I could go to the mess, and so I went to the Cable Deck and squeezed into my favourite place, between two frames and the hull of the ship. Hermes crashed into the waves, and, occasionally spray would be blown into the deck. I smoked a cigarette and contemplated life: soon, we would be in Australia again, this time on the west side. I need to get a woman again; it had been a long time since I had had a good shag. The memory of Sandra was always very clear in my mind, and thinking of her always brought an erection. I didn't know if I would see her again; I would never be able to find her house, so if she wanted to see me, then she would know when the Hermes got back into Cape Town, and she could take the initiative. I did not fuck her at that time, but did so many times in my dreams since we left. I was still writing to Sheila, and she was excited we were going back there and a big party was being planned. I would surely fuck her next time, and I would do it a bit differently than the last time: I would employ some of the techniques Sandra had taught me. Time passed quickly with these thoughts, and it was soon time for the galley shutters to open and dinner to be dished up.

I took my place in the queue, got my platter, stocked, it and carried it through into the dining room. Budgie came and sat with me, and we were soon joined by Max, Mort and Don. Mealtimes were always a din; people clanking on their stainless steel platters, benches clumping on the deck and everyone chatting at once, with occasional shouting and guffaws of laughter. If the tannoy system hissed, it signalled an announcement was about to be made; every person on-board was sensitive to this hissing, and waited for the announcement to come. Such a hissing came, and the noise subsided. 'RPO McSnell, contact the Regulating Office,' the tannoy system said in its scratchy tones. The whole dining hall erupted in laughter. If you are summoned to the regulating office in such a manner it signifies, almost always, you are in the shit. The thought of McSnell having to report to the reg. office for a misdemeanour and being punished was, indeed, a humorous thought. I was the only one who didn't find this funny: I was worried. What did this mean? *Were McSnell and Thorn stuck in the shaft?* I asked myself. No-one had said anything about McSnell or Thorn; if it were known they were covered in piss, then this news would fly around the ship like wildfire. I took my platter to the scullery and deposited it in a tray to await its travel through the washing machine. I went to the mess, and laid on my bunk. Were they still in the shaft? Surely this could not be. Stuck in the shaft, covered in piss, for almost three hours! It didn't make sense. My first instinct was to see if the hatch was open or not, but maybe this was a trap. It would be unwise for me to be seen anywhere near there. I decided something was wrong, and I was genuinely worried they may be hurt. I did not clip the hatch shut, but it would not be possible to open the hatch whilst standing on the ladder. Why did they not come out of the small access hatch? That is why it's there. What if one fell off the ladder, and landed on the other at the bottom? What if they were both dead? I had to do something. I got up from my bunk, and left the mess. I walked through the dining hall and past the NAAFI shop. I took the port passageway, as I always did. The starboard passageway would take me past the reg. office. I was tempted, but stuck to my usual pattern. I went down the ladder in H section to the Stokers' mess, but instead of going around the ladder and down again to the workshop, I went into hotel switchboard. Again, I knew this would be empty and I would be undisturbed. I checked behind the switchboards to check no-one was hiding there, sleeping. All was clear. I picked up the telephone and put the ball bearing in my mouth. I dialled the Regulating Office and the call was soon answered. 'Master-at-Arms,' a voice announced.

I pinched my nose and mumbled, 'McSnell is in Sierra Air Conditioning plant.' Hastily, I put the receiver back on its hook, leaving the switchboard and standing at the bottom of the ladder and to one side. I could see above; people passing the hatch, going forward and going aft. Soon, the MAA came into view with Leading Regulator Wilson behind him.

'Get a stoker,' the MAA said, pointing to the ladder. I scooted around the ladder and down to our workshop. At this time of day, traffic was heavy in the main drag gangway; people were leaving their messes and returning to the places of work. The MAA stormed through the watertight doors and pounded the deck between. Everyone jumped to the side to let him pass.

By the time afternoon arrived, the news of McSnell and Thorn had spread through the ship. After receiving an anonymous tip of illegal drinking, they rushed to S Air Conditioning plant. They descended the ladder, but could not access the machinery space. That was when it rained piss. There was no escaping the soaking; they had to stand there and wait for the rain to stop. Finally, with sodden Number 8 shirts and hair plastered to their faces, they were able to look up and see the hatch closed. They ascended the ladder, with Thorn leading and McSnell behind him; Pricky could not lift the hatch—with one hand and still clinging to the ladder, it was difficult. McSnell got frustrated with his feeble efforts and demanded he have a go; trouble was McSnell was lower down the ladder, and it was not possible to change places. There was no option but to climb down the five decks, change places, and then climb up five decks again. With McSnell leading, they ascended with Pricky bringing up the rear. McSnell could not lift the hatch; he could raise it a few inches, but needed to go up a rung to raise it further. He could not go up and hold the hatch at the same time as everything was soaked with piss; the ladder became slippery, wetting their hands, their sandals sliding on the rungs and their feet sliding in their sandals. They never tried the manhole access hatch. Whilst at the top, McSnell shouted for help, as did Pricky, and yet they found their cries went unanswered. It was difficult to make yourself heard through the closed hatch and above the noise of the machinery below; it was useless to bang on the hatch because they only had their hands and fists. They paused for a moment at the top of the ladder to think. They clung on to the ladder by wrapping their arms around the risers. McSnell had the idea that maybe there was something in the machinery compartment which could be used to bang on the hatch. Again, they went down five decks and stood in four inches of my piss. They struggled with the door clips, but the two I had forced closed they could not budge. These two were at chest-height, so they could not be kicked open. By this time, McSnell and Pricky were desperate. They must have been there for more than half an hour. In desperation, they decided to have another go at the hatch above. They soon found they could not climb the ladder; the leather of their sandals had absorbed my piss, and expanded it like a sponge, the sandals no longer fitting their feet—to attempt to climb a ladder would be crazy. Up one deck, and you may get away with it; this was five decks, and if you slipped near the top, then it really is curtains. They waited at the bottom for two and a half hours more, sloshing around in my urine, which had matured over several days in the heat of the small store above.

The MAA had gathered interest as he marched aft; curious onlookers followed to see what was happening. They arrived at the hatch, and the MAA instructed the stoker to open it. He lifted the hatch, and the stench of ammonia stung the back of his nose and caused him to drop the hatch shut immediately. The MAA stepped back and ordered L. Reg. Wilson to give a hand to the stoker and, together, they lifted the hatch and latched it to its bracket. The smell of urine filled the air, and everyone covered their noses. The MAA peered down at his pathetic-looking staff at the bottom of the shaft. 'What the fuck are you two doing?' the MAA boomed. The pair tried to explain, but nothing made sense to the MAA. 'Come up here,' he shouted down at them again. Communication was difficult. The machinery noise was one problem, and the echo that bounced from the sides of the shaft was another. The MAA could see they were making no effort to climb the ladder, and couldn't understand why. 'Go and see what's happening,' he said to the stoker. The stoker was wearing steaming boots because his place of work was a machinery space, like most stokers. The stoker climbed into the hatch, took a deep breath, as if he were in a swimming pool, and disappeared down the shaft. By now, a number of people were watching, their attention being drawn by the presence and loud voice of the MAA. They all covered their noses against the foul-smelling air. The stoker re-emerged, and climbed from the hatch.

'Master,' he said breathlessly, 'someone threw piss on them and closed the hatch.'

'So why won't they fucking come out?' the MAA queried wondrously.

'They need their steaming boots, Master,' the stoker explained. 'Their sandals are all fucked up. 'The MAA turned to the Leading Regulator and told him to get their steaming boots for them.

'Tell them,' he began, indicating the two at the bottom of the shaft, 'to clean themselves up and see me in my office.'

So that's what happened. McSnell and Thorn had to remain there until Wilson returned. News of the incident flooded around the ship, and people flocked to peer down at them, giggling and holding their noses as they did so. When they emerged, they had to walk along the main drag to get to their mess. The smell followed them and hung in the air.

In the mess, everyone was talking of the incident: it certainly was of great interest to all. No-one liked McSnell and most people liked Thorn even less. Everyone wondered who did it and how they did it.

'Wasn't you, Clarkie?' Spanner asked me, and when I didn't answer immediately, he asked, 'Was it?'

'Wish it was, mate,' I told him. 'I'd love to pour piss over the pair of them.'

The tannoy hissed, and we all cocked an ear. 'Anyone who was in the vicinity of four sierra passageway this morning between 09:00 and 09:30, report to the Regulating Office.'

Everyone knew what this was about, and mumbled their own whereabouts at that time. 'I was in the galley,' I told Spanner. I knew I would be on McSnell's suspect list, and I wouldn't be the only one. I expected to be summoned to the reg. office at some stage, but I wasn't. Time passed, and we got closer to Western Australia.

A new notice appeared on our noticeboard, and I was detailed to be part of the Procedure Alpha party. When entering or leaving Harbour, the Flight Deck is lined with sailors in uniform, standing at ease; this is procedure Alpha. Our mess had the responsibility of lining the deck from the island to the starboard forward corner; I had never done this before so, in a way, I was looking forward to it. Spanner had always told me of how you could smell the fannies of all the girls that waited on the shore for the ship to berth. Needless to say, he would be grinding his fist into his scrotum as he said this, and his eyes would narrow at the thought of what could be. The problem really was the length of time you had to stand there, without moving, whilst the ship entered harbour and manoeuvred into place by the dockyard wall. *Oh, well. We shall see*, I thought.

21: Fremantle

Western Australia looked flat. We had already entered the channel making our approach. It was a beautiful day, and the sun shone brightly, and a warm wind blew across the Flight Deck. The Hermes powered her way forward, following the directions of the pilot boat in front.

I watched the landscape go by with more and more buildings as we approached the dock. After what seemed like an eternity, our space at the jetty could be seen. Spanner was right about one thing: there was an abundance of females awaiting the arrival of the ship. I could not smell their fannies, though. As the ship came to an almost halt in front of our berthing place, I began to smell the perfume of the ladies. This stirred my loins, and I felt I was becoming to think like Spanner more and more. Mooring lines were thrown across, and made fast; we were then dismissed. I wanted to linger a while, but had to help with the Upper-Deck lighting, and I was also duty EM, so no shore leave for me tonight. I went to the mess and got changed quickly, and then to help drag the Upper-Deck lighting equipment up to the Flight Deck. We had already extracted this from the store, and placed close to the hangar, where we could take it up with the aircraft lift. I went into the store the day before to ensure no evidence of my previous antics were around; everything was okay, except for the faint smell of piss in the air. I left the door open and stayed there for a long time, pretending to sort things out. I looked down the shaft, towards the Air Conditioning compartment—it was clean, dry, and sweet-smelling. I pitied the poor guys who would have had to clean all the mess up; no doubt McSnell would have selected his most hated, from a punishment muster, and sent them to do the job. *Lateral damage*, I thought as a comforting justification for my deed.

The lights were rigged and all worked well; they would not be switched on until darkness came, which would be well into the evening, as we were in the height of Summer here. After the excitement and bustle of my mess mates showering and getting their civvies out of storage, preening themselves and saying goodbye to me, the mess went quiet. I checked in at Kilo switchboard; Mick Briggs was on watch. He sat back in a chair with his feet on the edge of the table and knees bent. He was reading a book, which was supported by his knees, and was looking at it with his head slightly cocked to one side. His eyes looked over the book, at me, and then back to the book. He said nothing. 'I'm going for supper,' I told him. 'You can get me in the mess if you need me.' He nodded whilst still reading.

I had supper and then lay on my bunk afterwards. My mind was wandering over recent events when I heard the hiss of the tannoy system open. 'EM Clark, Quarterdeck,' the speakers told me. I jumped up and ran to the phone at the foot of the access ladder. I dialled the number for the Quarterdeck, and the Quarter Master answered.

'Duty EM here.'

'Hang on,' he replied. I waited. 'We don't need no EM.'

'I just heard a pipe,' I told him.

'Hang on,' he said again. He came back on the line a moment later. 'No, we don't need no duty EM.'

'Oh. Okay, then.' I hung up.

Some minutes later, the hiss came again followed by: 'EM Clark, Quarterdeck.' Confused, I went back to the phone and dialled the same number.

'Duty EM here,' I said again.

'We don't need no Duty EM.'

'Well, you just piped for me again.'

'Oh, are you EM Clark?' he asked.

'Yes.'

'Ah, okay. Well, we have your auntie here,' he informed me.

Auntie? I thought. *I don't have an auntie.* 'No, mate,' I told him. 'I don't have no auntie.'

'Hang on. Are you Christopher Paul Clark?'

'Yes,' I confirmed.

'Well, it's your fucking auntie here.'

'I still don't have no auntie here,' I told him.

'Hang on,' he said again. He came back on the line. 'She said from Kingscliffe and Blatherwyke.'

Just the mention of those words was enough to almost stop my heart. We used to live in Kingscliffe when I was first born, but Blatherwyke haunted me. My upper arms sprouted goose-bumps and, for some strange reason, there was a tightening ache in my scrotum. My mind was carried back to Blatherwyke: I was then only a boy of seven or eight years old.

When entering the small village of Blatherwyke from the road from Kingscliffe, the first two houses on the right were semi-detached and stood alone without neighbours for a great distance beyond. In the first house lived a family with children I often played with; in the second lived Mrs Dams with her son Albert. Albert was an odd character: he had a pointed nose and chin, and his eyes were oriental in their shape. His face was rubicund from working outside in all weathers. However, he never seemed to work, except in the garden. I never knew his age, and always considered him younger than his years but, by this time, he was in his fifties.

His mother was a sweet old lady, whom I loved to be with; I would visit them often. Albert would be in the garden, or in the shed at the top of the path leading from the house. I say at the top of the path because this path inclined from the house in a series of steps and walkways made from broken paving slabs intermixed with bricks, stones and pieces of marble. The garden was always colourful with marigolds, geraniums, roses, primroses, pansies, and all sorts of boarder plants in the Spring and Summer, rich with greens from cabbages and sprouts and other vegetable produce later on.

I loved to see Albert in his shed; he was always doing interesting things, like trying to fix radios or clocks. The place would be strewn with mechanical bits in various modes of strip down; he had rigged up a light powered from a car battery, and would listen to an old car radio, which hung from strings above his bench. The speaker was hung next to it. Flower pots were all over the place with seeds and seedlings ready in line for the next stage of their evolution. Albert had a bunk at the back of the shed, and he often laid there, resting. Sometimes, he would be sleeping as he was on this particular day, all those years ago, when I visited. I ran back down the garden path, and gently pushed open the kitchen door, which stood ajar. Mrs Dams was in her usual position by the AGA stove in a rocking chair, gazing out the window, which overlooked the garden. 'Hello, Christopher,' she said cheerily as her cool blue eyes turned to me. She was a very small lady, with white hair that was always tied in a bun at the top of her head. Her face was small also, and the skin had a silky softness about it that held her beauty. She had no teeth, so her lips tended to be sucked into her mouth as she surveyed me. 'I suppose Albert is sleeping, then?' she enquired, not really expecting an answer. 'Do you want a bun?'

'Yes, please,' I replied as I looked around the kitchen for anything new or exciting. The kitchen was small with a door, opposite the door I had entered, which lead into the parlour. I had never been in the parlour, but guessed it housed a fancy sofa and soft chairs, and also a dining table, polished highly. I was sure there would be a large carpet with polished floorboards creating a margin to the walls around it. Paintings would hang on the walls, maybe with some plates like my mum had; the fireplace would be the focus of attention and be ready for the incendiary match.

Two more doors were on my right: these were wooden doors, which could have easily been made from floorboards. They were painted white, but the ageing paint had turned yellow and bordering on brown, where hands had opened them over the years. One led to a staircase—I had never gone through this door, either—the other to a pantry, where all the food stuff was stored. 'You'll have to get them for me,' she said, pointing with a bony, crooked finger to the pantry door. 'I can't get around these days like I used to. They are in the tin.' I opened the pantry door and took the tin; I knew this tin, as I had seen it many times before. Mrs Dams made the most wonderful current buns. Sometimes, I would catch her in the act of mixing the mix, and she would let me spoon out the remains after she had loaded the cups of a baking tray. I carried the tin and sat on a stool beside the AGA opposite her. I levered off the lid, and was disappointed to see only two buns. 'I need to make some more, but can't get about at all,' she said. 'My legs are painful, and I can't walk so well. It's a devil of a job even getting to the Lavvy.' The 'Lavvy' was the toilet, which was outside across the yard from the kitchen door. It was a bucket in a box, which was emptied once a week by men from a smelly lorry that we all jeered at and held our noses at as it passed. I didn't know what to say, so said nothing, and munched on my bun. I balanced the tin on her lap for her to take the other, but she just let it sit there. Normally, she would get the tin from the pantry herself and bring out a small churn of fresh milk and give me a glass; the milk here always tasted wonderful. Albert would get it each morning from the dairy farm opposite the house. 'How's your mum?' she asked, surveying me closely.

'Okay,' I said as I finished the bun. 'She's at work, but I'm going to meet her at the bottom of the hill when she comes home.'

'That'll be nice,' she said, as her eyes dropped away from me and she seemed to sink further into the chair. This was the first time I had seen her like this: normally, she was cheerful, spritely and bright, but now, she seemed distant and pensive. 'Come and see me next Thursday,' she said, turning towards me as I stood, ready to leave. I had to return to Forty Foot on the following Sunday, so Thursday was okay. She raised her finger to me as she said this, and added, 'Promise me, Christopher, you will come on Thursday.'

'I will,' I replied, and then left. Thursday was some days away, and during this intervening period, my mum told me Mrs Dams was very ill. She was in a bed in the front room (this was the parlour), as she couldn't get up the stairs.

That particular Thursday, I could not find Albert in the garden, or in his shed. I pushed open the kitchen door, but no-one was inside. The door to the parlour was open slightly, and I hesitated before I pushed the door further. There was a large bed in the middle of the room and a small grey head on white fluffy pillows. 'Hello,' I said, hesitantly.

The head turned towards me and I was shocked to see the sunken eyes and grey skin. Her lips flopped around her gums as she said, 'Christopher.' I walked closer to the bed, and looked at this pitiful face. No hair in a bun now; it was like straw, and tangled around her head. I knew she was dying; I knew I would never see her in her chair by the AGA, or making current buns ever again. There was a fidgeting under the bed, like a ferret trying to escape, and then a hand appeared from under the sheets, close to her chin. Bony fingers reached out to me, and I stepped forward to take her hand. It was cold, but the fingers squeezed me a little and her eyes closed.

The room was not as I expected, even with the bed in the middle: piles of old newspapers were stacked against the wall; no paintings on the wall, only dirty, old wallpaper, peeling where the joins were; cobwebs in the corners; the fireplace boarded up. There was an old sideboard cluttered with pieces of crockery, tins, books, papers, and on top, a musical instrument that had a small piano keyboard on one side and at the end, a mouthpiece to blow into. When played, it sounded like a mouth organ. I once saw Albert with this in his shed, and he was trying to play it, but he couldn't. I wanted to have a go, but he wouldn't let me. Mrs Dams must have sensed me looking at it, and she said, 'Take it. Albert drove me mad with it.'

'Thank you,' I said with real excitement, and ran over to pluck it from its surroundings. I resisted the urge to blow into it, as I didn't want to annoy her. 'Thank you, Mrs Dams. Thank you very, very much,' I said in my childish way. I wondered if that is why she wanted me to be there today: to give me this thing. Never mind; I was very pleased with it. I looked back to her, but her head had not moved; it was motionless on the pillow.

'Come tomorrow,' she said. 'Come tomorrow, Christopher.'

'I will,' I assured her, and watched as she sank into a sleepy world. I could see she was still breathing, so at least it was still this world.

The next morning, when I arrived, Albert was in his shed. 'Now, then?' he said as a manner of greeting as he saw me at the shed door. His voice was squeaky and nasally, which seemed to be the only way he would be able to speak with such a pointed nose. He was dressed in his normal tweed jacket, checked shirt, knitted tie, ex-army surge trousers, boots, and gaiters, plus a trilby hat, with a feather, on his head. I had never seen him without this hat; even when sleeping in the shed, he wore his hat.

'What you doing, Albert?'

'Waiting to milk the cows. Want to come with me?' he asked expectantly.

'Maybe,' I said. 'Have to see Mrs Dams first.'

'Oh,' he said, and the busied himself with some gadget on his bench.

I turned and ran down the path into the house. I slowly eased my way across the kitchen to the parlour door, which, again, was ajar. 'Come in, Christopher.' Mrs Dams' voice surprised me from within. I opened the door, and saw this dying lady sat up in bed with a big smile on her face. The usual brightness of her eyes had returned, and the bun re-established on her head. Her hands were held together on her lap, and she idly twiddled her thumbs. I was so surprised by the difference, and also so pleased.

I knew I was beaming as I said, 'Hello, Mrs Dams.' I then felt safe to add, 'How are you? 'She didn't answer, but reached a hand out to me. I walked forward and took it. She placed her other hand on mine and squeezed warmly. I leant against the bed as she pulled me gently towards her.

'Christopher, I have something I have to say to you, and you must be a strong boy.' Her eyes were burning into me, and I somehow felt afraid. 'The angels have been to see me, and tell me I have to tell you this.' She squeezed my hands some more, as if in reassurance.

'Okay.'

'Everyone has family secrets,' she informed me. Mrs Dams went on to tell me that my father once had an affair with a travelling girl, who was staying at the youth hostel next to the Red Lion pub in Kingscliffe. This affair ended up with this young girl being pregnant. The girl came from far away and could not return home in this condition because of the shame it would bring to her family and the ruin to her career. My father agreed to look after this girl until she gave birth, and then my mum would look after the baby and bring it up as her own. That baby was me, and the girl came from Australia.

A lot of what Mrs Dams told me that day I did not understand. A lot I didn't believe; I believed she was mad. I was young, and couldn't understand at all why she should be so hurtful. I said very little, but watched her face as she told me these things. Finally, she said, 'I have to go now, and you should go, too.' She lowered her head to the pillow and closed her eyes. She slept.

I watched her for some time. I saw the wrinkles around her eyes and mouth disappear; she looked serene. I backed away and left the house. I didn't go home; I went to one of my favourite fields and climbed the big oak tree in the middle. I decided I would forget about what Mrs Dams had told me; I thought she was cruel to say such things. Did an angel really go to see her, and if so, why was she told to tell me such a story? Why didn't the angel come and see me and tell me herself?

That evening, Albert came to our house. I was completing a jigsaw puzzle on the carpet in front of the fire. Albert was invited in, and he took his hat off to reveal a white, balding pate with long strands of wispy lank hair stuck to it. He informed my mother that his mother had died that afternoon. I already knew this.

'I'll come down right now,' I informed the Quarter Master, and hung up the phone. All the words Mrs Dams told me came flooding back. She said an angel had told her to tell me; I remember thinking she was cruel and mad. What if it was true? Who can this woman be? I stepped onto the Quarterdeck and reported to the Quarter Master. He indicated the lady, who stood a little way away. She was tall and slim, and wore a light flower-print skirt that billowed gently in the breeze. She wore a white blouse that tucked into the waist of her skirt; I think her hair was light brown and wavy. I have no recollection of any other of her features. She was with a man, and I think there were two small children there as well. She introduced me to the man, but I don't know if she told me his name or anything. She was talking to me, but I was not understanding what she said. She was mentioning names, some I knew, some I didn't. She mentioned Mrs Dams, but I don't know why. She asked me if I could go with her to her home, but I had to say no because I couldn't go ashore; I was on-duty. She asked if I could go the next day and I said I would. She gave me some money, and asked if I would get her some English cigarettes. I told her we could only take twenty-five ashore a night. She gave me much too much money, but she said to give her the change tomorrow. She said she would come for me at 13:00 the next day.

I had a troubled night: she knew too much to be a nobody. She knew Mrs Dams. Why did she know Mrs Dams? Could it be that this woman was, in fact, my mother? I know my brother and I are different, so very different in many ways: he has blue eyes, fair hair, and light skin; I am dark, with dark hair and brown eyes. Finally, I went to sleep with the thought that, tomorrow, many questions would be answered.

At 13:00 the next day, I was ready. I sat in the mess, waiting for the call; I could not sit still. I decided to go to the Quarterdeck and wait there. There was no sign of her, and there were no messages left for me. I went to the jetty to wait. I would see her approach or a car would turn up. I didn't want to look at my watch, and I didn't want to know the time; I wanted this woman to come back again. I had her cigarettes and her change. As I waited, I convinced myself that she really must be my mother; nothing else made sense. No-one had ever told me I had an auntie in Australia. If I had an auntie in Australia, why did no-one ever mention her? In any case, how did she know I was on-board this ship?

She knew my name and lots of other things, and she knew Mrs Dams. Someone must be giving her information.

I saw Budgie, Don, and Max saunter down the forward gangplank and knew it must be gone 16:00; they could not go ashore before this time. A feeling of true sadness overwhelmed me: she was not coming. I thought I might cry; in fact, I wanted to cry. I wanted to be angry also, but really, I wanted to cry. I took a deep breath, and walked away from the ship. Once again, I felt low; lower than a snake's belly in a wheel rut. My head was down, and I was scuffing my feet along the concreted ground of the dockyard. I tried to pretend it didn't matter, even though it *did* matter. I knew my pals were catching up with me, so took deep breaths and cleared my mind. 'Coming with us tonight, Chris?' Budgie asked me, putting a friendly hand on my shoulder.

'Sure,' I told him cheerfully. 'That's why I've been waiting for you.' Budgie told me that yesterday, they went into Perth and met some girls in a bar there. The girls told him to get some friends together, and they would have a party; so off we went. We had to take a train to Perth, so stopped off at a bar on the way to the station. The bar was similar to the one Budgie and I had visited in Sydney: no decorations and no girls. We were a little bit older now, but still looked too young to buy beer, but it didn't seem to matter too much. I was confident to go to the bar and ask. If they said no, then someone else would go and get the beer. I think the barmen knew this. 'Give me a fucking pitcher, mate, please,' I asked, remembering the correct terminology. He gave me the beer, and asked how many glasses I needed. I gave him some money from the change I should have given to either my mother or my auntie, and he gave me some back. I began to feel better; the depression of being stood up was receding.

The train ride was scenic. We passed close to the sea, and was told some of the best surfing in the world could be had at these beaches. The sea was wild and rolled in on giant waves, rolling over and over, and then disintegrating in a total mess of white foam and spray. Perth City was different from Sydney: the buildings were not so high; the streets were much wider, and traffic was less. Everything seemed more sedate; bars were more akin to those in England, and women were allowed in. Budgie led me to the bar where he had met the girls the night before. It was a big place, with a polished wooden bar, not like the stainless steel versions I had come to associate with Aussie. Wooden-turned pillars supported a shelf above the bar, where glasses were waiting to be used. Pint mugs hung from hooks beneath the shelf; a barman—beautifully framed between the bar, pillars and the shelf—stood with one hand leaning on the bar and the other atop a pump for beer. He stood in front of a mirrored wall, where shelves carried all manner of bottled spirits and smaller glasses behind him. He wore a white apron, and had a broad smile of greeting on his face. His hair was receding slightly, and his wide eyes cause his forehead to line with wrinkles. His smile was slightly lopsided, but revealed sparkling white teeth. 'Hello, lads,' he greeted us; he had a strong Glaswegian accent. 'What'll it be?' Fingers and Bob were already here playing darts in a far corner of the bar; Mort and some other guys from the mess looked on. Don went to the jukebox, exhaling smoke from his cigarette and squinting with one eye whilst he surveyed the records on offer. Glen Campbell sang about how he drove the main road, searching in the sun for an overload, whilst Don made a choice of what we were to hear next. I never put money in jukeboxes; to me, it was a waste, as there was always someone else who would. We got our pitcher of beer, and sat down with Mort and the rest; some of the girls that Budgie talked of filtered in and sat around us. There was a variety: good-looking, ugly, fat, and indifferent. I was not going to join the melee and sniff around them as the others were doing; I had been rejected once today, and that was enough. The talk was we would be invited back to someone's house, where a party was being prepared; I would wait and see what happened then.

'Chris Clark, my 'ole mate!' Parky greeted me with open arms. I was sat in a lounge chair, and he sat on my knee, embracing me. 'Fancy a JC?' he asked, drawing reference to the last time we drank them in Singapore. He was clearly drunk.

'Not today, pal,' I told him. 'I nearly got in the shit last time.'

'Yeah, but some fucker got McSnell, though,' he said, giving my neck another hug. 'I would have loved to see that.'

'Yeah, me too.'

Parky got up and went to the bar. He had come in with Jonah, who would, no doubt, have some words with his fellow countryman behind the bar.

We all stayed in this bar for some time. More girls joined us and more people filled the place; finally, the word got around of where we should all go afterwards. People started to disperse. After a while, and in danger of being left behind, Parky and Jonah grabbed me and we piled into a taxi. The house was a townhouse on three floors: the rooms were numerous and large. The main living room was on the first floor, and was full of people drinking and smoking. Some were dancing, some were talking, and some embracing each other with hands roaming up and down the back. The air smelled of sickly-sweet perfume, mixed with smoke, which hung in a cloud from the ceiling. I heard, for the first time, the lyrics *the world is just a great big onion*, and thought, *how strange*. Someone gave me an opened can of beer, which was ice-cold in my hand, and I squeezed onto a sofa and tried to catch more lyrics of the song. A girl had moved to give me space to wedge myself between her and the arm of the sofa; I did not pay her any attention. I had already seen she was not particularly good-looking: she had short hair and wore jeans. To me, women should have long hair and wear skirts; you can run your hand up the thigh of a girl in a skirt. With jeans, it's a nightmare. For me, I could not get the events of yesterday and today out of my mind; I could not join in with the spirit of the run ashore. I was no longer sad—it was just that I was preoccupied, and not following exactly what was going on around me. However, I was enjoying being with my friends, and watching their antics trying to win favours of various girls. I was enjoying the beer and the effect it was having on me; it seemed to elevate me to a level where reality was becoming detached. I probably could have stayed, slumped on this sofa, until I passed out.

'What do you do on the ship?' the girl next to me asked, leaning against me to get my attention. I looked at her face, which was round and chubby. She had pale blue eyes, which beamed into my face. It seemed there was too much flesh on her cheeks and the skin was pulled tightly over it. Her mouth was a small, straight line, with thin lips painted red. Her short, black, curly hair was styled with a fringe that came down her forehead and covered her eyebrows. However, the lines of broken scars criss-crossing the eyebrows could not be missed. They were newly healed and still an angry red. Her eyes were on mine, challenging me not to look away.

'I'm an Electrical Mechanic,' I told her.

'Ooh,' she said, wriggling a little. 'A brainy boy. Where do you come from? 'This was always a question I never really knew how to answer. No-one has ever heard of Forty Foot, and in the past I have answered 'Ramsey', but then I am invariably asked is that Ramsey Isle of Mann or do you mean Romsey in Hampshire. I always found it safer to say Peterborough.

'Peterborough,' I answered.

'Ooh, where's that?' she asked in her squeaky little voice.

'Two hours' north of London.'

'Ooh,' she said. I was about to ask her where she came from, but she beat me to it. 'I come from Portsmouth,' she told me proudly.

'Really? We sailed from Portsmouth.'

'Yes, I know. My dad used to be in the Navy.'

'Really?' I said, faking amazement.

'He was a Leading Regulator. 'I wondered if he ever got piss poured over him. We sat, almost glued together, whilst we asked and answered each other's questions. She had recently been in a car crash and had forty-seven stitches in her face; she also broke her collarbone, but that had healed now. I told her I had broken a collarbone, on two separate occasions, and so knew how painful that was. She told me she was sixteen years old and had lived in Australia for a year. Bobby Goldsboro began to sing *Honey.*

'Do you want to dance?' I asked her. I was waiting for a slow one before I asked her, so I could get her close and do some exploring with my hands. I prised myself from between her and the end of the sofa, and reached out a hand to help her up. She was nearly as tall as me; she was bordering on being fat—some might say she *was* fat. Her blouse was sleeveless, in fact, almost like a vest. An expanse of shoulders and neck was on show—a fat neck and fat shoulders. The neck seemed only to be a stump sitting on the shoulders with her face sitting on it. There was no form to the neck or shoulders, no muscle definition or dimples. Her shoulder bra straps were tight and embedded within her flesh; she didn't have a fat belly, though. It wasn't flat, but sufficiently rounded. Her tits were small, and I could see they were held tightly by the bra. Her thighs were big; the denim of her jeans was pulled tight at the top of them, and no light could be seen between them. The thighs rubbed together as we shuffled onto the dancing area. I held her close as we smooched around. She also held me close, and her hands were caressing my back. I could feel her bra strap through the thin material of her vest and this, too, was pulled tight, causing her skin to roll above and below it. When my hands roamed up and down, she responded by burying her face in my shoulder and neck. I could feel her breathing; she was getting turned on. Mary Hopkin followed Bobby Goldsboro, recalling *Those Were the Days*. She now had both arms about my neck, caressing the back of my head. I was able to drop my hands and felt the waistline of her jeans, or where the excess flesh rolled over it; a bit lower, and I found the hemline of the vest. I let my hands rest a while; the next move would be a good indicator of what could follow. I slid my hand under her vest, up a little, and I was touching the contours of her back. Her skin was cold and yielding under my palm. If anything, I felt her press closer to me. I was now getting turned on. I let my hand explore her bra strap; I investigated the clip, and considered I could flick this apart with no trouble at all. Both sides would fly apart and release the strained flesh of her back. The thought of what it would do at the front turned me on further. We were pressing our bodies close together and swaying from side-to-side. I now had two hands inside her vest, exploring her back. As I ran my thumbs down her flanks, she shuddered, and held me tighter. I had the distinct feeling I could actually end up fucking this girl tonight. The tempo of the music changed with the Lemon Pipers and *Green Tambourine*. We stood apart and held hands. Neither of us wanted to jerk around on the dance floor, so we sidled off to the side. We went outside to a small balcony, which had a good view of the wide avenue and city. We embraced each other and snogged. Her tongue explored mine, and my hands found the mounds of her breasts. I pinned her to the wall and pressed my erection to her tummy; she responded to its stiffness by pulling me in tighter. People came on to the balcony and went. Some lingered for a while, doing the same as us. 'We need to find somewhere more private,' I whispered huskily in her ear. She looked into my face, searching for something. I maintained eye contact, but was reminded of the scars and how pretty she was not. Her lipstick had smudged, the fringe swept away. I didn't care; I would still fuck her. She took my hand, and I followed her inside. She went to a door by the entrance, and we both went in. There were two single beds full of clothes; it was as if someone was in a hurry to unpack a suitcase, and had just tipped it up and emptied the contents there. In the corner was a toilet and a small wash basin. She locked the door behind us, and saw me looking at the toilet.

'Don't worry,' she said, 'people don't use this much.' We then embraced again and snogged some more. I pulled her down so we were sitting on the bed. Still kissing and fumbling, I manoeuvred her so we were lying on the bed, facing each other. I pushed a bundle of clothes to the floor, and she did the same. We both kicked off our shoes; I had an arm around her neck and the other inside her vest at the back. I found the bra clasp, played with it a while, then I flicked it open. I caressed the skin where the strap had been, and felt the small indentations disappear. I eased her over so she was more on her back. I was now able to slide my hand round to her tummy, and then up to her breasts. She shuddered as I touched her nipples. I remembered what Sandra told me—'spend time with the breasts'. So I did; rubbing, caressing, pinching, flicking, and massaging. Her breathing got deeper and more husky. She writhed around beneath me. *Now must be the time*, I thought. I let me hand slide down to the waistline of her jeans. It was embedded by her fat, but I was able to force my fingers inside. I played with the metal button with my thumb, and when I was ready, I pushed the button through the retaining hole, which I was supporting with my fingers on the underside. I caressed the exposed belly with the reverse side of my fingers, which were still in the same position. I pushed the open waistband from side to side, but it could not open much because of the zip. The next step would be another crucial one. I decided to go back to the tits and fiddle with them some more. Again, I could feel her arousal, which replaced the tension I was feeling undoing the jeans button. After a while, I went back to her midriff, caressing all the way, and found the tang of the zip. I held it with finger and thumb and slowly forced it down. *So far, so good,* I thought. I was then able to open the front of her jeans wide and place my hand inside. I could feel the elastic of her knickers, and let my hand linger for a while. Suddenly, her hand clamped over mine, and she turned to face me.

'Chris,' she breathed, 'I have never done this before.'

So what? I thought. there has to be a first time for everything. I didn't think I should say that, though.

'Look,' I said, 'you don't have to do anything.' I slid my hand up to her breasts again. 'I can go back to the party and drink beer, if you want me to.' I was calling her bluff.

'No!' she said urgently, 'I want you to stay with me.' I smiled inwardly, and she relaxed. When I ventured down with my hand again, she removed her arms from my neck and took hold of her jeans, lifted her buttocks, and pushed the garment down. She then kicked them free from her legs. I played with her breasts some more until I felt her relax. I then explored her panty line and the furry mass inside; her legs parted to give me easier access, and I felt the crevice of her vagina. I let my finger follow the valley and when I pushed a little, my finger slipped in. It was warm and wet. I did not push my finger all inside, as I would have done in the past; I searched for the clitoris. When I touched it, she stiffened and shuddered as I massaged it and I felt the gristliness of it. I was so hard; I could shoot my load at any moment. I rolled over, sat up, and removed my trousers. Once more beside her and my hand between her legs, she pushed me away slightly. 'You won't tell anybody, will you, Chris?' she pleaded.

'No. Of course not,' I reassured her.

'I might have a baby,' she said.

'No,' I said. 'I'll pull it out when it comes.' I removed her panties, and found her clitoris again. She was soon breathing hard and waiting for me to be inside her. I penetrated her gently; I wanted to get it all the way in before I had to pull it out again. I looked into her face, and her eyes were tightly shut. Her mouth was open, and she was panting. I pushed some more and her face screwed up. She was pretty ugly at this stage. Her fist went up to her mouth and she bit into it. I pushed again and was all the way in. She grunted, and her fist was stifling a scream. I now wanted to come out a little. She shuddered beneath me and I could feel her legs go rigid. *Is this an orgasm?* I wondered. Was she having an orgasm? It must be an orgasm. She was reacting in a similar fashion as Sandra had when her backside was to the kitchen sink and she was pulling my face into her fanny. The shuddering stopped, but she was still biting her fist. I withdrew a little, and went forward again. She reacted to every movement I made. Another couple of thrusts and I felt it coming. From deep within me, I was about to erupt. I jerked my cock out and spurted my juices on her belly. I then slumped to her side, panting. We laid there for a while. Finally, she released the fist from her mouth.

'Chris,' she called, 'promise me you won't tell anybody.' I assured her, but I lied.

I got up and pulled on my trousers and shoes. She was just sitting up on the bed, as if in a daze. I went to the door and she said, 'I need to clean up a little.'

'Okay,' I said, and unlocked the door.

'Chris,' she called. I looked back at her. 'You never asked me my name.'

'Don't worry. Names are not important.' I let myself out.

The party was breaking up, and a lot of people had already left. I found another can of beer and went out to the balcony to sip at it. Miss Portsmouth came out and put her arms around me. This irritated me, but I tolerated it. 'My dad will be coming for me soon,' she said. 'Do you want to come back to our house for the night?' I didn't fancy being under the same roof as an ex-Leading Regulator. Whilst he may not have known I had fucked his daughter, he would have thought I'd have made a pretty good attempt to do so.

'No. I have to be back on-board.'

'Will you stay with me till he comes?' she asked. 'He should be here in about an hour.'

'Of course I will,' I told her by way of comfort. I would find as many beers as I could during the next hour, and so not have to buy any in a bar. Miss Portsmouth told me her name was Janice. She asked if she could write to me, and would I write back. I told her it would be a good idea. Janice's father came, and she introduced me to him; he asked me if I would go for a drink with him and he would drop me off at the station afterwards. He further told me he would pay, so I agreed. Her father was okay. His name was Roy, and he had served seven years. He then worked for the prison service after that and got a transfer to Australia. We stopped off at a bar by the station, and he insisted on buying me rum. I was soon really drunk and wanted to go. He must have sensed this, as he told Janice to say goodbye to me, and they left. It was getting late, and the last train would be leaving soon. I bought a ticket and slumped on a carriage bench. The rocking motion sent me to sleep, and I dreamed of fucking Janice again.

I woke up gently. My head ached, which I'd got accustomed to by now; it always did after I had been out drinking. But now, my neck ached and my back was sore. It was light and quiet. Panic suddenly overcame me, and I sat bolt-upright. I was still in the train carriage, but it was not moving. I looked about me, and nobody else was in the carriage. I looked outside and could see many other carriages, along with box cars and aggregate rail trucks. I walked up and down the carriage, and realised there was no carriage in front and none behind. It was clear this carriage had been parked up at some siding and no-one realised I was on-board. I opened the door and climbed down to the ground; I walked around the carriage, but no-one was around. In one direction there seemed to be more buildings, so I set off towards them. After a while, I could see the station ahead of me, so I knew I had chosen the right way. As I approached the station, a man came out on to the platform and stood looking at me, his fists on his hips. As I neared him, he shouted at me, 'What the fucking 'ell do you think you're doing?'

'I'm on my way to the dockyard. I fell asleep on the train and just woke up down there,' I said, pointing.

'Dockyard? What fucking dockyard?' Surely there could be only one dockyard in Fremantle.

'Where the big Aircraft Carrier is,' I told him.

'Mate,' he said, 'that's fucking Fremantle.'

'I know. That's why I'm here. Which way do I go?' I was still on the track and he was on the platform in front of me. He was pointing across the track and up towards the underside of the platform roof.

'What the fuck does that say, mate?' I followed his pointing finger. To my horror, I saw the sign hanging from the iron supports of the roof: Perth Central, it said.

'This is Perth?' I asked him in disbelief.

'Fucking right there, cobba.'

'But I left here on the last train last night.'

'Well, you must have come back on the same train afterwards,' he explained. 'I suppose you were fucking pissed and fell asleep.' Then he laughed; a deep, throaty laugh.

'When's the next train to Fremantle?'

'No trains today, mate. Fucking Sunday.' I was just looking at him wide-eyed and open-mouthed. 'No fucking trains on a Sunday.'

'Where can I get a taxi?'

'No taxis today, mate,' he informed me again. 'Fucking Sunday.'

'I have to be on-board by seven-thirty,' I told him, sounding rather pathetic.

'No fucking chance, mate.'

'How long does it take to walk?' I was desperate.

'Half a fucking day,' he told me. 'Here!' he said, extending a hand down to me to pull me up to the platform. 'I have to go to the rail yard in Fremantle today, no reason why I can't leave now and drop you off.' This was incredible. He was offering to give me a lift! 'Can we get there before half seven?'

'Not without speeding.' He looked at me and realised I really had to be there by 07:30. 'Come on,' he said, and we marched off. 'Anyway,' he said to me, as we set off in his car, 'no speed cops today.' We looked at each other and together said, 'Fucking Sunday.' We both laughed at this.

He pulled up at the bottom of the gangway and I jumped out, said thanks, and ran up it. McSnell was there, standing next to the Bosun's Mate. Mostly, a member of the reg. staff would be there when leave was about to expire. Sometimes, if you were late, the Bosun's Mate would let you have your station card, and so you'd get away with being adrift.

I could see three things: first, I had one minute to spare; next, I could see my station card in McSnell's hand; and third, the look of disappointment on McSnell's face knowing his chance of 'getting' me had been dashed. He could not bring himself to hand the card to me. Instead, he replaced it in the box and he left the deck. 'You're lucky,' the Bosun's Mate told me 'He's got it in for you.'

'Not today, though,' I told him. 'Fucking Sunday.'

22: The Party

After a few more days, we left Australia. I went into Perth one more time, but didn't see Janice. I took the train back to Freemantle, but made sure I didn't sleep. We explored Fremantle more, and I managed to keep out of trouble.

There was another round of job changes, and I was transferred to the switchboard section. This was a fairly interesting section: we worked on generators and all the switchboard equipment. Another responsibility we had was to bring on the shore supply cables when we were in Harbour. We would be getting all the things ready on the Weather Deck as we entered, and so could not be available for Procedure Alpha. We therefore had all the benefits, but did not need to stand still for hours without talking.

We had to fall into a routine of watch-keeping. This took us out of the normal daily routine of things, but there were lots of benefits. There were times when we did not need to get up with the rest of the mess, and there were times we could legally be in the mess during working hours. The best thing, though, was when we were alongside after a period of watch-keeping, we would have twenty-four hours off. This means we could go ashore one day at 12:00, and not return until 12:00

the following day.

We were on our way now to South Africa, once again, and there were a number of us who would be returning to girls we had met during our first visit the previous year. A lot of these girls also knew each other, and they all wanted to throw a party for us. We were all excited about this, and had visions of getting our end away for the last time before returning to the UK. The party would be held at Sheila's place, where she lived with other girls, who worked for the bus transport company. She was in charge of the house, and so she would be the one who said when the party would be held. Sheila was waiting for me to confirm when I would be able to get ashore before she finalised this date; things for us are a bit clearer now, so I was able to tell her when it should be.

Once again, Spanner and I were seated opposite each other in Hotel switchboard, and our writing pads in front of us. Spanner had borrowed an LP, and he set it in motion on his portable player. It was a compilation of recent records.

I took my pad and on the first page wrote *My Darling Kay*. I turned the next page and wrote *My Darling Dianne*, and on the following page I wrote *My Darling Sheila*. 'What the fuck you doing?' Spanner asked me.

'I'm writing three letters at once,' I told him. 'Saves me having to copy one out twice when I am finished. You could use carbon paper.' He looked at me, so I explained. 'You write two letters, and they are both to Mary. 'I could see him thinking about it. He wrote on one page, turned the sheet, and wrote on another. He was doing the same as I. We both fell silent whilst we thought of things to include in our letters.

'You know, Clarkie, Mary's mum doesn't like Mary hanging around with Sheila.'

'Really?' I said. 'Why's that, then?'

'Dunno. She thinks Sheila's a bit of a loose woman.' I thought about this for a while, and recalled how easy it was for me to get her going. All I needed to do was kiss her neck, or suck her earlobe, and she would be writhing against me.

'Does she think she's on the game or something, then?'

'No, I don't think so. Dunno, really.'

'If she has loads of boyfriends, why would she be so interested in me?' I asked him. He shrugged. 'Well, as long as I get my end away, I couldn't give a fuck, really.'

'You'd fuck anything you would, Clarkie,' he said. 'That girl in Perth was like the back end of a bus.'

'You don't look at the mantelpiece when you're poking the fire.'

'What if you knew that Sheila had been fucking a load of other men?' Spanner asked. 'Would you still fuck her?'

'I couldn't care less, as long as I get my end away.'

'But you could catch all sorts of things,' he said. 'What would happen if you caught a dose, just before we get back to Pompey, and then you give it to Kay?' I thought of this for a while. Many of the guys on-board had caught something, and squeezed yellow puss up from cocks. They just went to the sickbay, got a jab, and took doses of Mist Pot Cit every morning for a week or so. Drink loads of water and no alcohol, is what they were told.

'What about you?' I retaliated. 'You've been with prozzies and fucking Kai Tais.' He looked at me. 'You could have a dose as well,' I accused.

Spanner looked hurt. In a meek voice, he said, 'I check every day, but I'm okay.' We fell silent for a while. 'I'm going to give blood when I get back,' Spanner told me. 'You can do it at Vicky Barracks. They always test it, and if there's anything wrong, then they'll let you know.'

'Good idea. I'll do the same.'

I wrote on my pad; *Fremantle was good fun. I met some people from Portsmouth and some from Scotland. They have black swans in Fremantle.* I duplicated this on each of the other two pages. When I looked up, Spanner was looking at me with an expectant look in his eye. I told him what I had written, and he busied himself with his pen.

The Moody Blues were singing. 'This is a beautiful song,' I said to Spanner.

He looked at me with amazement. 'It's fucking crap, man,' he said. 'A fucking load of shite.'

'Why do you say that, then?'

'Well, listen to the fucking words!' He started to recall them. 'Knights in white satin,' he said sarcastically. He was looking at me, and I just looked blankly at him, not knowing his point. He continued: 'Every fucker knows knights don't wear white satin!' My eyebrows involuntarily raised. 'They wear shining armour and chainmail,' he said with emphasis. 'I've never seen a fucking knight in white fucking satin!' Spanner was prodding his finger on the desk as he said this. My jaw was beginning to drop now. 'And, what's this about never reaching the end? Never reaching the end of what? No, man,' he said, 'it's a fucking load of crap.' I was wondering how to tell him, but he continued. 'You should listen to Joan Baez or Bob Dylan. They have fucking good words.'

'Spanner,' I said calmly, 'it's not Knights with a *K*. It's nights with an *N*,' I informed him. I could see he was thinking about this. 'And the white satin is the sheets.' He looked at me. 'Never reaching the end means that the guy went to bed, with white satin sheets on the bed at night, and he couldn't sleep!' Spanner shrugged, picked up his pen and began to write. He lifted the page and wrote again. 'What did you put?' I asked.

He picked up his pad and read, 'We are on our way to Cape Town now.' He then threw the pad back down on the table. I picked up my pen and wrote, *We are on our way to Cape Town now*, and duplicated this on the other two sheets. Spanner was feeling a bit hurt and by not commenting on his contribution to the letter, but including it in my letters, I hoped to comfort him a little. After a while, he said, 'Anyway, what's this about the fucking letters?' he challenged.

Mystified, I asked, 'What letters?'

'The letters in the fucking song.' He was pointing to the record player. 'Letters I've written never meaning to send. Why write a fucking letter if you don't mean to send it? It's like us, coming down here, writing these fucking letters, and then tossing them overboard.'

'You are right, Spanner. It's a fucking stupid song,' I agreed, as a way to comfort him. We both sat in silence for a while; then I leant forward to write. As I wrote, I spoke the words out loud so Spanner could copy them if he wanted. *They say the sea can be quite rough here, but today, it's fine.*

Spanner did copy my words, but I don't think he liked them too much. In fact, I didn't, but it filled another line. Spanner leant forward to write, and recited as he wrote. I copied. *Maybe we will see some whales soon.* 'I'm going to finish off now,' I told him, and said aloud as I wrote, *I miss you very much and can't wait to hold you in my arms again. All my love, Chris xxxxxxx.* I copied this on the other two pages. At the bottom of Sheila's letter, I told her the date for the party when both Spanner and I would not be on duty; in fact, it was the day I was off for twenty-four hours. Some people would not be happy because they would be on duty, but it would not be possible to pick a date when we were all off.

With my new job, I was able to see South Africa and the approach to Cape Town. Again, I was in awe of the beautiful sight: the top of Table Mountain was clear, and the black rock glistened in the sun. Spanner and I had arranged to meet Sheila and Mary in the Navigator's Den. Spanner had qualified for all-night leave, and I could enjoy the same privilege because I was a watch-keeper.

We got ashore much later than we hoped, but maybe that was a good thing: less time to drink, too much before we met the girls later. The Navigator's Den was exactly as I remembered it. I had a bottle of Cape Brandy in my sock; we bought Coke from the bar and wandered around to the area where we first met Sheila and Mary. My heart was pounding in anticipation; I was really excited, and looking forward to seeing her again. They were sat in the same seats as before; both looked up at us and smiled brightly as they removed the handbags and coats from the seat next to them that they were reserving for us. I sat down, and Sheila threw her arms about my neck and hugged me close. 'It's really good to see you again, Chris,' she said, looking intently at me. Her eyes shone brightly from her small, round face, and her lips looked luscious—painted red and shining. I looked across, and could see Spanner and Mary were still held in an embrace and looking at each other, as we had. I surreptitiously retrieved the brandy and recharged our glasses. 'You have changed,' Sheila told me. 'You seem much older now.'

'Really? I know I have grown a bit taller, but I'm still me,' I said, hoping she would still fancy me.

'Yes, I know,' she murmured, snuggling up closer to me. We talked a lot about our trip, but had to modify certain parts of it. I didn't tell her about the brothel or the Kai Tais, and certainly not about Janice. We also talked of the party which was arranged for us. She told me there were lots of her friends coming, who had already met some of our friends from the mess, as well as other people on-board.

'That's Maggie and Brenda.' She pointed, and I saw Fingers and Bob with two girls. 'Maggie always gets drunk,' she informed me, whispering in my ear as if they may hear us with all the noise of the club. So, now I knew who Maggie Steaming was. She didn't look too drunk from where I was sitting. She was leaning against Fingers, and she had a drink in her hand. Bob had his arms around Brenda, who was smiling broadly. Brenda was taller than Bob and she had an enormous chin: it was far too big for her face, and exaggerated the movement of her lips as she spoke. I had seen Don earlier, and knew he had been keeping in touch with Janet, although they were nowhere to be seen at the moment. Sheila said she wanted to dance, so we got up and left Spanner and Mary to look after the table and handbags. Sheila and I held each other close and swayed with the sound of Dionne Warwick and *The Valley of the Dolls*. Just being close to her was enough to make blood run to my cock, causing it to stiffen and strain against my clothes. I knew she could feel it, and pushed her tummy on to it. My hands explored her back, and she breathed harder as I touched the bare flesh of her shoulders and neck. After a while, the music gathered pace, and we decided to return to our seats. As we got to the table section of the club, Maggie was coming towards us, so we squeezed to the side to let her pass. She stopped when she reached us, and looked at me with a big smile on her face. 'Fingers can't come to the party,' she said, pouting at Sheila. 'He has to stay on the ship. 'Maggie was blonde. Her hair was long and had thick, languid curls. She had big blue eyes, which seemed bloodshot, and she wore too much eye makeup. Her lips were full with lipstick that needed attending to. She was as tall as me. 'You must be Chris. I'm Maggie.'

'Hi, Maggie,' I said. I moved back amongst some chairs to allow her to pass. Even so, it was a squeeze, and as she passed, she caressed the front of my trousers with her hand. Her eyes lit up as she realised I had a hard-on. It took all the willpower I possessed not to react to her touch or to her reaction. She squeezed me gently as she went past.

'She will be drunk again soon,' Sheila told me as we took our place at our table. It was clear Sheila was unaware of what Maggie had done to me. Spanner and Mary got up to dance, and we had our small corner to ourselves. We got close, kissed and cuddled; it was an effort to keep my hands from disappearing under her clothes and to keep my manhood inside my trousers. Spanner and Mary came back to save the day: we chatted and drank our brandy. Things were a little fuzzy by the time the music stopped and security men came around, inviting us to leave. The girls ordered a taxi, and we all piled in. They dropped Spanner and I off at the gangway and we said our goodbyes.

'Fucking 'ell, man,' Spanner said, grabbing and grinding his scrotum as we mounted the gangplank. We retrieved our station cards and moved off towards our mess. 'Eh! You know that fucking Maggie? She grabbed my balls one time when I went passed her,' he told me. 'I couldn't fucking believe it. We had just come off the dance floor, and she was there with Fingers.' He was still grinding away at the front of his trousers and added, 'She needs a fucking good fucking, she does, mate.' I decided it wouldn't be right to inform him he had not been the only one to receive this treatment.

The party was in full swing when Budgie and I got there. I found Sheila and gave her a kiss. She dragged me into the kitchen and wrapped her arms around me, pressing her body hard against me. 'I have to do this,' she said, indicating the trays of food and titbits being prepared. 'Here,' she said, taking a beer from the fridge, 'don't have too many. I might need you later.' There was a glint in her eye.

The house was large: the entrance steps led up to a veranda going off to the left and right; straight on was the lounge. Through the door to the left was the dining area; a large dining table stood with eight chairs surrounding it. To the right was the lounging area; three large sofas were positioned around a low coffee table. The back of one sofa formed the boundary of this area; the other two were against a wall. Interspersed were four lounge chairs, which were low and inviting. Across the lounge, directly in front of the entrance door, was a doorway to a long passageway that ran from left to right along the length of the house. To the right were six doors off the passageway; each was an entrance to a small bedroom. Opposite the lounge door was the kitchen, and to the left, next to it, was the bathroom and toilet.

Budgie and I had stopped off at several places on our way here and, had already consumed several beers, so we were well on the way. I slumped on the end of the sofa by the lounge door through to the passageway; it was a good vantage point, as I could see who was coming and going, and also who went to the toilet. Sheila kept breezing past, passing round trays of small sausages, sandwiches and snacky things. She gave me a kiss each time she passed. Several people were already drunk, and were sleeping on the sofas and chairs. Loud music issued from a record player, and some people were dancing on the floor area of the dining room. I watched women's arses wobble beneath their skirts, and observed breasts jiggling up and down with their movements. Two ceiling fans whirred, distributing second-hand smoke evenly about the room; Sheila kept bringing me beer, and would sit with me from time-to-time. We would embrace, grope each other, and get turned-on; then she would have to return to being the host. A lot of people were here from her work, and all wanted to speak with us sailors. I could not be bothered; I was too drunk, really. From time-to-time, my head would topple forward and I'd doze off for a while, always waking with a start. The arm of the sofa was wooden; it was not padded, as the sofas in Mary's house. I was resting my arm and hand on the wood, and then I felt something warm pressing against my hand. Maggie was standing just inside the passageway door, next to the arm of the sofa. The back of her knee was pressing against my hand. She wore black leather boots that stopped short of the knees; her skirt started just above the knee, and the soft flesh of the reverse side of the kneecap was pressing against my hand. I did not move my hand, but just let it be caressed. There was a movement of her knee; she was moving it against my hand. She was also pushing against it and I could feel her pulse. Her back was to me, and she was talking to another girl, whom I did not know. I moved my hand slightly, returning her caresses, just rotated it a little. She took the pressure off my hand to allow this movement; she wanted me to be touching her. I rubbed my little finger up the backside of her leg. I increased the movement of my hand, and still she stood there. I increased the movement, working towards the hemline of her skirt. She must have known I was doing this; I let my hand disappear beyond the hemline. Still, she remained still, although she was swaying slightly. I turned my hand to caress her leg with my palm. The palm of my hand was now on the inside of her thigh. My fingers spread out and I moved my thumb up and down on the back of her thigh. I was now getting turned on by this. It was also risky, as I could have been seen if someone looked in my direction. I let my hand go higher. My thumb felt the crease of her flesh where the leg gave way to the buttock. I ran my thumb over the curve of the larger muscle. The knuckle of my first finger abutted her underwear. The hidden secret, encased in her panties, yielded to the pressure of my hand. It was warm and soft. I massaged it a little, and she seemed to arch her back, putting more pressure on my hand. I could feel the prickliness of pubic hair through the garment; someone approached, and she had to move to allow them to pass. I returned my hand to the wooden part of the sofa as if nothing had happened. Maggie walked unsteadily to the front door and leaned against the frame work. I sniffed my hand, where it had contacted her, and was instantly reminded of being on my knees in front of Sandra. I got to my feet and steadied myself. I walked across the room and stood behind Maggie, who was smoking a cigarette. I let my left hand rest on her buttocks and whispered in her ear, 'Do you want a good fucking?' Her head turned slightly and before she said anything, I went on. 'Next time you go to the bathroom, just give me the nod, and I'll give you a good fucking.' I was being brazen.

'A good fucking?' she asked me.

'Yeah, a good fucking.'

'Okay,' she said, and turned her face forward again.

I went into the kitchen, where Sheila was chatting with some of her work friends. I got another beer, a small sandwich, gave her a kiss, and returned to the lounge. Maggie had moved from her position by the door, but I couldn't see her. Don was laid out on one of the sofas, snoring away. I went out onto the veranda, and there were several couples embracing each other and groping, much the same as Janice and I had done in Perth. Bob was there with his hands up the front of Brenda's blouse, fondling her ample breasts. Brenda looked embarrassed when she saw me looking, and pulled Bob in closer to try and hide his activity. Her jaw was open with heavy breathing, and her chin looked as if it was a giant weight hanging on her face. I went back to my position on the sofa, next to the passageway door. I resumed the routine of drinking and dozing, head nodding forwards and snapping back. Then, I saw Maggie approaching the door with a stagger to her gait. 'Come on, then,' she said, although I couldn't hear this, with all the noise, but I could read her lips, and the beckoning of her head was unmistakable. She went through the door and turned left. I struggled to get up and stood for a moment; the passageway was clear, although I could see people in the kitchen. I went into the bathroom and locked the door behind me. Maggie was sat on the toilet with her knickers about her knees. Her left elbow was resting on the hand basin, and her right hand held the crotch of her knickers. She gestured, with her finger, for me to approach her. I did, and she explored the front of my trousers with her hand. She unzipped me, and I undid the button, holding the waistline together. My trousers fell to the floor and my erect penis sprang up and, wobbling, pointed itself towards her. She took it in her hand and examined it with her eyes. I slid a hand down the front of her blouse and inside the left bra cup. The flesh was warm and soft. I squeezed it gently, and felt the nipple go hard on my palm. She leaned her head forward and licked the end of my cock. I nearly exploded. She took my cock into her mouth, and I exploded. Maggie made some grunting, choking sounds as she tried to get more of me in her mouth. My hand reached in the other bra cup, and I massaged the other breast. She then pushed me away gently and almost vomited in the sink. She gagged and spit. 'You still have to fuck me,' she said as she wiped her mouth.

'Don't worry, 'I said, as I pushed my cock in her face. She grabbed it again and rubbed it gently. I was still hard, but the urgency had dissipated. I reached down inside her blouse and inside the top of her skirt to her rounded belly; I could feel the line where her pubic hair started. Her hand clamped on mine.

'I have to pee,' she told me, and there was a gushing sound and a splashing as her urine flowed from her body and crashed into the water at the bottom of the toilet. I forced my hand down further and felt the warm liquid flow through my fingers. I covered her fanny, causing her piss to squirt in all directions. She screeched in delight and, again, took my cock into her mouth. When no more fluid flowed, she stood up, moved against the basin, and leant against it. She kicked off her knickers and placed her left leg on the rim of the bath; she then pulled me towards her and guided me in. Just like that, I was inside her. She held me tight as I thrust away at her. I pulled the blouse up and pulled the bra up over her breast; her tits swung down and separated slightly. I got them both in my hands and played with them: I gyrated them, lifted them, pulled them, pushed them, squeezed them, and even became aggressive with them. I lifted them by the nipples, and Maggie squeaked, stifling laughter and screams. She let her leg drop, and we disengaged. She turned around and thrust her backside towards me. She bent forwards, put her hand between her legs, and grabbed hold of me, and guided me in again. Her tits were swinging free and felt wonderful in my hands—one in each hand. A knock came at the door, and we froze. 'I'm having a fucking piss!' Maggie shouted.

'Well, hurry up,' someone replied. 'You've been in there ages.'

'Fuck off!' Maggie said, and with that we continued. She stood up and we came free again. 'Come on,' she said. She dragged the bathroom mat to the middle of the floor, threw some bath towels on top, and sat on it. 'Come on,' she said reaching up for me. She laid back and opened her legs wide. 'Fuck me now, Chris,' she said. 'Fuck me, fuck me fuck me.' I lay on top of her and was inside her again. I was rigid and stabbing my cock into her. She was writhing beneath me and kicking with her feet. There was another knock at the door, which forced us to be silent.

'Fuck off!' Maggie shouted again. 'I'm finishing soon,' she added. 'Come on, Chris, baby. Fill me up.' I resumed the stabbing, and it didn't take long before I shot another load inside her. We were both panting when another banging on the door sounded. It was a man.

'For fuck's sake, Maggie. You're not the only one who has to piss, you know.'

'Fuck off!' Maggie shouted once again, 'You can go outside to piss if you're that desperate.'

I pulled my trousers up; they were still round my ankles. Maggie pulled the bra down over her tits and adjusted them in their supports. She smoothed down her blouse and skirt. She picked up her knickers and crumpled them up in her hand. 'Let's go,' she said. She unlocked the door, opened it and flew out. I followed. Three ladies stood outside the door with their mouths open, and, in disbelief, watched as we disappeared into the lounge.

I went through the lounge and out to the veranda. I don't know what happened to Maggie; she seemed to have disappeared. There were fewer people around now: more people were crashed out, and fewer people were dancing. I didn't see Sheila as I passed through the lounge, but guessed it would not be long before she had found out about Maggie and I. I was thinking about leaving when I saw Janet at the end of the veranda. She was on her own, and just staring out to the garden. Janet was the girl Don had been writing to; I always thought it strange that anyone would fancy Don, especially someone as beautiful as this girl. I walked down the veranda to where she was standing. 'Hi,' I said. She didn't say anything, but shrugged a little. 'Why are you on your own?' She turned to look at me. She was a very beautiful girl, with clear skin and pale blue eyes.

'Because your mate is pissed and passed out,' she said, obviously annoyed. She had turned to me momentarily, but was now looking out to the garden again. I had noticed something, though: it looked as if a front tooth was missing.

'Well,' I said, 'maybe he was tired.' She shrugged at my feeble attempt to excuse him.

'I think I'm going to go soon,' she said. I thought of Sheila, and considered it may be a good idea if I went also. After all, I had got my end away, so number one objective had been achieved.

'Where do you live?'

'Oh, it's up the hill,' she said with a casual wave of her hand.

'Is it walking distance?'

'It's a long way,' she said, 'and I don't want to walk by myself, and there're no taxis till it starts to get light.'

After a while to think, I said, 'I'll walk with you, if you like.'

She looked at me again, and I was ready for when she opened her mouth to confirm if, indeed, she had a missing tooth. 'But you are with Sheila,' she said, and I was right. A front tooth at the top was missing. Now, my mind was full of thought. What happened to her tooth? What happened to Maggie, and did Sheila know about what happened? If Sheila did know, then she would be pissed off with me, and I certainly didn't want to fight with her—or anyone else, for that matter. I was looking out to the garden now, leaning on the balustrade with my elbows. 'Don said he'd take me home, but...' She didn't finish. The next question in my mind was: would Janet let Don fuck her if he took her home? Maybe I could fuck her, if I took her home. It was clear that Janet did not know I had been in the toilet with Maggie, so maybe it would be a good idea to get away before she found out.

'Yeah,' I said, 'I thought I was with Sheila, but she seems to be more interested in the people she works with. Spent all the time in the kitchen with them.'

'Oh. I thought she really fancied you.'

'I think she fancies everyone.' There was a pause; then I spoke again. 'So Shall we go?'

She turned to me again. 'Sure you don't mind?' Clearly not worried about her missing tooth. We went down the steps and into the street. I looked back casually to note no-one seemed to notice we were leaving.

As we walked away from the house, Janet folded her arms and shuddered slightly against the cool morning air. I used this as an excuse to put my arm around her, and she let me do so. She told me she lived with her parents and two elder brothers, who worked for one of the mining companies close to the city. We never talked about her tooth, or the gap where it used to be.

We arrived at her house, and she indicated I should be quiet. We entered the house via a kitchen door; she then led me through to a large lounge and looked about. No-one was around. We went back to the kitchen, and she asked if I wanted a drink. She took Coke out of the fridge and Cape Brandy from a shelf above the kitchen table. She blended the two together, dropped in a couple of ice cubes, and we went back to the lounge. I went to a sofa, sat down, and leant back against the soft comfort of the support. Janet came and sat next to me, leaned against me, and then tucked her feet up under her. Her head rested on my shoulder, and her empty hand rested on my thigh. I put my arm around her and we sat in silence, sipping at our drinks. When she finished, she looked up at me, and asked if I wanted another. I looked into her beautiful face, and gently kissed her lips. She then put an arm about my neck, and we kissed passionately. We both put down the empty glasses and kissed some more. I explored her body through her clothes. I caressed her arms, back and shoulders, and she didn't flinch when I ran my hand across her breasts. Finally, she got up and went to the kitchen for more drinks. When she returned, she put the condensation-covered glasses on to a side table and told me to wait. She went upstairs and returned moments later with a blanket. There was no need for instruction; we both laid ourselves out on the sofa and covered ourselves with the blanket. We resumed our kissing and exploration. Janet responded to my every move, encouraging me to continue. Again, I remembered Sandra's words: 'take time with the tits'. I did. I caressed them through the thin material of her blouse; I then unhooked her bra without removing it. I pushed the supporting garment up and caressed her breasts again through the nylon material of the blouse. I knew the roughness of the material would add a greater sensation to her nipples, which grew hard beneath my fingers. Her left leg was over my right thigh, with her knee nudging my elbow. I put a hand on her knee, and her skin was silky soft. I ran my hand down her thigh to her rounded buttocks. No knickers! She must have taken them off when she went upstairs, or maybe she wasn't wearing any all night. I let my fingers find their way to the crevice between her legs, and gently followed the furry valley. She was now trying to undo my trousers, but only had one hand as the other was about my neck. I let her struggle whilst I gently pressed my finger inside her. She was wet; slippery wet and so very warm. We were both breathing in gasps. She had freed my cock, and was rubbing it gently; I found her pleasure button and massaged it, causing her to writhe against me to increase the intensity. She pulled my stiff penis down whilst reaching up with her knee so her crotch would be in the correct position. She rubbed her clitoris with the end of my cock, which drove me crazy. The roughness of her wiry pubic hair mixed with the warmth and moistness of her insides was an electrifying sensation. Soon, I was all inside—inside deep. In and out and in and out. I reached down to massage her clit as I was fucking her. She went wild, thrusting her hips against me. Suddenly, she stiffened and gripped my neck so hard I thought it would break. A couple more thrusts, and I exploded inside her. We both relaxed. Our breathing returned to normal, but I was still inside her. 'I need the toilet,' she said, breaking the spell. She rolled over me and off, and I came out of her. She adjusted her skirt as I watched her go towards the stairs. I pulled up my trousers and sorted myself out. When she came back, I was drinking my Brandy and Coke, and she joined me. 'I hate to tell you,' she said, 'but you have to leave before my brothers get up.' I was relieved she said this, as I was ready to go. I had fucked her, and didn't want to sit around kissing and cuddling anymore.

'Okay,' I said, 'I have to be back on-board anyway. 'I got up and finished my drink.

'Will you be able to find your way back?'

'Sure,' I said. She came to the door with me, and we kissed goodbye.

I set off down the road. I did not know exactly which way to go, but decided if I kept going downhill, I would eventually come to the sea and the road that ran alongside the shore; it would be easy to find the dockside from there. I was on an ego high. I had fucked two women in one night! Neither had asked to see me again, and it seemed that's all they wanted to do: just to be fucked.

I walked downhill, turned some corners, and walked downhill further. I was walking in a residential area; all the houses were big. They were set in their own ground, and neither one looked like the other. It was beginning to get light; stars were disappearing, and a warm glow appeared in the eastern sky. I turned another corner and some things were familiar; some trees, a wall, and a gate. Beyond the gate, steps ran up to a veranda and an open door to a lounge. I was back at Sheila's house. I went in. Don was gone from the sofa, but Bob was on another under a blanket with Brenda. Both were fast asleep. The other two sofas had sleeping bodies lying on them. The kitchen was a mess, with food remnants all over the place, along with glasses with a variety of liquids still in them at various levels. Ashtrays full and overflowing, spilling filthy dog-ends on table tops and floors. No-one was in the bathroom; the last bedroom, at the end of the passageway, belonged to Sheila. The door was not fully closed, so I pushed it open. I did not know what I would find: maybe Sheila would be getting fucked by someone. The thought of this made me feel a pang of jealousy. The bed ran from left to right on the wall opposite the door. By the head of the bed was a night table and next to that, on the left-hand wall, was a small hand basin. There was a wardrobe, desk and chair against the right-hand wall. I could see Sheila in the bed, covered with a sheet. She was lying on her front with her head facing the door. I assumed she was sleeping. I didn't know whether to stay or leave. I didn't know if I should go and wake her and apologise for disappearing. I didn't know what she knew about Maggie. 'Hello,' she said to me sleepily.

'Hello,' I said, and slowly crept into the room. *Not violently angry then*, I thought. As I approached the bed, she raised her head and turned it away from me. Now she was facing the wall.

'Where have you been?'

'I had to take Janet home.' I told her. 'She was very upset because Don passed out.' I was waiting for Sheila to say something but she remained silent. 'She was frightened to go by herself and couldn't get a taxi. I'm sorry I didn't tell you, but I didn't think I would be that long.'

She still didn't say anything. I reached onto the bed with my hand and slid it towards her shoulder. She flinched slightly when I touched her. 'Then I got lost on my way back.' I told her. I slid my hand over her shoulder blade; her skin felt warm and smooth. I could feel the rise and fall of her body as she breathed. 'All the streets around here look the same,' I explained. My hand had crept to the nape of her neck and I kneaded it gently.

'What about Maggie?' she asked. *Shit*, I though. *What do I say now?*

'Oh, I didn't take her home,' I said, in all innocence. I moved my hand down to the area crossed by the bra strap when worn. She was not wearing one now. Her back was wonderfully warm and smooth. I let my hand travel further down. Sheila made no objection to the travel of my hand; I knew to touch her skin is enough to make her breathing quicken. I could sense her breathing was not as shallow as when I entered the room.

'They say you were in the toilet with her,' she said. *Uh oh*, I thought. *Here we go.* I moved my hand to the small of her back just as it inclined to the mounds of her buttocks.

'She had a problem with the zip of her boot,' I lied. I was moving my hand now along the waistline of her waist towards the right flank. I felt her back muscles tense a little. I did not want to go too far to where the ticklish spot is, so I stopped and moved it across to the other side. 'She went to clean off some vomit from her boot, and got a flannel trapped in the zip.' I explained. I was pleased I had thought of such a plausible answer so readily. 'I was waiting my turn outside when she asked me to help her.'

'Why was the door locked?' she asked me. My hand now glided up the mound of her buttocks, and the bony muscular hardness of her back turned into a soft, forgiving expanse of soft muscle. My hand was forced to rotate as it reached down. My fingers fell in the valley between the two mounds.

'It wasn't locked,' I said. 'There was no need to lock it.' Now I would go on the offensive 'I only helped her to release the flannel from her zip. Poor woman was drunk and was getting in a state.' She rolled away from me and raised herself up on her right elbow.

'You didn't fuck her, did you, Chris?' Sheila asked me directly.

'Of course I didn't,' I lied. 'I only helped her with her zip. 'She looked at me, then dropped her head on to the pillow.

Finally, her face softened and she asked, 'Do you want to come in here? 'She was raising the sheet invitingly, revealing two full breasts. I shut the door, got undressed, and joined her in her bed. I remembered to spend time on the tits, but it wasn't necessary: she was willing and ready. I played with her body, knowing she was getting more turned on with every movement of my fingers and hands. When I found her clit, she shuddered with endless orgasm. Finally, I fucked her, and we lay together and slept.

Mid-morning we awoke, and I ventured out into the rest of the house. Bob was in the kitchen, picking through the scraps for something to eat; I looked into the lounge, but no-one else was around. 'Where's Chin?' I asked.

'Fucked off,' Bob said with a non-caring shrug of his shoulders.

'Come on, let's go,' I said.

Bob was on the same shift pattern as me, so we didn't have to be on-board until mid-day. I said goodbye to Sheila, said I'd see her again, and that I would continue to write. As it happens, I didn't see her again, nor did I ever reply to any of her letters.

Bob wanted to know what happened in the bathroom with Maggie. Bob was close friends with Fingers, so I decided to stick to the same story of the flannel and zip. I don't think he believed me, but I didn't care.

There was a notice on the main noticeboard, appealing for blood donors. A unit was coming to the jetty the following day, and all volunteers should report there. I decided to go. I didn't say anything to anyone else, but in line was Spanner and Bob. We all looked at each other, and knew our donations were for selfish reasons.

23: Homeward

The Hermes sailed out of Table Bay into the Atlantic Ocean. A right turn headed us North towards England. We stowed all the shore supply cables and secured lockers and link boxes. Bob and I watched Cape Town fall back behind us, and then we went below.

From time-to-time, people in the mess would play cards for money. This activity was not allowed, so when it happened, someone has to keep an eye on the access ladder in case the reg. staff visit or the Chief Elec. Normally, pontoon could be played, or three card brag. If we played then, normally, a limit would be set. I had heard that big money was played for in the other side of the mess where the Seniors were located, many of whom were Leading Hands - and their pay was greater.

However, a new game appeared on the scene—Shoot. The dealer would put money in the kitty; he could choose how much he put in. It could be just a few pennies or, in rare instances, a few pounds. The dealer would then deal three cards to each player. Normally, there would be between four and eight players. Each player, in turn, would then decide if they wanted to bet or not. The bet was that the player would have a higher card than the next one the dealer would turn over. He could choose how much he wanted to bet; this could be a small amount, or the total amount of the pot. If the dealer turned over a card of a lesser value, the player could take from the pot the value of his bet. If he lost, he added his bet to the pot, increasing the size of the kitty. To 'Shoot' would be to bet the value of the pot. If you won, you took all the money, that round would be over, and the cards passed to a new dealer. If you lost, you doubled the pot. If the dealer could last for three rounds of bets, then he claimed the pot, and passed the cards on. Statistically, the dealer had a better chance of winning; a player could only ever have three suits, so if the forth suit was turned up for his bet, he would lose. The dealer was also least at risk, as he could choose to only put a small amount in the kitty to start off with, and should a number of players 'Shoot' and lose, then the pot would be very valuable in the end. Unlike pontoon, or brag, you could not put a limit on this game; if a number of people lost their bets before you, then the pot would hold a lot of money. If you wanted to 'Shoot', you were risking a lot of money.

I got into trouble with this game. We played for some time, and I was losing; even when I was the dealer, I was losing. I had borrowed money to continue in the game because I 'felt' my luck would turn. I had borrowed my next two weeks' pay, and still, I played. The final dealer placed a large sum in the pot, and people were betting big. I had to be cautious because I only had a small sum in front of me; first time around, I bet half the amount of money I had—and lost; second time around, I bet the remaining money I had—and lost again; on the third deal, I was dealt an Ace of Spades and an Ace King of Clubs. If I bet, I needed the card to be black; if it was red, I would lose. My bet was less than a fifty/fifty chance; it was possible that twenty-six red cards could turn up. I had three black cards, so only twenty-three would give me a win. There was a load of money in the pot; no-one knew, at that stage, how much. I watched the dealer approach me, and noticed the three players before me were all given red cards. It was my turn. My heart thumped against the side of my chest; my breaths were really only gasps. I gripped my hands between my knees. The dealer looked at me, the pack of cards in his left hand. He had pushed forward a card with his left thumb, ready to take with his right hand if I chose to bet. I looked at the card, and knew I had to decide. 'Shoot,' I blurted. I knew people thought me crazy. I had lost a lot of money, and was in debt. I could not afford to lose again. I was crazy! The dealer turned the card over, and threw it, face up, in front of me. It was the Jack of Spades. I exploded, 'Yes!' and almost jumped through the ventilation trunking above our heads. I was so relieved, I almost cried. I turned my cards over, and everyone gasped. It was a crazy bet to take with so much money at stake; in one hand, I had retrieved the money I had lost. I was able to pay my debt, and there was some left over. I said a silent prayer because I could not begin to think of what would have happened if I had lost. I made a vow that I would never play cards again for money. And I never did.

Life continued without too much excitement. The duty watch list was promulgated for when we arrived at Portsmouth, and I was relieved to note I was not duty first night in. I lay on my bunk and could feel the power of the Hermes as it thrust through the water at high speed; it rumbled up from the keel of the ship and through my back, adding a vibration to the rocking motion of the ship. We were now directly on our way to Portsmouth. The squadrons and all the aircraft had left, and we had no missions to complete. Our remaining time at sea could almost be measured in hours; just two more nights. I smoked a cigarette and listened to The Beatles singing from the ship's tannoy system. I felt contented.

I had achieved an objective of visiting Singers and Honky Fid, and now felt some way near being a real sailor. I had been drunk in every place we visited, stood before the Captain and Commander, and received punishment for a variety of misdemeanours. I cleaned more copper boilers than anyone ever had, thanks to the influence of one RPO McSnell. Mind you, I got my revenge for that; I had also shagged a few women; three on one night the last time in Cape Town. That had to be some kind of record.

I was looking forward to seeing Forty Foot again, but only to see my childhood friends and brag, just to let them know what I'd been up to and show off all my tattoos.

Kay wrote to me, and said she would be there when the ship

docked, and we could stay for a couple of days at a friend of her family who had a flat in Southsea. So, my first night's shag was assured. Kay had written to me almost every day, and whenever post was brought on-board, there would always be a pile for me. Dianne wrote a few times, but she didn't write so well: she just told me about the weather in Portsmouth, how the team was doing and that she missed me, and really looked forward to my return. I always answered her letters, whenever I replied to Kay's, but never took the initiative to write first. I received the last letter in Cape Town, which she had written a week or so before arrival there. We had no plans to meet, and I assumed she would think I would go home for leave before meeting up with her. I had thought of Dianne often, and hoped I would be able to give her a good shagging sometime during the coming weeks. I had never done that; I think she was worried that once I had fucked her, I would lose interest in her and neglect her. She was very experienced, and I had heard many stories about her. I guess she had learned by experience that once a guy had got what they wanted, they were off. She didn't want that with me, so I was not allowed to go the final step. However, I would persevere and eventually, I would fuck her and then, I'd be off.

I often thought of Rosie and our last meeting at Southsea sea front. She was so fucked up: she wanted me to fuck her because she had placed me in her mind when being abused by her family. It seemed it was something that she needed to somehow clear her mind, of all the wrong-doing, before she disappeared into the oblivion of a gypsy marriage. She must have thought, from me, it would be something special. but being fucked is being fucked. I remember Sandra telling me to make my girlfriend laugh and give her an orgasm, and she would love me forever. Before I left on this voyage, I didn't know that girls *had* orgasms: certainly Kay had never had one. Well, not that I know of. I didn't even fully understand the bit about making them laugh. Should I be telling them a joke whilst on top? I didn't think I made Kay laugh. The thing about love was something I didn't really understand: I had read books about people being in love, and within the stories there always seemed to be tragedies. One would die or one would meet someone else, and so one would end up pissed off and sad. There were all other emotions described, like heart-racing when you see your loved one, light-headedness, and the overwhelming desire to be with them and them only. I guessed I didn't love anyone. I remembered at St Vincent some of the boys crying at night because they missed their mothers. I had seen some men in the mess really upset when receiving a letter from their girlfriends, telling them they had found someone else, or others who had stopped receiving letters altogether. I knew not to be around those people for a while.

Being in love with your mother has to be different than being in love with a girlfriend; I guess that's the big difference. Mothers are family, and girls are friends. I supposed you had to be friends first before you could be in love. Spanner was my friend and so was Budgie; people like Mick and Fingers were guys I knew fairly well, but we didn't spend hours together talking and swapping jokes. With Spanner and Budgie, we had a laugh; we were happy to be together; we didn't want anything from each other, only to enjoy each other's company and pass the time. Maybe, I reasoned, you need to be friends like that with a girl before you could be in love.

I guessed that was what Sandra meant about making her laugh: friends, together, laugh. I didn't know why I was with Kay, except for what I could get out of her. She was beautiful, so it served my ego to be seen with her and show her photo around. I couldn't be with her for long, though: after a few days, I needed a change of scenery. Kay was more intelligent than Dianne, but she soon bored me. Dianne was thick—really, really stupid. She worked as a waitress in a restaurant, and we couldn't talk about much when we were alone together. It was okay in the Victory playing darts, because that's something of interest we shared; she had also introduced me to Portsmouth football club, and I enjoyed going with her to see live matches. I looked forwards to our moments of intimacy, when I would feel her tits and get my hands inside her knickers. She would tease me and make me make a mess in my pants, or about me if she got my cock out. I always lived in hope that 'tonight's the night', but so far, not yet. I would fuck her, though.

Rosie, though, was uneducated. She'd never been to school; she couldn't write or read, yet being with her and talking to her seemed to be wonderful. Our conversations, though only a few and very interspersed, left me always with a feeling of wonderment about her. She was intelligent and knowing; she said things that made me think. She was also sad; she asked me to fuck her, but she wanted more from me than that. Somehow, she had a fantasy in her mind of me associated with the incest of her family. It seemed she needed to realise that fantasy before she could move on to the rest of her life. For me, to fuck her wouldn't make the memories go away, but maybe if she could associate them with me, in a physical sense, then afterwards it would be like losing a boyfriend because we both know we had no future together. I really didn't know, but it did make me think.

The thought of fucking Rosie excited me. She was a stunning beauty, and she was maturing well for someone so young. Last year, her breasts were already full and she had a gorgeous curve to her hips and buttocks. I didn't know when this would be, but I did know she would make it happen; she would just appear and the time would be right.

I would have to make it special, though; I would *want* to make it special. As Sandra had told me, I would take her in my arms and caress her; I would gently let my hand run down her back, caress her neck and run my fingers through her beautiful hair. I would kiss her lips gently, not crushing them against her teeth; I would kiss her cheeks, eyes and nose. I would pamper her face with my lips; my hands would run up and down her flanks, feeling the flair of her hips, the rise of her ribcage and swelling of her breasts. I would eventually free her breasts and allow a moment for her to enjoy that freedom, before I would encroach upon their softness. I would gently cup them, allowing my thumb to flick across the nipple. 'Spend time on the breasts', Sandra had told me, and I would do just that. Caressing gently, fondling, flicking, and tenderly nipping the nipple end. I would kiss her chin, then throat, and her shoulders and chest. I would kiss from one breast to the other, taking the nipple in my mouth and suckling like a baby would. My hands would be around her back, travelling up and down, but each time lower to explore to globes of her soft buttocks. I would kiss her breast bone and make my way down to her navel; I would lick inside, where she was once connected to her mother. I would be between her legs with my hands around her. I would kiss the gentle mound of her tummy, and further down till I felt the tickle of her pubic hair on my chin. My nose would rub gently in the valley of soft flesh against the hood protecting her magic button. Then, I would lick her: I would lick her where she pisses from, but I would not be disgusted by it as I had been when Sandra told me to do the same all those months ago. I would know the joy this gave to a girl, and I would lick and suckle until I felt her gasping and thrusting and finally, the involuntary shudder of an orgasm. Then, I would fuck her. I would have to think of other things like fishing in the lake at Forty Foot or playing football with my mates, think of anything to stop me shooting my load too soon. I would be making love to Rosie because she deserved it.

'What you doing, Clarkie?' Bob Walkinson boomed at me, breaking my thoughts. 'You can have my beer the next two nights if you do me a sub first night in.'

'Piss off!' I replied abruptly. 'My girlfriend's coming down, and she'll need a good fucking.'

Bob pushed my feet aside and sat on my bunk. 'Come on, man,' he pleaded.

'Sorry, mate. Someone has to be on-duty first night in, and you got the short straw.'

'It's the Chief Elec., he's got it in for me, 'he said, sulking.

'Bob,' I said, sitting up and pushing up against him 'you are on duty first night in because you joined in Singers. You didn't do the whole trip.'

'So what?'

'The Chief Elec. is a good egg,' I told him. 'All Senior Rates should be like him.'

'Fuck it,' Bob said in resignation. 'I'm depressed. I feel low, lower than whale shit.' Well, that's a variation on the wheel rut. I liked it. Bob got up and sauntered round to his side of the mess.

The day of arrival came, and everyone seemed happier. More smiles could be seen around, and generally, people were jollier. We went early to the Weather Deck to prepare the shore supply cables. We watched France come into view and get bigger as we sailed along the narrowing channel. We turned around the Isle of Wight, and we could see Southsea; we scrutinised every detail, trying to see what had changed. We passed the Fun Fair, and squeezed through the entrance of the harbour. Isle of Wight ferries waited to depart from the berths in front of the railway station. The wooden planks of the station, painted with black tar, looked the same as the first time I had crossed the harbour on my way to StVincent, which seemed an absolute eon ago. I could see the Victory pub, where Dianne would be tonight. She would wonder if I would be in; she would be waiting for me in anticipation. We could see all the pubs along the Hard up to the main dockyard gate. We watched the masts of Nelson's HMS Victory glide past as we penetrated further into the harbour. Finally, Fountain Lake Jetty came into view: it was full of colour; it was full of people; it was full of fanny. Wives had come to meet husbands; girlfriends had come to meet boyfriends; family came to meet family; and friends to meet friends. Predominantly women were there, waving, cheering, shouting, jumping up and down and waving flags and banners. Tugs pushed the bulk of the Hermes to the jetty, and we began to smell the fragrance we had all missed at sea. The closer we got, the more detail we could see. Faces began to show detail; we could see legs in miniskirts and bulges pushing out the front of woollen jumpers and coats of the ladies wearing them. Then I saw Kay. My heart skipped a beat as I recognised her square jaw and straight nose; she wore a red beret hat that flopped down on one side. She was looking up at the Flight Deck, where the guys were lining the deck. She was looking for me, but I was about twenty feet in front of her. I raised my hands and cupped them around mouth, like a funnel, to transmit my voice. I was about to shout her name when, not three feet from her, I saw no other than Dianne. She, too, was looking up with a broad smile on her face. She wore a Pompey football scarf.

I began to realise I had a problem. My hands returned to my sides, and then another thunderbolt hit me: just behind Kay and Dianne stood Rosie, who was not looking up to the Flight Deck—she was looking directly at *me*. I panicked and had to think fast. 'Bob!' I called.

'What?'

'You still want me to stay on-board and do your duty?'

'Fucking right I do.'

'Two days' worth of beer?'

'Of course.'

'Okay then.'

'Really?' he exclaimed in disbelief.

'Really.'

'Clark, you're a fucking hero!'

ABOUT THE AUTHOR

Christopher P Clark was brought up in a small village in the Fens of England, badly educated and destined for a life of crime. He joined the Royal Navy where he had a second chance of education. He served 17 years, mostly in the submarine service. On leaving the Navy he was employed by a company selling light house equipment. He travelled the World installing new equipment and converting old systems to solar power. Chris then joined the printing industry followed by the packaging industry. In the early nineties he started his own business. He went bust twice and then got the formula right and made some money. He was married twice, divorced twice and lost all his money twice. In 2007, aged 56, he packed all his possessions into the back of a motor home and moved to Spain. Chris built his own house, single handed, where he now lives with his new beautiful Colombian wife. There are many stories to tell. HMS Hermes was just two years of a very interesting life – which has not yet finished.

Printed in Great Britain
by Amazon

47633211R00215